Political Realism in Apocalyptic Times

From climate change to nuclear war to the rise of demagogic populists, our world is shaped by doomsday expectations. In this pathbreaking book, Alison McQueen shows why three of history's greatest political realists feared apocalyptic politics. Niccolò Machiavelli in the midst of Italy's vicious power struggles, Thomas Hobbes during England's bloody civil war, and Hans Morgenthau at the dawn of the thermonuclear age all saw the temptation to prophesy the end of days. Each engaged in subtle and surprising strategies to oppose apocalypticism, from using its own rhetoric to neutralize its worst effects to insisting on a clear-eyed, tragic acceptance of the human condition. Scholarly yet accessible, this book is at once an ambitious contribution to the history of political thought and a work that speaks to our times.

Alison McQueen is Assistant Professor in the Department of Political Science at Stanford University. She writes on the history of political thought, religion in early modern political thought, and political realism. Her work has been published in *Journal of Politics*, *Perspectives on Politics*, *European Journal of Political Theory*, *Political Theory*, and *Critical Review of Social and Political Philosophy*. She is the recipient of the American Political Science Association's Leo Strauss Award for the best dissertation in political philosophy (2012). She has held fellowships at Princeton's University Center for Human Values and the Stanford Humanities Center.

Political Realism in Apocalyptic Times

ALISON MCQUEEN
Stanford University

CAMBRIDGE
UNIVERSITY PRESS

University Printing House, Cambridge CB2 8BS, United Kingdom

One Liberty Plaza, 20th Floor, New York, NY 10006, USA

477 Williamstown Road, Port Melbourne, VIC 3207, Australia

314-321, 3rd Floor, Plot 3, Splendor Forum, Jasola District Centre, New Delhi - 110025, India

79 Anson Road, #06-04/06, Singapore 079906

Cambridge University Press is part of the University of Cambridge.

It furthers the University's mission by disseminating knowledge in the pursuit of education, learning and research at the highest international levels of excellence.

www.cambridge.org
Information on this title: www.cambridge.org/9781316606544
DOI: 10.1017/9781316588307

© Alison McQueen 2018

This publication is in copyright. Subject to statutory exception and to the provisions of relevant collective licensing agreements, no reproduction of any part may take place without the written permission of Cambridge University Press.

First published 2018
First paperback edition 2018

A catalogue record for this publication is available from the British Library

ISBN 978-1-107-15239-7 Hardback
ISBN 978-1-316-60654-4 Paperback

Cambridge University Press has no responsibility for the persistence or accuracy of URLs for external or third-party internet websites referred to in this publication, and does not guarantee that any content on such websites is, or will remain, accurate or appropriate.

This book is dedicated to the memory of David McQueen and Jennifer McQueen

Contents

List of Figures		*page* ix
Acknowledgments		xi
1	Introduction	1
2	Understanding the Apocalypse	22
3	Machiavelli's Savonarolan Moment	63
4	Hobbes "At the Edge of Promises and Prophecies"	105
5	Morgenthau and the Postwar Apocalypse	147
6	Conclusion	192
References		206
Index		228

Figures

2.1	Nero conquering Armenia, Sebasteion at Aphrodisias, first century AD.	*page* 35
2.2	Claudius conquering Brittania, Sebasteion at Aphrodisias, first century AD.	36
3.1	Sandro Botticelli, *Mystic Crucifixion*, c. 1500.	77
3.2	Luca Signorelli, *Apocalypse Sequence*, 1499–1502.	78
3.3	Luca Signorelli, *Apocalypse Sequence*, 1499–1502.	79
4.1	Frontispiece of *Leviathan*, "Head" edition, 1651.	140

Acknowledgments

We rarely do our best thinking alone. I have many people to thank for thinking through this project with me. Susan Buck-Morss supervised the doctoral dissertation that became the basis for this book. She consistently pushed me to see the project with new eyes, to find the strange in the familiar, and to take seriously the way in which images do important political theoretical work. Peter Katzenstein brought his sharp critical eye and wide-ranging intellect to every part of this project. And, as he has done for so many, Peter modeled what it means to be a generous scholar and teacher.

It was in a class with John Najemy that I first began to formulate my ideas on Machiavelli. The reading I offer in this book owes much to these early conversations, to John's own wonderful work on Machiavelli and Renaissance Florence, and to the careful attention he brought to multiple drafts of that chapter. The project benefited from John's rare combination of a breadth of vision and an eye for detail. I must acknowledge a special debt to Jason Frank. Had it not been for several seminars and many conversations with Jason, I would not have realized that I was a political theorist. He consistently saw more in this project than I knew was there. When I would turn to Jason in frustration, he would send me back to work with a renewed sense of enthusiasm. One could not ask for more.

A number of people read the manuscript in its entirety at various stages. I would like to thank David Bates, Joshua Cohen, David Como, Robert Fredona, Kinch Hoekstra, Victoria Kahn, Isaac Kramnick, Josiah Ober, Stephen O'Leary, Rob Reich, and William Scheuerman. More recently, several anonymous reviewers carefully read the manuscript and offered invaluable responses, criticisms, and corrections.

Many other people read one or more chapters and offered useful feedback. I would like to thank Dwight Allman, Samuel Arnold, Eric Beerbohm, Charles

Beitz, Richard Bensel, Peter Breiner, Jonathan Bruno, Allen Carlson, Douglas Dow, Dan Edelstein, Matthew Evangelista, Michael Frazer, Amy Gais, Giovanni Giorgini, Joshua Goldstein, Benjamin Gregg, Randal Hendrickson, Burke Hendrix, David Johnston, Risa Kitagawa, David Laitin, Melissa Lane, Harvey Mansfield, Al Martinich, Lida Maxwell, John McCormick, Eric Nelson, Philip Pettit, Arlene Saxonhouse, Shalini Satkunanandan, John Scott, Quentin Skinner, Steven Smith, Travis Smith, Brent Sockness, Anna Stilz, Leif Wenar, and Yves Winter. I would also like to thank audiences at the various conferences and workshops where these chapters were presented. All remaining errors are, of course, the result of malevolent Fortune.

For their friendship and support during the highs and, more importantly, the lows of this project, I would like to thank Emilee Chapman, Lauren Davenport, Helena de Bres, Jennifer Hadden, Louis-Philippe Hodgson, Hallie Liberto, Jonathan Kirshner, Margaret McKinnon, Josiah Ober, David Plunkett, Lucas Stanczyk, Silvana Toska, and Leif Wenar.

I owe Burke Hendrix a special debt of gratitude. He saw this project develop from its earliest stages. The book benefited from his encouragement, questions, and gentle requests for clarification. He helped me see the humor in an often gloomy subject.

The book also benefited from the financial and institutional support of the Cornell School of Graduate Studies, Cornell's Mario Einaudi Center for International Studies, Princeton's University Center for Human Values, the Social Sciences and Humanities Research Council of Canada, Stanford University, Stanford's McCoy Family Center for Ethics in Society, and Stanford's Brown Faculty Fellowship.

Robert Dreesen at Cambridge University Press patiently supported this book from the outset. Julia Hrischeva and Nitesh Srivastav saw the manuscript smoothly through the production process. Wendy Nardi brought a sharp eye to copyediting.

Earlier versions of parts of Chapters 3 and 5 appeared, respectively, as "Politics in Apocalyptic Times: Machiavelli's Savonarolan Moment" in *Journal of Politics* 78, no. 3 (2016), pp. 909–24, and as "Salutary Fear? Hans Morgenthau and the Politics of Existential Crisis," *American Political Thought* 6, no. 1 (2017), pp. 78–105. Earlier versions of some brief passages of Chapter 1 appeared in "Political Realism and the Realist 'Tradition,'" *Critical Review of International Social and Political Philosophy* 20, no. 3 (2017), pp. 296–313 and "The Apocalypse in U.S. Political Thought," *Foreign Affairs* (July 18, 2016), https://www.foreignaffairs.com/articles/united-states/2016-07-18/apocalypse-us-political-thought. Earlier versions of some brief passages of Chapter 5 appeared in "On Hans J. Morgenthau's 'The Twilight of International Morality,'" *Ethics* 125, no. 3 (2015): 840–2. Earlier versions of some brief passages of Chapter 6 appeared in "Apocalyptic Thought in the Age of Trump," *Foreign Affairs* (November 20, 2016), https://www.foreignaffairs.com/articles/

Acknowledgments

2016-11-20/apocalyptic-thought-age-trump. I am grateful to all of these journals for allowing me to reproduce the relevant portions of those texts here.

Finally, I owe a special debt to my family. My parents, Nancy and David McQueen, first nurtured the skills and habits of scholarly work – reading, writing, and asking questions (not necessarily in that order). My aunt, Jennifer McQueen, supported and encouraged me throughout my early academic career. She was proof that it is possible to be a compassionate realist. My father and my aunt both died as this project was still unfolding. I dedicate this book to their memory.

I

Introduction

Apocalyptic Times

As May 21, 2011 approached, radio evangelist Harold Camping preached a message of cosmic hope and despair. A cross-country billboard campaign urged Americans to "Save the Date!" and announced the "Return of Christ. May 21, 2011." On this day, he warned, a small group of the faithful would be taken up to heaven in the rapture.

From their celestial perches, they would watch a wave of divine destruction circle the globe and massacre the unfaithful. Earthquakes would devastate the world, opening the graves of sinners and spewing forth their bodies to be "desecrated and shamed."[1] Those still alive would weep and wail as famines, plagues, and wars ravaged the earth for five months. As God wreaked his terrifying final judgment, nearly seven billion new corpses would be strewn around the world.[2] No one would be left to bury them. God would have won his final victory over the forces of evil.

Camping's predictions described the apocalypse. They were his interpretation of the story told in Revelation, the final book of the Christian Bible. This is the story of a world that is corrupt and beastly. A world ruled by power, greed, and deceit. A world in which moral goodness and religious devotion are mocked and punished. But the end of this world is imminent. Revelation foretells a transformation both gruesome and sublime. Four horsemen will bring war, conquest, famine, and death. All the great cities will be destroyed by violent earthquakes. The stars will fall from the sky and the earth will run with

---

[1] Scott James, "From Oakland to the World, Words of Warning: Time's Up," *The New York Times*, May 19, 2011, www.nytimes.com/2011/05/20/us/20bcjames.html.
[2] Dan Amira, "A Conversation With Harold Camping, Prophesier of Judgment Day," *New York Magazine: Daily Intelligencer*, May 11, 2011, http://nymag.com/daily/intelligencer/2011/05/a_conversation_with_harold_cam.html.

rivers of blood. At the end of this divine carnage, Christ will grant eternal life to the chosen and eternal torment to the damned.

These hallucinogenic images have avalanched down through the centuries to our secular age.

When we speak of apocalypse today, we describe cataclysms – from nuclear war to climate change – that are of human making and not divine. What is common to ancient and contemporary ideas of apocalypse is an imminent and cataclysmic end to the known world and the arrival of a radically new future. Apocalypses position us at a rupture in time, at the edge of a great transformation. Nothing will be the same again.

When the world failed to end on May 21, Camping and his followers, some of whom had quit their jobs and liquidated their assets, were widely mocked.[3] They were exactly what most people expect an apocalyptic group to be – marginal, religious, and wrong.

We imagine apocalyptic believers as vulnerable people who, under the direction of a charismatic leader, have gathered in a rural bunker to await the end of the world. Or worse, we picture people who have cut themselves off from mainstream society to pursue their doomsday expectations to a violent end. There are certainly examples that look like this. The mass suicide of more than 900 members of the Peoples Temple at Jonestown, Guyana in 1978 was motivated by this group's apocalyptic beliefs. The Branch Davidians, who were locked in a fifty-one-day armed standoff with the FBI near Waco, Texas in 1993, were motivated by an ideology of the end times.

In 1995, members of Aum Shinrikyo, a Japanese group whose beliefs incorporate elements of yoga, Buddhism, and Christian apocalypticism, released sarin gas in the Tokyo subway system, killing thirteen people and severely injuring many others. In 1997, thirty-nine members of Heaven's Gate, a group that combined Christian apocalypticism with beliefs about the salvation of the soul through UFO transport, committed mass suicide.

More recently, the Islamic State of Iraq and Syria (ISIS) has used extremist readings of Sunni doomsday theology to recruit thousands of followers in a campaign of territorial expansion, violence, subjugation, and enslavement in Iraq and Syria. The group's leaders and recruits portray the wars in the Middle East as the "final battles of the apocalypse," after which the Caliphate will be restored and prophecy fulfilled.[4]

These movements caused far more destruction of life and property than did Camping's May 21 group. But like that group, they reinforce our preconceptions about apocalyptic movements. In each case, followers were motivated by

---

[3] Jesse McKinley, "Despite Careful Calculations, the World Does Not End," *The New York Times*, May 21, 2011, www.nytimes.com/2011/05/22/us/22doomsday.html; Jesse McKinley, "An Autumn Date for the Apocalypse," *The New York Times*, May 23, 2011, www.nytimes.com/2011/05/24/us/24rapture.html.
[4] William McCants, *The ISIS Apocalypse: The History, Strategy, and Doomsday Vision of the Islamic State* (New York: St. Martin's Press, 2015), 99.

Apocalyptic Times

charismatic leaders with beliefs about the imminent end that are difficult for most outsiders to understand, let alone accept.

Yet as we will see over the course of this book, apocalyptic beliefs are not exclusively held by marginal groups.[5] They are embraced by those in the highest positions of political power. Consider George W. Bush's presidential rhetoric in the aftermath of the terrorist attacks of September 11, 2001. The two decades prior to the attacks, Bush said, had seemed like "years of relative quiet, years of repose, years of sabbatical." The terrorist attacks brought this familiar world to an end. Suddenly, the past looked different. During these "years of relative quiet," dark forces had been at work.[6] We had now awoken to a new world.

Bush's rhetoric initially appears quite different from Camping's – it seems to lack Camping's overtly biblical references. But when we take a closer look, we can see that it tells a similar story. Camping and his followers expected that May 21, 2011 would be the end of time and the cataclysmic birth of a new world. Bush also described a rupture in the temporal continuity of history. The 9/11 attacks were a "day of fire."[7] They heralded a new world in which different rules of state practice applied. Previously unacceptable forms of political violence were now necessary to win a war against "evil."[8]

Like Camping, Bush was sure about the direction of history. Camping expected God's justice to wind its way around the world, destroying the damned wherever they may be hiding. For Bush, the "untamed fire of freedom" would spread to the "darkest corners of the world." It would burn "those who fight its progress."[9] The United States-led military campaign in Afghanistan was originally called Operation Ultimate Justice before being renamed Operation Enduring Freedom. Americans were told that the campaign would seek out terrorists wherever they were hiding. While they may initially "burrow deeper into caves and other entrenched hiding places," American troops would soon "drive them out and bring them to justice."[10] To non-Christian audiences, these images

---

[5] As Stephen O'Leary notes, "apocalyptic arguments made by people of good and sincere faith have apparently succeeded in persuading millions; it is unfair and dangerous to dismiss these arguments as irrational and the audiences persuaded by them as ignorant fools." And along similar lines: "A brief survey of the history of apocalyptic discourse shows that its appeal has historically cut across class lines. The audience of those receptive to prophecy and its interpreters included emperors, peasants, merchants, farmers and factory workers, the educated and the uneducated alike from Isaac Newton to Ronald Reagan." Stephen D. O'Leary, *Arguing the Apocalypse: A Theory of Millennial Rhetoric* (New York: Oxford University Press, 1994), 4, 9.

[6] George W. Bush, "Inaugural Address," The American Presidency Project, January 20, 2005, www.presidency.ucsb.edu/ws/index.php?pid=58745.

[7] Bush, "Inaugural Address."

[8] George W. Bush, "Address Before a Joint Session of the Congress on the State of the Union," The American Presidency Project, January 29, 2002, www.presidency.ucsb.edu/ws/?pid=29644.

[9] Bush, "Inaugural Address."

[10] George W. Bush, "Address to the Nation Announcing Strikes Against Al Qaida Training Camps and Taliban Military Installations in Afghanistan," The American Presidency Project, October 7, 2001, www.presidency.ucsb.edu/mediaplay.php?id=65088&admin=43. See also: William E. Connolly, *Capitalism and Christianity, American Style* (Durham: Duke University Press Books, 2008), 39–68.

might not have carried any special meaning, beyond the familiar promise that American military power would be both effective and decisive. To many Christians, however, Bush's statement might well have evoked Revelation, where sinners "hid in the caves and among the rocks of the mountains, calling to the mountains and rocks, 'Fall on us and hide us from the face of the one seated on the throne and from the wrath of the Lamb [Jesus]; for the great day of their wrath has come, and who is able to stand?'"[11] The apocalyptic undertones of Bush's speeches may not be as obvious as those of Camping's, but they are there for those able and willing to hear them.

Camping called upon his followers to put their trust in God's plan for history. May 21, 2011 would mark the beginning of a terrifying battle between good and evil that would inaugurate a new and better world. Bush asked Americans for a similar act of faith: "We Americans have faith in ourselves, but not in ourselves alone. We do not...claim to know all the ways of Providence, yet we can trust in them, placing our confidence in the loving God behind all life and all history."[12] Bush's apocalyptic narrative absorbs the September 11 attacks, which might initially have raised questions about the progressive direction of history. The attacks become the terrifying birth pangs of a new world.[13]

Bush is not the only American president to put contemporary events into an apocalyptic narrative. Even before assuming office, Abraham Lincoln cast the looming civil war in overtly apocalyptic terms. Drawing on the imagery of the bowls of God's wrath from Revelation 16, he said that it seemed to him "as if God had borne with this thing (slavery) until the very teachers of religion had come to defend it from the Bible to claim for it a divine character and sanction; and now the cup of iniquity is full, and the vials of wrath will be poured out."[14]

More than seventy years later, Theodore Roosevelt used the same rich stock of apocalyptic imagery to link his own battle against "special privilege" to Lincoln's resistance to slavery. In 1912, as the Republican National Committee seemed set to award the party's nomination to William Howard Taft, Roosevelt gathered his supporters in Chicago the night before the convention. He urged the cheering crowd to fight for a country in peril: "Fearless of the future; unheeding of our individual fates; with unflinching hearts and undimmed eyes; we stand at Armageddon and we battle for the Lord."[15]

Amid global conflagrations and the ever-looming threat of nuclear annihilation, Ronald Reagan was drawn to similar visions of a final battle. While

---

[11] Rev. 6:15–17. New Revised Standard Version (NRSV).
[12] George W. Bush, "Address Before a Joint Session of the Congress on the State of the Union," The American Presidency Project, January 28, 2003, www.presidency.ucsb.edu/ws/index.php?pid=29645#axzz1UZTKZP00.
[13] Antoine Bousquet, "Time Zero: Hiroshima, September 11 and Apocalyptic Revelations in Historical Consciousness," *Millennium* 34, no. 3 (2006): 761.
[14] As quoted in Isaac Newton Arnold, *The History of Abraham Lincoln, and the Overthrow of Slavery* (Chicago: Clarke & Co., 1866), 689.
[15] Theodore Roosevelt, "The Case Against the Reactionaries (June 17, 1912)," in *Selected Speeches and Writings of Theodore Roosevelt*, ed. Gordon Hunter (New York: Vintage, 2014), 159.

governor of California, he confided to a political associate that the recent coup in Libya was "a sign that the day of Armageddon isn't far off." Reagan downplayed these beliefs when he became president. But his Secretary of Defense Caspar Weinberger was more forthright: "I have read the Book of Revelation and yes, I believe the world is going to end – by an act of God, I hope – but every day I think that time is running out."[16] Bush's apocalyptic rhetoric is therefore by no means politically unique.

And consider the more secular apocalyptic rhetoric that Donald Trump used in the 2016 United States presidential campaign. "Our country is going to hell," he warned, claiming that the United States faced economic collapse, the disintegration of its vital infrastructure, and looming annihilation at the hands of "radical Islamic terrorists." In short, it was the apocalypse: "If we don't get tough, and if we don't get smart, and fast, we're not going to have a country anymore." The time to act is now "because later is too late."[17] The 2016 election was "a moment of reckoning" and a "crossroads in the history of our civilization."[18] If voters heeded his call, Trump promised, there was hope. The country's "problems can all be fixed, but…only by me."[19] Casting himself in the role of a messiah, Trump promised to lead the United States away from Armageddon and make the country "great again."[20] Trump's rhetoric borrows from the narrative of apocalypticism, while shedding much of its Christian imagery.

Even if we recognize that it need not always be religious, we might still conclude that apocalypticism is uniquely attractive to Republicans or those on the political right. But consider this statement by environmentalist James Lovelock: "The evidence coming in from the watchers around the world brings news of an imminent shift in our climate towards one that could easily be described as Hell: so hot, so deadly that only a handful of the teeming billions now alive will survive."[21] Lovelock draws on the religious language of doomsday to convey the threat of global climate change.

He is not alone. Former Vice President Al Gore uses biblical imagery to describe a secular day of reckoning. After showing devastating images of

---

[16] As quoted in Paul Boyer, *When Time Shall Be No More: Prophecy Belief in Modern American Culture* (Cambridge: Harvard University Press, 1992), 142, 141.
[17] "Transcript of the New Hampshire GOP Debate, Annotated," *Washington Post*, February 6, 2016, www.washingtonpost.com/news/the-fix/wp/2016/02/06/transcript-of-the-feb-6-gop-debate-annotated/; "Read Trump's Speech on the Orlando Shooting," *Time*, June 13, 2016, http://time.com/4367120/orlando-shooting-donald-trump-transcript/.
[18] "TRANSCRIPT: Donald Trump's Speech Responding To Assault Accusations," *NPR.org*, October 13, 2016, www.npr.org/2016/10/13/497857068/transcript-donald-trumps-speech-responding-to-assault-accusations.
[19] "Full Transcript: Donald Trump NYC Speech on Stakes of the Election," *POLITICO*, June 22, 2016, www.politico.com/story/2016/06/transcript-trump-speech-on-the-stakes-of-the-election-224654.
[20] Repurposing a slogan from Ronald Reagan's 1980 presidential campaign, Trump's campaign promised to "Make America Great Again."
[21] James Lovelock, *The Revenge of Gaia: Earth's Climate Crisis and the Fate of Humanity* (New York: Basic Books, 2006), 147.

climate catastrophe in the 2006 documentary film *An Inconvenient Truth*, he notes that they are "like a nature hike through the book of Revelations [sic]." He concludes his 2009 book *Our Choice* on a similar note, with a poem that combines references to melting ice caps, ocean acidification, and species extinction with one of the most ominous images of the Christian apocalypse: "Horsemen ready their stirrups."[22] Lovelock and Gore, no less than Camping, Bush, and Trump, convey apocalyptic visions of the end of the world.

And yet, one might think, surely there is a difference between religious and secular expectations about the end of the world, even if the latter are often clothed in scriptural garb. Today's environmentalists, for example, like the antinuclear activists of the Cold War, are not describing some fantastical apocalypse outlined in the Bible and transposed into the contemporary world. They are talking about the *real* apocalypse – an impending end supported by hard facts and data. The polar ice caps *are* melting. Rates of extreme weather events *are* on the rise. Yet as we shall see, the terrors nourished by the Christian apocalypticism of early modern Europe were real enough for those who experienced them. Believers saw signs of an impending end that seemed every bit as incontrovertible to them as evidence of environmental doom is to many today.[23]

Whether held by the marginal or the powerful, whether overtly religious or seemingly secular, apocalyptic beliefs share an expectation of the coming cataclysmic end of the world and the arrival of a radically new future. It is a terrifying and captivating vision.

Political Realism in Apocalyptic Times

This book began with a concern about the prevalence of apocalyptic rhetoric in post-9/11 political discourse. I discovered that this was a concern that I shared with members of a particular tradition of political thought. In the autumn of 2002, when an American-led invasion of Iraq seemed likely, the *New York Times* ran an op-ed advertisement criticizing the Bush administration's case for the invasion. The signatories were scholars of international security and about half of them were self-identified political realists.

That is, they are the contemporary social scientific heirs of a tradition that is focused on power and interest, suspicious of moralizing, and attentive to

---

[22] Al Gore, *Our Choice: A Plan to Solve the Climate Crisis* (Emmaus, PA: Rodale Books, 2009), 28.
[23] Frank Kermode makes a similar point in a comparison of fears of nuclear annihilation and older forms of apocalyptic expectation. Frank Kermode, *The Sense of an Ending: Studies in the Theory of Fiction (with a New Epilogue)* (New York: Oxford University Press, 2000), 182–83. This, of course, is not to deny that the epistemological statuses of these portents differ or that environmentalists might have more warrant for their expectations than did Christians in Renaissance Florence and seventeenth-century England. It is merely to suggest that the *experience* of these hopes and fears and the agents' *own estimation* of how warranted these feelings were could well have been roughly equal in all cases.

the limits of political action. In the history of political thought, this approach is most strongly associated with such thinkers as Thucydides, St. Augustine, Niccolò Machiavelli, Thomas Hobbes, David Hume, Friedrich Nietzsche, Max Weber, and Carl Schmitt. In international relations, it is linked with E. H. Carr, Hans Morgenthau, George Kennan, Kenneth Waltz, and John Mearsheimer.

In brief, the realist case against military intervention in Iraq was that the war was not in America's national interest – that the real threat was Al Qaeda, and that there was no good evidence of Saddam Hussein's cooperation with this organization; that a costly war would divert resources from the fight against Al Qaeda; that an effective invasion and state-building effort would cost too much in American and Iraqi lives and resources; that a war would almost certainly spread instability in a region essential to America's security and interests; and that the United States lacked a "plausible exit strategy."[24] Many of these worries were prescient. Looking back, some wondered whether the political realists in this debate were like "Hegel's Owl of Minerva, their wisdom only taking flight at dusk – when most of the damage ha[d] been done."[25]

But the realist case against the war went beyond claims about national interest. It also included worries about the worldview behind the argument in favor of war. John Mearsheimer, for instance, suggests that the Bush administration's case for war drew from an idealistic worldview historically associated with Woodrow Wilson. This worldview rests on a Manichean division of the world into good (democratic) and bad (non-democratic) states. Once all states are brought to democracy either by internal pressures, shining foreign exemplars, well-meaning international encouragement, or external coercion, there will be enduring peace. The worst that we should fear after this "end of history" is boredom.[26]

An earlier generation of political realists went further. They recognized an apocalyptic belief structure in Wilsonian idealism, which shared Revelation's hope for a final escape from conflict and the arrival of a permanent peace. For E. H. Carr, "Woodrow Wilson's [own] moral authority was built up on the conviction, shared by himself, that he possessed the key to a just, comprehensive and final settlement of the political ills of mankind. It is noteworthy that almost

---

[24] "War with Iraq Is Not in America's National Interest," ad published in *The New York Times*, September 26, 2002, www.bear-left.com/archive/2002/0926oped.html. The signatories included, for instance: Michael C. Desch, Robert Jervis, John Mearsheimer, Randall Schweller, Stephen van Evera, Stephen Walt, and Kenneth Waltz. See also: John J. Mearsheimer and Stephen M. Walt, "An Unnecessary War," *Foreign Policy*, no. 134 (2003): 50–59.
[25] Brian C. Schmidt and Michael C. Williams, "The Bush Doctrine and the Iraq War: Neoconservatives Versus Realists," *Security Studies* 17, no. 2 (2008): 209.
[26] John J. Mearsheimer, "Hans Morgenthau and the Iraq War: Realism versus Neo-Conservatism," *openDemocracy*, May 19, 2005, www.opendemocracy.net/democracy-americanpower/morgenthau_2522.jsp. See also: Francis Fukuyama, *The End of History and the Last Man* (New York: Free Press, 1992), 330.

all religions agree in postulating an ultimate state of complete blessedness."[27] Similarly, Hans Morgenthau casts Wilson's promise that World War I would be a "war to end war" as the "expression of an eschatological hope deeply embedded in the very foundations of liberal foreign policy."[28]

These kinds of intriguing remarks prompted me to embark on a more sustained investigation of realist responses to apocalypticism. What I expected to find were curt dismissals. What I in fact found was a history of more uneasy and sustained realist encounters with the apocalypse.

The three thinkers that I examine here represent epiphanic moments in this history. Niccolò Machiavelli (1469–1527), Thomas Hobbes (1588–1679), and Hans Morgenthau (1904–1980) are all defining members of the realist tradition.[29] They all wrote during times when powerful political, social, and religious actors were announcing the imminent end of the world. Apocalyptic expectations were not uncommon after the rise of Christianity. But the periods in which Machiavelli, Hobbes, and Morgenthau wrote were ones in which these hopes and fears emerged in particularly sharp relief and held immense political sway.[30] Machiavelli wrote in the context of Dominican friar

---

[27] Edward Hallett Carr, *The Twenty Years' Crisis, 1919–1939* (New York: Harper and Row, 1964), 90.
[28] Hans J. Morgenthau, *Scientific Man vs. Power Politics* (Chicago: University of Chicago Press, 1946), 52.
[29] While Machiavelli and Hobbes do not self-identify as political realists, contemporary realists and students of realism tend to look back on these earlier thinkers as intellectual predecessors. See, for example: Steven Forde, "Varieties of Realism: Thucydides and Machiavelli," *Journal of Politics* 54, no. 2 (1992): 372–93; David Boucher, *Political Theories of International Relations: From Thucydides to the Present* (Oxford: Oxford University Press, 1998), 90–167; Thomas L. Pangle and Peter J. Ahrensdorf, *Justice Among Nations: On the Moral Basis of Power and Peace* (Lawrence: University Press of Kansas, 1999), 125–61; Jack Donnelly, *Realism and International Relations* (Cambridge: Cambridge University Press, 2000), 13–15, 24–26; Michael C. Williams, *The Realist Tradition and the Limits of International Relations* (Cambridge: Cambridge University Press, 2005), 19–51. Hans Morgenthau did self-identify as a realist. However, scholars such as William Scheuerman and Michael C. Williams have questioned and sought to complicate this identification. See: Williams, *The Realist Tradition*, 82–127; William E. Scheuerman, *Hans Morgenthau: Realism and Beyond* (Cambridge: Polity Press, 2009), 1–10; William E. Scheuerman, "Was Morgenthau a Realist? Revisiting *Scientific Man vs. Power Politics*," *Constellations* 14, no. 4 (2007): 506–30. I discuss important concerns about tradition-building below.
[30] If this work were primarily concerned with making a causal argument for the effect of periods of heightened apocalypticism on political realism as such, choosing only realists who wrote during such periods would pose a clear selection problem. If we wanted to understand the effect of periods of heightened apocalypticism on realist commitments, so the suggestion goes, we would want to include in the analysis at least one political realist who did not write in a period of heightened apocalypticism. I have two thoughts to offer in response to this potential worry. First, the addition of a realist who did not write in a period of heightened apocalyptic expectation would, at best, make for an awkward and completely insufficient proxy for the kind of social scientific research design that allows for robust causal inferences. Second, and more importantly, my goal is not to make a causal argument about two general phenomena (political realism and

Political Realism in Apocalyptic Times

Girolamo Savonarola's disturbing apocalyptic visions about the future of Florence. Although Savonarola was executed in 1498, the apocalyptic hopes and fears to which he gave voice would continue to shape Italy well into the sixteenth century.

Thomas Hobbes developed his political thought against the backdrop of both radical and Royalist attempts to cast the English Civil War in apocalyptic terms. This apocalypticism persisted during the Protectorate, when visions of doomsday were wielded both by and against Oliver Cromwell. Working much later, Hans Morgenthau wrote his most influential works on international politics in the aftermath of the Holocaust and in the shadow of nuclear war. Yet with a few notable exceptions, interpreters have given little attention to these thinkers' apocalyptic contexts.[31]

Over the course of this book, I show that attending to the apocalyptic circumstances in which Machiavelli, Hobbes, and Morgenthau wrote does three things. First, it prompts us to consider aspects of their work that we might otherwise neglect. For instance, the final two books of Hobbes's *Leviathan* continue to receive comparatively little attention by scholars of the history of political thought.[32] These are chapters in which Hobbes engages in detailed scriptural arguments that, at first blush, can seem largely unconnected to the political arguments outlined in the first two books of the work. However, as I show in Chapter 4, these scriptural arguments are central to Hobbes's political project. He uses them to combat the revolutionary apocalypticism of the English Civil War and to make Christianity's most radical expectations safe for political order and civil peace.

Second, an attention to the apocalyptic context in which these thinkers wrote casts the more familiar parts of their work in a new light. For example, seen alongside Savonarola's visions of the end times, the final chapter of Machiavelli's *Prince* begins to look less like a strategic ploy to curry favor with the

---

apocalypticism). It is, at least in part, to see how looking at their engagement with apocalypticism casts these thinkers' work in a new light, sometimes in ways that affirm and other times in ways that challenge their identification as political realists. In so doing, I occasionally make causal suggestions about the impact of a confrontation with apocalypticism on a particular thinker's realist commitments. These suggestions are supported, to the extent possible, with contextual and textual evidence specific to that thinker and time.

[31] John G. A. Pocock has given apocalyptic beliefs some treatment in his work on Machiavelli and Hobbes. John G. A. Pocock, *The Machiavellian Moment: Florentine Political Thought and the Atlantic Republican Tradition* (Princeton: Princeton University Press, 2003), 83–113; John G. A. Pocock, "Time, History and Eschatology in the Thought of Thomas Hobbes," in *The Diversity of History: Essays in Honour of Sir Herbert Butterfield*, ed. J. H. Elliott and H. G. Koenigsberger (Ithaca: Cornell University Press, 1970), 149–98.

[32] Pocock wryly notes: "The two books in which Hobbes expounds Christian faith and its sacred history are almost exactly equal in length to Books I and II [of *Leviathan*]; yet the attitude of too many scholars towards them has traditionally been, first, that they aren't really there, second, that Hobbes didn't really mean them." See: Pocock, "Time, History and Eschatology," 161–62. However, as I note in Chapter 4, there are now important exceptions to this trend.

Medici and more like an apocalyptic exhortation of despair and redemption. Third, tracing these thinkers' responses to hopes and fears about the end of the world prompts us to consider the rhetorical and normative challenges of responding to catastrophes today.

Finding any kind of sustained attention to apocalyptic ideas in the works of Machiavelli, Hobbes, and Morgenthau may seem surprising. To see why, we need to understand a bit more about the tradition of political thought to which these thinkers are seen to belong. Political realism is a distinctive family of approaches to the study, practice, and normative evaluation of politics.[33] Despite their differences, these approaches tend to share four commitments. First, realists think that there is something distinctive about politics. It is a realm of activity with "its own character, purposes, and means."[34] For realists, this distinctiveness shapes the relationship between ethics and politics. Some hold that politics is an amoral realm, while others claim that it is a realm with its own moral rules that are distinct from those in other spheres, while still others claim that politics is a realm in which conventional or universal moral rules must be overridden and "good" political actors must dirty their hands. For instance, Machiavelli advises rulers that they must "not depart from good, when possible, but know how to enter into evil when necessary."[35]

Second, realists think that politics is agonistic or conflictual. They attribute this disagreement to a variety of causes, including human nature and the limits

---

[33] Over the past decade, there has been a revival of interest in realism within political theory. This revival is most strongly associated with the work of Bernard Williams and that of Raymond Geuss. See: Bernard Williams, "Realism and Moralism in Political Theory," in *In the Beginning Was the Deed: Realism and Moralism in Political Argument*, ed. Geoffrey Hawthorn (Princeton: Princeton University Press, 2005), 1–17; Raymond Geuss, *Philosophy and Real Politics* (Princeton: Princeton University Press, 2008). For an influential statement of realism's core commitments, see: William A. Galston, "Realism in Political Theory," *European Journal of Political Theory* 9, no. 4 (October 1, 2010): 385–411. See also: Duncan Bell, ed., *Political Thought and International Relations: Variations on a Realist Theme* (Oxford: Oxford University Press, 2009); Karuna Mantena, "Another Realism: The Politics of Gandhian Nonviolence," *American Political Science Review* 106, no. 2 (May 2012): 455–70; Alison McQueen, "The Case for Kinship: Political Realism and Classical Realism," in *Politics Recovered: Essays on Realist Political Thought*, ed. Matt Sleat (New York: Columbia University Press, 2018), chapter 10; Alison McQueen, "Political Realism and the Realist Tradition," *Critical Review of International Social and Political Philosophy* 20, no. 3 (2017): 296–313; Enzo Rossi and Matt Sleat, "Realism in Normative Political Theory," *Philosophy Compass* 9, no. 10 (October 1, 2014): 689–701; William E. Scheuerman, "The Realist Revival in Political Philosophy, or: Why New Is Not Always Improved," *International Politics* 50, no. 6 (November 2013): 798–814; Joel Alden Schlosser, "Herodotean Realism," *Political Theory* 42, no. 3 (June 1, 2014): 239–61; Matt Sleat, *Liberal Realism: A Realist Theory of Liberal Politics* (Manchester: Manchester University Press, 2013); Matt Sleat, "Realism, Liberalism and Non-Ideal Theory or, Are There Two Ways to Do Realistic Political Theory?," *Political Studies* 64, no. 1 (2016): 27–41.

[34] Sleat, "Realism, Liberalism and Non-Ideal Theory," 32.

[35] Niccolò Machiavelli, *The Prince*, trans. Harvey C. Mansfield (Chicago: University of Chicago Press, 1998), chapter 18, 70.

Political Realism in Apocalyptic Times

of rationality, competing identities and interests, and value pluralism.[36] Morgenthau, for example, locates the causes of conflict in human nature – our lust for power and will to dominate. This "aspiration for power over man" is, for Morgenthau, both a cause of conflict and "the essence of politics."[37] Whatever the causes of conflict, realists hold that our disagreements are not primarily intellectual and will not tend to be resolved through "the unforced force of the better argument."[38] Politics is necessary "because we have to live and act alongside those with whom we disagree."[39] At their best, political institutions can channel and manage this disagreement. But they cannot eliminate it.

Third, political realists tend to prioritize the requirements of order and stability over the demands of justice. They see order as a fragile accomplishment. Because disagreement and conflict are ineradicable, order and stability are always vulnerable. They should never be understood as "once-and-for-all achievements."[40] While they may be fragile, order and stability are often necessary preconditions for pursuing other political values, such as justice. In real-world political contexts, "justice purchased at the expense of order is likely to prove self-defeating."[41] This priority of order is best illustrated by Hobbes. His Leviathan state must, above all else, provide a stable solution to the anarchy, conflict, and violence of our natural condition. Without order and stability, we are in no position to realize justice.

Fourth, realists reject as utopian those approaches which seem to deny the distinctiveness of politics and the persistence of disagreement and conflict.[42] Realists take aim at theories that fail to take seriously the psychological, sociological, and institutional constraints on political action. Inattentive to these constraints, utopian thinkers offer inadequate, and even dangerous, guidance for political reform.[43] Machiavelli famously contrasts his approach in *The Prince*

---

[36] On human nature and the limits of rationality, see: Geuss, *Philosophy and Real Politics*; Mark Philp, *Political Conduct* (Cambridge: Harvard University Press, 2007); Carl Schmitt, *The Concept of the Political: Expanded Edition*, trans. George Schwab (Chicago: University of Chicago Press, 2007). On competing identities and interests, see: Bonnie Honig, *Political Theory and the Displacement of Politics* (Ithaca: Cornell University Press, 1993); Chantal Mouffe, *On the Political* (London: Routledge, 2005). On value pluralism, see: John Gray, *Two Faces of Liberalism* (New York: The New Press, 2000); David McCabe, *Modus Vivendi Liberalism: Theory and Practice* (Cambridge: Cambridge University Press, 2010).
[37] Morgenthau, *Scientific Man vs Power Politics*, 45.
[38] Jurgen Habermas, *Between Facts and Norms: Contributions to a Discourse Theory of Law and Democracy*, trans. William Rehg (Cambridge: MIT Press, 1998), 306.
[39] Sleat, *Liberal Realism*, 44.
[40] Philp, *Political Conduct*, 62.
[41] Galston, "Realism in Political Theory," 9. I assess the nature of the realist claim for the priority of order and stability over justice in more depth in: McQueen, "Case for Kinship."
[42] Galston, "Realism in Political Theory"; Laura Valentini, "Ideal vs. Non-Ideal Theory: A Conceptual Map," *Philosophy Compass* 7, no. 9 (September 1, 2012): 654–64.
[43] For arguments that, at the conceptual level at least, realism's target is best seen as moralism rather than utopianism, see: McQueen, "Political Realism and the Realist Tradition"; Sleat, "Realism, Liberalism and Non-Ideal Theory," 35–36.

with that of those who imagine "republics and principalities that have never been seen or known to exist in truth; for it is so far from how one lives to how one should live that he who lets go of what is done for what should be done learns his ruin rather than his preservation."[44] Morgenthau goes so far as to suggest that the struggle between utopianism and realism is the main plot of modern political thought.[45] This anti-utopianism is seen by many to be the most characteristic feature of political realism. In the field of international relations, realism is sometimes defined almost entirely in terms of its opposition to utopianism.[46]

In its Judeo-Christian form and many of its secular variants, apocalypticism is a kind of utopianism. It is a utopianism premised on a belief in the imminent end of the known world and the arrival of a radically new and *better* future.[47] Understanding it in this way, we might expect that political realists would limit themselves to merely opposing or dismissing apocalyptic expectations.

Instead, as we will see over the course of the book, Machiavelli, Hobbes, and Morgenthau pursue persistent and unsettled encounters with apocalypticism. At times, their realist commitments are deepened and enriched through these encounters. At other times, these commitments are challenged and disrupted. None of these thinkers merely oppose or dismiss apocalypticism. They appreciate it, they confront it, and they use it. They see its dangers and its possibilities.

Studies of apocalypticism give us similar reasons to be surprised upon finding this sort of engagement with hopes and fears about the end of the world. Histories of apocalypticism tend to divide their subjects into two groups: apocalypticists and anti-apocalypticists. For instance, in *Heaven on Earth* (2011), Richard Landes marks a clear division between apocalyptic "roosters" who announce

---

[44] Machiavelli, *Prince*, chapter 15, 61.
[45] Hans J. Morgenthau, *Politics Among Nations: The Struggle for Power and Peace*, 2nd ed. (New York: Alfred A. Knopf, 1954), 3.
[46] See, respectively: John A. Vasquez, *The Power of Power Politics: From Classical Realism to Neo-traditionalism* (Cambridge: Cambridge University Press, 1998), 36; Stefano Guzzini, *Realism in International Relations and International Political Economy: The Continuing Story of a Death Foretold* (London: Routledge, 1998), 16; Robert Gilpin, "The Richness of the Tradition of Political Realism," in *Neorealism and Its Critics*, ed. Robert O. Keohane (New York: Columbia University Press, 1986), 304. These kinds of characterizations are testaments to the enduring influence of E. H. Carr on international relations theory. Carr's *The Twenty Years' Crisis* identifies realism as both a successor to utopian idealism in the *study* of international relations and as an intellectual disposition and *political stance* that is always a reaction to perfectionist projects. See: Tim Dunne, "Theories as Weapons: E. H. Carr and International Relations," in *E. H. Carr*, ed. Michael Cox (Basingstoke: Palgrave Macmillan, 2000), 222. Contemporary realists in political theory and political philosophy position their approach as an antidote to political moralism, ideal theory, or "high liberalism." See, for instance: Geuss, *Philosophy and Real Politics*; Glen Newey, *After Politics: The Rejection of Politics in Contemporary Liberal Philosophy*, 2001 (Houndmills: Palgrave Macmillan, 2001); Williams, "Realism and Moralism in Political Theory."
[47] In Chapter 5, I argue that some strands of secular nuclear apocalypticism entertained hopes about a new and better world after the apocalypse.

the imminent end of the world and anti-apocalyptic "owls" whose conservative feathers are ruffled by these radical enthusiasts. As roosters await the coming cataclysm, owls advise caution "and counsel against hasty enthusiasms."[48]

Many other scholars of apocalypticism implicitly affirm this binary. This makes it difficult for them to classify thinkers who seem neither wholly apocalyptic nor entirely anti-apocalyptic.[49] For instance, (St.) Augustine is often cast as an anti-apocalyptic thinker.[50] But, as we will see in Chapter 2, he attempts to negotiate the dangers of apocalypticism while never fully disavowing expectations about the end times. Augustine is both an apocalyptic and an anti-apocalyptic thinker.

The easy binary of apocalypticism versus anti-apocalypticism is what Stephen Holmes, in another context, calls the "tyranny of false polarities"[51] – a stylized and misleading antithesis that prevents an accurate account of the range of possible positions. Given two mutually exclusive options, one would have to class political realists as anti-apocalyptic owls. Their insistence on the inescapability of conflict and their anti-utopianism seem to make realists profoundly hostile to expectations of radical world transformation. However, as we will see, the realist response to apocalypticism makes easy classification impossible. Like Augustine before them, Machiavelli, Hobbes, and Morgenthau are drawn to elements of the apocalyptic narrative at the same time as they attempt to negotiate its dangers.

Central Argument

The central argument in this book is that Machiavelli, Hobbes, and Morgenthau respond to apocalypticism in ways that are far more complex than an easy and reflexive opposition. These responses take two forms. The first is *rejection* – a principled and considered turn away from apocalypticism and toward a tragic worldview. This worldview opposes an apocalyptic certainty about the direction of history with a cyclical understanding of political time. Tragedy emphasizes the ease with which virtuous actions can produce terrible consequences,

---

[48] Richard Landes, *Heaven on Earth: The Varieties of the Millennial Experience* (New York: Oxford University Press, 2011), 47.
[49] For an exception, see: Catherine Keller, *God and Power: Counter-Apocalyptic Journeys* (Minneapolis: Fortress Press, 2005).
[50] See, for instance: Bernard McGinn, *Visions of the End: Apocalyptic Traditions in the Middle Ages* (New York: Columbia University Press, 1998), 26; O'Leary, *Arguing the Apocalypse: A Theory of Millennial Rhetoric*, 73–76. For more nuanced treatments, see: Paula Fredriksen, "Apocalypse and Redemption in Early Christianity: From John of Patmos to Augustine of Hippo," *Vigilae Christianae* 45, no. 2 (1992): 160–68; Robert A. Markus, *Saeculum: History and Society in the Theology of St Augustine* (Cambridge: Cambridge University Press, 1970), esp. 1–71.
[51] Stephen Holmes, *Passions and Constraint: On the Theory of Liberal Democracy* (Chicago: University of Chicago Press, 1995), 28.

insists on the limits to effective political action, and warns of the impossibility of final and enduring political settlements.[52] This is the response adopted by Machiavelli in his later work and by Morgenthau in his earlier work. In both cases, rejections are the result of a serious and troubled encounter with apocalypticism.

The second approach is *redirection* – drawing on the rhetorical and imaginative resources of apocalypticism to combat its enthusiastic excesses. It is an approach that fights apocalypse *with apocalypse*. This is the tack taken by Hobbes to make his case for the Leviathan state and by Morgenthau in his later writings on nuclear weapons. For both Hobbes and the later Morgenthau, this attempt to redeploy apocalyptic ideas puts pressure on these thinkers' realist commitments. Both use hopes and fears about the end of the world to secure adherence to political orders that promise perpetual peace.

Taken together, Machiavelli's, Hobbes's, and Morgenthau's responses offer us a series of meditations on how best to respond to ongoing and prospective catastrophes. They also reveal the deep challenges that realists face in dealing with hopes and fears about the end of the world. Neither rejection nor redirection is a fully adequate response. The turn to tragedy that characterizes the strategy of rejection has the advantage of being consistent with political realism's core commitments. Yet in its insistence that political time is cyclical and that there is no relief from the familiar patterns of conflict and loss, tragedy has difficulty confronting radically new circumstances. As we shall see, Morgenthau's tragic worldview left him with few tools to grasp the novel threat of thermonuclear war.

But redeploying doomsday prophecies is also risky. Political realists are right to be wary of apocalypticism. Visions of the end times can be highly motivating. They have the potential to rouse audiences to confront profound injustices – from slavery to environmental catastrophe. Those who deploy them may be eminently well motivated. By presenting us with terrifying images of imminent scourges and doom, they aim to shake us from our complacency and give us the moral courage to act together in the name of justice. But these benefits come with moral and political risks. Apocalyptic visions seek to achieve their political ends by terrifying us into action. While the fear they elicit may sometimes be salutary, it is not a reliable spur to action. As we will see, apocalypticism can just as easily prompt political withdrawal and resignation.

---

[52] On the features of the tragic mode from literary and historical perspectives, see: Northrop Frye, *Anatomy of Criticism* (Princeton: Princeton University Press, 2000), 35–42; Hayden White, *Metahistory: The Historical Imagination in Nineteenth-Century Europe* (Baltimore: Johns Hopkins University Press, 1973), 7–11. For a discussion of tragedy in political theory, see: J. Peter Euben, *The Tragedy of Political Theory: The Road Not Taken* (Princeton: Princeton University Press, 1990). For a discussion of the place of tragedy in the realist tradition, see: Richard Ned Lebow, *The Tragic Vision of Politics: Ethics, Interests and Orders* (Cambridge: Cambridge University Press, 2003).

Approach and Method

This project sits at the intersection of the history of political thought and the history of international relations thought. This intersectional approach makes it possible to trace the intellectual trajectories and recurrent dilemmas of a tradition that has its roots in the canonical works of the history of Western political thought but whose contemporary proponents tend, with a few notable exceptions, to be scholars of international politics. While international relations thinkers tend to look back to the works of Machiavelli, Hobbes, and Morgenthau as classic articulations of a political realist tradition that continues to exercise considerable influence over the field, they are generally content to leave detailed investigations of the first two thinkers to political theorists. For their part, political theorists have largely left the analysis of Morgenthau's thought to their colleagues in international relations.[53] Working across the boundaries between these two fields, this project aims to bring these thinkers into productive conversation.

My approach to the three figures covered in this book is broadly contextualist. Because contextual research in the history of political thought has been dominated by a set of methodological commitments first systematically articulated and defended by Quentin Skinner, it may be helpful to identify the points at which my approach aligns with and departs from his. Like Skinner, I begin with the assumption that "the *text* itself" is not "the self-sufficient object of inquiry and understanding."[54] Understanding a work like *The Prince*, *Leviathan*, or *Scientific Man vs. Power Politics* requires an attention to the context in which it was produced, and more particularly to the range of meanings and visual vocabulary available to its author.[55]

For instance, it is difficult to imagine that one could fully understand the detailed scriptural arguments in *Leviathan* – why they take the form that they do and why Hobbes would have thought it necessary to offer them – without an account of the ways in which scripture was deployed polemically in the political and religious debates of seventeenth-century England. Similarly, it would be difficult to fully understand this work's iconic frontispiece without knowing something of the visual conventions of seventeenth-century frontispieces and representations of sovereign power.

I further share Skinner's conviction that even the most seemingly abstract works of political thought are not only philosophical arguments but also polemical interventions in the debates of their day. The arguments in these

---

[53] For an important and illuminating exception, see: Scheuerman, *Hans Morgenthau*.
[54] Quentin Skinner, "Meaning and Understanding in the History of Ideas," *History and Theory* 8, no. 1 (1969): 4.
[55] For an example of Skinner's attention to the question of visual vocabularies, see his discussion of frontispieces and emblems throughout Quentin Skinner, *Hobbes and Republican Liberty* (Cambridge: Cambridge University Press, 2008).

works "are never above the battle; they are always part of the battle."[56] In Machiavelli's, Hobbes's, and Morgenthau's respective times, the battle was at least in part about the imminent fate of the world. Finally, like Skinner, while I acknowledge that "a study of social context may *help* in the understanding of a text," I eschew a reductionist approach that treats the ideas in a text as epiphenomenal and that understands a political work *purely* "in terms of its social context."[57] Great political thinkers have the capacity to shift, transform, and reimagine the concepts, languages, and visual rhetoric of their times.

However, I depart from the strongest versions of contextualism on the question of doctrines or traditions of political thought. Skinner's early statements take a hard-line position on this question. He draws upon the work of R. G. Collingwood, who argues that philosophers are not concerned with a finite set of permanent questions to which thinkers of different eras have given particular answers that can easily be compared. Rather, "what is thought to be a permanent problem P is really a number of transitory problems p_1, p_2, p_3 ... whose individual peculiarities are blurred by the historical myopia of the person who lumps them together under the one name P."[58] Following Collingwood, Skinner argues that the questions with which thinkers are concerned transform themselves in subtle ways over time.

Historians of political thought commit a serious error, then, in assuming or arguing that there is such a thing as a realist doctrine or a realist tradition. Beyond failing to recognize the subtle but significant transformation of questions over time, a commitment to the reality of doctrines and traditions is problematic because it is based on a potentially unwarranted assumption that an "author must have had some doctrine, or a 'message,' which can be readily abstracted and more simply put."[59] The assumption may be unwarranted because attempts to think through political problems are difficult and often reflect some confusion and changes of mind. The works that result from such thinking often contain inconsistent arguments and competing themes.[60]

Faced with these scattered remarks, the doctrine-hunting or tradition-building interpreter is vulnerable to at least two kinds of error. First, she may be susceptible to a combination of confirmation and selection bias. She may, consciously or not, find in a thinker's work only those ideas that confirm his identification with the relevant doctrine or tradition. For example, if an interpreter approaches Thucydides as the originator of a realist tradition, she may

---

[56] Skinner, *Hobbes and Republican Liberty*, xv.
[57] Skinner, "Meaning and Understanding," 43.
[58] Robin G. Collingwood, *An Autobiography* (Oxford: Oxford University Press, 1939), 69. See also: Quentin Skinner, "The Rise of, Challenge to and Prospects for a Collingwoodian Approach to the History of Political Thought," in *The History of Political Thought in National Context*, ed. Dario Castiglione and Iain Hampsher-Monk (Cambridge: Cambridge University Press, 2001), 175–88.
[59] Quentin Skinner, "The Limits of Historical Explanations," *Philosophy* 41, no. 157 (1966): 209.
[60] Skinner, "Meaning and Understanding," 7.

Approach and Method 17

be inclined to attend only to those portions of the *History* (e.g., the Melian Dialogue, or the account of the civil war in Corcyra) that affirm this account, while failing to attend to those that do not.[61]

Second, she may impose a false coherence on the texts she is reading. Looking for evidence of a doctrine or membership in a tradition, the interpreter may slide almost imperceptibly into the project of "constructing doctrines more abstract than any which the writer in question might seem to have held, in order to dispose of inconsistencies in his opinions which would otherwise remain."[62] The result of such an interpretive project is "a history of thought which no one ever actually succeeded in thinking, at a level of coherence which no one ever actually attained."[63]

We must be vigilant about these sorts of errors because establishing traditions of political thought is such a tempting way to enhance the legitimacy of one's own position. Relating to one's own view on a question as an article of faith, one may be inclined to defend it by using the analysis of historical thinkers "to show how long and honourable an ancestry that faith has."[64] This is a particularly strong temptation for contemporary political realists because, as Michael C. Williams notes, "the claim that there is a Realist tradition" that stretches back to Thucydides "is a key component of claims about the continuing salience and wisdom of Realism itself."[65] If the Peloponnesian War was able to prompt a realist analysis as readily as has the Cold War, then realism's insistence that there are certain enduring facts about the political world (e.g., the inescapability of conflict) seems all the more warranted.

While these are valuable warnings about the dangers of overzealous doctrine-hunting and tradition-building, I think the concerns and the methodological implications are both overstated. There do seem to be basic normative questions that recur through time, admittedly in somewhat different articulations and from various points of view.[66] These include: What is the best regime? Who should rule? Under what conditions is political power legitimate? And, especially important for political realists: Which has primacy, justice or political order? While the political concepts deployed in these questions, the range of possible answers, and the criteria for evaluating plausible answers have undoubtedly varied across time and space, both the questions and the answers –

---

[61] Skinner, "Meaning and Understanding," 9–10. Skinner makes this point with reference to John Locke.
[62] Skinner, "The Limits of Historical Explanations," 210.
[63] Skinner, "Meaning and Understanding," 18.
[64] Crawford B. Macpherson, "The History of Political Ideas," *Canadian Journal of Economics and Political Science* 7, no. 4 (1941): 565.
[65] Williams, *The Realist Tradition*, 3.
[66] For an attempt to carve out a more modest version of the Collingwoodian claim about perennial problems, see: Samuel Freeman, foreword to *John Rawls, Lectures on the History of Political Philosophy*, ed. Samuel Freeman (Cambridge: Belknap/Harvard University Press, 2007), 103–04.

even when understood in their full contextual richness – retain a coherence through time. Political thinkers take part (albeit often not self-consciously) in an ongoing conversation.[67]

The three thinkers on whom I focus in this book are either self-identified political realists (Morgenthau) and/or have been classified and recognized as such by other self-identified political realists, across time and space (Machiavelli, Hobbes, and Morgenthau).[68] Of course, it would be foolish to deny that such self-identified political realists have been immune to the legitimizing aspirations of tradition-building or to insist that Machiavelli and Hobbes *intended* to contribute a political realist tradition. Nor do I intend to suggest that there are no substantial differences across the thought of Machiavelli, Hobbes, and Morgenthau or that these thinkers' realist commitments remain constant. The ways in which they respond to apocalypticism, for instance, sometimes deepen and sometimes challenge their realist commitments. However, the fact that important strands of Machiavelli's and Hobbes's arguments have been classified and recognized as realist in their character by self-identified realists gives at least a cautious warrant for talking about their place in a "realist tradition."[69]

So far, I have argued that it makes sense to talk about a realist tradition that persists through time. The concept of apocalypse also has a trans-historical coherence. In order to see this, we can use a thesis from political theology. Carl Schmitt offers the classic articulation of this argument:

All significant concepts of the modern theory of the state are secularized theological concepts not only because of their historical development – in which they were transferred from theology to the theory of the state, whereby, for example, the omnipotent God became the omnipotent lawgiver – but also because of their systematic structure, the recognition of which is necessary for a sociological consideration of these concepts. The exception in jurisprudence is analogous to the miracle in theology.[70]

---

[67] If his repeated references to a republican (or neo-Roman) tradition are anything to go by, Skinner himself seems to have warmed to something like this view. See: Quentin Skinner, *Liberty before Liberalism* (Cambridge: Cambridge University Press, 1998); Skinner, *Hobbes and Republican Liberty*.

[68] These are the criteria that Duncan Bell uses to define a liberal tradition. Duncan Bell, "What Is Liberalism?," *Political Theory* 42, no. 6 (December 1, 2014): 689–90. Exactly where to draw the relevant thresholds (e.g., how many self-identified realists must make the same classification and across how large a span of time?) are difficult questions that I cannot begin to address here. Bell sketches one possible answer and reviews some important considerations (9–10). I make a case for a similar approach to defining the realist tradition in McQueen, "Political Realism and the Realist Tradition," 307–309.

[69] Bell points out, quite rightly, that "it is productive to distinguish between the identities of agents and the arguments they invoke – between being an X (liberal, socialist, fascist) and employing arguments that are best characterised as X. The former is a claim about self-fashioning and the construction of personae, the latter about doctrine." Bell, "The Liberal Tradition," 10. While I agree with this point, affirming it semantically throughout the coming chapters runs the risk of substantial awkwardness. So, I do not.

[70] Carl Schmitt, *Political Theology: Four Chapters on the Concept of Sovereignty*, ed. Tracy B. Strong, trans. George Schwab (Chicago: University of Chicago Press, 2006), 36. This intertwining of the political and theological is central to Schmitt's intellectual and political project. For

Approach and Method

We need not accept the most expansive version of Schmitt's argument – that *"all significant concepts of the modern theory of the state are secularized theological concepts"* – to use it to track the fate of apocalyptic ideas through time.[71] Because theological and political concepts share a "systemic structure," they lend themselves to a genealogical approach.[72] We trace the transformation of concepts through time, attending to the possibility that there are "remnants of belief that are attached to our political concepts and maintained in our political practices."[73] Schmitt argues that with secularization, the ways in which divine authority was understood and negotiated were transferred to the confrontation with political sovereignty. What remains constant, however, is the systemic structure of the theological concept – the way in which it orders and narrates relations of authority. The "omnipotent God" is translated into "the omnipotent lawgiver," but the structure of the concept remains the same.

We now see how we can recognize the persistence of theological concepts through time. When tracing the trajectories of apocalyptic ideas in the works of modern and purportedly secular thinkers, for instance, we should not limit ourselves to overtly scriptural expressions of these ideas. As I suggest in the next chapter, such limits would fail to do justice to the enduring flexibility of apocalyptic beliefs, their capacity to adapt and endure in contexts very different from those in which they were first developed. Rather, we must look for the generic

---

Schmitt, there is an affinity between the theological and the political that emerges from their common expression as law and their shared alienation from liberalism. See: Carl Schmitt, *Crisis of Parliamentary Democracy*, trans. Ellen Kennedy (Cambridge: MIT Press, 1988), 39–50; Schmitt, *Concept of the Political*, 69–79; Michael Hollerich, "Carl Schmitt," in *The Blackwell Companion to Political Theology*, ed. Peter Scott and William T. Cavanaugh (Malden: Blackwell, 2004), 112.

[71] It is also possible to question the causal directionality of Schmitt's claim. First, perhaps both theological and political concepts reflect prior concepts or convictions (e.g., moral convictions). Call this the *common cause objection*. For example, it seems plausible that certain strands of apocalypticism are theological expressions of a moral conviction or hope that, despite bleak contemporary evidence to the contrary, moral progress is possible. Second, it is possible that theological concepts may in fact be theologized political concepts. Call this the *reverse causation objection*. For example, the theological concept of God's sovereignty, which is central to most Judeo-Christian apocalyptic narratives, could plausibly be a theologized rendering of some existing secular political concept of sovereignty, dominion, or power in the ancient world. However, we need not take a stand on the causal directionality of Schmitt's account to make some headway in accounting for the historical trajectory of apocalypticism. As I suggest in the next chapter, whatever the conceptual origins of apocalypticism, a system of beliefs that had once been expressed in a theologized form eventually came to be presented in secular ways.

[72] While the historical narrative that underpins Schmitt's argument rests uneasily with some of the fundamental commitments of Skinnerian contextualism, the genealogical approach does not. Skinner has, particularly in his later work, embraced a genealogical approach (though certainly not one with political-theological trappings). See: Quentin Skinner, "A Genealogy of the Modern State," *Proceedings of the British Academy* 162 (2009): 325–70. On Skinner's "genealogical turn," see: Melissa Lane, "Doing Our Own Thinking for Ourselves: On Quentin Skinner's Genealogical Turn," *Journal of the History of Ideas* 73, no. 1 (2012): 71–82.

[73] Paul W. Kahn, *Political Theology: Four New Chapters on the Concept of Sovereignty* (New York: Columbia University Press, 2011), 106.

structural features of apocalypticism – such as the narrative that it imposes on human events. These structural features are outlined in the concluding pages of the next chapter, which offers an analysis of the scriptural manifestations of apocalypticism in the Judeo-Christian tradition before abstracting from this account the basic structural features of these beliefs. This analysis allows us to recognize the powerful secular versions of apocalypticism at play in the works of Machiavelli, Hobbes, and Morgenthau and to trace an element of their thinking that has not been thoroughly explored in the history of political thought or international relations.

Plan

The argument of this book unfolds in five parts. Chapter 2 describes the canonical Judeo-Christian apocalypses, focusing on how they responded to their political contexts. These texts offer a radical critique of sovereign power, provide a powerful historical narrative that renders contingent events meaningful, and hold out the hope for a world without disagreement, conflict, or difference. The chapter then considers how (St.) Paul and (St.) Augustine, two early Christian thinkers whose arguments would shape the realist tradition, negotiate the dangers and possibilities of apocalypticism. I find in their work prototypical examples of the kinds of responses later used by Machiavelli, Hobbes, and Morgenthau. I conclude with an effort to conceptualize apocalypticism not as a text or a worldview, but as a social imaginary.

Chapter 3 situates Niccolò Machiavelli's work in the context of the apocalyptic excitement that gripped Florence in the late fifteenth century. The Dominican friar Girolamo Savonarola was at the center of this enthusiastic movement. I argue that Machiavelli's work bears the mark of this context. The final chapter of *The Prince* is, I suggest, an apocalyptic exhortation that resonates strongly with the Savonarolan message. Machiavelli gravitates toward this apocalyptic solution in *The Prince* because he has failed to master the contingency of the political world and to explain the crises plaguing Florence. Recognizing the dangers inherent in such a solution, Machiavelli rejects the apocalyptic mode and embraces a robustly tragic sensibility characterized by openness to the variability and struggle of the political world. Yet even Machiavelli's tragic turn is haunted by redemptive hope for a perpetual republic.

In Chapter 4, I locate Thomas Hobbes's political thought in the radical apocalypticism of the English Civil War. Hobbes responds to this threat not by rejecting the apocalyptic imaginary, but by redirecting it in the service of sovereign power. He fights apocalypse *with apocalypse*. I argue that Hobbes pursues two paths in his project – one that is overtly scriptural and another that is seemingly secular. His scriptural argument offers a deflationary reinterpretation of the end times, making its radical promises consistent with the demands of political order. Hobbes's political argument stages a secular apocalypse, in which the terror and chaos of the state of nature usher in an enduring commonwealth ruled by a mortal God. In pursuing these two paths, Hobbes does not escape apocalypticism, but rather redirects it and tries to return it safely into sovereign hands.

Chapter 5 sets Hans Morgenthau's work in the context of postwar American apocalypticism. The development of nuclear weapons and the possibility of large-scale human annihilation fueled both overtly religious and seemingly secular visions of the end times. Concerned primarily with the secular apocalypticism that underpins strains of liberalism and rationalism, Morgenthau initially pursues a strategy of rejection and offers a tragic response that, like Machiavelli's turn to tragedy, emphasizes the ongoing and undecided struggle that shapes political life. However, I argue that Morgenthau later abandons this tragic response, turning instead to the Hobbesian strategy of redirection, or fighting apocalypse with apocalypse. Through a close reading of his remarkable essay on "Death in the Nuclear Age," I map Morgenthau's attempt to fight the possibility of nuclear annihilation by staging an imagined apocalypse of his own. A tragic worldview, Morgenthau concludes, is not enough. One must constantly imagine the apocalypse to prevent it.

In the concluding chapter of the book, I revisit and evaluate these responses to apocalypticism and consider what guidance they might provide today as we think about how best to respond to catastrophes.

2

Understanding the Apocalypse

Introduction

After describing the catastrophic upheavals and divine judgment that will mark the end of the world, the book of Revelation concludes with a warning to anyone who would alter its prophecies. This warning has not been heeded. The message of Revelation has been reinterpreted, repurposed, and redeployed since the controversial decision to canonize it. While early Christians read the book as a revelation of the imminent fall of Rome, some contemporary American evangelicals read the same book as a revelation of the imminent destruction of secular cosmopolitan globalism.[1] The idea of the apocalypse has undergone a similar process of transformation. While its literal meaning is simply revelation, it has come to describe anything from the cataclysmic end of the world prophesied in the bible to the effects of nuclear war or global climate change to the more mundane inconveniences of severe winter storms.[2]

The idea of the apocalypse is flexible, migratory, and unstable. It resists the kind of conceptualization that would make its content narrowly specifiable and its behavioral effects predictable. This chapter attempts no such endeavor. Instead, we will attend both to apocalypticism's roots in the Judeo-Christian tradition and to its ability to transcend these origins and assume a central place in the modern Western imagination.[3] This chapter treats apocalyptic texts as

---

[1] This is the underlying narrative of the best-selling *Left Behind* series of novels by Tim LaHaye and Jerry B. Jenkins.
[2] The severe winter storm that hit the mid-Atlantic states in early February 2010 was widely dubbed the "Snowpocalypse."
[3] While this chapter, and indeed the book, focuses on a Western tradition of apocalypticism, the phenomenon itself is not exclusively Western. In addition, the label Western is used with some caution. What most scholars class as Jewish, Christian, or Western apocalypticism traces its roots back to non-Western sources such as Persian and Near Eastern mythology.

political works written in particular contexts. These works make visible the existing power relations of their times and urge responses to them, ranging from radical overturning to quietest accommodation. However, this chapter also goes beyond the textual sources of apocalypticism in the Judeo-Christian tradition. We will try to understand the concept of apocalypse in a way that helps us to recognize it even when it persists in forms that are very different from these original articulations. This contextual and conceptual work will help us to see both the overtly religious outbursts of apocalypticism in Machiavelli's and Hobbes's times and the more secular apocalyptic rhetoric and imagery to which Morgenthau was responding.

The chapter proceeds in three parts. First, it offers a contextual and political reading of the two canonical apocalyptic texts of the Judeo-Christian tradition – the books of Daniel and Revelation. We begin here because, taken together, these works are the primary textual sources of Western apocalypticism. Their themes and images have endured in contexts very different from those in which the books were originally written. In examining Daniel and Revelation, I draw heavily on historical and critical biblical scholarship to locate these works within their historical contexts and highlight the ways in which they imagine and respond to concrete political developments.

Second, the chapter examines two early Christian attempts by Paul and Augustine to contain the radical political potential of these apocalyptic texts. While interesting in themselves, these containment efforts have a larger significance for this book's project. Paul and Augustine are the two foundational figures of a Christian strand of political realism. Their early responses to apocalypticism will later be deployed by Machiavelli, Hobbes, and Morgenthau.

Finally, the third section of the chapter expands on a latent intuition in Paul's and Augustine's works – that the power and potential danger of apocalypticism lie in its capacity to captivate the imagination. We will explore what it might mean to understand the apocalypse not as a genre of literature, or even a worldview, but as an imaginary. This final section moves beyond the historical source material to understand the way in which certain fundamental features of apocalypticism recur through time to give us a shared way of envisioning our common world.

The Judeo-Christian Apocalypse

Let us begin gently with etymology. The word "apocalypse" comes from the Greek *apokalypsis*, meaning "revelation," "disclosure," or "uncovering." The book of Revelation identifies itself as "the *apokalypsis* of Jesus Christ," marking the first known use of the term to denote a literary genre.[4] In this sense, an apocalypse is a species of eschatology, a teaching about the "last things."

---

[4] Paul D. Hanson, "Apocalypses and Apocalypticism: The Genre," in *The Anchor Bible Dictionary*, ed. David Noel Freedman, vol. 1 (New York: Doubleday, 1992), 279.

In its concern with the end of history, eschatology is primarily focused on the cosmic fate of the world, rather than on the fate of the individual.[5] While apocalypses partake of this communal and cosmic orientation, they bring a sense of urgency and imminence to the end of history that is not a necessary feature of eschatology.[6] So, while all apocalypses are eschatological, not all eschatology is apocalyptic. Biblical scholars also typically draw another distinction between *apocalypticism*, a worldview or "symbolic universe," and *apocalypse*, a literary genre.[7] In what follows, I outline the origins and features of an apocalyptic worldview, as biblical scholars understand it, before considering the genre of apocalyptic literature and the political contexts to which it responds.

The apocalyptic worldview took shape gradually in response to the political crises that plagued ancient Palestine. This is worth stressing. The origins of the apocalyptic worldview do not lie "outside" of politics but are instead inescapably political. At the dawn of the Christian era, Palestine had suffered eight centuries of conflict and almost perpetual foreign domination. The inhabitants of the northern Kingdom of Israel and the southern Kingdom of Judah endured conquest, exile, foreign rule, and pressures for cultural assimilation. The worst blows came when the Assyrians destroyed the northern kingdom in 722 BCE and, after complex power struggles, the Babylonians captured the southern kingdom, first in 597 BCE and then decisively in 586 BCE. Along with the loss of political sovereignty, both conquests led to substantial deportations of Israelites from their homeland.[8] The Assyrians removed and dispersed the

---

[5] David L. Petersen, "Eschatology," in *The Anchor Bible Dictionary*, ed. David Noel Freedman, vol. 2 (New York: Doubleday, 1992), 576. Some theologians and biblical scholars refer to a personal or individual eschatology. However, the dominant usage refers to a communal fate and I will adhere to this usage in the book.

[6] As Bernard McGinn notes: "Every Christian view of history is in some sense eschatological insofar as it sees history as a teleological process and believes that Scripture reveals truths about its End... But there is still an important difference between a general consciousness of living in the last age of history and a conviction that the last age itself is about to end." See: McGinn, *Visions of the End: Apocalyptic Traditions in the Middle Ages*, 4.

[7] John J. Collins, "Apocalypses and Apocalypticism: Early Jewish Apocalypticism," in *The Anchor Bible Dictionary*, ed. David Noel Freedman, vol. 1 (New York: Doubleday, 1992), 283. There is some debate among Biblical scholars regarding the content of apocalypticism, much of which hinges on how we understand the concept of a worldview. John Collins understands apocalypticism as a "symbolic universe," while Paul Hanson argues for a more detailed definition of apocalypticism as "the symbolic universe in which an apocalyptic movement codifies its identity and interpretation of reality." Collins rightly notes that the problem with this more precise conceptualization is that "there is no automatic connection between apocalypticism and social movements. In many cases we know very little of the social matrix in which apocalyptic literature was produced." See: Paul D. Hanson, "Apocalypticism," in *Interpreter's Dictionary of the Bible, Supplementary Volume*, ed. Keith Crim, et al. (Nashville: Abingdon Press, 1976), 30; Collins, "Early Jewish Apocalypticism," 284.

[8] I use the terms "Israel" and "Israelites" here to refer to members of the twelve tribes that make up the Israelite *ethnos*, which eventually formed the kingdom of Israel. After this kingdom split into the northern kingdom of Israel and the southern kingdom of Judah upon the death of Solomon in 922 BCE, inhabitants of the northern kingdom would have been Israelites both by virtue of

people of the northern kingdom, replacing it with a settler population, while the Babylonians destroyed the Temple in Jerusalem and forced all but the poorest inhabitants of Judah into exile in Babylon.

These political circumstances raised difficult questions among Israelites who believed that they had entered a covenant with God in which he would give them protection in exchange for their obedience to his law. Why had God not leapt to Israel's defense? Why was he failing to uphold his side of the covenant? Ancient prophets such as Amos, Hosea, and Isaiah in the eighth century BCE and Jeremiah and Ezekiel in the sixth century BCE argued that Israel's sufferings were of its own making. The people had fallen away from God and were no longer devoted to keeping his law. If they returned to him, their sufferings would end and their political sovereignty would be restored.[9]

Over time, this position proved difficult to maintain. Suffering seemed to befall those who obeyed God's law as well as those who strayed. During the reign of Antiochus IV Epiphanes (175–164 BCE), those Israelites who were *most* pious and observant were the special targets of political persecution. The rise of the phenomenon of Jewish martyrdom raised new questions. Why would God punish those who had kept his law in the face of overwhelming political and cultural pressure to abandon it? The apocalyptic worldview developed, in part, as an answer to this question.[10] Bart Ehrman summarizes the outlines of this answer as follows:

God was still in control of this world in some ultimate sense, but for unknown and mysterious reasons he had temporarily relinquished his control to the forces of evil that opposed him. This state of affairs, however, was not to last forever. Quite soon, God

---

their membership in the *ethnos* and their political membership in the kingdom, while Judahites would have been Israelites solely by virtue of their membership in the *ethnos*. I am following Christine Hayes, *Introduction to the Bible* (New Haven: Yale University Press, 2012), xii.

[9] Bart D. Ehrman, *Jesus: Apocalyptic Prophet of the New Millennium* (Oxford: Oxford University Press, 1999), 120. The relationship between prophetic and apocalyptic worldviews is more complex and contested than the simple narrative I have presented in this paragraph and the following one suggest. For more detailed studies that capture some of the scholarly debate on this issue, see: Paul D. Hanson, *The Dawn of Apocalyptic: The Historical and Sociological Roots of Jewish Apocalyptic Eschatology* (Philadelphia: Fortress Press, 1975); John J. Collins, *The Apocalyptic Imagination: An Introduction to Jewish Apocalyptic Literature*, 2nd ed. (Grand Rapids: William B. Eerdmans, 1998); and, John J. Collins, "From Prophecy to Apocalypticism: The Expectation of the End," in *The Continuum History of Apocalypticism*, ed. Bernard J. McGinn, John J. Collins, and Stephen J. Stein (New York: Continuum, 2003), 64–88.

[10] While the political circumstances outlined here go some way to explaining why we see the rise of a fully developed apocalyptic worldview by the second century BCE, the ideational and mythological roots of this worldview can be traced, in part, to ancient Near Eastern myth and Persian eschatology. The extent and nature of these influences are contested among biblical scholars. See: Richard J. Clifford, "The Roots of Apocalypticism in Near Eastern Myth," in *The Continuum History of Apocalypticism*, ed. Bernard J. McGinn, John J. Collins, and Stephen J. Stein (New York: Continuum, 2003), 3–29; Anders Hultgård, "Persian Apocalypticism," in *Continuum History of Apocalypticism*, ed. Bernard J. McGinn, John J. Collins, and Stephen J. Stein (New York: Continuum, 2003), 30–63.

would reassert himself and bring this world back to himself, destroying the forces of evil and establishing his people as rulers over the earth. When this new Kingdom came, God would fulfill his promises to his people.[11]

The apocalyptic worldview is a political theodicy – an attempt to understand the oppression, dispersion, and loss of sovereignty that plagued the Israelites, without delegitimizing the authority of God. More broadly, it is an attempt to situate contemporary political circumstances within a sacred worldview, thereby endowing them with divine significance. We find evidence for this worldview in the book of Daniel, discussed later, the Dead Sea Scrolls from the Essenes in Qumran, and various non-canonical Jewish writings from the second century BCE through the end of the first century CE.

While there is some disagreement among biblical scholars about the content of the apocalyptic worldview, most agree that it has the following features. First, it embraces a cosmic dualism. Worldly reality is defined by the conflict between good and evil forces. The former are a small minority, while the latter are an overwhelming majority. God and his angels are aligned on the side of good, light, and life. God's cosmic adversary, Satan or the Devil, and his demons are aligned on the side of evil, darkness, and death. For those on earth, neutrality is impossible. One stands either with the divine forces of good or with the demonic forces of evil.[12]

Second, this cosmic dualism corresponds to a chronological dualism. Time is divided into two eras – the present age and the promised future.[13] The present era is dominated by the forces of evil, which cause the good to suffer through war, famine, and death. For mysterious reasons of his own, God has ceded control over history to evil powers. However, he will soon irrupt into the world, bringing time to a close, annihilating the forces of evil, and reestablishing his sovereignty over the earth.[14]

Third, the apocalyptic worldview is marked by a pessimistic historical determinism; supernatural agents control the direction of human affairs.[15] The prophesied end will happen independently of human agency.[16] Even worse, the

---

[11] Ehrman, *Jesus*, 120–21.   [12] Ehrman, *Jesus*, 121.
[13] This historical dualism is more complicated in the Christian tradition. Some early Christians saw the resurrection of Jesus as the beginning of the prophesied end of the world. However, the Kingdom of God had clearly not yet been established. It would come only with the *parousia*, or Jesus' return to earth, which many saw as imminent. Thus, some early Christians saw themselves as living in a kind of "middle time" between the resurrection and the *parousia*. Through the resurrection of Jesus, the future eschatological age had already begun to impinge upon the present. This is clearest in Paul's writings. See: 1 Cor. 15:23–24; 1 Thess. 1:10.
[14] Ehrman, *Jesus*, 121.   [15] Collins, "From Prophecy to Apocalypticism," 85.
[16] It is worth emphasizing the crucial distinction between classical Jewish prophecy and apocalypticism. Despite their disturbing predictions of divine wrath, prophets such as Jeremiah do not see the future as closed or determined. They urge Israel to return to God precisely because they think that human choices affect the direction of history. The apocalyptic worldview, on

The Judeo-Christian Apocalypse

forces of good will continue to be the targets of persecution and oppression until God intervenes to decisively reassert his sovereignty.[17]

Fourth, this "denouement of history" will culminate in a final act of divine redemption and universal vindication.[18] God will annihilate the forces of evil and transform the cosmos. He will create a new heaven and a new earth. He will then preside over a day of universal judgment, rewarding the faithful with membership in his kingdom and condemning the wicked to eternal damnation.[19]

Finally, the apocalyptic worldview has a sense of urgency and imminence. The "triple drama of crisis-judgment-vindication" will happen very soon.[20] Those with an apocalyptic worldview see themselves as living at the edge of time. Any day now, they will witness the closure of history and the dawn of a new world order.

Not all apocalypticists wrote apocalypses. For instance, there is strong evidence that Jesus shared the apocalyptic worldview, even though he did not write any apocalyptic works.[21] We therefore need to distinguish between the apocalyptic worldview and the apocalypse as a literary genre. While biblical scholars disagree on the generic features of a written apocalypse, the following abstract definition is often taken as a solid starting point: "'Apocalypse' is a genre of revelatory literature with a narrative framework, in which a revelation is mediated by an otherworldly being to a human recipient, disclosing a transcendent reality which is both temporal, insofar as it envisages eschatological salvation,

---

the other hand, assumes that the future is written. Human actions cannot change the course of history. An individual may repent, return to God, and join the forces of good. But, in so doing, he is only taking steps to ensure *his own* salvation. He cannot, either acting individually or in concert with others, prevent or avoid the coming crisis, judgment, and vindication.

[17] Ehrman, *Jesus*, 121–22. [18] Collins, "From Prophecy to Apocalypticism," 85.

[19] Ehrman, *Jesus*, 122.

[20] The quoted phrase is from: Bernard J. McGinn, "Revelation," in *The Literary Guide to the Bible*, ed. Robert Alter and Frank Kermode (Cambridge: Harvard University Press, 1990), 526.

[21] For instance, Mark reports the following statement: "But in those days, after the suffering, the sun will be darkened, and the moon will not give its light, and the stars will be falling from heaven, and the powers in the heavens will be shaken. Then they will see the Son of Man coming in clouds with great power and glory. Then he will send out the angels, and gather his elect from the four winds, from the ends of the earth to the ends of heaven ... So, when you see these things taking place, you know that he is near, at the very gates. Truly I tell you, this generation will not pass away until all these things have taken place" (Mark 13:24–30). See also: Mark 8:38–9:1; Matt. 13:40–43. Unless otherwise noted, all biblical quotations in this chapter are from the New Revised Standard Version (NRSV). The apocalyptic interpretation of Jesus' teachings was popularized in academic circles by Albert Schweitzer, *The Quest of the Historical Jesus*, trans. W. Montgomery (London: Adam and Charles Black, 1910). More recently, a version of this reading has been taken up in Ehrman, *Jesus*. John Dominic Crossan offers a forceful argument that Jesus did not have a Jewish apocalyptic worldview. This argument rests on an assertion that the sources in the gospels are not the earliest writings on the life of Jesus and that a more accurate picture of his life can be found in even earlier extra-testamentary materials. This argument is open to challenge because its dating of these non-canonical gospels is somewhat speculative. See: John Dominic Crossan, *Jesus: A Revolutionary Biography* (San Francisco: Harper, 1994).

and spatial insofar as it involves another, supernatural world."[22] This definition draws attention to both the form of apocalyptic literature (e.g., its plot and narrative framework) and its content (e.g., its otherworldly mediator). John J. Collins, the chair of the group of scholars who crafted the definition, has since offered an important clarification. While the definition implies that all apocalypses have both a temporal *and* a spatial dimension, Collins suggests that most apocalyptic literature emphasizes one over the other.

On this view, therefore, we can divide apocalypses into at least two distinct groups. Otherworldly journeys are spatial. They explore the relationship between the earthly and heavenly realms. An angelic being gives a human protagonist a tour of heaven, illuminating the supernatural sources of earthly reality. The first portion of the non-canonical book of Enoch, for example, is an otherworldly journey. This form is also central to various strains of mysticism and well-known works of literature, such as Dante's *Divine Comedy*.

Historical apocalypses, on the other hand, are temporal. They sketch the direction of history. A human protagonist receives a symbolic revelation about the future, the meaning of which is often explained by a supernatural interpreter. While both have spatial elements, the second half of the book of Daniel and the entirety of the book of Revelation are primarily historical apocalypses.[23] Apocalypses of this type are the central textual and imaginative sources for the religious apocalyptic movements to which Machiavelli and Hobbes are responding. We will focus our attention on these historical apocalypses.

The two most developed and influential biblical apocalypses are in the books of Daniel and Revelation, which display most of the features of the apocalyptic genre and all the elements of the apocalyptic worldview outlined earlier. In what follows, I give brief summaries of the context, structure, and contents of each book, followed by observations about their political relevance. Any account of such complex and symbolically dense works must resort to simplification. The discussion I offer imposes some artificial coherence on texts that are often frustratingly elaborate and obscure. My aim is not to be interpretively exhaustive, but rather to draw out the narrative structures, images, and political themes that persist in later manifestations of apocalypticism, particularly during the historical periods in which Machiavelli, Hobbes, and Morgenthau wrote.

The book of Daniel contains the only fully developed apocalypse in the Hebrew Bible. The nature and status of the book are subject to some debate in the Judeo-Christian tradition. In the Hebrew Bible, Daniel is placed among the *Kethuvim* (Writings), reflecting the late date of its composition and

---

[22] John J. Collins, "Towards the Morphology of a Genre: Introduction," *Semeia* 14 (1979): 9. This definition incorporates input from a group of scholars in the Apocalypse Group of the Society of Biblical Literature's Genres Project.
[23] Collins, "Early Jewish Apocalypticism," 283; Collins, "From Prophecy to Apocalypticism," 77. The vertical/horizontal distinction is from: McGinn, "Revelation," 526.

The Judeo-Christian Apocalypse

perhaps also a sense that it should not be accorded the status given to the books known as the Prophets.[24] Christians, on the other hand, have been eager to assign the book a more prominent place, situating it among the Prophets in their Bible. The reason for this enhanced status is that the book of Daniel has had an important impact on the development of several elements of Christian doctrine. First, it is the only text in the Hebrew Bible that makes unambiguous reference to bodily resurrection and judgment after death, a belief that is central to the Christian tradition.[25] Second, it is the source of the figure identified as "one like the son of man," a cosmic judge who descends on the clouds to earth.[26] Early Christologies see Jesus in this role. Finally, as we shall see later, several of the images and symbols in Daniel are further developed in the book of Revelation.

The book of Daniel recounts the heroic exploits and revelatory visions of its eponymous protagonist. The text includes two distinct genres. Chapters 1 through 6 are "court legends," third-person narratives of Daniel's courageous deeds in the courts of foreign rulers. In this portion of the book, Daniel is an interpreter of the dreams and visions of others. Chapters 7 through 12, which are narrated in the first person, describe a series of prophetic visions. Collectively, these chapters are an apocalypse in the literary sense.[27] Here, Daniel is himself a visionary, the recipient of revelations about the end times.

The reader is told that Daniel lived during the time of the Babylonian Exile. But critical biblical scholars agree that the book was compiled and composed much later. Specifically, there is substantial agreement that the apocalyptic part of Daniel was written sometime between 167 and 164 BCE.[28] This dating

---

[24] This may have been a determination based purely on considerations of genre. Daniel is not identified as a prophet anywhere in the book. However, as Laurence M. Wills explains, it may also have reflected a discomfort within the rabbinic tradition with the place that Daniel occupied in the Christian tradition, particularly the early church's tendency to see "prefigurations of Christ and Christian resurrection" in the book. Also, as Wills continues, "Jewish tradition was sometimes critical of what appeared to be a positive relationship between Daniel and Nebuchadnezzar." See: Lawrence M. Wills, "Daniel: Introduction and Annotations," in *The Jewish Study Bible, Tanakh Translation*, ed. Adele Berlin and Mark Zvi Brettler (New York: Oxford University Press, 2004), 1642.

[25] Isa. 26:19 ("Your dead shall live, their corpses shall rise") and Hos. 6:2 ("After two days he will revive us; on the third day he will raise us up, that we may live before him") seem to suggest a resurrection. However, as John J. Collins notes, they "are more probably speaking metaphorically of the restoration of the Israelite people." See: John J. Collins, "Daniel, Book of," in *The Anchor Bible Dictionary*, ed. David Noel Freedman, vol. 2 (New York: Doubleday, 1992), 35.

[26] Dan. 13:7.

[27] The interpretive difficulties posed by the change of genre are compounded by the fact that Dan. 1:1–2:4a, 8–12 are in Hebrew, while Dan. 2:4b–7:28 are in Aramaic. These linguistic shifts do not coincide with the genre division. For a summary of scholarly attempts to deal with bilingual nature of the text, see: Collins, "Daniel," 31.

[28] This dating is unusually precise. Contemporary critical scholars tend to accept the case that was first made by the third-century philosopher Porphyry, whose argument (which survives only in

suggests a very particular historical context. In 175 BCE, Antiochus IV Epiphanes succeeded his brother as ruler of the Seleucid Empire. In two military campaigns financed through taxes levied on Judea and the pillage of the Temple at Jerusalem, Antiochus attempted to wrest control of Egypt from the Ptolemies before threats from Rome forced his withdrawal. Upon his return, he strengthened an existing program of cultural and religious assimilation. With the support of some Hellenized Jews, Antiochus systematically outlawed Jewish religious practices and began a campaign of violent persecution aimed at ensuring the hegemony of Greek culture and institutions.[29] For many faithful Jews, the final straw came in 167 BCE when Antiochus installed a statue of Zeus in the Temple in Jerusalem. The stage had been set for a guerrilla campaign that would later become known as the Maccabean Revolt.[30] It is within the context of these policies of cultural assimilation and persecution that the apocalyptic message of Daniel took shape.

While the summary provided here focuses on the apocalyptic half of Daniel (chapters 7–12), there is a story in the early portion of the book that is essential for understanding this later material. Chapter 2 tells of an incident during Daniel's time in the court of the Babylonian king Nebuchadnezzar. The king has had a troubling dream and summons his interpreters, commanding them to tell him both the content of the dream and its meaning, on pain of violent death. Unsurprisingly, the interpreters find this task impossible. Facing the threat of imminent execution, Daniel prays to God and the mystery of the dream is revealed. Daniel recounts the dream to the king: "there was a great statue...its brilliance extraordinary; it was standing before you and its appearance was frightening. The head...was of fine gold, its chest and arms of silver, its middle and thighs of bronze, its legs of iron, its feet partly of iron and partly of clay."[31] A stone cut "not by human hands" struck the

---

the form of a citation in Jerome), was that the book of Daniel was accurate in its predictions up to but not beyond the reign of Antiochus IV Epiphanes (r. 175–164 BCE). The book is also especially detailed in its descriptions of the persecution of Jews between 167 and 164 BCE, which suggests that this was a matter of particular (and likely contemporary) concern. See: Collins, *The Apocalyptic Imagination*, 87–88.

[29] I use the term "Jew" here and later to denote "an adherent of the tradition of Judaism," who, in the context of the Book of Daniel, would have also been Judeans, or inhabitants of Judea. See: Hayes, *Introduction to the Bible*, xii. Such a terminological decision is certainly open to reasonable challenges. See, for instance: Steve Mason, "Jews, Judaeans, Judaizing, Judaism: Problems of Categorization in Ancient History," *Journal for the Study of Judaism* 38, no. 4 (2007): 457–512.

[30] Much of the summary given here comes from the (admittedly one-sided) account in 1 and 2 Macc. For an attempt to evaluate arguments about Antiochus' motives and to develop a new position on the issue, see: Erich S. Gruen, "Hellenism and Persecution: Antiochus IV and the Jews," in *Hellenistic History and Culture*, ed. Peter Green (Berkeley: University of California Press, 1993), 238–64.

[31] Dan. 2:32–33.

The Judeo-Christian Apocalypse

statue, breaking it in pieces and leaving it "like chaff of the summer threshing floors."[32] In its place, the stone grew into "a great mountain and filled the whole earth."[33] Daniel explains that the head of gold represents the Babylonian kingdom, while the other materials are three consecutive kingdoms of decreasing strength. The stone is the eternal kingdom of God that "shall crush all these kingdoms and bring them to an end."[34] Apparently untroubled by this looming destruction, the grateful Nebuchadnezzar rewards the interpreter and acknowledges the sovereignty of Daniel's God. Here, the annihilation of earthly kingdoms and the establishment of the kingdom of God are events that will occur in the distant future. There are still three kingdoms to come after Babylon's demise.

In contrast, the second half of the book is marked by a sense of apocalyptic urgency. Chapters 7 through 12 describe Daniel's visions of a future that would have been imminent for those living under Antiochus IV Epiphanes in the second century BCE. Chapter 7 revisits the theme of the four kingdoms in a vision that Daniel is reported to have had during the reign of "King Belshazzar."[35] This time, the kingdoms are portrayed symbolically as a series of beasts rising out of the sea, each more frightening than the last. The fourth beast emerges with ten horns, three of which are then uprooted to make room for a smaller, "arrogant" horn. God then appears in corporeal form, takes his seat on a fiery throne, and passes judgment on the four beasts.[36]

Ultimately, "one like a son of man" descends on "the clouds of heaven" and is granted "dominion and glory and kingship" over "all peoples, nations, and languages" by the Ancient One.[37] This kingdom will endure forever. An angelic figure then interprets the dream for Daniel. The four beasts represent four kingdoms. However, their power will not last and "the holy ones of the Most High shall receive the kingdom and possess the kingdom forever."[38] The angelic figure explains that the small, arrogant horn will persecute "the holy ones of the Most High."[39] This persecution will endure for three and half years, after which

---

[32] Dan. 2:34–35.   [33] Dan. 2:35.   [34] Dan. 2:44.
[35] This is one of several places in which the book of Daniel is historically inaccurate. Belshazzar was not a king. He reigned as a kind of prince regent when his father, Nabonidus, was absent.
[36] Dan. 7:9.
[37] Dan. 7:13–14. The NRSV translates the Aramaic "one like a son of man" as "one like a human being." The figure of the "Son of Man" is the subject of some debate. Here, it refers to an angelic figure that descends from heaven on clouds and presides over the eternal kingdom on earth. Non-canonical, first-century BCE, Jewish apocalyptic works also sometimes use the designation "Son of Man" to refer to a cosmic judge who will deliver Israel. See, for example: 1 Enoch 69. However, Jesus also refers to a figure he calls "the Son of Man," who will "gather his elect from the four winds" to admit them into the kingdom of God and condemn evildoers to "the furnace of fire" (Matt. 13:40–43). Some Christians believe that Jesus is referring to himself and that the figure mentioned in Daniel actually anticipates the Second Coming of Jesus.
[38] Dan. 7:18.   [39] Dan. 7:25.

the horn will be subject to divine judgment and stripped of his dominion.[40] To an audience living during the reign of Antiochus IV Epiphanes, the meaning of this angelic interpretation would have been clear. The four beasts are the kingdoms of Babylon, Media, Persia, and Greece, while the ten horns represent Alexander the Great's successors.[41] The small, arrogant horn is Antiochus IV Epiphanes, whose persecution will usher in a day of judgment and the establishment of the kingdom of God.

Subsequent chapters develop the themes introduced in this account. Chapter 8 offers a similar vision in which the four kingdoms are represented as animals and provides an angelic interpretation that confirms the identification of these kingdoms outlined earlier. Chapter 9 deals with a problem of apocalyptic chronology, reinterpreting Jeremiah's prophecy that Jerusalem would remain devastated for seventy years. Given that Jeremiah prophesied in the early sixth century and the later chapters of Daniel were written in the mid-second century BCE, in a time when Jerusalem remained under foreign control, some interpretive solution had to be reached. The angel Gabriel explains to Daniel that Jeremiah's message was a code intended to indicate not seventy years, but seventy *weeks* of years, or 490 years.[42] The description of the last week of this period is a thinly veiled account of Antiochus' persecutions and his profanation of the Temple.

The vision that spans the final three chapters of the book is an extended and detailed account of the final events of worldly history. Daniel is visited by an angelic being, with "eyes like flaming torches" and arms and legs "like the gleam of burnished bronze."[43] Speaking to Daniel with a voice "like the roar of a multitude," he explains that the worldly events of the Hellenistic wars are but a reflection of a battle in heaven between angelic "princes."[44] With the help of Michael, he is currently fighting the prince of Persia and will soon confront the

---

[40] The period of the little horn's reign is literally described as "a time, two times, and a half time." Interpreters take this to mean three and a half years, which was roughly the duration of Antiochus' persecution of the Jews. Also, as exactly half of seven (which was seen as a perfect number), three and a half denoted radical incompleteness. See: Amy-Jill Levine, "Daniel: Introduction and Notes," in *The New Oxford Annotated Bible, New Revised Standard Version with Apocrypha*, ed. Michael D. Coogan, 4th ed. (Oxford: Oxford University Press, 2010), 1249.

[41] This reading is confirmed by the angelic interpretation of a similar vision in the following chapter. Dan. 8:18–25.

[42] Other portions of Daniel also give precise date calculations of the period between Antiochus' persecutions and the end of time. In Dan. 8:14, we are told that the Temple will remain desolate for 2300 "evenings and mornings," which amount to 1150 days. In Dan. 12:11–12, we are given two different numbers of days: "From the time that the regular burnt offering is taken away and the abomination that desolates is set up, there shall be one thousand two hundred ninety days. Happy are those who persevere and attain the thousand three hundred thirty-five days." Of the latter passage, Collins notes that "the fact that two different figures are given strongly suggests that the second calculation was added after the first number of days had passed," a phenomenon that would become quite prevalent in later apocalyptic movements. See: Collins, "From Prophecy to Apocalypticism," 76.

[43] Dan. 10:6.   [44] Dan. 10:6, 13–20.

prince of Greece. Having explained the heavenly source of the Hellenistic wars, he then offers a summary of political history from the end of the Babylonian kingdom through to the reign of Antiochus IV Epiphanes, which is the subject of a more detailed set of predictions. The angel outlines Antiochus' rise to power, his military campaigns in Egypt, and his eventual withdrawal under Roman pressure before detailing the ruler's program of persecution.

Daniel is told that the ruler will abolish religious ceremonies and set up an "abomination that makes desolate," a reference to Antiochus' installation of a statue of Zeus in the Temple at Jerusalem. As these events unfold, "the wise among the people shall give understanding to many" but will also be the targets of violent persecution.[45] The angel then reveals (inaccurately, as it turns out) the circumstances of Antiochus' demise.

The vision concludes with an account of the end of days. After the death of Antiochus, "there shall be a time of anguish, such as has never occurred since nations first came into existence."[46] There will be a bodily resurrection and "many of those who sleep in the dust of the earth shall awake, some to everlasting life, and some to shame and everlasting contempt."[47] All of Daniel's people whose names are "found written in the book" will be delivered.[48] The angel then advises Daniel to keep the contents of this vision secret and "the book sealed until the time of the end," warning that in the meantime "evil shall increase."[49]

The book of Daniel is an "imaginative construction" of the historical crisis facing second-century-BCE Judeans. That is, it does not simply reflect or respond to the political events of its time. It also describes them metaphorically and locates them within a sacred worldview that endows them with divine significance.[50] For these reasons, the symbols and images that the text brings together would prove almost endlessly flexible and migratory. Less than two centuries later, they would provide some of the central imagery in the book of Revelation.

The author of that book identifies himself as John and tells us that he "was on the island of Patmos because of the word of God and the testimony of Jesus."[51] Most scholars agree that the author of Revelation is not John, son of Zebedee, one of Jesus' disciples.[52] Internal textual evidence suggests instead that he was an itinerant prophet in Asia Minor. He may well have been of Jewish

---

[45] Dan. 11:33.   [46] Dan. 12:1.   [47] Dan. 12:2.   [48] Dan. 12:1.
[49] Dan. 12:4. Stephen O'Leary notes that one of the unique features of the apocalyptic myth, particularly compared to conspiratorial discourse, is that the former "offers a temporal or teleological framework for understanding evil by claiming that evil must grow in power until the appointed time of the (imminent) end." See: O'Leary, *Arguing the Apocalypse*, 6.
[50] The notion of an "imaginative construction" is from Collins, *Apocalyptic Imagination*, 114.
[51] Rev. 1:9.
[52] John, son of Zebedee is reported to have been killed sometime before 70 CE and most scholars think that Revelation was written or compiled in the 90s CE. In addition, the author of Revelation never identifies himself as a disciple of Jesus.

birth, perhaps even a refugee from the first Roman-Jewish War (66–73 CE).[53] Most critical biblical scholars agree that the book of Revelation was written or compiled during the latter part of the reign of the Roman emperor Domitian (r. 81–96 CE) and there is good internal textual evidence to support this claim.[54]

In contrast to the case of Antiochus IV Epiphanes, there is no proof that Domitian systematically persecuted Christians for their faith. Nevertheless, there were other political circumstances that may well have made both Jews and Christians profoundly uneasy. Barely a few decades had passed since the first Jewish-Roman war, which ended with the destruction of the Temple in Jerusalem in 70 CE.[55] Only six years before this, Nero had embarked on a campaign of violent persecution against Christians to deflect blame for the great fire in Rome.[56] Given the brutality and significance of both events, it would hardly be surprising if they continued to traumatize Jews and Christians in the mid-90s CE.

The ways in which the Romans visually represented their imperial triumphs would also have horrified many Jews and Christians. The Sebasteion at Aphrodisias was a visual celebration of the victories of Rome and the humiliation of subject territories. For example, a panel depicting Rome's conquest of Britannia shows the emperor Claudius grasping an anguished female captive by the hair. He jams her exposed body into the ground as he prepares to deliver a fatal blow (see Figure 2.1). A similar panel depicts Nero subduing Armenia (see Figure 2.2).[57] Even without a systematic campaign of persecution, this gendered theater of imperial humiliation might well have left Jews and Christians feeling acutely vulnerable.

---

[53] John's knowledge of the Hebrew Bible and the similarities between Revelation and earlier Jewish apocalypses, such as the book of Daniel, suggest that John may well have been Jewish. The fact that he seems to have known Greek, Hebrew, and possibly Aramaic suggests that he was a native of Palestine, as there is little reason to think Jews in the Diaspora would have learned Hebrew or Aramaic. For a review of debates about authorship, see: Adela Yarbro Collins, *Crisis and Catharsis: The Power of the Apocalypse* (Philadelphia: Westminster Press, 1984), 24–53.

[54] In Revelation, Rome is equated with Babylon. We find this equation in various non-canonical Jewish apocalypses from the same period, all of which indicate that the reason for this association is that Rome, like Babylon previously, destroyed the Temple and waged war on Jerusalem. This evidence suggests that Revelation was written sometime after 70 CE. See: Collins, *Crisis and Catharsis*, 57–58.

[55] The first Roman-Jewish war began under Nero (r. 54–68) and continued under Vespasian (r. 69–79).

[56] Collins, *Crisis and Catharsis*, 99–100. The persecution of Christians under Nero took place between 64 and 68 AD.

[57] Elaine Pagels, *Revelations: Visions, Prophecy, and Politics in the Book of Revelation* (New York: Viking, 2012), 12. Steven Friesen suggests that both panels drew on representations of the conquest of the Amazons. See: Steven J. Friesen, *Imperial Cults and the Apocalypse of John: Reading Revelation in the Ruins* (Oxford: Oxford University Press, 2001), 173–74.

The Judeo-Christian Apocalypse

FIGURE 2.1. Nero conquering Armenia, Sebasteion at Aphrodisias (first century AD). Photo by Dean Stevens.

Another source of distress may have come from the imperial cult, which cast emperors and their families as gods and called upon those under Roman authority to worship them.[58] The imperial cult had helped to secure the loyalties of

---

[58] There is a lively scholarly debate about the extent to which Christians in Asia Minor should be seen as oppressed and/or persecuted. Adela Yarbro Collins, whose work I have drawn upon here, argues that some Christians were very likely still traumatized by Nero's persecutions and the first Roman-Jewish War. This trauma was compounded by the pressure to participate in the imperial cult. Elisabeth Schüssler Fiorenza argues that the oppression and colonial exploitation of Christians in Asia Minor were even more serious than Yarbro Collins suggests. Leonard Thompson, on the other hand, argues that there is little evidence of this kind of pervasive

FIGURE 2.2. Claudius conquering Brittania, Sebasteion at Aphrodisias (first century AD). Photo by Dean Stevens.

provinces far from the center of the empire and was enthusiastically embraced by many people living in Asia Minor.[59] Tied as it was to polytheism and the worship of political sovereigns, the imperial cult was likely very troubling to

> oppression and cautions that Revelation should be seen not as a reflection of the social reality in Asia Minor, but as John of Patmos' attempt to alienate his audience from their social context. See: Collins, *Crisis and Catharsis*, 99–104; Elisabeth Schüssler Fiorenza, *The Book of Revelation: Justice and Judgment* (Minneapolis: Fortress Press, 1985), 126–27; Leonard L. Thompson, *The Book of Revelation: Apocalypse and Empire* (New York: Oxford University Press, 1990), 164–67, 171–85.
> [59] Collins, *Crisis and Catharsis*, 101.

The Judeo-Christian Apocalypse

devout Christians and Jews. Even worse, one of the deified emperors whom some would have been called upon to worship was Titus. As a military commander, he had laid siege to Jerusalem and destroyed the Temple.[60] Christians and Jews were being asked not just to obey but to worship their conquerors. This is the context in which John of Patmos wrote the book of Revelation.

The text begins with John's overpowering encounter with the risen Jesus, who is identified as "one like the Son of Man."[61] In terms that echo the description of the angelic being that mediates Daniel's apocalyptic vision, Jesus is described as having eyes "like a flame of fire," feet "like burnished bronze," and a voice that is "like the sound of many waters."[62] He tells John to "write what you have seen, what is, and what is to take place after this."[63] The book of Revelation accomplishes each of these tasks in turn. It begins with an account of John's vision of the risen Jesus ("what you have seen"). It then continues with a record of Jesus' messages to the seven churches of Asia Minor, assessing their current situation, praising the faithful, and admonishing those who have strayed ("what is"). The bulk of Revelation is devoted to the third task and describes a series of visions of the end times ("what is to take place after this").[64]

The literary structure of the work poses interpretive difficulties. The repetitive sequences of visions make a literal interpretation of the narrative challenging. The world is repeatedly beset by a series of plagues – let loose first by the opening of seven seals, then by the sounding of seven trumpets, and subsequently by the pouring out of seven bowls – and at the end of each the world is destroyed, only then to be found back intact, ready to be beset anew by even more terrible tribulations. These repetitive visions make it impossible to chart the narrative on a linear chronological timeline.

We can alleviate these interpretive difficulties, however, if we assume that the book has a recapitulative structure that repeats the core elements of Revelation's message: "(a) persecution, (b) punishment of persecutors, and (c) salvation of the persecuted."[65] The bulk of the narrative proceeds in cycles, each of which brings the reader's focus back to the edge between the precarious present and the imminent end. The summary of these visions offered later is not meant to be exhaustive, but rather to give the reader a sense of the "imaginative construction" that John of Patmos puts upon the events of his time, the criticism of

---

[60] See: Friesen, *Imperial Cults*, 46, 53. Friesen's argument here is based on archeological evidence. There was a statue of Titus at the temple of the Sebastoi at Ephesus.
[61] Rev. 1:13.   [62] Rev. 1:14–15.   [63] Rev. 1:19.
[64] I am borrowing this convenient approach to the summary from: Bart D. Ehrman, *The New Testament: A Historical Introduction to the Early Christian Writings* (New York: Oxford University Press, 2008), 471.
[65] Adela Yarbro Collins, "The Book of Revelation," in *The Continuum History of Apocalypticism*, ed. Bernard J. McGinn, John J. Collins, and Stephen J. Stein (New York: Continuum, 2003), 199. There are, of course, numerous other ways to interpret the narrative structure of Revelation. See, for instance: Fiorenza, *The Book of Revelation*, 170–77.

sovereign and imperial power that runs through the text, and the captivating nature of some of its most enduring images.

After Jesus dictates his letters to the seven churches of Asia Minor, John is taken up to heaven, where he sees God seated on a throne. Gleaming as if he were made of gemstones, God is surrounded by four heavenly beings in animal form and twenty-four enthroned elders, who fall at his feet and "cast their crowns before the throne" in a gesture of worship and an acknowledgment of his complete sovereignty.[66] God holds a scroll with seven seals on which is written the future history of the world. When no one worthy to open the scroll can be found in heaven or on earth, John begins to weep. However, he soon sees Jesus, figured as a "Lamb standing as if it had been slaughtered."[67] The worthy Lamb takes the scroll from God, opening it one seal at a time. As each seal breaks, new terrors are unleashed upon the world. Four horsemen bring war, conquest, famine, and death. With the opening of the sixth seal, a great earthquake turns the sun black and the moon to the color of blood. The stars fall to earth and the sky vanishes "like a scroll rolling itself up."[68] The opening of the seventh seal brings complete silence.

It also inaugurates a violent narrative recapitulation, as another sequence of terrifying catastrophes begins. This time, John sees seven trumpeting angels, who inflict a series of disasters that recall the plagues let loose on Egypt in the book of Exodus: hail and fire destroy the land and trees, the sea turns to blood, the waters are poisoned, the light from the sun and the moon is darkened, an army of locusts with scorpion tails torture the unfaithful "who will seek death but will not find it,"[69] and finally a massive cavalry of fire- and sulfur-spewing horses lay waste to a third of mankind. The sounding of the seventh trumpet signals an end to these terrors and the beginning of the Kingdom of God.

However, it also heralds another terrifying vision. Satan, in the form of a dragon, waits hungrily while a woman "clothed in the sun" and wailing in the anguish of childbirth brings forth a son, "who is to rule all the nations with a rod of iron."[70] Denied his messianic feast, the dragon wages a war against Michael and his angels in heaven, but is defeated. He is then thrown to earth and makes war on God's children. Standing at the edge of the sea, he looks out as a seven-headed beast emerges from the water and assumes the power and the throne of the dragon. The beast will be worshipped by the entire world, "given authority over every tribe and people and language and nation."[71] Yet the duration of his rule will be limited to a (symbolic) period of three and a half years, as we are told in Daniel. To John's audience, the identity

---

[66] Rev. 4:10. The description of God's throne echoes those in Ezek. 1:5–11; Isa. 6:1–4. Steven Friesen cites this description as an example of the way in which John did not limit himself to the use of preexisting models and imagery, but "created powerful new ones through a *recombinant mythic method* whereby pieces of various models were conjoined in new ways." See: Friesen, *Imperial Cults*, 174. Emphasis mine.
[67] Rev. 5:6.   [68] Rev. 6:14.   [69] Rev. 9:6.   [70] Rev. 12:1, 12:5.   [71] Rev. 13:7.

The Judeo-Christian Apocalypse 39

of this beast would have been clear. It is Rome. Its seven heads on which are inscribed "blasphemous names" are those emperors who were worshipped as gods.[72]

A second beast then rises out of the earth, exercising "all the authority of the first beast on its behalf" and commanding all peoples to worship its predecessor, perhaps a reference to the Roman imperial cults.[73] The second beast also requires that all people wanting to participate in the economy bear a mark signifying the numerical equivalent of the beast's name – 666.[74] After this terrifying vision, John once again offers the faithful some reassurance. He describes Jesus swinging his sharp sickle over the earth, reaping an eschatological harvest, trampling the grapes of wrath, and producing a flow of blood "as high as a horse's bridle, for a distance of about two hundred miles."[75]

Seven more angels then appear and each pours out a bowl of God's wrath, plunging the world into new terrors: painful bodily sores, bloody water, scorching heat, darkness, drought, a plague of frogs, and an earthquake so violent that it destroys Babylon and all other cities. John then describes a more detailed vision of the destruction of Babylon. The city is figured now as a "great whore...with whom the kings of the earth have committed fornication, and with the wine of whose fornication the inhabitants of the earth have drunk."[76] The whore herself is also "drunk on the blood of the saints and the blood of the witnesses of Jesus."[77] The angel translates the vision for John, telling him that the seven heads of the beast are the seven mountains on which the whore is seated. This leaves no doubt as to her identity. She is Rome, the city of seven hills.

John then witnesses the divine destruction of Babylon, which is followed by a gruesome heavenly feast where all are invited "to eat the flesh of kings, the flesh of captains, the flesh of the mighty, the flesh of horses and their riders, the flesh of all, both free and slave, both small and great."[78] Strengthened by this meal, Jesus and his forces then decisively defeat "the beast and the kings of the earth" in a cosmic battle. Satan is imprisoned in a bottomless pit for a thousand years and the martyrs and saints are resurrected to rule with Jesus on earth. At the end of this millennium, Satan is released and gathers his forces for war. But they are quickly consumed by heavenly flames and thrown into a lake of fire to be tortured for eternity.

---

[72] Rev. 13:1.   [73] Rev. 13:12. See: Friesen, *Imperial Cults*, 146.
[74] As Adela Yarbro Collins explains, "many of the coins in circulation in Asia Minor bore the image of the emperor with divine attributes and his name. This aspect of the vision expresses the offense caused by the virtual necessity of using such coins for strict monotheists and strict interpreters of the commandment against images." The number 666 itself is thought by some to be a reference to Nero, following a system of alphanumeric equivalencies in the Hebrew and Greek alphabets. This reference, along with Revelation's preoccupation with persecution, led (and continues to lead) some scholars to date the book to the 60s AD. See: Collins, "The Book of Revelation," 205.
[75] Rev. 14:20.   [76] Rev. 17:2.   [77] Rev. 17:6.   [78] Rev. 19:18.

With the forces of evil vanquished, John once again sees Jesus enthroned. There is a second bodily resurrection, this time of the dead who are not among the ranks of the martyrs and saints. They stand before Jesus and await judgment. All are rewarded or punished for their deeds, according to the list of the redeemed contained in the book of life. The damned are thrown into the lake of fire, while the elect remain to rule with Jesus on earth for eternity. There is now "a new heaven and a new earth; for the first heaven and the first earth had passed away, and the sea was no more."[79] A gleaming New Jerusalem descends from heaven – a home in which God will dwell with this people. In this eternal kingdom, he "will wipe every tear from their eyes. Death will be no more; mourning and crying and pain will be no more, for the first things have passed away."[80] God's people will be forever secure, the gates of the city "will never be shut... and there will be no night there."[81] John then concludes his revelation with a warning from Jesus that the contents of this book should not be sealed, "for the time is near... Surely I am coming soon."[82] Thus concludes the book of Revelation and the Christian Bible.

Daniel and Revelation are both books pregnant with interpretive possibilities. For the purposes of this chapter, however, let us focus on three broad themes, all of which help account for the enduring political power of these works. These three themes are also central to the contexts and the works of Machiavelli, Hobbes, and Morgenthau.

First, both biblical texts present us with a criticism of sovereign and imperial power. In both, this power is imagined as a beast. Daniel sees four beasts emerge from the sea, each representing one of the empires that conquered and occupied the eastern Mediterranean between the eighth and second centuries BCE. John collapses these four sea beasts into one – a seven-headed monster crawling out of the sea, ready to assume the power and authority of Satan. In Revelation, Rome becomes "the ultimate empire, combining all the destructive characteristics of its predecessors."[83]

To their ancient authors and audiences, however, these beastly images would have carried additional meaning. Ancient Near Eastern mythology describes a primordial struggle between a rightful God and the beasts of the sea. It is a battle between divine order and primeval chaos.[84] These mythological images are taken up in a new form in the Hebrew Bible. God crushes a great multi-headed sea beast called "Leviathan" at the beginning of creation, overcoming the dark forces of chaos and providing the conditions for earthly order. His followers remind God of this feat when they plead with him for deliverance: "You divided the sea by your might; you broke the heads of dragons in the waters. You crushed the heads of Leviathan; you gave him as food for the creatures of the wilderness."[85] In Isaiah, we are told that God will once again battle the

---

[79] Rev. 21:1.   [80] Rev. 21:4.   [81] Rev. 21:25.   [82] Rev. 22:10, 20.
[83] Friesen, *Imperial Cults*, 202.   [84] Collins, "From Prophecy to Apocalypticism," 74.
[85] Ps. 74:13–14. The same beast is also called "Rahab." See: Ps. 89:10; Job 26:12–13; Isa. 51:9.

great sea monster as a preliminary to the restoration of Zion: "On that day the Lord with his cruel and great and strong sword will punish Leviathan the fleeing serpent, Leviathan the twisting serpent, and he will kill the dragon that is in the sea."[86] The slaying of this Leviathan is necessary for the establishment and renewal of divine order on earth.

So, when Daniel and John of Patmos cast sovereign power as a sea beast, they are presenting a more thoroughgoing criticism than we might initially think. Sovereign power is allied with the forces of primeval chaos. The promise of order offered by Hellenic institutions or the *Pax Romana* is illusory. Worldly empires are antithetical to divine order. Despite any appearances to the contrary, the world is radically out of joint and it will not be righted until God eliminates the forces of chaos and makes his sovereignty manifest on earth. With the establishment of the Kingdom of God, not only does John see "a new heaven and a new earth" but also that "the sea [is] no more."[87] The source of primeval chaos and the home of Leviathan are forever destroyed.

Second, both Daniel and Revelation suggest that God's sovereignty is, at least in part, *sovereignty over history*. Those suffering the persecutions of Antiochus IV Epiphanes or the traumas of Roman rule may well have seen themselves as the victims of radically contingent and inexplicable events. But both Daniel and John of Patmos make these events meaningful by locating them in a cosmic story that culminates in the reassertion of divine power. Both books offer a spatial and a temporal meaning for earthly events. On a spatial level, they cast the events on earth as the product of actions in heaven. Daniel sees the Hellenic wars as earthly shadows of heavenly battles between angelic princes, while John of Patmos reveals that Satan's reign of oppression on earth is the product of the dragon's conflict with angelic forces in heaven. On a temporal level, both books bring narrative coherence to history. The sequence of empires and the apocalyptic timetables in the book of Daniel make over 500 years of conquest and persecution meaningful. They allow his audience to locate its current predicament in apocalyptic time, to recognize that Antiochus' reign will be short and that the violent persecution of Jews will soon end. While God may have temporarily ceded his control over worldly history, he has revealed its outlines to his followers so that they may make narrative sense of their place in time.

Revelation collapses the longer historical vision of Daniel, a feat achieved metaphorically by combining the latter's four sea beasts into one terrifying creature. The result, as Adela Yarbro Collins explains, "is a reduction of attention to history and a focus on the terrors of the recent past and the present."[88] John of Patmos puts his audience in the last great crisis before the end times, allowing them to see Roman oppression as a prelude to the kingdom of God.[89] In spite of these temporal differences, both Daniel and Revelation achieve the same

---

[86] Isa. 27:1. [87] Rev. 21:1. [88] Collins, "The Book of Revelation," 203.
[89] Friesen, *Imperial Cults*, 159.

narrative goal. They offer a vision of the end that brings retrospective coherence to political events that seem threatening, inexplicable, and contingent.

Finally, both works demonstrate that one of the benefits of this cosmic denouement is that difference, conflict, and moral complexity will be eliminated. In Daniel, the borders and distinctions between groups melt away. The son of man will rule over "all peoples, nations, and languages," his total dominion guaranteed by the complete servitude and obedience of all his people.[90] The differences of race, nationality, and language will be obliterated as God gathers his people back from the corners of the earth to be ruled as one. This theme is even more pronounced in Revelation. With the restoration of divine order on earth, not only is evil abolished, but so too are all the previous markers of difference. Jesus promises his faithful followers "a new name" and new clothes – the white garments that befit those who are glorious and exalted.[91] Only once the elect have completely surrendered to his transformative omnipotence will they be fit to be pillars in God's temple and to share the throne of Jesus.[92] With evil vanquished and worldly differences eliminated, the New Jerusalem will descend from heaven "prepared as a bride adorned for her husband" and there shall be no more death, no more tears, and no more pain.[93] Without fear of conflict, evil, or ambiguity, the gates of the city will remain forever open. God's final assertion of earthly sovereignty destroys all the boundaries, differences, conflicts, and moral complexity that define the political world. Revelation and Daniel offer their audiences not only the promise of a world without persecution but also a seductive vision of a world without politics.

Containing the Apocalypse

The visions in apocalyptic texts have a troubled place within the Judeo-Christian tradition. While they may well have offered hope and consolation to those struggling to make sense of a dark world, they also generated radical enthusiasms that proved difficult to control. As we will see in this section, these difficulties were a central preoccupation for Paul and especially for Augustine, two of the founding figures in the Christian realist tradition. Both thinkers developed responses to apocalyptic enthusiasm that would later be used and adapted by political realists such as Machiavelli, Hobbes, and Morgenthau.

The radical political potential of Daniel and Revelation is not immediately obvious. Neither book explicitly encourages active agency on the part of its audiences. Daniel's politics are overtly quietist. While the text was written and compiled during the period of the Maccabean revolt, its author offers little support for this outright challenge to sovereign and imperial power. Instead, he celebrates "the wise," who "shall give understanding to many" but also "fall by sword and flame, and suffer captivity and plunder."[94] By promising a bodily

[90] Dan. 7:14, 27. [91] Rev. 2:17, 3:5. [92] Rev. 3:12, 21. [93] Rev. 21:2, 4.
[94] Dan. 11:33.

resurrection, Daniel consoles potential martyrs and frees them from a fear of violent death.[95] But the author certainly does not urge them to political action. He distinguishes the wise from those who rely on military force and are of "little help," likely a thinly veiled reference to the Maccabees.[96] Similarly, John of Patmos does not encourage active revolt against Rome. The battle of the end times will be fought by Jesus and his angels against Satan and his demons. Babylon will be destroyed by God "in a single day," rather than by the plodding and precarious efforts of mere men.[97] Believers will exercise their agency through prayer, prophecy, and martyrdom.[98]

However, despite their explicit quietism, the texts contain the potential for political radicalism. First, any discouragement of active political agency has to overcome the force of a set of terrifying images that cast sovereign power as the primeval force of chaos. The success of the message of quietism assumes an audience capable of accepting that they are living through a period of profound crisis and that their political sovereign is the chaotic antithesis to divine order. It further assumes that, faced with this interpretation of the facts, audience members will be willing to limit their role in the eschatological drama to patient endurance and martyrdom. While Daniel and Revelation have inspired some quietist movements, history suggests these competing demands are just as easily resolved in favor of radical and violent enthusiasm.[99]

Second, as we have seen, both texts deploy a dense network of symbols, which may ultimately prove difficult to control. Especially as part of a public performance or reading, the use of imagery and symbolism allows the audience to experience for themselves the revelation that is being "'re-presented' or re-actualized for them."[100] Like the author of the apocalypse, the audience can attempt to decode the cryptic symbolism and imagery, thereby reliving the experience of the author and appropriating the revelation for themselves. Yet

---

[95] Collins, "Daniel," 35.
[96] Levine, "Daniel," 1256, n. 11:33–34. See also: Collins, "From Prophecy to Apocalypticism," 75.
[97] Rev. 18:8.
[98] There are two passages in Revelation that are potentially ambiguous on this point. The account of the final eschatological battle between the beast and the Lamb tells us that "those with [the Lamb] are called and chosen and faithful" (17:14). Earlier, John of Patmos describes the 144,000 followers of the Lamb, who follow him "wherever he goes" (14:4). It is not at all clear in the text that these followers will join Jesus in the eschatological battle. As Adela Yarbro Collins notes, "these two passages...seem to show that the author was aware of [a] tradition [for instance, in the apocalyptic materials among the Dead Sea Scrolls] that the elect would fight in the last battle. But they are just glimpses of such an idea and are not at all emphasized. The dominant conception of the final holy war is similar to that of Daniel, where people will participate in the new order brought about by the eschatological battle but not in the battle itself." See: Adela Yarbro Collins, *Cosmology and Eschatology in Jewish and Christian Apocalypticism* (Leiden: Brill, 1996), 207.
[99] John J. Collins, "The Zeal of Phinehas: The Bible and the Legitimation of Violence," *Journal of Biblical Literature* 122, no. 1 (2003): 17.
[100] David E. Aune, "The Apocalypse of John and the Problem of Genre," *Semeia* 36 (1986): 90.

because it invites interpretation, this dense symbolism guarantees that the apocalyptic text is almost infinitely flexible.[101] It can be – and indeed has been – appropriated for both quietist and activist ends.

Third, the violent imagery in both texts is ambiguous. Those who remain on earth for the final tribulations are subjected to terrors and tortures that are so unbearable that they cause their victims to envy the dead. The wicked are afflicted, consumed, and trampled until the earth is soaked in their blood. A quietist interpretation suggests that this "violent imagery was apparently intended to release aggressive feelings in a harmless way," providing a catharsis for the faithful and the powerless and urging moral and spiritual reform on those who had grown too comfortable with imperial rule.[102] Yet the symbolic flexibility of apocalyptic works offers no interpretive guarantees. These works' ambiguous treatment of violence treads a fine line between the cathartic and the inflammatory.[103]

Among early Christians, the thinkers most attuned to the potential dangers of apocalyptic rhetoric and imagery are Paul and Augustine – the two foundational members of a Christian strand of political realism.[104] Both share with later realists a pessimistic view of human nature and a concern with the imperative of political order. Paul saw in human nature a tragic conflict between our intentions and our actions: "For I do not do the good I want, but the evil I do not want is what I do ... So then, with my mind I am a slave to the law of God, but with my flesh I am a slave to the law of sin."[105] For Augustine, humanity has been condemned by original sin to both suffer and commit great evils. Our

---

[101] Paula Frederiksen, *From Jesus to Christ: The Origins of the New Testament Image of Christ* (New Haven: Yale University Press, 2000), 33.
[102] Yarbro Collins, *Crisis and Catharsis*, 171.
[103] Adela Yarbro Collins acknowledges this. See: *Crisis and Catharsis*, 171.
[104] More than anyone else, Reinhold Niebuhr is responsible for making visible and shaping a Christian realist tradition that looks back to Paul and Augustine as foundational thinkers. Niebuhr is particularly interested in Paul's conception of human nature, which centers on the persistence of sin even in the face of sincerely held moral and religious ideals. Augustine more fully develops this account of human nature and adds to it a concerted attention to "the social factions, tensions, and competitions which we know to be well-nigh universal on every level of community." See: Reinhold Niebuhr, "Augustine's Political Realism," in *The Essential Reinhold Niebuhr: Selected Essays and Addresses*, ed. Robert McAfee Brown (New Haven: Yale University Press, 1986), 124. On the centrality of Paul to Niebuhr's conception of human nature, see: Richard Crouter, *Reinhold Niebuhr: On Politics, Religion, and Christian Faith* (New York: Oxford University Press, 2010), 41–58. On Niebuhr's Christian realism, see: Robin W. Lovin, *Reinhold Niebuhr and Christian Realism* (Cambridge: Cambridge University Press, 1995), esp. 1–32. Niebuhr is undoubtedly engaged in a bit of retrospective tradition-building to legitimize his own position. However, the pessimistic account of human nature and the preoccupation with questions of power and the imperative of political order in the work of both Paul and Augustine mean that there are some "family resemblances" between their thought and that of later (self-identified) realists, Christian or otherwise.
[105] Rom. 7:19, 25.

love of "futile and harmful satisfactions" dooms us to a life of misery.[106] For both thinkers, this evil is the root cause of human conflict.

The purpose of political order is to contain this conflict and punish this evil.[107] Paul calls on everyone to "be subject to the governing authorities," which are "instituted by God." Political resistance will incur divine judgment, "for rulers are not a terror to good conduct, but to bad."[108] Similarly, Augustine points to political authority as evidence that God has not wholly abandoned his people. Just as parents and educators cane stubborn children, secular sovereigns exist to punish sin, to "overcome ignorance and to bridle corrupt desire."[109] So much do we want an escape from evil and chaos that we prefer "subjugation at the hands of victors to total destruction by the devastation of war."[110]

This commitment to the problem of political order sits uneasily with an apocalyptic worldview. While he wrote before the composition of Revelation, Paul nonetheless had to contend with the apocalypticism that captivated many early Christians. According to some of the accounts in the gospels, Jesus told his followers that the end times were imminent. Some among them would "not taste death until they see that the kingdom of God has come with power."[111] As a zealous convert to the teachings of Jesus, Paul's despair about human nature sits alongside a radical hope for the Second Coming (the *parousia*). Paul accepted and urged others to accept the imminence of the end times. But he always resisted the temptation to engage in precise chronological speculation.

His earliest epistle, the first of his letters to the Thessalonians, bears this out. The letter suggests that some of those whom Paul had converted during an earlier visit to Thessalonica had died, leading to questions about the status of these deceased brethren at the *parousia*. Paul comforts his readers by telling them that "through Jesus, God will bring with him those who have died."[112] He reaffirms the imminence of the end times, suggesting that "we who are alive" will witness them.[113] But while the *parousia* is imminent, it will nevertheless come suddenly and unexpectedly, "like a thief in the night."[114] At one moment, there will be "peace and security," while in the next "sudden destruction will come upon [the wicked], as labor pains come upon a pregnant woman, and

---

[106] Augustine of Hippo, *Concerning the City of God Against the Pagans*, trans. Henry Bettenson (Harmondsworth: Penguin, 1972), book XXII, chapter 22, 1065. All subsequent citations to this volume will be in the following format: XXII.22, 1065.

[107] While this position is elaborated in far more detail in Augustine's work, it is also present in Paul's epistle to the Romans: "for [the ruler] is God's servant for your good. But if you do what is wrong, you should be afraid, for the authority does not bear the sword in vain! It is the servant of God to execute wrath on the wrongdoer" (13:4).

[108] Rom. 13:1, 3. Biblical scholars are quick to point out that this famous passage may not be representative of Paul's views on sovereign power. See, for instance: 1 Cor. 2:6–8; 15:24–26. However, for our purposes, Rom. 13 is an accurate summary of what many take to be Paul's contribution to a particular kind of "theology of the state."

[109] Augustine, *City of God*, XXII.22, 1066.   [110] Augustine, *City of God*, XVIII.2, 762.

[111] Mark 9:1.   [112] 1 Thess. 4:14.   [113] 1 Thess. 4:15.   [114] 1 Thess. 5:2.

there will be no escape!"[115] The faithful of Thessalonica will be armed and ready for this surprise, for they are "children of light and children of the day." In preparation for the *parousia*, they will "put on the breastplate of faith and love, and for a helmet the hope of salvation."[116] They must always live, as John Donne would put it centuries later, as if "this present were the world's last night."[117] Morally and spiritually prepared, the Thessalonians could look forward to the imminent end as the time when their faith would be rewarded and their suffering redeemed.

However, this message of apocalyptic hope seems to have encouraged enthusiasm and disorder in Thessalonica. A second letter that purports to be by Paul suggests that some Thessalonians thought that the end times were at hand.[118] They had quit their jobs and become a burden to others.[119] Paul condemns this "disorderly" and "undisciplined" behavior, reminding his audience that while he and his fellow missionaries were in the community, they worked for their meals and were a burden to no one.[120] His theological argument in the letter defers the apocalypse by providing a list of events that must precede it. A "lawless one" is currently restrained but will be revealed. He will exalt himself "above every so called god or object of worship" and take "his seat in the temple of God, declaring himself to be God."[121] This figure, whose coming "is apparent in the workings of Satan," is already operating covertly.[122] Once the agent of restraint (the *katéchon*) is removed, the lawless one will be revealed and Jesus will annihilate "him by the manifestation of his coming," thereby initiating the cosmic battle of the end times.[123] The "lawless one" is often taken to be the Antichrist, an agent of Satan analogous to the false prophet of Revelation. The identity of the *katéchon* is less clear. Paul tells the Thessalonians that they "know what is now restraining" the lawless one. Interpreters have suggested that Paul is referring to a false prophet, an emperor, or the Roman Empire itself. As we shall see in Chapter 4, the identity of this figure is a matter of debate both historically and among contemporary political theologians. For our purposes here, it is sufficient to stress that when faced with end-times enthusiasm, Paul sought to temporally displace the apocalypse and return his audience to normal time.

In the centuries that followed, Christianity was transformed from a messianic sect of Judaism into a powerful religious and political institution. In 312

---

[115] 1 Thess. 5:3.   [116] 1 Thess. 5:8.
[117] John Donne, "Holy Sonnet XIII," in *The Complete Poetry and Selected Prose of John Donne*, ed. Charles M. Coffin (New York: Modern Library, 1952), 252.
[118] Biblical scholars debate whether Paul wrote 2 Thessalonians. For our purposes here, the debate over authorship is not particularly important. The letter forms part of an at least somewhat coherent Pauline tradition of political thought and political theology.
[119] 2 Thess. 3:6–15.
[120] 2 Thess. 3:8. The word that is translated as "idle" in the NRSV is *ataktos*, which means "disorderly" or "undisciplined." I have therefore opted for those words here.
[121] 2 Thess. 2:4.   [122] 2 Thess. 2:9.   [123] 2 Thess. 2:8.

CE, Constantine I converted to Christianity and, in the following year, issued an edict of religious toleration. Christianity's allegiance with imperial power meant that it urgently "had to come to terms with its foundational prophecy ('The kingdom of God is at hand!'), especially as it was embodied in the Book of [Revelation]."[124] Early attempts to neutralize the political threat of apocalypticism tended to adopt one of three strategies: to acknowledge that the end was imminent while explaining its postponement, to divest the relevant texts of any literal meaning and embed them in the politically neutral ground of allegory, or to reject these texts altogether.[125] Among these attempts at neutralization, that of Augustine stands as the most theologically sophisticated and historically significant.[126]

Two aspects of Augustine's historical context made this work especially urgent. First, the area of North Africa in which Augustine preached and wrote was full of enthusiastic Christians with apocalyptic expectations.[127] For many of these apocalypticists, the world was nearing its close. Based on a peculiar but persistent interpretation of Jewish and Christian scripture, these believers estimated that the end of days would occur when the world was 6,000 years old. Estimating that Christ had been born in the world's 5,500th year, they expected the apocalypse in 500 CE. It was less than a century away.[128]

Had they not been activated by a political crisis, these beliefs might have remained innocuous. After all, the apocalypse was looming but not imminent. But a development in the early fifth century gave these hopes and fears a new urgency. In 410 CE, Alaric and the Visigoths sacked Rome. They pillaged the city, sending refugees to calmer regions such as North Africa. These refugees would have been burdened with terrifying memories of violence and destruction.

The apocalyptic significance of this event cannot be overstated. Constantine's conversion transformed Christianity from a religion of the oppressed into a religion of political power and empire. The Christian view of Rome changed

---

[124] Fredriksen, "Apocalypse and Redemption," 151.
[125] Fredriksen, "Apocalypse and Redemption," 152–55. I am using the word "strategy" here to refer to a *rhetorical strategy*, or an appeal to the rational capacities, normative commitments, or emotional and imaginative sensibilities of one's audience.
[126] Augustine's work drew heavily on that of the Donatist theologian Tyconius, who reinterpreted Revelation and "provided the point of departure for what is most brilliant and idiosyncratic in Augustine's own theology." See: Fredriksen, "Apocalypse and Redemption," 157. Tyconius' commentary on Revelation has been lost. However, scholars have been able to reconstruct some of its central moves by tracing citations of Tyconius in the work of later scholars, including Augustine.
[127] Fredriksen, "Apocalypse and Redemption," 151.
[128] For a thorough analysis of the connection between apocalyptic predictions and Christian chronology, see: Richard Landes, "Lest the Millennium Be Fulfilled: Apocalyptic Expectations and the Pattern of Western Chronography 100–800 CE," in *The Use and Abuse of Eschatology in the Middle Ages*, ed. Werner Verbeke, Daniel Verhelst, and Andries Welkenhuysen (Leuven: Leuven University Press, 1988), 137–211.

dramatically. No longer the Whore of Babylon, the Roman Empire came to be seen as "chronologically and geographically coextensive" with the church.[129] The *Pax Romana* was widely understood as the world's final age. So, if one wanted to calculate when the world would end, one simply had to figure out when Rome would fall. Among pagans, Rome was the "eternal city" that enjoyed divine protection. As long as the city endured, "then, the Empire (meaning the world) must survive."[130]

The fall of Rome therefore carried apocalyptic significance. Among many Christians, particularly in North Africa, it was the beginning of the terrifying sequence of events described in Revelation. For pagans, who had been the victims of repressive Christian persecution in the closing decades of the fourth century, the destruction was Rome's punishment for abandoning its ancient gods. Some Christians were even tempted to accept this pagan interpretation. If the pagan gods could wreak this kind of destruction, perhaps they should be heeded.[131] The combination of religious enthusiasm and political crisis created a climate of rampant apocalypticism in North Africa. It fell to Augustine, among others, to try to defuse it.

Augustine uses a three-part strategy in his response to this Christian apocalyptic enthusiasm. First, he espouses a tragic view of worldly history. While the world will eventually end at some point, our worldly life is marked by inescapable conflicts whose recurrence is guaranteed by human vice. The fall of Rome is simply another terrible misfortune of the sort that plagues any earthly city. And Rome has seen its fair share of misery before. In 388 BCE, the Gauls invaded and "butchered the senators or as many of them as they could find in all the rest of the city, apart from the Capitol – the citadel which alone was defended by some means or other."[132] In this respect, the Visigoths were less severe, sparing "so many of the senators that the real surprise is that they wiped out any of them."[133] Rome was also torn apart by internal strife in Sulla's civil wars (88–87, 83–82 BCE), which resulted in widespread death and destruction of property. Augustine's list of Roman woes, while by no means historically exhaustive, places the latest destruction in tragic perspective. The sack of Rome is simply an isolated and contingent event, devoid of any kind of apocalyptic or cosmic significance. It is precisely the sort of recurrent crisis one should expect in a world mired in sin and misery.[134] Augustine's conclusion, as J. Kevin Coyle

---

[129] Kevin J. Coyle, "Augustine and Apocalyptic: Thoughts on the Fall of Rome, the Book of Revelation, and the End of the World," *Florilegium* 9 (1987): 4.
[130] Coyle, "Augustine and Apocalyptic," 3.   [131] Coyle, "Augustine and Apocalyptic," 4.
[132] Augustine, *City of God*, III.29, 130.   [133] Augustine, *City of God*, III.29, 130.
[134] Augustine asks in a letter to an apocalyptically minded colleague: "When...has the earth not been devastated by wars at different times and in different places?" See: Augustine, *The Works of Saint Augustine* [Electronic Edition], vol. 2, no. 3, trans. Roland Teske (Charlottesville: InteLex, 2001), Letter 199, para 35, 344, http://pm.nlx.com/xtf/view?docId=augustine_iii/augustine_iii.00.xml;chunk.id=div.aug.pmpreface.1;toc.depth=2;toc.id=div.aug.pmpreface.1;

neatly summarizes, is that "far from being the ultimate catastrophe, the fall of Rome in 410 was simply another sad event in human history – a position that panders to neither total defeatism nor reverent fantasy."[135] By occupying a tragic middle ground between defeatism and fantasy, Augustine evinces a disposition toward the world that will be cultivated by other political realists such as Niccolò Machiavelli and Hans Morgenthau.

Second, Augustine transforms expectations about the end times into an account of the current struggles of the Church. Toward the end of *City of God*, he considers the portion of Revelation that describes the millennial reign that is initiated by the binding of Satan and the resurrection of the saints and martyrs. He notes:

> [Some people] have been particularly excited...by the actual number of a thousand years, taking it as appropriate that there should be a kind of Sabbath for the saints for all that time, a holy rest, that is, after the labours of the six thousand years since man's creation...Scripture says, 'With the Lord, one day is like a thousand years and a thousand years is like one day' [2 Pet. 3:8], and, on this assumption, there follows, after the completion of six thousand years – six of these 'days' – a kind of seventh day of Sabbath rest for the final thousand years.[136]

With some exegetical maneuvering, Augustine concludes that the span of one thousand years is symbolic, standing "for the whole period of this world's history, signifying the entirety of time by a perfect number."[137] He also applies an allegorical interpretation to the first resurrection, concluding that it is the rebirth of the individual soul "which comes here and now through baptism."[138] In contrast, the second resurrection is corporeal and will come at the end of days, as outlined in Revelation. The interval between the two resurrections is the millennium, the indefinite worldly period of the current church. While this church is a mixed body, housing both sinners and saints, for the righteous it is "even now...the kingdom of Christ and the kingdom of heaven."[139] With a rapid interpretive sleight of hand, Augustine then asserts that the terrifying Beast of Revelation, previously identified with Rome, is better understood as the hostile world in which Christians find themselves, surrounded by "the people of the unbelievers."[140] This spiritual and allegorical interpretation transforms expectations of the imminent end into an account of the *immanent* reality of

---

hit.rank=0;brand=default. All subsequent citations to this volume will be in the following format: 199.35, 344.

[135] Coyle, "Augustine and Apocalyptic," 10.   [136] Augustine, *City of God*, XX.7, 907.
[137] Augustine, *City of God*, XX.7, 908.   [138] Augustine, *City of God*, XX.7, 906.
[139] Augustine, *City of God*, XX.9, 915.
[140] Augustine, *City of God*, XX.9, 917. To be clear, Augustine does not definitely say that the Beast is not Rome. But his suggestion that it represents "the people of the unbelievers" among whom faithful Christians must live severs the image's connection to any *particular* empire.

the current church.[141] In so doing, it divests the apocalypse of its urgent appeal and tames one of its most terrifying images.[142]

Third, Augustine combines this allegorical interpretation of the millennium with a reassertion of God's ultimate sovereignty over history, effectively deferring the end times by locating them in an unknowable future. In an argument with distinctly Pauline echoes, he reasons that while Revelation may provide us with a general outline of apocalyptic events, the specific chronology is known only to God. In his correspondence with an apocalyptically inclined bishop in Dalmatia, he finds himself consistently returning to Jesus' admonition to his eager followers: "It is not for you to know the times or periods that the Father has set by his own authority."[143] The date of the apocalypse is not something that may be subjected to any useful speculation. Augustine therefore calls upon all those obsessed with chronological conjecture to "relax your fingers, and give them a rest."[144]

While we cannot know its date, we do know the sequence of events that will occur at the end of time. Apart from his reinterpretation of the millennial rule of Christ and his saints, Augustine affirms the general outline of the apocalypse given in Revelation, including the persecution of believers, the return of Christ, the resurrection of the dead, and the Day of Judgment.[145] Turning away from the dense symbolism of Revelation to the comparatively lucid ground of the gospels, he also considers what we can reasonably know about the apocalypse from Jesus himself. As Matthew reports, Jesus is perfectly clear about the prerequisite for the end of days: "And this good news of the kingdom will be proclaimed throughout the world, as a testimony to all the nations; and then the end will come."[146] While we cannot be sure when the end will come, we can be sure that it will not come until the gospel has been preached throughout the world.

---

[141] This formulation of the strategy is borrowed from McGinn, "Revelation," 528. McGinn adapts it from: Kermode, *Sense of an Ending*, 25–26. Paula Fredriksen characterizes the strategy differently, though no less accurately, when she writes that Augustine de-eschatologizes the events and images of the end times, "transposing them back into the present." See: Fredriksen, "Apocalypse and Redemption," 163.

[142] A related strategy that I have not mentioned here is Augustine's reading of the Apocalypse as an allegory for the internal spiritual struggle against vice. See: O'Leary, *Arguing the Apocalypse*, 74.

[143] Acts 1:7. Augustine and his correspondent disagree about the interpretation of the passage. The Bishop of Hippo seems to have adopted the old strategy of substituting repetition (of the biblical passage) for methodical persuasion. See: Augustine, *Works*, 197.1, 320; 197.2, 321; 197.4, 321; 199.1, 330; 199.7, 332; 199.10, 334; 199.13, 334; 199.18, 336; 199.22, 338; 199.24, 339; 199.33, 344; 199.35, 345. The passage also has a certain pride of place as the final biblical citation in *City of God*, XXII.30, 1091.

[144] Augustine, *City of God*, XVIII.53, 838. Augustine is referring to the ancient practice of dactylonomy ("finger counting") that was widely used before the adoption of Arabic numerals.

[145] Augustine, *City of God*, XX.30, 963.   [146] Matt. 24:14.

This gives Augustine vast chronological leeway. In the fifth century, there would have been many "inaccessible and inhospitable places" on earth.[147] The gospel would necessarily be slow to spread and credible accounts of its progress would be unlikely. Even if we did have reliable reports that the gospel was in fact spreading to the farthest reaches of the world, all we could conclude is that the end is *closer*. We could not name its time.[148] While we may know the general outlines of the apocalyptic sequence, the fundamental obscurity of God's chronology means that we cannot "impose a plot on time."[149] So, Augustine affirms much of the account given in Revelation and the gospels, while divesting it of its subversive potential in the here and now. In so doing, he uses a strategy later taken up by Hobbes.

To sum up, beginning with Pauline worries about the dangers of apocalyptic enthusiasm, Augustine offers a series of sustained exegetical attacks on predictions of the imminent end. While it certainly did not prevent continued apocalyptic outbursts throughout the Middle Ages, this approach became the orthodox interpretation of Revelation and "virtually defined the content of all future Catholic commentaries."[150] Politically, it provided an exegetical response to the radical political potential of apocalyptic expectations and contributed to the ambitious project of reconciling Christianity's foundational prophecy with sovereign and imperial power. Along with Paul's writings, Augustine's response offers us a first taste of the strategies that would be used by later political realists such as Machiavelli, Hobbes, and Morgenthau in negotiating the apocalyptic enthusiasms of their respective times.

The Apocalyptic Imaginary

For both Paul and Augustine, the danger of the apocalypse is not just one of scriptural misunderstanding. Both thinkers are responding to the effects that apocalyptic ideas and visions have in the world. In Paul's time, some Thessalonians were so captivated by the expectation of an imminent end that they stopped working and became a burden to others. They were "disorderly" and

---

[147] Augustine, *Works*, 197.4, 321.   [148] Augustine, *Works*, 197.4, 321.
[149] Fredriksen, "Apocalypse and Redemption," 166.
[150] Fredriksen, "Apocalypse and Redemption," 166. There had been a powerful consensus among twentieth-century medieval historians that Augustine's exegetical efforts had been so successful that not only was apocalyptic expectation banished from official theology, but also that its popular enthusiasms were effectively controlled until Joachim of Fiore produced a radically new eschatological account in the twelfth century. Richard Landes, among others, have challenged this consensus by pointing to numerous medieval apocalyptic movements, particularly those that coalesced around 1000 CE. Landes's work is an important reminder of the need to separate official church doctrine from local beliefs. He notes: "millennium was indeed local, but universally so; official doctrine was indeed 'universal,' but barely penetrated local culture." See: Richard Landes, "The Fear of an Apocalyptic Year 1000: Augustinian Historiography, Medieval and Modern," *Speculum* 75, no. 1 (2000): 106, n. 33.

"undisciplined." In fifth-century North Africa, accounts of the sack of Rome lent a worldly specificity and imminence to existing apocalyptic speculations. For Augustine, the effects of these expectations could be devastating. Invoking Paul's second letter to the Thessalonians, Augustine reasons that apocalyptic enthusiasm breeds disappointment. Inevitably, the time of the expected end would pass without incident and believers "would think that other false promises had been made to them, and they would give up hope about the reward of faith."[151] In short, the prophetic basis of Christian belief could unravel.

Augustine therefore calls upon the faithful to await the end not with captivated enthusiasm but with a comparatively sober "sincerity of faith, firmness of hope, and...ardor of love."[152] His response tries to undermine the most enthralling elements of the Judeo-Christian apocalypse – its sense of urgency, its beastly imagery, and its seemingly infinite ability to anticipate the crises of the present. Both Paul and Augustine are centrally concerned with the capacity of the apocalypse to capture the imagination and spur the faithful to potentially dangerous enthusiasms and disappointments.

I think we should take this ancient intuition seriously. We should understand the apocalypse not only as a genre of literature or as a historical text, but as an imaginary – a way of making sense of our world. Apocalypses captivate us with terrifying images of cruelty and justice. Through the ages, these images have passed down through the collective psyche. They resonate for people with no knowledge of the texts of Daniel and Revelation. Understanding the apocalypse as an imaginary helps us respond to these extraordinary facts.

Biblical scholars and students of religion often invoke the "apocalyptic imaginary" and the "apocalyptic imagination." But they rarely explain what they mean by these terms.[153] We may be able to make some conceptual progress if we set aside the apocalyptic for a moment and begin with the imaginary. In contemporary social and political theory, an imaginary is a "set of meanings, symbols, values, narratives, and representations of the world through which people imagine their existence."[154] While the imagination is commonly understood as a faculty that inheres in the individual, an imaginary is shared and contextual. It exists at a "more or less subconscious level" and shapes the way in which people make sense of and situate themselves in their common world.[155]

---

[151] Augustine, *Works*, 198.15, 335. [152] Augustine, *Works*, 198.15, 335.
[153] See, for example: Collins, *Apocalyptic Imagination*, 1–42; Richard K. Emmerson and Ronald B. Herzman, *The Apocalyptic Imagination in Medieval Literature* (Philadelphia: University of Pennsylvania Press, 1992), 1–35. For an important exception, see: Catherine Keller, *Apocalypse Now and Then: A Feminist Guide to the End of the World* (Boston: Beacon Press, 1996), 1–35.
[154] Chiara Bottici, "Imaginary, The," in *Encyclopedia of Political Theory*, ed. Mark Bevir, vol. 1 (Thousand Oaks: SAGE, 2010), 685.
[155] Bottici, "Imaginary," 686.

The Apocalyptic Imaginary

The philosopher and social theorist Charles Taylor captures all of these dimensions in his description of a "social imaginary."[156] For Taylor, an imaginary encompasses "the ways people imagine their existence, how they fit together with others, how things go on between them and their fellows, the expectations that are normally met, and the deeper normative notions and images that underlie these expectations."[157] These interpersonal and normative expectations are shaped by "wider perspectives on where we stand in space and time: our relation to other nations and peoples...and also where we stand in our history, in the narrative of our becoming."[158] An imaginary is not primarily the textual, theoretical, or self-consciously reasoned ways in which people think about the world. Rather, it involves the "way ordinary people 'imagine' their social surroundings, and this is not often expressed in theoretical terms, but is carried in images, stories, and legends."[159] While the imaginary may be carried in these forms, it necessarily exceeds any concrete representation. It exists as a "largely unstructured and inarticulate understanding of our whole situation."[160]

Taylor's conception of an imaginary offers a useful starting point for understanding the place of the apocalypse in the social and political world. He distinguishes between canonical texts and official doctrines, on the one hand, and social imaginaries, on the other. Texts and doctrines are, like abstract theories, "often the possession of a small minority, whereas what is interesting in the social imaginary is that it is shared by large groups of people, if not the whole society."[161] However, Taylor also asks us to look for the ways in which texts and doctrines sometimes shape imaginaries when "taken up and associated with social practices."[162] In Augustine's time, those trying to make sense of the sack of Rome took up the texts of Daniel and Revelation and used them as a basis for collectively making sense of their circumstances. In so doing, they changed some of the meaning that those texts had for them. Understanding the apocalypse as an imaginary helps us to capture this.

But the influence between text and imaginary runs in both directions. The social imaginary and the textual, theoretical, and doctrinal ideas that animate it shape one another.[163] The same is true of the lived belief in the apocalypse and its scriptural basis. Apocalyptic texts give voice to an apocalyptic imaginary, while the imaginary's progress through the world changes the meaning those texts have across time and space. They change the revelation. This ongoing negotiation between text and imaginary may help to explain the continued

---

[156] There are other conceptualizations of the imaginary in psychoanalytic theory (Jacques Lacan) and social theory (Cornelius Castoriadis). I focus on Taylor here for the accessibility of his approach and because, as we shall see later, his theorization falls victim to an instructive pitfall.
[157] Charles Taylor, *Modern Social Imaginaries* (Durham: Duke University Press, 2004), 23.
[158] Taylor, *Modern Social Imaginaries*, 27.   [159] Taylor, *Modern Social Imaginaries*, 23.
[160] Taylor, *Modern Social Imaginaries*, 25.   [161] Taylor, *Modern Social Imaginaries*, 23.
[162] Taylor, *Modern Social Imaginaries*, 29.   [163] Taylor, *Modern Social Imaginaries*, 30.

power of works that were intended to address situations very different from our own.

Following Taylor, we can also see how understanding the apocalypse as an imaginary helps us to capture some of its enduring appeal. We use imaginaries to understand our world. They provide the imaginative and narrative context "within which particular features of our world show up for us in the sense they have."[164] One of the ways in which imaginaries do this is by *emplotting* our collective lives. Imaginaries fashion events and experiences into stories and reveal them to be stories "of a particular kind."[165] What previously seemed like incomprehensible happenings start to make sense to us as part of a plot in which we are the protagonists. The apocalyptic stories of Daniel and Revelation cast the crises of the present as preludes to a permanent escape from contingency and conflict. These stories discern in current events signs of this imminent transformation. They expect the arrival of an extraordinary figure who will usher in a new world. For many ancient Jews and Christians, this apocalyptic story gave meaning to the events and experiences of their lives and offered the consolation required to endure them.

However, there are limits to Taylor's conception of an imaginary. While he makes frequent reference to symbols and iconography, his examples are almost exclusively focused on texts and narratives. For this reason, he never quite realizes the full potential of his core concept.[166] He has little to say about the visual dimensions of imaginaries. Yet understanding these aspects more clearly helps us to see why some imaginaries can be so resilient and politically explosive. Susan Buck-Morss suggests that this is a broader problem with the way many scholars think about imaginaries. We tend to reduce them to "little more than the logic of a discourse, or worldview."[167] While Taylor's conceptualization is helpful, as far is it goes, we can usefully supplement it with a more robust appreciation for the ways in which images help us to metaphorically order the world.

We see clear examples of this metaphorical capacity in the familiar images of sovereign power within the history of political thought – the divine father, the body politic, the Leviathan, or the machine. These images are prior to more specific forms of articulation or understanding. Michael Walzer explains, "the image does not so much reinforce existing political ideas (though it may later be used for that purpose) as underlie them... Thus the image provides a

---

[164] Taylor, *Modern Social Imaginaries*, 25.
[165] White, *Metahistory*, 7. See also: Kermode, *The Sense of an Ending* (2000).
[166] For instance, the following observation about the Tiananmen demonstrations in 1989 is little more than suggestive: "This sense of standing internationally and in history can be invoked in the iconography of the demonstration itself, as in Tianenmen in 1989, with its references to the French Revolution and its citation of the American case through the Statue of Liberty." See: Taylor, *Modern Social Imaginaries*, 27–28.
[167] Susan Buck-Morss, *Dreamworld and Catastrophe: The Passing of Mass Utopia in East and West* (Cambridge: MIT Press, 2000), 11–12.

starting point for political thinking, and so long as it is effective, no other starting point is possible."[168] At the heart of what Taylor calls the "largely unstructured and inarticulate understanding of our whole situation" is therefore a store of images and associations that captivate our collective imagination. While they may remain unacknowledged, they nevertheless order the social and political landscape. When deployed overtly in the service of political ends, they may also secure belief and provoke adherence. Any account of a social imaginary must therefore look at the complex of metaphors and signifiers through which power is organized and belief is elicited.

This more imagistic conception of an imaginary helps us to recognize the ways in which apocalypticism is something more than simply a genre of revelatory literature or a worldview. It allows us to see the effects of the extraordinary semiotic qualities of apocalyptic texts. An illuminator of a tenth-century commentary on Revelation characterizes its visions as "picture-making words."[169] Given the density of symbolic imagery in Revelation, it is hardly surprising that it is one of the most illustrated books of the Bible and has had a central place in the history of Western art.[170] Yet the words of the text have an imaginative power that exceeds any attempt to specify their concrete meaning in a coherent statement or a particular visual representation.

Edmund Burke captures this power of "picture-making words" when he compares the effect of a drawing to that of an affecting verbal description in the context of a broader discussion of the aesthetic experience of the sublime. He explains:

> If I make a drawing of a palace or a temple, or a landscape, I present a very clear idea of those objects; but then... my picture can at most affect only as the palace, temple, or landscape would have affected in reality. On the other hand, the most lively and spirited verbal description I can give raises a very obscure and imperfect *idea* of such objects; but then it is in my power to raise a stronger *emotion* by the description than I could do by the best painting.[171]

Similarly, the imagery of apocalypse always seems to lose something of its power when rendered into any determinate visual form. Revelation's rich but incoherent riot of images gives the book tremendous affective power. For, as Burke observes, "great clearness" is often "an enemy to all enthusiasms whatsoever."[172]

---

[168] Michael Walzer, "On the Role of Symbolism in Political Thought," *Political Science Quarterly* 82, no. 2 (1967): 194.

[169] Mary Carruthers, *The Craft of Thought: Meditation, Rhetoric, and the Making of Images, 400–1200* (New York: Cambridge University Press, 1998), 152.

[170] Frances Carey, ed., *The Apocalypse and the Shape of Things to Come* (Toronto: University of Toronto Press, 1999).

[171] Edmund Burke, *A Philosophical Inquiry into the Origin of Our Ideas of the Sublime and Beautiful with Several Other Additions*, in *On Taste, On the Sublime and Beautiful, Reflections on the French Revolution, Letter to a Noble Lord* (New York: Collier, 1909), 53.

[172] Burke, *Sublime and Beautiful*, 54.

The rolling up of the sky like a scroll, the seven-headed beast emerging from the sea, or the trampling of the grapes of wrath are most powerful as "obscure and imperfect" ideas that can be inflected with the more particular terrors or hopes of one's own context. The overflowing semiotic resources of the imaginary seem to guarantee the apocalypse a remarkable resilience. While particular expectations of the end might be disconfirmed, the apocalypse itself is never discredited because its narrative and imagery will always find further events with which to resonate.[173] The plagues of locusts, which for early Christians would have recalled God's punishment of Egypt in the book of Exodus, today become the allegory for the effects of global climate change.

With these further specifications to the concept of an imaginary, it becomes easier to recognize the ways in which apocalypticism might become unmoored from its scriptural origins. As the example of locusts and global climate change suggests, elements of the apocalyptic imaginary continue to recur today in locations far from their original theological roots, often in purportedly secular interpretations of the world. The apocalyptic imaginary has travelled beyond conditions in which its core features are believed to be literally true, or even recognized as the products of biblical sources. The apocalyptic imaginary, even in its fully religious form, rarely rises into complete awareness by those who draw upon its resources to make sense of the world. For this reason, it can shape the understandings of those who do not even recognize the ways in which its individual elements were originally seen to be linked. For those who lived within explicitly Christian eras, where apocalyptic belief in at least some form was central to the coherence of the sacred worldview, the semiotic potential of these resources was often tremendously powerful. For those who have followed them in time, these resources remain nonetheless; once loosed upon the world, their semiotic richness makes them extraordinarily difficult to contain.

In the coming chapters, I will not assume that apocalyptic thinking must necessarily be grounded in a Judeo-Christian theology. Rather, we will see instances in which elements of this imaginary have shaped the thinking of self-consciously secular political actors as well as those motivated by profound Christian enthusiasm. Here, let me offer a general conception of the apocalyptic imaginary that draws out its central structural elements, without presuming that these elements must continue to take their original theological form. In either its theological or secular form, I conceptualize an apocalypse as *an imminent and cataclysmic end to the known world, along with its attendant "evils." It is a rupture in the apparent temporal continuity of history, a revelatory moment around which the past is given meaning and a radically new future is announced*. This conceptualization focuses on elements of apocalypse that are present in, but ultimately transcend, the Judeo-Christian tradition.

---

[173] Fredriksen, *From Jesus to Christ*, 83; Kermode, *Sense of an Ending*, 8–9.

The Apocalyptic Imaginary

Let us break this concept of apocalypse down. First, the end of the world is always *imminent*.[174] It will come soon, generally within the lifetime of the conveyer or audience of the apocalyptic message. This sense of imminence is clearly present in the early Christian tradition. As we have seen, some of the accounts in the gospels suggest that Jesus expected the world to end within his own generation. The books of Daniel and Revelation have a similar sense of imminence. Daniel anticipates that Antiochus' reign is drawing to a cosmic close, while Revelation concludes with the warning and hope that "the time is near."[175] Contemporary secular apocalyptic movements also share a sense of imminence. For instance, those who expect that the world will end in environmental devastation tend to insist that such an end will come soon, or at least sooner than we think.[176] As we shall see in Chapter 5, the nuclear apocalypticism of the 1950s and 1960s was centered on the expectation of imminent annihilation. These different manifestations of the apocalyptic imaginary share a "discursive construction of temporality" which situates its audience at the end of the known world.[177]

Second, an apocalypse is *cataclysmic*.[178] In the Judeo-Christian tradition, the earth is consumed by plagues and fire, which clear the way for a New Jerusalem. In Revelation, the spiraling narratives of destruction are rife with images of catastrophic natural disasters, rotting flesh, excruciating torture, and ravenous beasts, which serve to present "the unrepresentable" – the divine consumption of the world and most of humanity.[179] This cataclysm is a form of creative destruction, the preparatory work for building a new world. On a

---

[174] Richard Landes, "Roosters Crow, Owls Hoot: On the Dynamics of Apocalyptic Millennialism," in *War in Heaven/Heaven on Earth: Theories of the Apocalyptic*, ed. Stephen D. O'Leary and Glen S. McGhee (London: Equinox, 2005), 21–22, 26–27.

[175] Revelation 22:10.

[176] Such an insistence is supported by the science on the contemporary effects of climate change, as well by theories about abrupt climate change. The increasing focus on climate change as a contemporary and imminent problem, rather than a comfortably distant one, is reflected in: Intergovernmental Panel on Climate Change (IPCC), *Climate Change 2014: Impacts, Adaptation, Vulnerability* (Cambridge: Cambridge University Press, 2014).

[177] O'Leary, *Arguing the Apocalypse*, 14, 13.

[178] The historian Richard Landes has offered the most developed conceptualization of apocalyptic beliefs outside the religious and biblical studies literature. While his conceptualization has influenced my own, I depart from him on the question of the cataclysmic nature of the apocalypse. For Landes, an apocalypse can be classified as cataclysmic or transformational. The latter type of apocalypse involves collective, voluntary world transformation. However, I think that here Landes falls victim to a problem that he himself has diagnosed in the work of other scholars of apocalypticism – a tendency to "subsume the apocalyptic component under the millennial." I would class transformative visions as millennial, for reasons I will explain in more detail. Here, it is worth noting that transformative visions rarely seem to possess the emphasis on imminence that Landes and many other scholars classify as central to the concept of apocalypse. See: Landes, "Roosters Crow," 26.

[179] This notion of presenting "the unrepresentable" is borrowed from: Keller, *Apocalypse Now and Then*, 6.

secular level, political and economic ideologies with apocalyptic dimensions similarly emphasize the creative power of annihilation. For instance, the destructive and cleansing powers of revolution in certain strains of Marxist thought share much with the focus of the apocalyptic imaginary on the pregnant potential of cataclysm.[180] In contrast, most (though certainly not all) environmental or nuclear scenarios of apocalyptic annihilation treat their cataclysms as purely world-destroying.

Third, an apocalypse brings *an end to some real or perceived evil*. For Christians, the apocalypse marks the end of sin and suffering and the arrival of an era in which the elect will live with God on earth, where "death will be no more; mourning and crying and pain will be no more, for the first things have passed away." Given the symbolic flexibility of the images of evil in both Daniel and Revelation, religious enthusiasts have rarely suffered from a shortage of contemporary analogs for the dragons, beasts, and whores that populate the apocalyptic landscape. In secular accounts of the apocalypse, the content of the evil that is to be purged is similarly variable. It may include human abuse of the natural environment, political or economic arrangements, or dangerous weapons and technologies.[181] Common to these visions of the apocalypse is the idea that the annulment of time is "the redemptive solution to the problem of evil."[182]

Fourth, an apocalypse is a moment of *rupture* in the apparent temporal continuity of history. The accounts of the apocalypse in Daniel and Revelation describe the irruption of God into human time. This marks a radical break that dissolves the distinction between secular and divine history. After this, God will dwell among humans on earth, and time, as such, will no longer exist. Even secular apocalypses have this ruptural quality. They are "a temporal break and

---

[180] Norman Cohn was the first to make a sustained argument about the apocalyptic character of certain strains of Marxist thought. See: Norman Cohn, *The Pursuit of the Millennium: Revolutionary Messianism in Medieval and Reformation Europe and Its Bearing on Modern Totalitarian Movements*, 2nd ed. (New York: Harper and Row), 308–14. Comparatively less scholarly attention has been focused on the cataclysmic apocalyptic dimension of certain strains of neoliberal economic and political thought. For a controversial but thought-provoking discussion on this question, see: Naomi Klein, *The Shock Doctrine: The Rise of Disaster Capitalism* (New York: Picador, 2008), 3–25.

[181] In most (though not all) variants of apocalypticism, religious or secular, the end of evil requires the sorting out of people such that only an elect remain to enjoy the new world. In the Christian apocalyptic narrative, this sorting out is done by Jesus on the Day of Judgment. In secular apocalyptic narratives, particularly those animating totalitarian political projects, ideological elites take responsibility for sorting out the saved and the damned. The analysis of the apocalyptic underpinnings of Nazism in Chapter 5 provides an example of this phenomenon. Secular apocalypses that lack some notion of redemption – for example, some visions of nuclear or environmental apocalypse – also tend to lack a commitment to the idea of a chosen elect who will remain after the apocalypse. While some accounts of nuclear or environmental apocalypse envision survivors, this remnant is rarely seen to be providentially chosen because of its moral character. Survivors are left by chance, having escaped a sudden death only to endure a more lengthy and painful one. The 1959 film *On the Beach* is illustrative in this regard.

[182] O'Leary, *Arguing the Apocalypse*, 33.

The Apocalyptic Imaginary

omnipresent point of reference" around which the past is understood anew and a previously unimaginable future lays itself out before us.[183] An apocalypse therefore differs from other events that might be collectively or individually devastating, such as death. These events are given meaning by sacred and social "rituals that symbolically affirm social continuity."[184] In contrast, an apocalypse simply cannot be absorbed into ritual or calendric time. It always exists as both a rupture in and an end to time.

Finally, an apocalypse is *revelatory*. In an instant, it discloses both the meaning of the past and "the shape of things to come."[185] In Daniel and Revelation, the apocalypse is revelatory in another sense – it is a transcendent reality conveyed to Daniel and John of Patmos respectively through a vision mediated by an angelic figure. Once this vision has been communicated and interpreted, the upheavals, conflicts, and persecutions of the past and the present cease to be the unaccountable contingencies of history and become instead the birth pangs of a new world. Suffering becomes the narrative prelude to redemption and renewal. Similarly, secular apocalypses reveal a present filled with signs of the imminent end – rising temperatures, species extinction, economic crises, or conflicts between nuclear powers. An apocalyptic interpretation reveals these events to be signs of an inevitable and imminent world transformation.

Understanding the apocalypse as an imaginary allows us to recognize the possibility of many potential apocalypses. The apocalyptic imaginary includes the overtly theological apocalypses in which God irrupts into history, initiating a bodily resurrection in which the saved are granted immortality and the damned are condemned for eternity. However, it also includes secular apocalypses in which humans alone bring about the end of the world. As I have outlined it here, the apocalyptic imaginary is not committed to a particular vision of the postapocalyptic world. Christian accounts of the apocalypse envision a millennial kingdom and, eventually, a world in which the elect dwell with God. Yet there is disagreement within the Christian tradition about whether the postapocalyptic world would be hierarchical or radically egalitarian.[186] There are similar debates among secular apocalypticists, whose postapocalyptic scenarios range from the totalitarian to the anarchic. However, with secularization comes another option – that the entire physical world, or at least all human life, will be destroyed. The apocalyptic imaginary includes these scenarios as well.

At this point, the apocalyptic imaginary may well seem overly capacious. Yet it is important to stress that it does not encompass all possible forms of eschatological expectation. The centrality of imminence, cataclysm, and rupture to

---

[183] Bousquet, "Time Zero," 741.
[184] John R. Hall, Philip D. Schuyler, and Sylvaine Trinh, *Apocalypse Observed: Religious Movements and Violence in North America, Europe and Japan* (New York: Routledge, 2000), 4.
[185] This phrase is taken from the title of H. G. Wells's 1933 science fiction novel. See also: Carey, ed., *The Shape of Things to Come*.
[186] Landes, "Roosters Crow," 25–26.

the apocalyptic imaginary means that it necessarily excludes the beliefs of progressive millennialists. Progressive millennialism includes a variety of narratives about the future, all of which are linked by the expectation of a coming better age on earth that will be achieved through gradual human transformation, rather than through an imminent and destructive cataclysm.[187] The various agrarian utopian communities that developed in Europe and the United States in the nineteenth century were the products of such beliefs. Similarly, the narratives of progress that lie at the heart of liberal political thought often have a progressive millennialist bent, particularly when they take the form of arguments about "the end of history."[188] Here, the expected transformation is not achieved through ruptural catastrophe or violence and it is rarely cast as imminent. This means that while there are elements of progressive millennialism that partake of the apocalyptic imaginary, particularly its revelatory qualities and the emphasis on the purging of evil, expectations of gradual transformation involve separate categories of belief and very different visions of the future.

Yet this distinction should not blind us to the dynamism of beliefs, narratives, and images of the end of the world. There are several historical cases in which progressive millennialism has transformed into full-throated apocalypticism. The case of the Anabaptists at Münster between 1533 and 1535 is a prime example. This group's beliefs, along with the narratives and imagery that shaped them, shifted from transformational and pacifist to violent and cataclysmic when the expected future did not come.[189] There was a similar shift for large numbers of Western Franks when hopes for the arrival of Jesus were dashed at the turn of the first millennium.[190] While these groups did not originally draw on the full resources of the apocalyptic imaginary to make sense of their world, they turned to this imaginary when their prophecies failed. As we shall see in Chapter 5, this is precisely the kind of transformation that Hans

---

[187] Richard Landes has a category of millennial belief that he calls "transformational apocalypticism." He explains that groups with these beliefs hold that the end of the world is imminent (which is Landes's key reason for calling them apocalyptic) but also that the new world will come about through human transformation, rather than cataclysm. While various kinds of natural catastrophes may play an important role for the groups Landes might classify as transformational apocalypticists, in my view, these events serve as signs of the coming apocalypse, rather than as constituent features of the apocalyptic moment itself. Such signs are often used to convince people to transform themselves in preparation for the end of the world. Because they lack the belief in the constitutive role of cataclysm, I would classify such groups as progressive millennialists. Landes's most extensive case study of such a group is the Peace of God movement in southern France in the 990s. See: Richard Landes, "What Happens When Jesus Doesn't Come: Jewish and Christian Relations in Apocalyptic Time," in *Millennial Violence: Past, Present and Future*, ed. Jeffrey Kaplan (London: Frank Cass, 2002), 245–59.

[188] Fukuyama, *The End of History and the Last Man*. Fukuyama's account of the "end of history" is certainly eschatological, but it is not apocalyptic. Also, while not itself easily classified as liberal, Fukuyama's story shares with liberal political thought a progressive account of history and a commitment to liberal democracy as the best political regime.

[189] Landes, "Roosters Crow," 30.

[190] Landes, "What Happens When Jesus Doesn't Come," 245–59.

The Apocalyptic Imaginary

Morgenthau worried about. The beliefs and narratives of such interwar idealists as Woodrow Wilson, at least on a political realist reading, may begin as a kind of secular progressive millennialism centered on the hope for a world without war. However, these expectations become apocalyptic when they begin to focus on the need for a final and decisive battle for a singular humanity. Because the apocalyptic imaginary shares narrative and symbolic resources with progressive millennialism, this shift is often easy.

Even when progressive millennialist beliefs become apocalyptic, they need not erupt in violence. In fact, overt public eruptions of apocalyptic hostility are relatively rare. This does not mean, however, that the imaginary is not at work. In any historical period, there are groups that accept the current political, economic, or moral order "'under protest' even if that protest is, provisionally, silent. They await eagerly the moment when the rules will change, and change dramatically."[191] The apocalyptic imaginary gives these groups a way to understand their current circumstances and envision a new world. They can legitimize their expectation of an imminent cosmic transformation by appealing to the "signs of the times." For those captivated by the apocalyptic imaginary, the world is "overflowing with meaning and purpose."[192] History ceases to be a realm of unaccountable contingency and becomes a determined process subject to eschatological interpretation. The apocalyptic imaginary rescues suffering, oppression, and cultural discontent from the threat of meaninglessness and makes time reliable.[193]

It allows believers to take everything – political events, cultural shifts, economic downturns, changes in the weather, particular dates – to be signs of an imminent transformation. In short, believers become *semiotically aroused*. As Landes summarizes:

> From the people they meet, to the texts they read, to events that happen around them, everything coheres as part of a huge apocalyptic plan, crystalline in its clarity and glorious in its implications. Sometimes the plan is nefarious – an international conspiracy by the forces of evil to enslave mankind; sometimes benevolent – the dawn of a new age. In any case, whereas it once existed only in the shadows, scarcely discernable, the signs of its advent are now legible, visible, clear to anyone with discernment.[194]

As we have seen in the case of Judeo-Christian apocalypticism, the symbolic flexibility of texts such as Daniel and Revelation guarantees believers a continued source of cosmic analogs that can be made to correspond to almost any contemporary figure or event. For secular apocalyptic believers, this semiotic arousal may work at the level of an unconscious habit or subliminal practice. While they may "not perceive any possible connection between an old text

---

[191] Landes, "Roosters Crow," 31.   [192] Landes, "Roosters Crow," 33.
[193] Cathy Gutierrez, "The Millennium and Narrative Closure," in *War in Heaven/Heaven on Earth: Theories of the Apocalyptic*, ed. Stephen D. O'Leary and Glen S. McGhee (London: Equinox, 2005), 47.
[194] Landes, "Roosters Crow," 33.

and the current reality... they may be inclined to *expect* the burning of rainforests, for instance. And they may feel some mix of foreboding and inevitability about 'the environment.'"[195] Whether they are sacred or secular, all apocalyptic believers exist in a world charged with meaning and at the edge of a cosmic transformation. The shape of this transformation is fundamentally unimaginable at the same time as it haunts the collective imagination.

Conclusion

In sum, the Judeo-Christian apocalypse emerged in response to specific political circumstances in the Eastern Mediterranean and Asia Minor. The books of Daniel and Revelation offered their audiences powerful criticisms of sovereign and imperial power, a historical narrative through which persecution and trauma could be made meaningful, and the seductive promise of a new world purged of suffering. Yet the dense and flexible symbolic resources in these works have allowed them to capture the imaginations of audiences in circumstances that are very different from those of antiquity.

Within the early Christian tradition, those thinkers most concerned with the radical political potential of apocalypticism are Paul and Augustine – two figures who would later come to be the foundational voices of a Christian strand of political realism. Both Paul and Augustine take seriously the effects that apocalypticism has in the world, its capacity to captivate the imagination and impel people to potentially subversive forms of enthusiasm. Together, these writers deploy three strategies of which later political realists will also avail themselves: acknowledging the reality of the apocalypse while deferring its arrival, divesting the apocalypse of its most captivating and terrifying images, and embracing a tragic view of history that eschews apocalyptic cerainty.

Following an intuition in Paul's and Augustine's works, I have argued that the apocalypse is best conceptualized as an imaginary. It is part of the stock of narratives, myths, and images through which we make sense of our world together. As I have suggested here, the apocalyptic imaginary persists not only for those who believe in the literal truth of Jewish and Christian scriptures, but also for purportedly secular political thinkers and audiences. The chapters that follow trace the troubled encounters of three political realists with the apocalyptic imaginary. As we shall see, these encounters are not primarily undertaken at the level of texts, doctrines, or policies, but rather through the images, symbols, and narratives with which we envision our political landscape.

[195] Keller, *Apocalypse Now and Then*, 8.

3

Machiavelli's Savonarolan Moment

Introduction

Addressing a city rocked by a recent regime change and the threat of foreign invasion, the Dominican friar Girolamo Savonarola warned Florentines: "God's dagger will strike, and soon...Do not make a jest of this...if you do not do what I have told you, woe to Florence, woe to the people, woe to the great and small!"[1] At the height of the Renaissance, many citizens expected a divine scourge that would violently transform Florence into a New Jerusalem. While Savonarola was at the center of this enthusiastic movement, the apocalypticism that captivated Italians and Florentines was much broader and deeper than the preaching of a single man. The "Savonarolan moment," as I refer to it here, was a time at which a divine transformation of Florence seemed possible and even inevitable. Political upheaval and prophecy combined to transform a hope for a better world into an expectation that God would burst into secular history and build his heavenly kingdom on earth.

I will argue that Niccolò Machiavelli's work bears the mark of the Savonarolan moment. The final chapter of *The Prince*, I will suggest, is an apocalyptic exhortation that reiterates the Savonarolan message in a secular way.[2]

---

[1] Girolamo Savonarola, Sermon on Psalms III (13 January 1494[5]), in *Selected Writings of Girolamo Savonarola: Religion and Politics, 1490–1498*, trans. Anne Borelli and Maria Pastore Passaro (New Haven: Yale University Press, 2006), 74–75.

[2] This portion of the chapter's argument builds on the work of those who have stressed a prophetic dimension, a providential logic, and a messianic expectation in the final chapter of *The Prince*. I want to insist that these features of the final chapter are tied to its apocalyptic emplotment. For discussions of the prophetic dimension of the chapter, see: Albert Russell Ascoli, "Machiavelli's Gift of Counsel," in *Machiavelli and the Discourse of Literature*, ed. Albert Russell Ascoli and Victoria Kahn (Ithaca: Cornell University Press, 1993), 252–57; John M. Najemy, *Between Friends: Discourses of Power and Desire in the Machiavelli-Vettori Letters of 1513–1515* (Princeton: Princeton University Press, 1993), 206–14; Mark Jurdjevic, *A Great and Wretched City:*

Machiavelli concludes *The Prince* with an apocalyptic exhortation because he has failed to make the apparent contingency of the political world intelligible by containing it with analytical categories, ordering it with general rules, or analogizing it with metaphors for fortune. Offering evidence of the work's failure to deliver on these aspirations, I argue that its exhortation amounts to a final attempt to understand Italy's political situation by fashioning it into a familiar apocalyptic story. Yet Machiavelli ultimately rejects this apocalyptic solution. In the *Discourses on Livy*, he turns instead to a tragic sensibility that is epistemologically humble and wary of redemptive politics. Even in the *Discourses*, however, there are strange hints of apocalyptic hope. Machiavelli could never fully abandon the seductive promise of the Savonarolan moment.

This chapter proceeds in three parts. First, I sketch the context of the Savonarolan moment in Renaissance Florence, focusing on the preaching of the Dominican friar and then broadening the analysis to the ways in which the apocalyptic imaginary transcended Savonarola himself. Second, I offer a close reading of *The Prince*'s final chapter, drawing out the resonances between Machiavelli's exhortation and the Savonarolan moment. I also consider why a work that begins with apparently empirical and anti-utopian goals culminates in an apocalyptic exhortation. Third, I trace how Machiavelli rejects the apocalyptic imaginary in the *Discourses* and instead embraces a tragic sensibility.

The Savonarolan Moment

Prophecy flourished during the Italian Wars of the late fifteenth through mid-sixteenth centuries.[3] The climate of crisis and the ease with which prophecies could now be printed and disseminated meant that they became part of popular culture. One persistent prophecy predicted that a 1484 conjunction of Saturn and Jupiter would unleash unimaginable events.[4] But many prophecies were more overtly apocalyptic. Fashioning the events of the recent past, present, and imminent future into a story modeled on those in Daniel and Revelation, apocalyptic prophecies predicted an imminent and violent end to the known world and the arrival of a better future.

Girolamo Savonarola (1452–1498) was at the center of this apocalyptic moment in Florence. Savonarola's early life made him an unlikely candidate

---

Promise and Failure in Machiavelli's Florentine Political Thought (Cambridge: Harvard University Press, 2014), 30–32. For a discussion of the providential logic of the chapter, see: Mario Martelli, "La Logica Provvidenzialistica E Il Capitolo XXVI Del Principe," *Interpres* 4 (1982): 262–384. For a discussion of the messianic expectation of the chapter, see: Miguel Vatter, "Machiavelli and the Republican Conception of Providence," *Review of Politics* 75, no. 4 (2013): 605–23.

[3] Ottavia Niccoli, *Prophecy and People in Renaissance Italy*, ed. Lydia G. Cochrane (Princeton: Princeton University Press, 1990), 3–29.

[4] Niccoli, *Prophecy and People*, 136–39; Donald Weinstein, *Savonarola: The Rise and Fall of a Renaissance Prophet* (New Haven: Yale University Press, 2011), 39–40.

for the role of apocalyptic prophet of a Florentine millennium. He was born in Ferrara, the son of a businessman and the grandson of a learned physician and medical writer. He received a humanist education and earned a Master of Arts degree at the University of Ferrara. In the spring of 1475, the young Savonarola surprised his family when he ran away to join the Observant Dominican friary in Bologna. He explained this decision in a letter to his father, writing that he could no longer stand "the great wickedness of the blind people of Italy, especially when [he] saw that virtue had been completely cast down and vice raised up." In a world rife with sin, Savonarola thought he had been called to become a "knight militant" for Christ.[5]

He first came to Florence in 1482–1487 as a lecturer in theology. His preaching failed to attract many followers–"only some simpletons and a few little women," as he later recalled.[6] However, Savonarola soon found inspiration in the apocalyptic imaginary. His *Prayer for the Church* (1484), written during a battle for papal succession after the death of Sixtus IV, poses a stark apocalyptic choice between the renewal of the Church and the triumph of the devil. Later that year, while visiting the Convent of San Giorgio, Savonarola was inexplicably struck by "about seven reasons" why the church faced an imminent scourge and eventual renewal. His Lenten sermons at San Gimignano in 1485 and 1486 expanded on this theme and came alive with frightening biblical imagery. By the time he left his lectureship in 1487 to begin several years as an itinerant preacher, he had still not shared these visions with the Florentine people.[7]

In 1490, Savonarola returned to Florence. His superiors had assigned him to the convent of San Marco at Lorenzo de' Medici's request and with the young philosopher Pico della Mirandola's recommendation. Savonarola's apocalyptic conviction was now much stronger.[8] He was more certain that he was a prophet[9] called to preach the imminent apocalypse, urge penitence, and seek the renewal of the Church. His election as prior of San Marco in 1491 allowed him to reform his community of friars, while his fiery apocalyptic sermons attracted a substantial following among Florentines. The swelling crowds at his sermons meant Savonarola had to find ever-larger venues for these gatherings.[10] Florence was receiving his apocalyptic message with rapt attention.

---

[5] Girolamo Savonarola, Letter to his father (25 April 1475), in *A Guide to Righteous Living and Other Works*, trans. Konrad Eisenbichler (Toronto: Centre for Reformation and Renaissance Studies, 2003), 36.

[6] Savonarola, Ruth and Micah, Sermon IV (18 May 1496), as quoted in: Alison Brown, "Introduction," *Selected Writings of Girolamo Savonarola: Religion and Politics, 1490–1498*, trans. Anne Borelli and Maria Pastore Passaro (New Haven: Yale University Press, 2006), xv.

[7] Weinstein, *Savonarola*, 36–37.   [8] Weinstein, *Savonarola*, 76.

[9] The earliest evidence of this self-perception is in a letter Savonarola wrote to his mother in 1490. In explaining why he must continuously travel, he references Luke 4:24 and writes "no-one is a prophet in one's own country, so much so that even He was not accepted in His own country." See: Savonarola, Letter to his mother (25 January 1490), *Guide to Righteous Living*, 39.

[10] Konrad Eisenbichler, introduction, *Guide to Righteous Living*, 7.

Florentine receptiveness to the Savonarolan message was not merely the product of the friar's rhetorical or prophetic skill. The political situation at the end of the fifteenth century made Florentines particularly open to apocalypticism. In April 1492, Lorenzo the Magnificent died, leaving behind a gathering political storm fueled by a brittle regime and an increasingly vocal and dissatisfied elite. Lorenzo's son Piero assumed power and excluded many of the city's most powerful citizens from his inner circle, leading to fears that his power would eventually become tyrannical.[11]

This domestic unrest was compounded by a foreign threat. In the early 1490s, rumors of a French invasion were spreading through Italy. Charles VIII was coming to make good his inherited claim on the Neapolitan kingdom, with a force whose size and strength were unimaginable to Italians.[12] In 1494, the French were en route and sought Florentine assistance in easing their way through Tuscany. But Piero chose to maintain the Florentine alliance with Naples. As the French approached, the young Medici leader tried to both preserve the Neapolitan alliance and avoid overtly antagonizing the French. Internal dissatisfaction with the Medici regime grew and Charles's forces marched from Milan to Tuscany. Piero now realized that he had to negotiate with the French. On October 26th, he met with Charles and made substantial concessions on behalf of Florence, surrendering the city's fortresses in Pisa, Livorno, Pietrasanta, and Sarzana.

Florence was at a breaking point. Its citizens were outraged at Piero's surrender of the fortresses and worried about the impending arrival of an army that had already laid waste to a nearby town. The city's executive body, the Signoria, called an emergency meeting of the regime's top officials. Most of the inner circle was now prepared to abandon Piero. But with the French threat still looming, they decided to dispatch a delegation headed by Savonarola to persuade Charles either to avoid coming through Florence or, if he insisted on doing so, to restrict the size and movements of his force.[13] They reached no firm agreement. However, during Savonarola's absence, Piero was successfully ousted from power. Sixty years of Medici dominance had ended and a politically disorganized Florence awaited the French army. This is the political context in which Savonarola's apocalyptic message took hold.

In his early apocalyptic sermons, Savonarola offered a vivid picture of an apocalypse without worldly redemption in which Florence would be God's primary target. While the friar envisioned the reform of the Church and a universal

---

[11] John M. Najemy, *A History of Florence 1200–1575* (Malden: Wiley, 2006), 375–80.
[12] Donald Weinstein cites a figure, taken from a late nineteenth-century French source, of forty thousand effectives armed with one hundred siege guns. See: Donald Weinstein, *Savonarola and Florence: Prophecy and Patriotism in the Renaissance* (Princeton: Princeton University Press, 1970), 114.
[13] The reasons why Savonarola was chosen for this mission are not entirely clear. By this time, he was a prominent figure in Florence and had gained substantial public credibility by seeming to have predicted the city's political calamities in his apocalyptic sermons.

The Savonarolan Moment

conversion to Christianity, these changes merely heralded the Last Judgment. They did not suggest the imminent creation of a better world on earth.[14] This deep pessimism put Savonarola at odds with other apocalyptic prophets in Florence, who also predicted tribulations but saw them as necessary preludes to worldly renewal.[15]

Reflecting back, Savonarola recalled the mood of these early apocalyptic sermons: "I am the hailstorm that shall break the heads of those who do not take shelter."[16] The friar's focus in these sermons was on the corruption of the Church, which he took to be a sign of an imminent apocalypse.[17] Like many of his contemporaries, he pointed to the Turks as alternatively the Antichrist or a divine apocalyptic scourge.[18] Yet as his sermons evolved, the friar's focus became much more local. During Lent in 1491, Savonarola delivered what he later called his "terrifying sermon," in which he singled Florence out for the worst of God's apocalyptic wrath. The city would no longer be known as *Florentia*, but "turpitude and blood and a den of robbers."[19]

As rumors of a French invasion spread, Savonarola no longer had to cast the Turks as the agents of God's fury. Charles VIII, Savonarola explained as the French approached Tuscany, was the apocalyptic scourge the friar had predicted. The French invasion was only the beginning of the terrifying sequence of apocalyptic events of which the friar had warned. With a tone of reproach, he told his listeners: "long before anyone had heard the noise or smelled any of today's wars, moved by people from beyond the Alps, great tribulations were announced to you. You also know that not two years have passed since I told you: '*Behold the sword of the Lord falling on the earth quickly and swiftly.*' Not I, but God predicted it to you. And, look, it has come to pass and it is here."[20]

Florence had not heeded these warnings. Again, Savonarola reproached his audience: "God has spoken and you did not want to listen to Him. If the Turks had heard what you have heard, they would have done penance for their sins."[21]

---

[14] Donald Weinstein, "Millenarianism in a Civic Setting: The Savonarola Movement in Florence," in *Millennial Dreams in Action: Essays in Comparative Study*, ed. Silvia L. Thrupp (The Hague: Mouton, 1962), 188; Donald Weinstein, "The Myth of Florence," in *Florentine Studies: Politics and Society in Renaissance Florence*, ed. Nicolai Rubinstein (Evanston: Northwestern University Press, 1968), 40.

[15] Weinstein, "Myth of Florence," 40.

[16] As quoted in Roberto Ridolfi, *The Life of Girolamo Savonarola*, trans. Cecil Grayson (New York: Knopf, 1959), 32.

[17] Other recurring themes include social injustice and the moral corruption of the wealthy. See: Weinstein, *Savonarola and Florence*, 98–99.

[18] Weinstein, *Savonarola and Florence*, 94.

[19] As quoted in Weinstein, *Savonarola and Florence*, 98.

[20] Savonarola, Haggai, Sermon I (1 November 1494), in *Guide to Righteous Living*, 89. Emphasis in original. The translator has translated the italicized portion from the Latin that appears in the original: *Ecce gladius Domini super terram cito et velociter*.

[21] Savonarola, Haggai, Sermon I (1 November 1494), in *Guide to Righteous Living*, 88.

Repentance and moral reform, the friar warned, would not stop the apocalyptic onslaught, but would offer some protection, if only in the form of martyrdom. If Florentines did not change their ways, he warned, they should not be surprised "afterwards, when the slaughter will come and everything will be in danger."[22] Thus construed, the looming invasion of the French took on immense prophetic significance. Faced with an imminent apocalypse, Florentines drew closer to Savonarola during these tense November days.

Charles entered Florence on November 17. His stay was tense. The city's inhabitants had practical, as well as prophetic, reasons to fear the king's retribution. Florence had opposed his Italian campaign and had very recently ousted his new Medici ally.[23] Playing the role of the conqueror and installing himself in the Medici palace, Charles exacerbated an already tense situation by demanding that the government allow Piero's return. Politically, the situation was defused with the drafting of an alliance between Florence and France and a promise on behalf of the city's officials that they would consider allowing Piero to return.[24] When Charles still seemed reluctant to leave, Savonarola was sent to persuade him. Wielding a crucifix and casting Charles as God's chosen minister, the friar exhorted the king to continue his divine mission to Naples as quickly as possible.[25]

In presenting Charles's mission in this way, Savonarola drew on a well-established prophetic tradition centered on the hope for a second Charlemagne who would prepare the way for the apocalypse by taking Italy, renewing the Church, and finally moving East to conquer and convert the infidel, thereby reducing "the world to a single sheepfold under one shepherd."[26] Charles was prepared to be persuaded by such an argument. His Italian campaign had been spurred by apocalyptic fantasies of his role as a second Charlemagne, recalled to the king by Neapolitan and Milanese envoys in the French court.[27] Charles and his army promptly left Florence and their departure was widely seen as a miracle. Savonarola was celebrated by many as the savior of the city.

---

[22] Savonarola, Haggai, Sermon I (1 November 1494), in *Guide to Righteous Living*, 94.
[23] Weinstein, "Millenarianism in a Civic Setting," 191.
[24] Najemy, *History of Florence 1200–1575*, 379–80.
[25] Weinstein, *Savonarola and Florence*, 115.
[26] Weinstein, *Savonarola and Florence*, 113. The origins of the myth of a second Charlemagne lie in the preaching of the French Franciscan Jean de Roquetaillade. Writing in the aftermath of the terrible French defeat at Poitiers in 1356, Roquetaillade predicted an outpouring of divine wrath, as a combination of plagues and popular revolutions swept over the earth, stripping the church of its wealth and paving the way for the rule of Antichrist in Rome and Jerusalem. These terrors would end by 1367, with the rise of a reforming pope and the election of the king of France as Holy Roman Emperor. The king would be a second Charlemagne, conquering the world and presiding over a period of unprecedented peace. See: Marjorie Reeves, *The Influence of Prophecy in the Later Middle Ages: A Study in Joachimism* (Oxford: Oxford University Press, 1969), 320–31.
[27] Weinstein, *Savonarola and Florence*, 112.

Florence was spared the divine scourge that the friar had predicted. Savonarola's popularity soared and his sermons continued to whip the city into a state of heightened apocalyptic expectation. Now, the dominant theme was earthly renewal rather than worldly annihilation.[28] No longer singled out for the worst of the tribulations, Florence would now be the site of an apocalyptic rebirth. Because Florence was "the navel of Italy," this renewal would flow outward.[29] In Christian terms, Florentines were God's elect, a chosen people who would be shielded from the worst of the divine violence.

However, this status was conditional. Savonarola again urged Florentines to purify themselves of their sins and to "attend to the common good of the city." If Florence heeded the friar's apocalyptic plea, its rewards would be temporal, as well as spiritual. He predicted "Florence will become richer and more powerful than she has ever been, and her empire will expand into many places." Yet Savonarola did not abandon the apocalyptic themes of scourge and tribulation. Divine violence was a prerequisite for the friar's promised renewal. He warned: "God wants to renew His Church – do not doubt this at all – and He will renew it, and He will do so with the sword of tribulations – and soon!"[30] At best, Florence's elect status would protect the penitent from the worst of the tribulations. The unrepentant and the unconverted would be the primary targets of God's sword.[31] Only after this apocalyptic purge would Florence become the New Jerusalem.[32]

Florence's renewal would be political, as well as spiritual. As the constitutional crisis spurred by the forced departure of Piero de' Medici worsened, Savonarola propelled himself into the political arena, marrying prophetic

---

[28] Savonarola scholarship owes much to Donald Weinstein for recognizing this important shift in the friar's preaching. Savonarola himself obscures this shift in the retrospective account he offers in *Compendium Revelationum*, in which he offers a retrospective account of his apocalyptic preaching.
[29] Savonarola, Psalms, Sermon III (13 January 1495), *Selected Writings*, 62.
[30] Savonarola, Aggeus, Sermon XIII (12 December 1494), in *Selected Writings*, 153.
[31] Savonarola, Psalms, Sermon III (13 January 1495) in *Selected Writings*, 69–70.
[32] I think that Donald Weinstein confuses matters by classifying Savonarola's "post-Charles" apocalypticism as "postmillenarian." Weinstein does this because he sees Savonarola as placing "the age of regeneration within historical time, before the Second Coming and the Last Judgment." Based on my review of Savonarola's sermons, it is not at all clear that he can be so easily classified. First, as Weinstein himself notes, while Savonarola urges Florentines toward spiritual reform, he does not think that human action alone can bring about the millennium. Divine intervention is still necessary. This intervention will come in the form of apocalyptic tribulations and violence. This narrative already separates Savonarola's message from those commonly classified as postmillennial or postmillenarian. Second, in the sermon from which I quote at the end of the paragraph, it seems clear that the spiritual reform Savonarola is urging on Florence is not meant to establish the city as a millennial kingdom right away. Rather, it is to guarantee penitent Florentines some protection from imminent apocalyptic violence. A fully realized millennial kingdom may only be achieved, Savonarola seems to be suggesting, after a period of tribulation. See: Weinstein, *Savonarola and Florence*, 165–66; Savonarola, Psalms, Sermon III in *Selected Writings* (13 January 1495), 69–70.

yearning with republican traditions. The friar laid the foundation for this marriage in a series of principles: "that you fear God and seek the light of His grace...that no citizen should seek to be first or superior to the others but [all] should be content, each within his own degree and limit, as I have said...that the angels and the blessed are in Paradise, each within the limits God has given him, without seeking more beyond; in this way you would be an ordered city like the celestial one."[33] He urged Florentines to adopt a holy republic, modeled on the Venetian constitution[34] and with the Great Council at its heart.[35]

While Savonarola was not the only voice that shaped the constitution of 1494, he did imbue it with a sacred importance and locate it within a divine history.[36] Florence was to be both a temporal republic and a spiritual monarchy, with Christ as its king.[37] In practical terms, this meant that Savonarola envisioned a republican government imbued with the Christian moral purpose of stamping out sin and making social reforms. The practice of sodomy was the government's first target. It eliminated fines in favor of corporal punishment or death as the sentence for this crime.[38] This agenda of moral reform brought Savonarola support both within the Council, and among Florentines more broadly.[39]

The legislative process was not the only way in which Savonarola and his supporters instituted their reforms. When the Great Council found itself unable

---

[33] Savonarola, Aggeus, Sermon XXIII (28 December 1494), in *Selected Writings*, 167.

[34] On the strange power that the idealized image of Venice exercised on the Florentine political imagination, see: Pocock, *The Machiavellian Moment*, 99–103. As Pocock points out, part of the appeal of the Venetian constitutional model might have been its very ambiguity. To some, it was the paradigmatic mixed government, while to others it was an unapologetic aristocracy.

[35] The Great Council was a sovereign legislature comprised of approximately 3,500 citizens whose membership was determined based on whether a given individual was a citizen himself, or his father, grandfather, or great-grandfather had held, or had been drawn for, a seat in one of the three main executive offices of the government. This body had power over elections, taxes, and city finances. For a more detailed account of the political reforms of this period, see: Najemy, *History of Florence*, 381–90.

[36] Najemy, *History of Florence*, 394.

[37] Savonarola, Aggeus, Sermon XXIII (28 December 1494), in *Selected Writings*, 171.

[38] Najemy, *History of Florence*, 395.

[39] It is difficult to estimate the extent of this support. As Lorenzo Polizzotto rightly points out, contemporary estimates of the size of the crowds at Savonarola's sermons cannot be taken as indicators of the extent of the friar's support. One cannot assume that attendance at a sermon is necessarily an indicator of support for the religious and political ideas advanced by the friar. We do have an idea of the support that Savonarola had within the Great Council. In December 1494, there were approximately 400 Savonarolans in the Council, accounting for about one-ninth of total members. Yet these estimates may understate the influence Savonarola's supporters had over legislation. As Polizzotto explains, Savonarola had built up a lot of good will when his prophecies were seen to have been fulfilled and when he helped shape the new government. He also had the support of some Medicean factions, whom he had intervened to protect after Piero was ousted. Finally, there were numerous gifted politicians in the Savonarolan ranks who garnered substantial support from different groups. See: Lorenzo Polizzotto, *The Elect Nation: The Savonarolan Movement in Florence, 1494–1545* (Oxford: Clarendon Press, 1994), 12–17.

The Savonarolan Moment

to initiate the total renewal for which Savonarola had hoped, he turned to roving gangs of boys, which targeted prostitutes, homosexuals, and the wealthy, urging them to reform.[40] These gangs pursued the spiritual purification that Savonarola had promised would ready the city for apocalyptic tribulations. Through political and moral reform, Savonarola and his supporters were determined to transform Florence into a holy republic, the New Jerusalem that would fulfill God's apocalyptic plans.

This transformative agenda reveals an interesting ambiguity around the question of agency in Savonarola's apocalyptic thought. In keeping with Christian doctrine, Savonarola casts God as the primary agent of apocalyptic transformation. The friar is often at pains to stress that he is merely God's messenger. Referring to his early prophecies of apocalyptic tribulation, he stresses, "Not I, but God predicted it to you." Yet this role of mediator is more central to the apocalyptic drama than Savonarola sometimes suggests. He explains, "if God had not enlightened me, you would not have been enlightened through my many sermons, and you have been enlightened more exclusively than any other place."[41] Just as Florentines have been singled out for a special role in the apocalypse, Savonarola is the chosen agent of God, capable of enlightenment so that he in his turn may enlighten.

While the primary apocalyptic agent may be God, Savonarola is hardly a *mere* messenger. He sees himself as a father and a shepherd to penitent Florentines.[42] But it is in Savonarola's maternal metaphors that one gets the most interesting glimpse of the friar's conception of his own role in a renewed and politically transformed Florence. He asks: "Florence, am I also not to you like a mother to her little child? I have suffered and suffer many pains and many afflictions to give you birth and to lead you to Christ. I have also been like your wet-nurse in raising you and counseling you about what is good for you and about your health."[43] While he could never abandon a commitment to God as an omnipotent agent in the apocalyptic drama, the friar nonetheless carves out a central role for himself in the tribulations and renewal of Florence.

Savonarola was tortured and executed by the Florentine government in 1498. His resistance to top-down institutional changes within the Church and his increasingly pointed criticisms of the pope had led to his excommunication

---

[40] Violence seems to have been rare in these encounters. Shaming and the threat of public exposure appear to have been the main weapons deployed by these groups of boys. Richard Trexler suggests: "Though the friar recognized the boys' very potential for violence deterred immorality, he counted on less violent inducements: the threat of official action, the shame perpetrators felt when they behaved immorally in the presence of children, and most significant, the example that the boys showed adults. In perfect marching order, small bands of innocents moved from place to place with saintly manners and dress, impressing their own innocence upon their elders." See: Richard C. Trexler, *Public Life in Renaissance Florence* (New York: Academic Press, 1980), 475.
[41] Savonarola, Haggai, Sermon I (1 November 1494), in *Guide to Righteous Living*, 89.
[42] Savonarola, Haggai, Sermon I (1 November 1494), in *Guide to Righteous Living*, 91–92.
[43] Savonarola, Haggai, Sermon I (1 November 1494), in *Guide to Righteous Living*, 92–93.

the previous year. However, the friar had remained undaunted. He had continued to call for the moral and spiritual renovation of the Church. In his 1498 Lenten sermons on the book of Exodus he had identified Pope Alexander VI with both Pharoah and Antichrist, casting himself as the Moses who would lead Florence out of bondage.[44] An enraged pope and a power shift in favor of Savonarola's opponents led to his execution by hanging and burning on May 23, 1498. Yet the apocalyptic story to which he gave an enduring voice took on an independent life. Signs of looming tribulation were being spotted everywhere and itinerant preachers continued to announce the apocalypse throughout Italy.[45] Sixteen years after Savonarola's death, it was still possible for Machiavelli to write to Francesco Vettori lamenting that "there is nothing to tell you about from these parts except prophecies and proclamations of calamities."[46]

In conceptualizing these events, rhetoric, and images as a "Savonarolan moment,"[47] I do not mean to suggest that the apocalyptic enthusiasm that captured the Florentine imagination was completely defined by the spiritual and political aspirations of a single man or bounded by the very brief period between the beginning of Savonarola's apocalyptic preaching in 1490 and his execution eight years later. Rather, I am drawing on J. G. A. Pocock's account of "the Machiavellian moment" of republican founding. Pocock asks us to interpret the Machiavellian moment in two ways. The first is rhetorical and experiential:

> It is asserted that certain enduring patterns in the temporal consciousness of medieval and early modern Europeans led to the presentation of the republic, and the citizen's participation in it, as constituting a problem in historical self-understanding, with which Machiavelli and his contemporaries can be seen both explicitly and implicitly contending. It became crucial in their times and remained so, largely as a result of what they did with it, for two or three centuries afterwards. Their struggle with this problem is presented as historically real, though as one selected aspect of the complex historical reality of their thought; and their "moment" is defined as that in which they confronted the problem grown crucial.[48]

Here, a "moment" refers to the *way* the problem of the republic's instability within time "made its appearance."[49] The relationship between the republic and its citizens is *presented* "as constituting a problem in historical self-understanding." However, the way these problems make their appearance is

---

[44] Girolamo Savonarola, *Prediche Sopra L'Esodo*, ed. Pier Giorgio Ricci (Rome: Belardetti, 1955).
[45] Niccoli, *Prophecy and People*, 89–120.
[46] Niccolò Machiavelli, Letter to Francesco Vettori (4 February 1514), in *Machiavelli and His Friends: Their Personal Correspondence* (Dekalb: Northern Illinois University Press, 2004), 278.
[47] I am borrowing the term from Marcia L. Colish, who is playing on Pocock's "Machiavellian moment." See: Marcia L. Colish, "Republicanism, Religion, and Machiavelli's Savonarolan Moment," *Journal of the History of Ideas* 60, no. 4 (1999): 597–616.
[48] Pocock, *Machiavellian Moment*, vii–viii.   [49] Pocock, *Machiavellian Moment*, vii.

not simply a reflection of "historical reality"; rather, it is in itself "historically real."

Nevertheless, Pocock seems at pains to distinguish between the rhetorical and experiential qualities of the Machiavellian moment and "the problem itself." In its second sense, then, the Machiavellian moment is:

> A name for the moment in conceptualized time in which the republic was seen as confronting its own temporal finitude, attempting to remain morally and politically stable in a stream of irrational events conceived as essentially destructive of all systems of secular stability. In the language which had been developed for the purpose, this was spoken of as the confrontation of "virtue" with "fortune" and "corruption" and the study of Florentine thought is the study of how Machiavelli and his contemporaries pursued the intimations of these words.[50]

Here, a moment is the historical point at which the republic is threatened with collapse. The early sixteenth century in Florence was one such moment, though not the only one. This second interpretation of a moment, however, is closely connected to the first. The historical circumstance of the republic at a given point in time is mediated through the language of virtue, fortune, and corruption. The problem itself can never be fully separated from the way it is presented.[51]

Similarly, when I use the term Savonarolan moment, I mean to describe both the historical point at which an apocalyptic transformation of Florence seemed possible in the late fifteenth through early sixteenth centuries and the way this possibility "made its appearance" and was presented. The invasion of Charles VIII, for instance, appears against the backdrop of an apocalyptic imaginary that expected an imminent end to the known world. The historical moment of the invasion is also rhetorically and imaginatively cast as a sign that this transformation is now at hand.

Like the Machiavellian moment, the Savonarolan moment is an attempt to find meaning and understanding in the face of radical contingency.[52] That is, both moments wrestle with a vertiginous combination of political indeterminacy, conditionality, and uncertainty.[53] Political outcomes such as institutional corruption or invasion by outside forces could have been different. These outcomes are also conditional on a host of other factors, many of which we do not understand. This makes it difficult to predict or even explain them. In the

---

[50] Pocock, *Machiavellian Moment*, viii.
[51] The discussion in the previous two paragraphs draws on the analysis of Helge Jordheim, "Conceptual History Between *Chronos* and *Kairos* – The Case of 'Empire,'" in *Redescriptions: Yearbook of Political Thought and Conceptual History*, vol. 11 (2007), 116–18.
[52] Pocock, *Machiavellian Moment*, vii–viii.
[53] I draw this three-part understanding of contingency from Andreas Schedler, who argues that indeterminacy, conditionality, and uncertainty are the three conceptual pillars of "the semantic architecture of 'contingency.'" See: Andreas Schedler, "Mapping Contingency," in *Political Contingency: Studying the Unexpected, the Accidental, and the Unforeseen*, ed. Ian Shapiro and Sonu Bedi (New York: New York University Press, 2007), 70.

face of these difficulties, we are left with the paralyzing sense that many of the events that shape our collective lives are underdetermined. The Machiavellian and Savonarolan moments grapple differently with this kind of radical contingency. The former seeks to restore the virtuous principles of the republic *within* secular time and to shore up the polity against the prospect of future corruption. The latter seeks to break with secular time and to prepare the polity to take a leading role in bringing history to a close.[54]

Just as Machiavelli was only "one of a number of greater and lesser men engrossed in the common pursuit" of republican founding, Savonarola was only one of many figures captivated by the apocalyptic imaginary. His eponymous moment both predated and survived him. The friar's apocalyptic message took shape in the context of a much larger revival of biblical prophecy in Italy. This revival was connected to a renewed interest in the apocalyptic prophecies of Joachim of Fiore, a twelfth-century Calabrian abbot, who proposed a Trinitarian model of history in which humankind would be brought to full fruition after apocalyptic tribulations and a period of false leadership by a priestly Antichrist.[55] Joachimism had been nurtured in late medieval Florence and was still popular in the late fifteenth century, as can be seen in the outpouring of Joachite prophecy during the approach of Charles VIII's forces.[56] As Marjorie Reeves notes, "the Joachimist marriage of woe and exaltation exactly fitted the mood of late fifteenth century Italy," where the humanist golden age confronted widespread apocalyptic expectation.[57] While Savonarola was not a close follower of Joachim and lacked the latter's sophisticated understanding of sacred history, the friar did draw on the well-established Joachimist "juxtaposition of tribulation and renewal," as well as the prophecies of a second Charlemagne that had developed among the Calabrian abbot's more recent followers.[58]

Savonarola was hardly the only apocalyptic preacher in late fifteenth-century Florence. When contemporary chronicler Piero Parenti noted the growth of terrifying apocalyptic preaching in Florence, he was not referring to Savonarola,

---

[54] Savonarola had republican commitments himself, to be sure, but his vision of a republican polity was never an end in itself. Rather, it was the necessarily worldly preparation for a cosmic transformation.

[55] On the role of the Antichrist in Joachim's thought, see: Bernard McGinn, *Anti-Christ: Two Thousand Years of the Human Fascination With Evil* (New York: Columbia University Press, 1999), 135–42. On Joachim's thought in its fullest form, see: Marjorie Reeves, *Joachim of Fiore and the Prophetic Future* (New York: Harper & Row, 1977).

[56] Reeves, *Joachim of Fiore*, 88.   [57] Reeves, *Influence of Prophecy*, 431.

[58] Reeves, *Joachim of Fiore*, 89. There is little evidence that Savonarola was well read in the works of Joachim or his followers. At times, the friar went out of his way to distance himself from a connection to Joachim, perhaps because the Church hierarchy saw the latter as having a dangerously revolutionary potential. Savonarola's engagement in worldly affairs also distances him from Joachim, who seems to have been content constructing elaborate prophetic conceptions of sacred history. Nevertheless, Marjorie Reeves concludes that despite these differences, "there can be little doubt that [Savonarola] belonged within the [Joachimite] prophetic tradition." Reeves, *Joachim of Fiore*, 90. See also: Weinstein, *Savonarola and Florence*, 95–96, 159, 175.

but rather to the Franciscan Domenico da Ponzo.[59] In this climate of apocalypticism, preachers vied for audiences. Those offering milder fare saw their crowds dwindle.

Florence was being whipped up into a state of semiotic arousal. Every event became a sign – a meaningful message about how the apocalyptic drama would unfold.[60] When a lightning bolt struck the cathedral shortly before the death of Lorenzo the Magnificent in April 1492, Savonarola interpreted the occurrence as a sign of an imminent divine scourge. Fra Domenico went even further, giving Florentines an August deadline to change their ways. If Florence did not repent, the streets would be rivers of blood.[61] Even Machiavelli concluded in retrospect that the lightning damage had been a sign that Lorenzo's "death would lead to the greatest calamities."[62] Savonarola was but one influential voice among many, pointing to the signs of God's imminent irruption into human history.

The friar's message also drew on well-established conceptions of Florentine identity. The city had long been seen as an elect nation. In the first written history of Florence, the thirteenth-century *Chronica de origine civitatis*, the city's special destiny is connected to its Roman origins – it was a *parva Roma*, or "little Rome." The *Chronica* also suggests that Florence had previously been reborn from the rubble of a divine scourge that had happened five hundred years after her founding.[63] While in the *Chronica* the city is rebuilt by the Romans, in a fourteenth-century account the Emperor Charlemagne is the agent of this rebirth. Here we see the origins of the linked destinies of France and Florence in apocalyptic prophecy. By the late fourteenth century, sources indicate that the city ceases to be a little Rome and assumes a special apocalyptic destiny in its own right. Various radical religious groups, furiously reworking Joachite ideas to suit the needs of a divinely chosen city, kept these prophecies alive. And, as Donald Weinstein has shown, these apocalyptic expectations were blended with conceptions of good government into "a single vision which seems to have functioned both as a model of a civic ethos and a promise of ultimate rewards."[64] It is this history of Florentine self-identity, at once prophetic and republican, that inflects Savonarola's later apocalyptic sermons.

Despite these connections to established traditions, it might still be tempting to see the Savonarolan moment as a marginal or fringe reaction to what would retrospectively be called the Renaissance. Such a conclusion would be misguided. The Savonarolan moment, particularly in its hopes for an apocalyptic rebirth, participated in and drew from the humanism that has come

---

[59] Najemy, *History of Florence*, 375.
[60] I am borrowing the term "semiotic arousal" from Landes, *Heaven on Earth*, 14.
[61] Weinstein, *Savonarola and Florence*, 127.
[62] Niccolò Machiavelli, *History of Florence*, in *The Chief Works and Others*, trans. Allan Gilbert, vol. 3 (Durham: Duke University Press, 1989), 1434.
[63] Weinstein, "Myth of Florence," 21.   [64] Weinstein, "Myth of Florence," 35.

to define this period in Florentine history. The idea of an enlightened people emerging from a period of darkness and ushering in a new age blended easily with the Savonarolan apocalyptic imaginary. Florentine exceptionalism lay at the center of the humanist conception of the city as a special place where history, culture, and art flourished as they could nowhere else.[65] Savonarola received broad support from humanist philosophers like Pico della Mirandola, Oliviero Arduini, and Marsilio Ficino.[66] Ficino proclaimed Savonarola a divine agent whose prophecies had been fulfilled and even welcomed Charles VIII to Florence as a second Charlemagne.[67] Ficino later rejected Savonarola, but he did so within the apocalyptic imaginary – denouncing the friar as the Antichrist who had led Florence astray.[68]

While this philosophical following demonstrates that Savonarola's messages resonated with learned humanists, the paintings of the period capture the apocalyptic imaginary most vividly. Sandro Botticelli's connections to Savonarola have been well established by art historians.[69] The artist was a devout follower of the friar and even threw some of his own paintings in one of the Savonarola's bonfires of the vanities. Botticelli's *Mystic Nativity* (1500/1) is inscribed with a message of apocalyptic anxiety and hope: "I Sandro painted this picture at the end of the year 1500 in the troubles of Italy in the half time after the time according to the eleventh chapter of St John in the second woe of the Apocalypse in the loosing of the devil for three and a half years. Then he will be chained in the twelfth chapter and we shall see him trodden down as in this picture."[70] Botticelli's *Crucifixion* (1498–1500) (see Figure 3.1) renders in visual and visceral form the scourge so often promised by Savonarola. Behind the crucified Jesus are fiery brands shooting downward from the skies, and the city of Florence, bathed in light and partially protected from tribulation.[71]

Lucca Signorelli's apocalypse at Orvieto (1499–1502) (Figures 3.2 and 3.3) is even more visceral. The multi-panel sequence visually interprets the apocalyptic

---

[65] Weinstein, "Millenarianism in a Civic Setting," 196.
[66] Another reason for the close connection between Savonarola and some humanist philosophers was the friar's interest in skepticism. Savonarola arranged for a complete translation of the writings of Sextus Empiricus and showed a deep interest in classical works. The skeptics' claims about the unreliability of natural knowledge suited Savonarola's prophetic cause. He argued, often with philosophical sophistication, that the only reliable knowledge was that provided by revelation. See: Richard H. Popkin, "Savonarola and Cardinal Ximines: Millenarian Thinkers and Actors at the Eve of the Reformation," in *Millenarianism and Messianism in Early Modern European Culture*, ed. Karl A. Kottman, vol. 2 (Boston: Kluwer, 2001), 16–20.
[67] Nancy Bisaha, *Creating East and West: Renaissance Humanists and the Ottoman Turks* (Philadelphia: University of Pennsylvania Press, 2006), 41.
[68] Marsilio Ficino, *Apologia contra Savonarolam*, in *Selected Writings of Girolamo Savonarola*, 355–59.
[69] See, for instance: Rab Hatfield, "Botticelli's Mystic Nativity, Savonarola and the Millennium," *Journal of the Warburg and Courtauld Institutes* 58 (1995): 89–114.
[70] The translation of the Greek is from Weinstein, "Myth of Florence," 15.
[71] Weinstein, "Myth of Florence," 16–17.

FIGURE 3.1. Sandro Botticelli, *Mystic Crucifixion*, c. 1500. Harvard Art Museums/Fogg Museum, Friends of the Fogg Art Museum Fund, 1924.27. Photo by Imaging Department © President and Fellows of Harvard College.

FIGURE 3.2. Luca Signorelli, *Apocalypse Sequence*, 1499–1502. Cappella di San Brizio, Orvieto. Courtesy of Art Resource, Inc.

events foretold in Revelation. One panel depicts the Antichrist pausing mid-sermon to receive intimate instructions from the devil. In another panel, winged demons torment the damned before forcing them into the fiery pits of hell. This remarkable sequence blends the typical Renaissance attention to the beauty and dignity of the human form with shocking divine violence. These images speak to a Renaissance to which scholars give too little attention – one captured by apocalyptic beliefs that saw totalizing divine violence as a prerequisite for spiritual rebirth.

The enduring power of this narrative is understandable. The prophecies of the Savonarolan moment fashioned an apocalyptic story from the crisis of Florentine politics at the end of sixty years of Medici rule. Narrated in this way, Florence's domestic political woes and looming foreign threats became necessary preludes to an imminent divine transformation. The apocalypticism of the Savonarolan moment promised an escape for a small elect from the frightening unpredictability of power politics. The friar did not offer the repentant complete protection from God's totalizing wrath, but rather the assurance that their suffering would be made meaningful through an apocalyptic rebirth. Drawing on the hopes and fears of his audience, Savonarola rendered imaginable that

FIGURE 3.3. Luca Signorelli, *Apocalypse Sequence*, 1499–1502. Cappella di San Brizio, Orvieto. Courtesy of Art Resource, Inc.

most unimaginable of events – the irruption of God into secular time. In so doing, he harnessed an apocalyptic imaginary that would continue to exert its power over Italy long after his death.

Machiavelli's Flirtation with Apocalypse

This Savonarolan apocalyptic enthusiasm had a profound effect on Machiavelli. Such a claim may strike some as unlikely, particularly those inclined to cast Machiavelli as the first modern political theorist, or as an unabashed realist who aims to break from medieval religious statecraft.[72] I want to suggest that

[72] This claim is made by a variety of political theorists, with vastly different intellectual agendas, seeking to construct a grand narrative of the history of political thought. See, for instance: Leo Strauss, "The Three Waves of Modernity," in *An Introduction to Political Philosophy: Ten Essays by Leo Strauss*, ed. Hilail Gildin (Detroit: Wayne State University Press, 1989), 81–98; Harvey C. Mansfield, *Machiavelli's Virtue* (Chicago: University of Chicago Press, 1996); Sheldon S. Wolin, *Politics and Vision: Continuity and Innovation in Western Political Thought*, expanded ed. (Princeton: Princeton University Press, 2006), 175–213. On the question of Machiavelli's modernity and originality more broadly, see: Isaiah Berlin, "The Originality

this influence is nonetheless plausible. First, it is not clear that Machiavelli held an entirely negative opinion of Savonarola. The formative influence of the friar on the political theorist may have been possible because Machiavelli held a view of Savonarola that is more positive than conventional accounts suggest. I make this case in the following paragraphs. Second, even if one is inclined to reject the first line of argument, it does not follow that Machiavelli was not attuned to (and even captivated by) the apocalyptic emplotment of Savonarola's political prophecy.

On the conventional account of Machiavelli's view of Savonarola, the political theorist could only react with suspicion and condescension to the friar's claims to prophetic knowledge.[73] However, this reading risks caricaturing both

of Machiavelli," in *Against the Current: Essays in the History of Ideas* (London: Hogarth Press, 1980), 25–79; Quentin Skinner, *The Foundations of Modern Political Thought, Vol. 1: The Renaissance* (Cambridge: Cambridge University Press, 1978), 128–38; Nathan Tarcov, "Quentin Skinner's Method and Machiavelli's Prince," *Ethics* 92, no. 4 (1982): 692–709; Donald McIntosh, "The Modernity of Machiavelli," *Political Theory* 12, no. 2 (1984): 184–203; Waller R. Newell, "How Original Is Machiavelli?: A Consideration of Skinner's Interpretation of Virtue and Fortune," *Political Theory* 15, no. 4 (1987): 612–34.

[73] See, for instance: Frederico Chabod, *Machiavelli and the Renaissance* (Cambridge: Harvard University Press, 1960), 1–2, 17–18, 94; Gennaro Sasso, *Niccolò Machiavelli: Storia Del Suo Pensiero Politico* (Bologna: Società Editrice Il Mulino, 1980), 13–26; Gennaro Sasso, *Niccolò Machiavelli, Volume 1: Il Pensiero Politico* (Bologna: Società Editrice Il Mulino, 1993), 25–53; Colish, "Republicanism, Religion, and Machiavelli's Savonarolan Moment," 611–15. These accounts are sometimes tied to broader arguments about Machiavelli's relationship to religion in general and Christianity in particular. Such broader arguments are subject to vigorous scholarly debate. Much of this debate has focused on the nature of Machiavelli's own beliefs and his view of the role of religion and Christianity in politics. The point on which most scholars can agree is that Machiavelli was a critic of the institution of the church (and of the papacy in particular) and of the interpretation of Christian doctrine that he thought prevailed in his own time. See: Niccolò Machiavelli, *Discourses on Livy*, trans. Harvey C. Mansfield and Nathan Tarcov (Chicago: University of Chicago Press, 1996), book I, chapter 12, pages 36–39; book II, chapter 2, pages 131–32. Future references will take the following form: I.12, 36–39. However, in considering these views in light of the rest of Machiavelli's thoughts, scholars reach radically divergent conclusions. We can divide these conclusions into five sets, not all of which are mutually exclusive. First, one position holds that Machiavelli's criticism of Christianity runs much deeper than a criticism of its contemporary institutional instantiation. This group of interpreters argues that Machiavelli rejected Christianity and Christian faith almost entirely. Many take this rejection as evidence of his modernity, immorality, or paganism. See: Clifford Orwin, "Machiavelli's Unchristian Charity," *The American Political Science Review* 72, no. 4 (1978): 1217–28; Leo Strauss, *Thoughts on Machiavelli* (Chicago: University of Chicago Press, 1958), 9–10, 12, 49–50, 175–92 and passim; Strauss, "The Three Waves of Modernity," 86–87; Guiseppe Prezzolini, *Machiavelli*, trans. Gioconda Savini (New York: Noonday Press, 1967). Second, another position holds that Machiavelli understood Christianity, and indeed all religions, in functional terms, as sets of beliefs that elicit behaviors that can either sustain or destroy political regimes. This interpretation leaves open the possibility that Christianity might be interpreted in such a way as to promote social order, cohesion, and citizen *virtù*. It also does not logically entail any position on Machiavelli's own religious beliefs. See: Berlin, "The Originality of Machiavelli," 37; J. Samuel Preus, "Machiavelli's Functional Analysis of Religion: Context and Object," *Journal of the History of Ideas* 40, no. 2 (1979): 171–90; Quentin Skinner, *Machiavelli* (New York: Hill

men, treating one as a thoroughly secular and modern theorist of power and the other as a politically impotent and utopian friar. If these caricatures are accurate, Machiavelli's reaction to Savonarola must be interpreted as either entirely negative or at best ambivalent.[74] While there is evidence for this view, it is not unambiguous. By revisiting what appear to be the strongest instances of Machiavelli's negative assessment of Savonarola, I aim to show how the hopes of the friar became the exhortations of the political theorist.

We find Machiavelli's most apparently negative assessment of Savonarola in a March 1498 letter to Ricciardo Becchi, a prominent politician and the Florentine ambassador to Rome. In June of the previous year, Pope Alexander VI, whom Savonarola had publicly criticized on numerous occasions, had

and Wang, 1981), 61–64. Third, a somewhat related position holds that Machiavelli held some Christian commitments but sought to radically adapt and reimagine Christianity in order to press it into service in creating, preserving, and renovating stable political orders. Machiavelli's project, on this interpretation, is to offer a vision of a new and distinctly political Christianity that is consistent with a robust republicanism. See: Sebastian de Grazia, *Machiavelli in Hell* (Princeton: Princeton University Press, 1989); Maurizio Viroli, *Machiavelli's God*, trans. Antony Shugaar (Princeton: Princeton University Press, 2010). Fourth, a position that extends some of de Grazia's suggestive but largely speculative interpretations holds that Machiavelli's political analysis is underpinned by central tenets of medieval Christian theology. See: Cary J. Nederman, "Amazing Grace: Fortune, God, and Free Will in Machiavelli's Thought," *Journal of the History of Ideas* 60, no. 4 (1999): 617–38. Finally, another position holds that Machiavelli's arguments and doctrines rely on secularized versions of Christian theology. See: Guiseppe Prezzolini, "The Christian Roots of Machiavelli's Moral Pessimism," *Review of National Literatures* 1, no. 1 (1970): 26–37. For one of the many interesting arguments that do not fit easily into any of these categories, see: Vickie B. Sullivan, "Neither Christian nor Pagan: Machiavelli's Treatment of Religion in the 'Discourses,'" *Polity* 26, no. 2 (1993): 259–80. While my own argument in this chapter – that, in the final chapter of *The Prince*, Machiavelli offers a secularized version of the Savonarolan apocalyptic imaginary that he rejects in his later writings – is closest to the fifth position, it does not take any stand on the sincerity of Machiavelli's religious beliefs. This is because I do not think that we can make reliable inferences about what a thinker believes on the basis of the words they choose to put on the page. However, the argument I offer in this chapter is not logically inconsistent with any of the others outlined earlier and could reasonably be held by many of their defenders. As a critic of Christianity, a religious functionalist, a somewhat unconventional and republican Christian, an inheritor of medieval theology, or a secularizer, Machiavelli might well have had reasons to initially fall prey to and later reject the Savonarolan message. The question of Machiavelli's own beliefs or his views on the proper relationship between Christianity and politics are largely orthogonal to this investigation.

[74] For arguments that Savonarola's influence on Machiavelli is an entirely negative one, see: Frederico Chabod, *Machiavelli and the Renaissance*, trans. David Moore (Cambridge: Harvard University Press, 1960); Gennaro Sasso, *Niccolò Machiavelli: Storia del suo pensiero politico*; Gennaro Sasso, *Niccolò Machiavelli*, vol. 1: *Il pensiero politico*; Peter Godman, *From Poliziano to Machiavelli: Florentine Humanism in the High Renaissance* (Princeton: Princeton University Press, 1998); Colish, "Republicanism, Religion, and Machiavelli's Savonarolan Moment." For arguments that Machiavelli's position on Savonarola is ambivalent at best, see: Maurice Cranston, *Political Dialogues* (London: British Broadcasting Corporation, 1968); Donald Weinstein, "Machiavelli and Savonarola," in *Studies on Machiavelli*, ed. Myron P. Gilmore (Florence: G. C. Sansoni Editore, 1972), 253–64; Silvia Ruffo-Fiore, *Niccolò Machiavelli* (Boston: Twayne, 1982).

excommunicated the friar and temporarily silenced him. However, a defiant Savonarola resumed preaching in February 1498, once again drawing large crowds. Machiavelli attended two of the friar's sermons on Exodus and provided Becchi with an account of their content and the effect they had on the friar's audiences. Machiavelli is focused on a shift in these sermons – from fear of an unnamed potential tyrant in Florence to sharp criticism of the pope. This shift, argues Machiavelli, is opportunistic. The friar has "changed coats" and, in Machiavelli's judgment, he "acts in accordance with the times and colors his lies accordingly."[75] One could see this assessment in an entirely negative light, as a condemnation of the friar's hypocrisy and demagoguery.[76] Yet I think such a judgment is too hasty. In many of his writings, Machiavelli sees an ability to change with the times, deceive, and cultivate appearances as rare and praiseworthy forms of *virtù*.[77] Furthermore, the detail and analysis that Machiavelli provides in the letter suggests, at the very least, a certain fascination with Savonarola and the prophetic words that bound his followers.[78]

Nevertheless, one might still insist that Machiavelli's assessment reduces Savonarola's prophetic claims to the status of mere lies. There are at least two responses here. First, as Mark Jurdjevic notes, Machiavelli "had a complex view of the relationship between duplicity and virtue."[79] Machiavelli praises Numa who, as second king of Rome, "pretended to be intimate with a nymph" so he might institute orders to make a crude and savage people virtuous.[80] Second, while he resists Savonarola's claim to prophecy here, in other works Machiavelli refrains from judgment. For instance, in the *First Decennale* (1504), he states simply that Savonarola was "inspired with heavenly *virtù*."[81] Focusing more

---

[75] Letter from Niccolò Machiavelli to Ricciardo Becchi (9 March 1498), in Machiavelli et al., *Machiavelli and His Friends: Their Personal Correspondence*, 10.
[76] Weinstein, "Machiavelli and Savonarola," 253–55; Colish, "Republicanism, Religion, and Machiavelli's Savonarolan Moment," 611. Machiavelli makes another charge of hypocrisy and opportunism against Savonarola when he notes that the friar instituted a law of appeal that he later failed to observe. See: Machiavelli, *Discourses on Livy*, I.45, 93. As is the case with changing one's lies to suit the times, this flexibility with regard to the law is treated as a political asset in *The Prince*. The great founders and refounders invoked in chapter 6, for instance, recognized that they had to act outside the fundamental laws (*ordini*) of their polities.
[77] Machiavelli, *The Prince*, chapter 18, pages 70–71; chapter 25, pages 99–100. Future references will take the following form: 18, 70–71. Alison Brown, "Savonarola, Machiavelli and Moses: A Changing Model," in *Florence and Italy: Renaissance Studies in Honour of Nicolai Rubinstein*, ed. Peter Denley and Caroline Elam (London: Committee for Medieval Studies, Westfield College, University of London, 1988), 65; John M. Najemy, "Papirius and the Chickens, or Machiavelli on the Necessity of Interpreting Religion," *Journal of the History of Ideas* 60, no. 4 (1999): 679–81; Mario Martelli, "Machiavelli E Savonarola: Valutazione Politica E Valutazione Religiosa," in *Girolamo Savonarola: L'uomo E Il Frate*, ed. Enrico Menestò (Spoleto: Centro Italiano di studi sull'alto medioevo, 1999), 147.
[78] Jurdjevic, *Great and Wretched City*, 16–26. [79] Jurdjevic, *Great and Wretched City*, 26.
[80] Machiavelli, *Discourses on Livy*, I.11, 35.
[81] Niccolò Machiavelli, *First Decennale*, in *The Chief Works and Others*, trans. Allan Gilbert, vol. 3 (Durham: Duke University Press, 1989), lines 157–59, 1448.

Machiavelli's Flirtation with Apocalypse

on the factional outcomes of Savonarolan rhetoric than on its truth claims, Machiavelli nonetheless takes the friar's heavenly inspiration as given.

In the *Discourses on Livy* (1516–1518?), Machiavelli addresses the question overtly. He recounts that the people of Florence were convinced of Savonarola's prophetic status, believing the friar spoke with God. Rather than denying this claim, or calling it a lie, Machiavelli refrains from judgment. While there was no evidence to support Savonarola's claim, Machiavelli does not "wish to judge whether it is true or not, because one should speak with reverence of such a man."[82] He echoes *The Prince*'s earlier assessment of Moses, whose prophetic status is not up for debate. We must simply admire Moses "for that grace which made him deserving of speaking with God."[83] So even if Machiavelli's initial assessment of Savonarola was negative, it may not have remained so.[84]

The direct comparison of Savonarola to Moses in *The Prince* is, of course, much to the disadvantage of the former, who is the paradigmatic unarmed prophet. While the friar successfully used his powers of prophetic persuasion to establish "new orders" in Florence, he had no recourse to violent force when these powers expired. People may be easily persuaded at first, but it is "difficult to keep them in that persuasion...When they no longer believe, one [must] make them believe by force." Unfortunately, Savonarola "had no [way to hold] firm those who had believed nor for making unbelievers believe."[85] It is tempting to see Machiavelli's assessment here as wholly negative. Yet Savonarola is in the best of company in this chapter of *The Prince*, grouped alongside the great founding legislators of myth and history – Moses, Cyrus, Theseus, and Romulus. Machiavelli treats Savonarola as a refounder of a state, a role that he holds in the highest regard.[86] Savonarola's goal is not in question. Rather, his limited means are the problem. Without force, he has no other way of maintaining himself than by keeping the support of the masses, who are by nature variable.[87] Seen in this way, Machiavelli's famous assessment of Savonarola is less a condemnation than a lament for the friar's inability to achieve his great task.

My own view is that Machiavelli did regard Savonarola in this more positive light. However, one need not agree to accept that Machiavelli's work may have

---

[82] Machiavelli, *Discourses on Livy*, I.11, 36.   [83] Machiavelli, *Prince*, 6, 22.
[84] On this point, see also: Weinstein, "Machiavelli and Savonarola," 255–57.
[85] Machiavelli, *Prince*, 6, 24. Mansfield translates the passages as "one can make them believe by force" and "he had no mode for holding firm."
[86] Machiavelli echoes this admiration in the *Discourses*, where he notes: "Florence, after '94 had been reordered in its state by the aid of Friar Girolamo Savonarola, whose writings show the learning, the prudence, and the virtue of his spirit." See: Machiavelli, *Discourses on Livy*, I.45, 93. See also: Weinstein, "Machiavelli and Savonarola," 256; Martelli, "Machiavelli E Savonarola," 123, 159; Najemy, "Papirius and the Chickens," 679–80; Pocock, *Machiavellian Moment*, 170–72.
[87] Thierry Ménissier, "Prophétie, Politique et Action Selon Machiavel," *Les Études Philosophiques* 3, no. 66 (2003): 305.

been shaped by the apocalyptic emplotment and imaginary of the Savonarolan moment. As I suggested in the previous section, the Savonarolan moment drew on and reinforced established prophetic traditions and elements of Florentine identity. It appealed to the masses and intellectual elites alike. Not everyone captivated by this apocalyptic imaginary held positive or even ambivalent views about Savonarola. Whatever Machiavelli's position on the friar, there are textual resonances between his works and the emplotment and expectations of the Savonarolan moment that are difficult to dismiss as accidental. Let us turn to these now.

The influence of the Savonarolan moment is clearest in the final chapter of *The Prince*, "An Exhortation to Seize Italy and to Free Her from the Barbarians." Machiavelli begins by explaining that he has now reached a point where he must consider "whether in Italy at present the times have been tending to the honor of a new prince, and whether there is matter to give opportunity [*occasione*] to someone prudent and [*virtuoso*] to introduce a form that would bring honor to him and good to the community of men."[88] He wastes no time in offering his answer: "it appears to me that so many things are tending to the benefit of a new prince that I do not know what time has ever been more apt for it."[89] This time, suggests Machiavelli, is an extraordinary one, a God-given *occasione* that calls for action.

Historically, the aftermath of the disruptions of 1512 was indeed a period of crisis and upheaval in Italy, but perhaps not one of any clear prophetic significance in a region that had been perpetually unstable since 1494. The Medici had been brought back to power in Florence by some of the city's radical nobles, aided by Pope Julius and a Spanish army, and Italy had been rocked by the bloody Battle of Ravenna, the descent of the Swiss into Italy, and the expulsion of the French by the Swiss and the Venetians. Like the period of crisis in which Savonarola preached, Machiavelli issues his exhortation at a time when Italy's uncertain future was at the mercy of foreign armies. And, like the friar, Machiavelli finds an apocalyptic story in what might otherwise have been just another political crisis for a city and a people increasingly accustomed to calamity. Like Savonarola's Florence, the Italy of Machiavelli's exhortation was "living through a moment of transhistorical crisis."[90]

Yet it is not just upheaval and uncertainty that make this the best time for princely intervention. Rather, it is what Machiavelli surprisingly casts as the complete degradation of Italy that provides the appropriate *occasione* for an extraordinary and prophetic act. For the *virtù* of Moses to be made visible, it was necessary "that the people of Israel be enslaved in Egypt." Similarly, for

---

[88] Machiavelli, *Prince*, 26, 101–02. Rather than translating *virtù* as "virtue" and *virtuoso* as "virtuous," as Mansfield does in this translation, I prefer to render the words in their original Italian in order to signal clearly their central and contested places in Machiavelli's work.

[89] Machiavelli, *Prince*, 26, 102.   [90] Jurdjevic, *Great and Wretched City*, 51.

the *virtù* of the Italian spirit to be made manifest, it is necessary "that Italy be reduced to the condition in which she is at present, which is more enslaved than the Hebrews, more servile than the Persians, more dispersed than the Athenians, without a head, without order, beaten, despoiled, torn, pillaged, and having endured ruin of very sort." Machiavelli picks up a theme first developed in chapter 6, where he explains that fortune gives *virtuoso* founders an *occasione* to act. Now he suggests that this *occasione* is not merely given by history or providence. It is also graced with divine favor. Italy's redeemer is "supported by God" and receives a degree of divine approval that at least equals that of the (re)founders of history and legend.[91] For Moses, Cyrus, and Theseus, finding their people devastated or dispersed presented an *occasione* for redemptive political action.[92] In his exhortation, Machiavelli asserts that the suffering of the Italians is even *worse* than that of the Israelites, Persians, and Athenians. Wounded and almost lifeless, Italy awaits a redeemer to cure her long-festering sores and restore her original vitality. This devastation is a sign of her readiness for salvation. Emplotted in this way, Italy's troubles become an *occasione* without precedent that demands an extraordinary act of redemption.

The nature of this redemptive act is both prophetic and apocalyptic.[93] Machiavelli does not just call for a great founder here. He calls for a redemptive prince, someone to save Italy "from these barbarous cruelties and insults" – to give form to the matter of a suffering people.[94] The chapter is suffused with the language of salvation. Italy's cause lacks neither the divine blessing nor the justice of its historical and mythological predecessors. And it will likewise be a justice forged in violence. Quoting Livy, Machiavelli writes, "for war is just to whom it is necessary, and arms are pious when there is no hope but in arms." Like Savonarola, Machiavelli gives various signs from God that the moment for an extraordinary rebirth is at hand. Beyond the empirical signs of Italy's devastation, there are the allegorical signs taken from the book of Exodus: "the sea has opened; a cloud has escorted you along the way; the stone has poured forth water; here manna has rained; everything has concurred in your greatness."[95] Not only do these signs indicate the existence of an extraordinary moment, they also suggest that the Italians are a chosen people, the Israelites

---

[91] Machiavelli, *Prince*, 26, 102.   [92] Machiavelli, *Prince*, 6, 23.

[93] Several interpreters have gestured at the apocalyptic qualities of the final chapter without subjecting them to much sustained analysis. See: Charles D. Tarlton, "The Symbolism of Redemption and the Exorcism of Fortune in Machiavelli's *Prince*," *The Review of Politics* 30, no. 3 (1968): 332; Weinstein, "Machiavelli and Savonarola," 262–63; Najemy, *Between Friends*, 207–14; Thomas M. Greene, "The End of Discourse in Machiavelli's 'Prince,'" *Yale French Studies*, no. 7 (1984): 69.

[94] Machiavelli, *Prince*, 26, 102.

[95] Machiavelli, *Prince*, 26, 103. Machiavelli is citing the miracles witnessed by Moses and the Israelites as they made their way to the promised land. The Exodus narrative was also central to Savonarola.

of the Renaissance.⁹⁶ They are an elect – chosen to suffer so that they can be redeemed.

These signs must not be dismissed as the accidents of a world governed by contingency. God or *Fortuna* must provide a prophet to interpret them. Savonarola saw himself as a prophet chosen by God to interpret the signs of a coming apocalypse to a Florence undergoing a scourge and eventual rebirth. The friar gave Florentines a narrative that emplotted the crises of the present as an apocalyptic story in which suffering would be redeemed in the establishment of a New Jerusalem with Christ as its king. For Machiavelli, the ruler who must act upon these signs will rely on a similarly powerful interpretation. The chapter calls for a redemptive prince who can give meaning to Italy's degradation by locating it in an apocalyptic story in which violence and suffering are the necessary prerequisites for a collective rebirth. The "barbarous cruelties" that Italy has endured demand both a meaning and an end. It is unbearable, Machiavelli seems to be suggesting, that such suffering be yet another accident of an inscrutable fortune.⁹⁷ It cries out for a prophetic interpretation and an apocalyptic emplotment.

Yet, as with Savonarola's prophetic message, the boundary between interpreting and enacting an apocalypse is blurred here. Savonarola confuses the question of apocalyptic agency by casting himself, on the one hand, as merely a messenger who announces events that will be carried out by God and, on the other, as an agent of Florence's sacred transformation. In his exhortation, Machiavelli puts God in the role he had assigned to fortune in the previous chapters. God signals an *occasione* for apocalyptic rebirth by offering signs that

---

⁹⁶ The invocation of Exodus here, along with Machiavelli's general preoccupation with Hebraic exemplars, leads Maurizio Viroli to suggest that the exhortation partakes more of "Exodus politics" than it does of "political messianism" or apocalyptic politics (to borrow a contrast from Michael Walzer). Viroli admits that the exhortation "shows some features of millenarianism" but ultimately argues that Machiavelli's invocations of Exodus here point less to the hope for a spontaneous apocalyptic transformation and more to "a people capable of achieving their own emancipation, through their own efforts and suffering, under the guidance of a great political founder...just like Moses." See: Maurizio Viroli, *Redeeming The Prince: The Meaning of Machiavelli's Masterpiece* (Princeton: Princeton University Press, 2013), 14–15. The founder and redeemer of chapter 26 is, on Viroli's account, a republican and emancipatory one. There are at least two points to be made in response to this suggestion. First, Exodus politics and messianic or apocalyptic politics are not easily separable. The book of Revelation draws heavily on the narratives and images of Exodus (e.g., in the seven plagues let loose by the trumpeting angels of Rev. 8–9), as does Savonarola's apocalypticism. Machiavelli's fascination with the figures and narratives of Exodus and his use of these figures in the final chapter are not in themselves evidence against a messianic or apocalyptic interpretation of the exhortation. Second, Machiavelli's invocation of an almost lifeless and wounded Italy awaiting a redeemer, a source of "matter...not lacking for introducing every form," and a people who would greet their redeemer with "obstinate faith," piety, and tears puts pressure on the vision of an emancipatory politics that Viroli discerns in the exhortation. See: Machiavelli, *Prince*, 26, 104, 102. See also: Michael Walzer, *Exodus and Revolution* (New York: Basic Books, 1985), 133–36.

⁹⁷ Tarlton, "Symbolism of Redemption."

Machiavelli's Flirtation with Apocalypse 87

the present is an extraordinary time. However, "the remainder" the redemptive prince must do himself. "God does not want to do everything, so as not to take free will from us and that part of the glory that falls to us."[98] The redemptive prince must become an agent of the apocalyptic transformation. Machiavelli blurs the line between the prophetic interpreter and the agent of salvation. The redemptive prince here boldly takes on the role that even Savonarola could never quite leave entirely to God – that of carrying out the apocalyptic transformation.[99] His success is guaranteed both by the prophetic signs Machiavelli describes and by an extraordinary ability to prompt a collective rebirth.

Just as Savonarola promised spiritual as well as temporal rewards to a chosen Florence, Machiavelli offers his redeemer prince not only God's favor but also unparalleled political power, buttressed by unconditional love and obedience.[100] He concludes: "I cannot express with what love he would be received in all those provinces that have suffered from these floods from outside; with what thirst for revenge, with what obstinate faith, with what piety, with what tears. What doors would be closed to him? What peoples would deny him obedience? What envy would oppose him? What Italian would deny him homage?"[101]

This is a striking promise. It suggests the redemptive transformation Machiavelli has in mind is, as he puts it earlier in the exhortation, "not very difficult."[102] No longer would the support of the masses be variable. Thirsting for salvation, Italians will provide a pliable and yielding matter for their redeemer's form. Like the biblical and Savonarolan apocalypses, Machiavelli's revelation ends in a millennium defined by absolute power and absolute love. This love is "a spontaneous submission to the prince's redemptive power: an acknowledgement of, and surrender to, his transformative omnipotence."[103] In Italy's ultimate redemption, the people offer themselves up for a collective rebirth after which the absolute power of the redemptive prince will be guaranteed by the absolute love of the radically altered masses. It marks an end to the variability, contingency, and contestation that define the political world.[104]

---

[98] Machiavelli, *Prince*, 26, 103.
[99] Cf. Vatter, "Machiavelli and the Republican Conception of Providence," 612.
[100] On the question of God's favor, cf. Erica Benner, *Machiavelli's Prince: A New Reading* (Oxford: Oxford University Press, 2013), 305–12.
[101] Machiavelli, *Prince*, 26, 105.   [102] Machiavelli, *Prince*, 26, 103.
[103] Najemy, *Between Friends*, 213.
[104] Miguel Vatter similarly discerns an eschatological and messianic logic to chapter 26. However, he hypothesizes that Machiavelli's inspiration does not come from Christian eschatology but rather from "medieval Arabic and Jewish political thought." See: Vatter, "Machiavelli and the Republican Conception of Providence," 607. This is a suggestive claim that connects Machiavelli to a largely underappreciated Hebraic strand in early modern political thought. (For exceptions, see: Eric Nelson, *The Hebrew Republic: Jewish Sources and the Transformation of European Political Thought* (Cambridge: Harvard University Press, 2010); Graham Hammill, *The Mosaic Constitution: Political Theology and Imagination from Machiavelli to Milton* (Chicago: University of Chicago Press, 2012)). While I am inclined to think that Vatter's

What has Machiavelli achieved in this exhortation? He has given meaning to the crisis and contingency of Italian politics by fashioning the events of his own time into an apocalyptic story. Echoing the emplotment of the Savonarolan moment, Machiavelli casts degradation as both the necessary prerequisites to and the revelatory signs of an imminent rebirth at the hands of a messianic figure. The suffering of Italians is made meaningful and its temporal horizon is narratively bounded. Appealing to a Florentine and Italian exceptionalism that casts his people as the Israelites of the Renaissance, Machiavelli's exhortation promises an escape from the unpredictability of power politics. In short, the final chapter of *The Prince* engages in a Savonarolan set of rhetorical maneuvers.

While this apocalyptic exhortation participates in and transforms the rhetoric of the Savonarolan moment, it can also seem inconsistent with the rest of *The Prince*. Surely this is just the emotional outburst of an Italian nationalist.[105] Perhaps it was even added later to gain the favor of the returned Medici.[106] Maybe Machiavelli's intention in the final chapter is satirical or

---

hypothesis rests on too sharp a distinction between Jewish and Christian messianism, the more immediate challenge to accepting it is his explicit avoidance of the contextual "question of the possible 'sources' that Machiavelli could have used in order to develop his interpretation of Jewish conceptions of divine providence" (609–10, n. 17).

[105] A popular nineteenth-century interpretation subject to occasional contemporary resurrections sees chapter 26 as an impassioned call for unification. See: Leopold von Ranke, *Sämtliche Werke*, Vol. 34: *Zur Kritik Neuerer Geschichtschreiber* (Leipzig: Duncker und Humblot, 1874), 171–72; Arthur L. Burd, introduction to *The Prince*, by Niccolò Machiavelli, ed. Arthur L. Burd (Oxford: Clarendon Press, 1891), 23–27; Friedrich Meinecke, *Machiavellism: The Doctrine of Raison d'État and Its Place in Modern History*, trans. Scott Douglas (New Haven: Yale University Press, 1962), 25–48; John Langton and Mary G. Deitz, "Machiavelli's Paradox: Trapping or Teaching the Prince," *The American Political Science Review* 81, no. 4 (1987): 1283. On this account, the final chapter is the key to the purpose of the *Prince* – the unification of Italy. The first twenty-five chapters pursue this goal by outlining the techniques of power politics necessary to achieve it, while the exhortation offers an emotional appeal toward the same end. The disjuncture between this chapter and the rest of the work is the product of a shift in style and tone, but not in aims. This view is subject to a variety of substantive objections. For instance, it has difficulty wrestling with the fact that Machiavelli seems far more focused on Italy's liberation from foreign invaders than he is on Italian unification. The latter concern is never mentioned explicitly. See: Hans Baron, "The Principe and the Puzzle of the Date of Chapter 26," *Journal of Medieval and Renaissance Studies* 21, no. 1 (1991): 86. An even more serious stumbling block is the fact that Machiavelli formulates the advice of the first twenty-five chapters as general rules that are as accessible to Italy as they are to its enemies. His analysis of the errors made by Louis XII in the king's Italian campaign, for example, could be used as easily by those wanting to divide and subjugate Italy as it could by those who wanted to unify and free it. This seems like strange decision for a writer whose ultimate goal is Italian unification. See: Ernst Cassirer, *The Myth of the State* (New Haven: Yale University Press, 1946), 143; Baron, "The Principe," 86.

[106] The dating of the last chapter of *The Prince* is a matter of significant debate in Machiavelli scholarship. The most detailed argument for the position that the final chapter of work, along with portions of the sixth chapter, were added later is offered by Mario Martelli. He argues that these sections must have been added in 1518, to influence Lorenzo de' Medici who, as some

strategic.[107] While subject to their own particular weaknesses, all of these interpretations struggle to take the religious and scriptural resonances of the exhortation seriously. Yet what would it mean to do this? And what might we uncover

> thought, was considering turning Florence into a formal principate. For Martelli, the chapter could only have been written when there was a hope for Italian "redemption" via a formalization of Medici rule. However, Gennaro Sasso has decisively countered this argument by pointing out that, on Machiavelli's *own terms*, the time for a redemptive intervention is when Florence and Italy are at their most devastated. This makes the period of upheaval in the aftermath of the upheavals of 1512 a more likely time for Machiavelli to have issued his exhortation than in the comparative calm of the subsequent years of Medici rule. See: Mario Martelli, "Da Poliziano a Machiavelli: Sull'epigramma dell'Occasione E Sull'occasione," *Interpres* 2 (1979): 230–54; Martelli, "La Logica Provvidenzialistica E Il Capitolo XXVI Del Principe"; Gennaro Sasso, "Il 'Principe' Ebbe Due Redazioni?," in *Machiavelli E Gli Antichi: E Altri Saggi*, vol. 2 (Milan and Naples: R. Ricciardi, 1988), 197–276. For a more detailed and nuanced account of the positions in this debate, as well as some original contributions to it, see: Najemy, *Between Friends*, 177–84.

[107] The classic articulation of the argument that *The Prince* is a work of satire is made by Garrett Mattingly. See: Garrett Mattingly, "Machiavelli's *Prince*: Political Science or Political Satire?" *The American Scholar* 27, no. 4 (1958): 482–91. Appealing to Machiavelli's admitted preference for republican government and his private evaluation of the political competence of the Medici, Mattingly argues that *The Prince* is a satire shot through with "mordant irony and sarcasm." The exhortation, on this account, is either the product of "an irony turned inward, the bitter mockery of misdirected optimism" or a suggestion to Machiavelli's republican compatriots that the "first sharp combat was not to be against the barbarians" but against tyrants closer to home (491). Like Mattingly, Mary Dietz insists that Machiavelli's republican commitments mean that we cannot take *The Prince* at face value. However, unlike Mattingly, she reads the work as a serious and strategic attempt to bait Lorenzo de Medici into committing political errors that would ultimately destroy his ability to control Florence. The final chapter of the work is intended to appeal to Lorenzo's vanity and to make him "not only Machiavelli's puppet, but the dupe of his own grandiose expectations of earthly power and political immortality" (796). See: Mary G. Dietz, "Trapping the Prince: Machiavelli and the Politics of Deception," *The American Political Science Review* 80, no. 3 (1986): 777–99. While both of these interpretations offer appealing portraits of Machiavelli, they have difficulty explaining why he would have expressed in his private correspondence sentiments so similar to those in the final chapter. Concerned about the growing power of the Swiss, Machiavelli echoes the dire worries of the exhortation in an August 1513 letter to Francesco Vettori: "I am ready to start weeping with you over our collapse and our servitude that, if it does not come today or tomorrow will come in our lifetime." See: Letter from Niccolò Machiavelli to Francesco Vettori (26 August 1513), in Machiavelli et al., *Machiavelli and His Friends*, 260. More than a decade later, as an alliance of northern and central Italian states and France sought to expel Spain, Machiavelli returns to the theme of divinely given opportunities and urges Francesco Guicciardini to use his political influence to "free Italy from long-lasting anxiety; eradicate those savage brutes, which have nothing human about them save their faces and voices." See: Letter from Niccolò Machiavelli to Francesco Guicciardini (17 May 1526), in Machiavelli et al., *Machiavelli and His Friends*, 386. This evidence also poses problems for Leo Strauss's interpretation of the final chapter as Machiavelli's attempt to redeem and excuse the "immoral policies" recommended in the preceding chapters and for Claude Lefort's interpretation of the final chapter as propaganda intended to provide "the prince with the themes the latter should use to mesmerize his subjects." See: Strauss, *Thoughts on Machiavelli*, 80; Claude Lefort, *Machiavelli in the Making*, trans. Michael B. Smith (Evanston: Northwestern University Press, 2012), 201.

if we examined the exhortation in relation to the preceding chapters? Such an examination reveals it is not at all surprising that *The Prince* ends in an apocalyptic exhortation.

However, before we proceed, let us consider another plausible interpretation that accepts an apocalyptic reading of the final chapter but nonetheless insists the exhortation is strategic. I think this interpretation does not allow us to see the full strangeness of the final chapter. But it deserves to be taken seriously. We might conclude, as Claude Lefort does, that Machiavelli is not here "speaking in his own name," but instead "providing the prince with the themes the latter should use to mesmerize his subjects."[108] On this account, Machiavelli is modeling the kind of apocalyptic and prophetic discourse that the Medici should deploy to hold Florence and pursue their larger Italian ambitions. This reading could be combined with one that reads *The Prince*'s early chapters as a warning to the Medici.

Quentin Skinner suggests such a warning lies beneath the conceptual typologies and general rules in the first part of the book. Consider three of Machiavelli's general rules: those who acquire their principality through fortune will have difficulty maintaining their status as princes (chapter 7); former republics are more difficult to hold than principalities (chapter 5); and it is easier to hold a former republic if one goes and lives there personally (chapter 5). Given that the Medici returned to power in 1512 with the help of the pope and a Spanish army, that Florence had formerly been a republic and had a long republican history, and that the Medici struggled to establish a personal presence in the city, it seems entirely plausible that there is "an undercurrent of specific warning and advice ... beneath the surface generalities of Machiavelli's text."[109]

Combining Skinner's insight with Lefort's, the text might be intended to alert the Medici to their profound vulnerability, offer advice about how best to maintain their rule, and model the kind of apocalyptic and prophetic rhetoric that might help captivate and subdue their subjects. Machiavelli might also have hoped this warning, advice, and demonstration of rhetorical skill would ease his own return to politics.

There are at least two challenges to such an interpretation. First, a purely strategic reading of the final chapter has difficulty explaining why Machiavelli would have echoed so much of the exhortation's tone and content in his private correspondence, where he presumably had no reason to want to model prophetic discourse.[110] Second, while *The Prince*'s typologies and general rules may well underscore the vulnerability of the Medici, it would be a mistake to underplay the depth and sincerity of Machiavelli's epistemological ambitions. On his account, the purpose of *The Prince* is to extract from historical

---

[108] Lefort, *Machiavelli in the Making*, 201. See also: Jurdjevic, *Great and Wretched City*, 32.
[109] Quentin Skinner, introduction to *The Prince*, by Niccolò Machiavelli, ed. Quentin Skinner, trans. Russell Price (Cambridge: Cambridge University Press, 1988), xiii.
[110] See n. 107.

examples a set of hidden laws and rules for princely behavior.[111] He records his "knowledge of the actions of great men, learned by me from long experience with modern things and a continuous reading of ancient ones." He suggests that he has "thought out and examined these things with great diligence," filtering them and reducing them "to one small volume."[112] He promises a systematic study that will make political contingency intelligible and subject to mastery by those who want to "hold empire over men."[113] In this sense, *The Prince* can be read as an extended answer to the challenge offered by Machiavelli's friend and regular correspondent Francesco Vettori, who insisted it was impossible to subject the political world to rational understanding and human control.[114] Reflecting on their earlier discussions of European politics, Vettori had gone so far as to observe: "it often appears to me that things do not proceed [according to reason], and because of this I judge it to be superfluous to speak of them, to discuss them, and to argue about them."[115] Machiavelli resists this suggestion in his responses to Vettori and in *The Prince*. What if we read the final chapter of *The Prince* as the peculiar outcome of the failure of these epistemological ambitions?

The opening chapters of the book insist on the possibility of political intelligibility. They are characterized by "the curt distinctions of a new, embracing political science."[116] Principalities are either hereditary or new. They are acquired through virtue, fortune, or crime. Machiavelli does his utmost to keep

[111] Ascoli, "Machiavelli's Gift of Counsel," 220.
[112] Machiavelli, *Prince*, dedicatory letter, 3.
[113] Machiavelli, *Prince*, 1, 5. See also: Felix Gilbert, "The Humanist Concept of the Prince and *The Prince* of Machiavelli," *The Journal of Modern History* 11, no. 4 (1939): 449–52; Greene, "The End of Discourse in Machiavelli's 'Prince,'" 57–60; Najemy, *Between Friends*, 176–214. It may well be that Machiavelli's preoccupation with the problem of contingency is connected to the revival of interest in Lucretius' *De Rerum Natura* in Renaissance Florence. In order to account for free will, Lucretius incorporated an element of indeterminacy, an unpredictable atomic "swerve," into his atomic theory. Given that there is a copy of *De Rerum Natura* (c. 1490s) in Machiavelli's own hand and that most of his annotations are concentrated in the portion of the poem dealing with atomic theory, it would not be unreasonable to suppose a connection between Machiavelli's interest in political and historical contingency and Lucretius' treatment of atomic indeterminacy, assuming, that is, that Machiavelli's interest in these ideas persisted through to the time at which he wrote *The Prince*. For discussions of the Machiavelli-Lucretius connection, see: Ada Palmer, "Reading Lucretius in the Renaissance," *Journal of the History of Ideas* 73, no. 3 (2012): 395–416; Alison Brown, *The Return of Lucretius to Renaissance Florence* (Cambridge: Harvard University Press, 2010); Paul Rahe, "In the Shadow of Lucretius: The Epicurean Foundations of Machiavelli's Political Thought," *History of Political Thought* 28, no. 1 (2007): 30–55.
[114] See, for instance, Vettori's letters of July 12 and August 20, 1513 in Machiavelli et al., *Machiavelli and His Friends*, 241–44; 251–56. For a discussion of this aspect of the Machiavelli-Vettori correspondence and its connection to the project of *The Prince*, see: Najemy, *Between Friends*, 136–214.
[115] Letter from Francesco Vettori to Niccolò Machiavelli (12 July 1513), in Machiavelli et al., *Machiavelli and His Friends*, 241.
[116] Greene, "The End of Discourse," 58.

analytical divisions precise and separate. Similarly, the lessons derived from historical and contemporary examples seem clear and categorical. Would-be conquerors must either eliminate or inhabit republics to hold them.[117] "Those who become princes from private individual solely by fortune become so with little trouble, but maintain themselves with much."[118] In the early chapters of *The Prince*, Machiavelli seems to be reaffirming the epistemological ambitions he had first sketched in his letters to Vettori. He intends to give meaning to history and to render the political world intelligible by wrenching lessons from its apparent contingency.

Yet the work fails to deliver on this promise. Rules that seem to have been extracted from history and expressed with unambiguous clarity are repeatedly qualified, generalizations complicated, and exceptions made. The project of historical and political intelligibility turns back on itself. Chapter 17 offers an illustrative example.[119] At the heart of the chapter is an apparently unambiguous lesson – it is better for a prince to be feared than loved. Yet, as the chapter moves forward, the rule becomes increasingly qualified, and ultimately less clear. After invoking Cesare Borgia's reputation for cruelty, which brought unity and peace to the Romagna, Machiavelli goes on to suggest that the prince should *nonetheless* "proceed in a temperate mode with prudence and humanity."[120] *While* the prince should make himself feared, he should do so "in such a way that if he does not acquire love, he escapes hatred."[121] The prince should deploy cruelty, *but* "he must abstain from the property of others."[122] *While* cruelty toward one's people should be tempered, a prince should not be so limited when dealing with his soldiers. The "inhuman cruelty" of Hannibal should be imitated because it promoted unity and discipline.[123] On this version of the military exception to the general rule, Scipio's leniency should have been his undoing. *However*, while "he lived under

---

[117] Machiavelli, *Prince*, 5, 21.   [118] Machiavelli, *Prince*, 7, 25.

[119] For an extended treatment of the problem that engages numerous other examples across the text, see: Greene, "The End of Discourse"; Ascoli, "Machiavelli's Gift of Counsel," 249–50, n. 64. Greene reads the breakdown of epistemological ambitions as a problem that gathers strength over the course of the text. This is a hard case to make. As Greene acknowledges, the correspondence between rule and example is far from exact in the early chapters of *The Prince*, where it is often confounded by extraordinary *virtù* (60). So, in what sense we are seeing a progressive breakdown instead of a failure from the outset is not clear. Similarly, the tendencies marshaled as evidence of a more pronounced breakdown in the last third of the book (e.g., a widening distance between precept and example; "the progressive recalcitrance of the precept to remain simple, pure, clear-cut"; the move from precept-qualification to precept-contradiction; and the reliance on *virtù* to bridge the gap) hardly, as Greene himself admits, seem peculiar to the final third of the book (60, 64–66). While I do not want to rule out the possibility that the breakdown is a progressive one, I am not convinced that Greene has made the case conclusively.

[120] Machiavelli, *Prince*, 17, 66. Mansfield translates this passage as "proceed in a temperate mode."

[121] Machiavelli, *Prince*, 17, 67. Mansfield translates this passage as "in such a mode that if."

[122] Machiavelli, *Prince*, 17, 67.   [123] Machiavelli, *Prince*, 17, 67.

the government of the Senate, this damaging quality of his not only was hidden, but made for his glory."[124] Not all of the rhetorical moves that Machiavelli makes in this chapter involve a qualification of its central rule. Yet the number of qualifications is suggestive of his difficulty in extracting clear guidelines from historical experience. At the beginning of chapter 20's treatment of fortresses, Machiavelli admits this difficulty, when he writes that "one cannot give a definite judgment on all these things unless one comes to the particulars." He nonetheless embarks on an ultimately futile attempt to discuss the matter in general terms.[125] These chapters are examples of the more general failure of *The Prince* to deliver on its author's epistemological ambitions.

We can identify a similar failure in Machiavelli's attempt to grapple with the idea of fortune. Throughout *The Prince*, he has tried to render the political world intelligible. He has tried to give the princely man of action the knowledge needed to deploy his *virtù* and to pull order and glory from apparent contingency. In the final chapters of *The Prince*, Machiavelli turns to a focused consideration of how this might be done. He has examined the interplay of *virtù* and fortune in earlier chapters. But, except in chapter 6, which foregrounds themes and ideas developed toward the end of the work, he tends to conceptualize *virtù* as a kind of ability and autonomy, and fortune as a form of dependence on others.[126]

Things get more complicated as Machiavelli reconsiders these themes beginning at the end of chapter 24, where he argues that princes who have held their principalities for many years "may not accuse fortune when they have lost them afterwards." Such men are not victims of fortune, but rather of their own laziness and lack of adaptive foresight. "Never having thought that quiet times could change (which is a common defect of men, not to take account of the storm during the calm), when later the times become adverse, they thought of fleeing and not defending themselves." These princes wait in expectation that their people will call them back.

While this may be an acceptable course of last resort, a prince should first consider more activist remedies. For, Machiavelli warns, "one should never fall in the belief you could find someone to pick you up. Whether it does not happen or happens, it is not security for you, because that defense was base and did not depend on you. And those defenses alone are good, are certain, and are lasting, that depend on you yourself and on your *virtù*."[127] Once again, Machiavelli conceptualizes *virtù* as autonomy. However, he has also provided a metaphor for the variation and contingency of fortune – but one that hardly renders these forces more intelligible. The effects of fortune, like a storm, cannot be prevented. One may prepare for them. Yet Machiavelli does not explain how a prince might prepare to confront fortune's unaccountable variation.

---

[124] Machiavelli, *Prince*, 17, 68.   [125] Machiavelli, *Prince*, 20, 83.
[126] For instance, see chapter 7 of *The Prince*.   [127] Machiavelli, *Prince*, 24, 97.

Furthermore, his weather analogy suggests a completely impersonal fortune, totally beyond human influence.[128]

Machiavelli's full engagement with fortune begins in the next chapter, which deepens the uncertainty, rather than relieving it. He seeks to counter the common opinion "that worldly things are so governed by fortune and by God, that men cannot correct them with their prudence." He admits that he has been attracted to this opinion, which is "believed more in our times because of the great variability of things which have been seen and are seen every day, beyond human conjecture."[129] Yet while the sheer variability of events in his own time seems to render the political world unintelligible, Machiavelli proposes to make variation itself subject to generalization and understanding. His motives here do not appear to come from the thought that such variation is inherently intelligible. Rather, he seeks to preserve autonomy and free will. It is not acceptable that fortune entirely governs worldly things. If that were true, there would be no clear relationship between actions and outcomes and men would cease to exercise their autonomy.[130] They might "not sweat much over things" and might surrender themselves to pure chance. If fortune is unintelligible, men might fail to act. To save free will and autonomy, Machiavelli arbitrarily proposes: "it might be true that fortune is arbiter of half of our actions, but also that she leaves the other half, or close to it, for us to govern."[131] This hypothesis hardly makes fortune more intelligible and gives no guidance to those who must act politically.

Machiavelli then shifts tactics, returning to a conception of fortune as an impersonal force that can nonetheless be mediated by human understanding and control. He likens fortune "to one of these violent rivers which, when they become enraged, flood the plains, ruin the trees and the buildings, lift the earth from this part, drop in another; each person flees before them, everyone yields to their impetus without being able to hinder them in any regard."[132] Fortune seems at its most inscrutable and unstoppable when the extraordinary happens and the river floods. However, in quiet times, prudent men may prepare for these extraordinary onslaughts by building dams and dikes. Technological mastery and foresight are the tools for overcoming fortune.

Yet *The Prince* is laden with examples of prudent leaders who are foiled by fortune in spite of themselves, or whose careful calculations are rendered

---

[128] Hanna Fenichel Pitkin, *Fortune Is a Woman: Gender and Politics in the Thought of Niccolò Machiavelli* (Chicago: University of Chicago Press, 1984), 148.

[129] Machiavelli, *Prince*, 25, 98. Here, Machiavelli echoes an observation he made in a September 1506 letter to Soderini: "I see that steering along a variety of routes can bring about the same thing and that acting in different ways can bring about the same end." See: Letter from Niccolò Machiavelli to Giovan Battista Soderini (13–21 September 1506), in Machiavelli et al., *Machiavelli and His Friends*, 134. If there is no correlation between means and ends, the project of crafting general political rules seems doomed.

[130] Pitkin, *Fortune Is a Woman*, 149; Najemy, *Between Friends*, 203.

[131] Machiavelli, *Prince*, 25, 98.   [132] Machiavelli, *Prince*, 25, 98.

Machiavelli's Flirtation with Apocalypse

meaningless when faced with a bold show of military force.[133] Once again, Machiavelli has illustrated the problem without making fortune more intelligible. He has explained *when* men should act – during calm times – but he has not adequately answered the question of *how* they should act.

The difficulty lies in the fact that the same action or disposition can produce wide variation in results in only marginally different circumstances.[134] Machiavelli responds to this vertiginous political contingency by offering another general rule: a prince must adapt his "mode of proceeding to the qualities of the times."[135] Men have been successful in their confrontations with fortune by being both bold and cautious, violent and artful, patient and impetuous. Their success depends on how well their chosen course matches the quality of the times.[136] Yet Machiavelli does not explain how we may know which trait matches any given time. One suspects this is something that may only be determined in retrospect, if then.[137] In an even more troubling move, he admits that man is fundamentally incapable of varying his nature with the times, "whether because he cannot deviate from what nature inclines him to or also because, when one has always flourished by walking on one path, one cannot be persuaded to depart from it." Were he capable of varying his own nature, a man could vary seamlessly with the times and "his fortune would not change."[138]

The necessity of this impossible human variability means that the cautious and prudent builder of dams cannot always succeed.[139] Indeed, here Machiavelli considers the example of Pope Julius II, who was not a cautious man but a bold one. Julius could match his actions with the times. However, he succeeded not because he was capable of a superhuman variability, but merely because he was fortunate enough to die before times changed. Had times changed while he was alive, "he would never have deviated from those modes to which nature inclined him" and would have come to ruin.[140] Machiavelli has led himself right back to the opinion he had intended to disprove.[141] Fortune remains impersonal

---

[133] Pitkin, *Fortune Is a Woman*, 151. [134] Ascoli, "Machiavelli's Gift of Counsel," 249.
[135] Machiavelli, *Prince*, 25, 99.
[136] Or, as he puts it in the September 1506 letter to Soderini: "because times and affairs often change – both in general and in particular – and because men change neither their imaginations nor their ways of doing things accordingly, it turns out that a man has good fortune at one time and bad fortune at another. And truly, anyone wise enough to adapt to and understand the times and the pattern of events would always have good fortune or would always keep himself from bad fortune; and it would come to be true that the wise man could control the stars and the Fates. But such wise men do not exist: in the first place, men are shortsighted; in the second place, they are unable to master their own natures; thus it follows that Fortune is fickle, controlling men and keeping them under her yoke." See: Letter from Machiavelli to Soderini (13–21 September 1506), in Machiavelli et al., *Machiavelli and His Friends*, 135.
[137] Robert Orr, "The Time Motif in Machiavelli," in *Machiavelli and the Nature of Political Thought*, ed. Martin Fleisher (New York: Atheneum, 1972), 199.
[138] Machiavelli, *Prince*, 25, 100. [139] Pitkin, *Fortune Is a Woman*, 151.
[140] Machiavelli, *Prince*, 25, 101. [141] Najemy, *Between Friends*, 206.

and unintelligible, leaving men unsure whether their actions will overcome it or lead to political ruin.

Attempting to salvage this endeavor, Machiavelli concludes by offering another metaphor that figures fortune not as an uncontrollable force but as an acquiescent victim. Resorting once again to a general rule, Machiavelli proclaims: "it is better to be impetuous than cautious, because fortune is a woman; and it is necessary, if one wants to hold her down, to beat her and strike her down. And one sees that she lets herself be won more by the impetuous than by those who proceed coldly."[142] The metaphor of fortune as a woman assigns to variability and contingency a nature that implies a course of action.

Having fixed the nature of fortune, Machiavelli has leveled the playing field somewhat. Man, with his inflexible nature, is now at less of a disadvantage. Yet the nature of the metaphor itself raises profound questions, beyond the usual ones connected to its misogyny and celebration of masculine mastery. The metaphor does not offer us an intelligible fortune. It merely suggests that brute force may sometimes contain her infinite variety.[143] Without intelligibility, however, the variability of the world remains mere contingency, contained occasionally by violence but fundamentally unknowable.

Is it not plausible that after this struggle to subject the contingency of the political world to human understanding Machiavelli might be drawn to the apocalyptic emplotment of the Savonarolan moment? If fortune cannot be understood by rules, calculations, or even metaphors, then even prudent princes have little hope for effective political action. The "great variability of things...beyond human conjecture" in Machiavelli's own times seems to call not for a prudent prince but for a prophet. Such a man seeks not to render the apparent contingency of the political world intelligible, but to discern in it signs of prophetic importance and endow it with a deeper meaning.

What appears to be a time of crisis and devastation becomes the narrative prelude to political rebirth. What appears to be the unaccountable variability of fortune becomes the sign of this imminent transformation. What appears to be contingency gains meaning and purpose in an apocalyptic story that promises a final escape at the hands of an extraordinary figure. Machiavelli's apocalyptic exhortation, on this reading, abandons the promise to make fortune's variability intelligible but holds out the more seductive hope that it can be given a meaning and an end in way that transcends human understanding at the same time as it transforms the political landscape of Italy. Seen in this light, the *Prince's* final chapter may represent an authentic if desperate moment of hope: hope that Italy's degradation holds the chance for a rebirth of ancient freedom and valor under a prophetic leader who knows how to grasp the potential of his moment.

---

[142] Machiavelli, *Prince*, 25, 101.   [143] Najemy, *Between Friends*, 206–07.

Fear and Longing

The apocalyptic solution for which Machiavelli pleaded at the end of *The Prince* offered to give suffering a meaning and an end, transform humanity, and transcend the political condition. If you are persuaded by this interpretation, it may be tempting to read the exhortation as a political failure and a betrayal of its author's republican,[144] radical democratic,[145] or agonistic[146] commitments. This is an understandable conclusion. The exhortation's conception of the people of Italy as pliable matter on which the redemptive prince may impose a form, its promise of the faithful and tearful submission to the will of a redemptive prince, and its vision of a polity built on faith, piety, and obedience all seem to bear out this reading.[147] Despite its radical call for redemptive political action, the final chapter of *The Prince* seems to replicate everything that is most objectionable about apocalypticism – its quietism, political escapism, and romance with final solutions.

In this section, I will suggest that by the time he wrote his *Discourses on Livy*, Machiavelli had begun to worry about this apocalyptic solution for some of these very reasons. In contrast to both *The Prince*'s epistemological optimism and the exhortation's recourse to the prophetic hope for a redemptive prince, the *Discourses* have a tragic sensibility. The work is epistemologically humble without being politically defeatist. It is also wary of the promises of redemptive politics.

Machiavelli is not conventionally seen as a tragic writer.[148] Yet, in a 1525 letter to Francesco Guicciardini, he signs as "Niccolò Machiavelli, historico, comico et tragico."[149] The first two parts of this identification are not controversial. As a historian, Machiavelli wrote several works, most notably *The*

---

[144] Maurizio Viroli, "Machiavelli and the Republican Idea of Politics," in *Machiavelli and Republicanism*, ed. Gisela Bock, Quentin Skinner, and Maurizio Viroli (Cambridge: Cambridge University Press, 1990), 143–172.

[145] John P. McCormick, *Machiavellian Democracy* (Cambridge: Cambridge University Press, 2011).

[146] Diego A. von Vacano, *The Art of Power: Machiavelli, Nietzsche, and the Making of Aesthetic Political Theory* (Lanham: Lexington Books, 2007).

[147] Cf. Benner, *Machiavelli's Prince*, 305–12; Vatter, "Machiavelli and the Republican Conception of Providence."

[148] For notable and interesting exceptions, see: Vickie B. Sullivan, introduction to *The Comedy and Tragedy of Machiavelli: Essays on the Literary Works*, ed. Vickie B. Sullivan (New Haven: Yale University Press, 2000), ix–xxi; Ronald L. Martinez, "Tragic Machiavelli," in *The Comedy and Tragedy of Machiavelli: Essays on the Literary Works*, ed. Vickie B. Sullivan (New Haven: Yale University Press, 2000), 102–19; Peter J. Euben, "The Politics of Nostalgia and Theories of Loss," in *Vocations of Political Theory*, ed. Jason A. Frank and John Tambornino (Minneapolis: University of Minnesota Press, 2000), 73–83; Giorgio Bàrberi Squarotti, *La Forma Tragica del "Principe" e Altri Saggi Sul Machiavelli* (Florence: L. S. Olschki, 1966).

[149] Letter from Niccolò Machiavelli to Francesco Guicciardini (after 21 October 1525), in Machiavelli et al., *Machiavelli and his Friends*, 371.

Florentine Histories, and his political arguments are supported with many historical examples. As a comedian, Machiavelli wrote *Mandragola* and *Clizia*, as well as the numerous amusing letters to his close friends. But Machiavelli's self-identification as a tragedian seems unusual, given that he wrote no works that are tragedies in the conventional sense of the term.[150] Yet his life was marked by political upheaval and crisis, which he often laments. For Roberto Ridolfi, one of his most passionate biographers, Machiavelli is a tragedian who takes contemporary Italy as his subject.[151] Machiavelli's later political writings, and particularly the *Discourses on Livy*, are also rich with the "techniques, scenes, and imagery of tragedy – tyrants, reversals of fortune, stunning acts of cruelty, prophetic dreams and visions, bitter laments."[152] In what follows, I highlight this dimension of Machiavelli's later work and consider how a tragic sensibility helps him to resist the allure of the apocalyptic imaginary.

A tragic sensibility acknowledges the unaccountable flux and variability of political life. It recognizes that efforts to guarantee stability and order produce temporary results at best.[153] Machiavelli's project in *The Prince* had been to subject the political world to understanding and control by containing it within analytical categories and ordering it with general rules. The early chapters of *The Prince* attempted to class political regimes into stable differential pairs – principalities or republics, new principalities or inherited ones, and so on.[154] The opening chapters of the *Discourses* signal a radically different approach.

In the *Discourses*, Machiavelli rejects the assumptions of conceptual and political stability implied by this earlier approach. Adopting the familiar Aristotelian typology, he explains that there are three types of good regime – principality, oligarchy, and republic. Yet these regimes are inherently unstable and liable to shift into a correspondingly bad regime. Each one is "similar to the next one to it so they can easily leap from one to the other. For the principality easily becomes tyrannical; the aristocrats with ease become a state of the few; the popular without difficulty converted into the licentious." The best political forms

---

[150] Sullivan, introduction, xi.
[151] Roberto Ridolfi, *The Life of Niccolò Machiavelli*, trans. Cecil Grayson (Chicago: University of Chicago Press, 1963), 219. Giorgio Bàrberi Squarotti reads *The Prince*'s many examples of man's battles with an adverse fortune and his inability to vary with the times as evidence of the work's tragic mode. While I agree with the characterization of at least some of Machiavelli's examples and think it could be extended to his conceptual treatment of the cardinal virtues, I think the epistemological commitments of *The Prince* – its ambition to make variation and contingency intelligible and susceptible to human control – are not consistent with a tragic sensibility. It is only after the failure of these epistemological commitments and Machiavelli's resort to an apocalyptic solution that he makes a turn to tragedy. See: Squarotti, *La Forma Tragica*. See also: Salvatore Di Maria, "Machiavelli's Ironic View of History: The Istorie Fiorentine," *Renaissance Quarterly* 45, no. 2 (1992): 248–70.
[152] Martinez, "Tragic Machiavelli," 110.   [153] Lebow, *The Tragic Vision of Politics*, 378.
[154] Najemy, *Between Friends*, 208–09. For an alternative reading that suggests that Machiavelli's discursive strategy involves introducing differential pairs into order to criticize them, see: Michael McCanles, *The Discourse of Il Principe* (Malibu: Undena, 1983), 11–39.

Fear and Longing 99

are temporary, "for no remedy can be applied there to prevent [them] from slipping into [their contraries] because of the likeness that the virtue and the vice have in this case."[155] Here, Machiavelli demonstrates a disposition toward the flux and variability of the political world that is distinctly tragic. Indeed, a central feature of the tragic form is an attention to the way in which virtue, when taken to excess, becomes vice.[156] Tragedy encourages an epistemological approach that does not abandon the project of understanding and negotiating this sort of inevitable variability. However, a tragic vision acknowledges how resistant the world is to human control.[157]

For Machiavelli, the tragic dimension of political order is tied to a cyclical conception of time borrowed from Polybius. Political regimes inevitably become corrupted and collapse in a cycle that repeats itself again and again. This conception of political time avoids apocalypticism's linear teleology and hope for a ruptural end. In Machiavelli's view, degeneration, decay and crisis are no longer the extraordinary and prophetic signs of an imminent apocalypse. Rather, we understand them by locating them within a cycle that has repeated itself throughout history and can therefore be rendered familiar, and even predictable.

However, I do not want to make too much of the idea of Polybian cycles or of the proposed solution of a mixed government, as both are applied unevenly in the *Discourses* and are totally absent from Machiavelli's other later works.[158] And while for Polybius "the cycle was a *physis*, a natural cycle of growth, and death through which republics are bound to pass," for Machiavelli it is also (and perhaps even primarily) the product of human inclinations and actions.[159] What Machiavelli undeniably shares with Polybius, however, is a broadly cyclical conception of political time. As he explains in *The Florentine Histories*,

---

[155] Machiavelli, *Discourses on Livy*, I.2, 11.
[156] Lebow, *The Tragic Vision of Politics*, 363. Shakespeare makes the same point with a horticultural analogy in *Romeo and Juliet*. The friar explains:

> Virtue itself turns vice, being misapplied,
> And vice sometime by action dignified.
> Within the infant rind of this weak flower
> Poison hath residence and medicine power.

See: William Shakespeare, *Romeo and Juliet*, ed. Jill L. Levenson (Oxford: Oxford University Press, 2000), act 2, scene 2, lines 21–24, p. 222.
[157] Northrop Frye, *Anatomy of Criticism: Four Essays* (Princeton: Princeton University Press, 2000), 206–207.
[158] John G. A. Pocock rightly notes that Machiavelli "played down the Polybian formula for stability and the Venetian myth of its attainment" and instead embraced the dynamic model offered by Rome. See: John G. A. Pocock, "'The Onely Politician': Machiavelli, Harrington and Felix Raab," *Historical Studies: Australia and New Zealand* 12, no. 4 (1966): 277. See also: Pocock, *Machiavellian Moment*, 189–90.
[159] Pocock, *Machiavellian Moment*, 77. See also: Gennaro Sasso, "Machiavelli E La Teroria Dell'anacylosis," *Rivista Storica Italiana* 70, no. 3 (1958): 333–75; Di Maria, "Machiavelli's Ironic View of History," 251–52.

In their normal variations, countries generally go from order to disorder then from disorder move back to order, because – since Nature does not allow worldly things to remain fixed – when they come to their utmost perfection and have no further possibility for rising, they must go down. Likewise, when they have gone down and through their defects have reached the lowest possible depths, they necessarily rise, since they cannot go lower.[160]

Machiavelli's project in the *Discourses*, as well as some of his other historical works, assumes there are perennial political problems. Familiar patterns repeat themselves. This is tragedy's cause for cautious optimism. However fragmentary and partial the resources of the past, we can use them now because human nature remains the same and "all people, everywhere and always, [have] led similar histories."[161] If problems and crises repeat themselves, then what may seem extraordinary or even apocalyptic becomes ordinary and familiar. This cyclical conception of time is often taken as evidence of Machiavelli's republicanism. But it is also possible to read it as evidence of his mature realism – his acceptance that political problems will repeat themselves indefinitely and that they will resist final settlement.

The constant in Machiavelli's musings on political time is the inevitability of decline. The world, explains Machiavelli, is eternal.[162] But earthly things rise, decline, and die in "a tragic drama played out again and again."[163] The reasons for this unavoidable decay have been well rehearsed by scholars of Machiavelli's republicanism. Citizens lose a sense of their founding virtues and pursue their own private good at the expense of the public good, political institutions are captured by private interests, and the republic becomes corrupt.[164]

Yet Machiavelli offers another reason for inevitable political decline. While founders should be considered among the most honorable of men, they tend to become dangerously emboldened by their past success. After a successful founding, they become "deceived by a false good and a false glory" and "almost all let themselves go, either voluntarily or ignorantly, into the ranks of those who deserve more blame than praise; and though, to their perpetual honor, they are able to make a republic or a kingdom, they turn to tyranny."[165] Past success, suggests Machiavelli, heightens the potential for future failure and political decline. Here, the cycles of political time are not extrinsic and impersonal forces. Rather, they are patterns in which humans are implicated. Machiavelli is invoking a tragic sensibility that emphasizes persistent human frailties and points to the dangers of hubris.

---

[160] Machiavelli, *History of Florence*, 1232.
[161] Edmund E. Jacobitti, "The Classical Heritage in Machiavelli's Histories: Symbol and Poetry as Historical Literature," in *The Comedy and Tragedy of Machiavelli*, ed. Vickie B. Sullivan (New Haven: Yale University Press, 2000), 178. On the fragmentary nature of our access to the past, see: Machiavelli, *Discourses on Livy*, I, preface; II.5.
[162] Machiavelli, *Discourses on Livy*, II.5, 138–39.
[163] Jacobitti, "The Classical Heritage," 187.   [164] Machiavelli, *Discourses on Livy*, III.1, 209.
[165] Machiavelli, *Discourses on Livy*, I.10, 31.

Fear and Longing

With this tragic sense of the limits to political action Machiavelli reconsiders the figure of the redemptive prince. He presents the reader with a situation that is structurally like the one he describes at the end of *The Prince* – a polity that is utterly degraded and devastated. In the language of republicanism, this is a profoundly corrupt polity. It exists outside the familiar cycles of growth and decline. Machiavelli suggests that the transformation and apocalyptic rebirth that he had hoped and pleaded for at the end of *The Prince* may simply be impossible. He reasons: "where [the matter] is corrupt, well-ordered laws do not help unless indeed they have been put in motion by one individual who with an extreme force ensures their observance so that the matter becomes good. I do not know whether this has ever occurred or whether it is possible."[166]

In light of the final chapter of *The Prince*, this is a remarkable admission. The redemptive figure Machiavelli had hoped for in that work was extraordinary and unprecedented – a figure that exists outside of history and can affect a transformation that has never occurred before and is not ordinarily possible. The transformative refounder in the *Discourses* seems similar. He is a charismatic leader who promises to renovate a devastated polity, transform its complacent masses, and innovate new orders "at a stroke."[167] However, the figure in *The Prince* performs a miracle that redeems his people's suffering, transforms them, and ushers in a new age. His transformative efforts meet with love, piety, and tears. By contrast, here in the *Discourses*, Machiavelli denies the possibly of such a miracle, revealing the promise of a transformative refounder to be both fraudulent and dangerous.

In the mode of rational deliberation rather than apocalyptic hope, Machiavelli considers the possibilities available to a corrupt polity. A political rebirth is only possible "through the *virtù* of one man who is alive [at the time]...As soon as such a one is dead, [the polity] returns to its early habit."[168] Here, the refounder is merely human. The rebirth he initiates allows new orders to be sustained, but only as long as he lives to guarantee them. Unable to effect a transformation of the people themselves, the refounder cannot protect his new polity from decay. While the millennial community hoped for at the end of *The Prince* was guaranteed by absolute love and piety, the reborn republic is destined for an eventual decay from which there is no apocalyptic exit.

Shifting from the mode of rational deliberation to that of normative evaluation, Machiavelli argues that even if a redemptive and prophetic leader were possible, he would not be worthy of our hope. Even if a single refounder could live an exceptionally long life or could arrange to be succeeded by someone who shares his *virtù* and political mission, the polity could only "be reborn with many dangers and much blood."[169] This is a clear allusion to the violence that would be required for the kind of collective redemption longed for

---

[166] Machiavelli, *Discourses on Livy*, I.17, 48.
[167] Machiavelli, *Discourses on Livy*, I.18, 51.
[168] Machiavelli, *Discourses on Livy*, I.17, 48.
[169] Machiavelli, *Discourses on Livy*, I.17, 48.

at the end of *The Prince*. There, rebirth requires spontaneous submission to the absolute power of a redemptive prince. Here, Machiavelli exposes the bloody work of any political endeavor aimed at total and eternal human transformation. The price of transformation is now too high.

Lurking behind Machiavelli's remarks in the *Discourses* is also a deeper fear that, instead of waiting for an *occasione* of devastation and suffering, a self-proclaimed redeemer might attempt to create one for himself with unimaginable force. The redemptive figure in *The Prince* is not a brutal agent, having conveniently come across an already devastated people. However, the transformative refounder of the *Discourses* unleashes a violence that may ultimately be irredeemable. Like a good tragedian, Machiavelli warns of the limits of political action and the perils of trying to exceed them.

Recognizing these limits need not engender political paralysis. Machiavelli's message is not one of retreat from the political world. Rather, the struggles with fortune and with human limits are the stuff of politics. The heroes of the *Discourses* are those who, like Romulus, found and refound polities knowing that they will eventually decay. All earthly creations, suggests Machiavelli, have limits to their lives.[170] Yet since fortune "proceeds by oblique and unknown ways," it makes little sense to withdraw from the world of politics. While the lives of states and men have limits, the aim should be "to live in a manner that would allow one to live out that limit."[171] As a tragedian, Machiavelli does not leave us despairing or encourage us to turn away from the world.

The kind of political action valorized in the *Discourses* aims neither to make the political world intelligible nor to achieve an eternal stasis. As Pocock notes, in the early chapters of the *Discourses*, Machiavelli makes "a series of decisions against studying the closed, aristocratic, defensive state – Sparta or Venice – which makes stability its only goal, and in favour of studying the dynamic, popular, warlike state – Livian Rome – which opts for liberty, expansion and dominion, even if this choice condemns it to ultimate decline and tyranny."[172] The *Discourses* embraces a model of politics in flux. Against an ideal of an eternal stillness, Machiavelli celebrates a Roman ideal of institutionalized antagonism and struggle. The "tumults between the nobles and the plebs," for instance, "were the first cause of keeping Rome free."[173] Rome negotiates political contingency internally by institutionalizing discord, courts it externally through imperial expansion, and thereby withstands the infinite variety of politics far better than do the stable and static models of Sparta or Venice. John McCormick goes so far as to suggest that, in this analysis of Rome, Machiavelli radically redefines stability "as something that is ensured by energy and movement, rather than harmony."[174] This political ideal of tumult and

---

[170] Machiavelli, *Discourses on Livy*, III.1, 209.   [171] Jacobitti, "The Classical Heritage," 180.
[172] Pocock, "'The Onely Politician,'" 277. See also: Machiavelli, *Discourses on Livy*, I.1, 2, 5, 6.
[173] Machiavelli, *Discourses on Livy*, I.4, 16.
[174] John P. McCormick, "Addressing the Political Exception: Machiavelli's 'Accidents' and the Mixed Regime," *American Political Science Review* 87, no. 4 (1993): 895.

movement is explicitly anti-apocalyptic. It eschews promises of eternal order, unity, and quiet. It rejects the hope of a final exit from the contingency and variability of politics.

As much as it turns away from the apocalyptic hope of the exhortation, the *Discourses* also reveals the Savonarolan moment's enduringly seductive power. Machiavelli's embrace of a vigorous and antagonistic politics is haunted by the lingering vision of an everlasting republic. He argues that there are no certain remedies for political disorders and that "it follows that it is impossible to order a perpetual republic, because its ruin is caused through a thousand unexpected ways."[175] Yet five chapters later, he writes with a kind of wistful longing for an extraordinary figure who, with a kind of cleansing violence "might renew the laws, and not only restrain [the republic] from running to ruin but pull it back [such that] it would be perpetual."[176] Like Savonarolan apocalypticism, the hope for an everlasting republic entails a final and decisive conquest of political contingency. If it were possible to halt the motion of fortune, Machiavelli explains, the result would be "the *true political* way of life and the *true quiet* of a city." To be sure, he goes on to acknowledge that this political quiet is impossible, "since all things of men are in motion and cannot stay steady."[177] Yet given Machiavelli's celebration of a Roman ideal of energetic and tumultuous politics, his hope for a perpetual republic and his wavering judgment about its possibility are troubling.

In these moments of hope, he longs for an anti-political ideal, one that represents – somehow – "the true political way of life," and that is characterized above all by its "quiet." This characterization resonates eerily with Augustine's description of the eschatological City of God as a place in which "we shall have the leisure to be still."[178] This haunting eschatological hope reveals some ambivalence in Machiavelli's tragic rejection of apocalypse. The captivating promise of the Savonarolan moment, once imagined, cannot easily be forgotten: a New Jerusalem in which suffering has been redeemed, contingency escaped, and discord silenced.

Conclusion

To sum up, the final chapter of *The Prince* is an apocalyptic exhortation. Having failed to render political contingency intelligible, *The Prince* concludes with a call not for a prudent prince but for a prophet. By locating the crises of Italy in an apocalyptic narrative, this redemptive figure promises to give political contingency both a meaning and an end – to transform Italy and transcend

---

[175] Machiavelli, *Discourses on Livy*, III.17, 257.
[176] Machiavelli, *Discourses on Livy*, III.22, 266.
[177] Machiavelli, *Discourses on Livy*, I.6, 23. Emphasis mine.
[178] Augustine, *Concerning the City of God against the Pagans*, 22.30, 1090; Paul Wright, "Machiavelli's City of God: Civic Humanism and Augustinian Terror," in *Augustine and Politics*, ed. Kevin L. Hughes and Kim Paffendorf (Lanham: Lexington Books, 2005), 325.

politics. However, Machiavelli later rejects this apocalyptic solution on both practical and normative grounds, turning instead to a tragic worldview.

Where does this leave the familiar reading of Machiavelli as a political realist? We need not completely abandon this interpretation. However, the analysis offered here does push toward a more nuanced account of Machiavelli's realism.

First, many interpreters treat *The Prince* as the primary locus of Machiavelli's realism and read the *Discourses* as an exclusively republican work. However, my interpretation of *The Prince* emphasizes the utopian and apocalyptic character of the work's concluding chapter. *The Prince* must culminate in an apocalyptic exhortation because the rest of the work has failed to achieve the goal of a narrow and underdeveloped political realism – to make an unruly politics intelligible and therefore susceptible to princely mastery. I find a much more developed and explicitly moral realism in the *Discourses*. This later work has a tragic sensibility that emphasizes the limits to political action and the dangers of trying to exceed them. Yet tragic realism does not demand that we withdraw from the world or acquiesce in evil. It urges continued political engagement, even if we are likely to fail.

Second, this reading suggests that Machiavelli's political realism is deeply contextual. It only fully develops through an attempt to reject the apocalyptic imaginary. Importantly, this is not simply a confrontation between Machiavelli ("the realist") and Savonarola and his followers ("the apocalypticists"). It is also a struggle that is internal to Machiavelli's own work. The tragic realism that Machiavelli eventually embraces takes shape only after an encounter with the apocalyptic imaginary.

Third, this interpretation complicates a conventional reading of Machiavelli that sees him as a thoroughly modern and secular realist – as a thinker whose commitment to charting the effectual truths of power politics marks a definitive break from the political thought of medieval Christianity. Machiavelli's political theological project and his confrontation with the apocalyptic imaginary makes it hard to place him firmly on either side of a premodern/modern divide.

Finally, and perhaps most importantly, I have pointed to lingering questions about the adequacy of tragic realism as a response to the apocalyptic imaginary. Machiavelli's turn toward a tragic sensibility in his later work is a rejection of apocalypticism and its fantasies of final solutions. But this rejection is incomplete. He never loses hope that a perpetual republic might bring an end to political tumult. For all its sensible maturity, Machiavelli's tragic realism cannot dispel the captivating hope for a world without politics.

As we will see in the next chapter, Thomas Hobbes will opt for a different strategy. He will not turn away from the apocalyptic imaginary. Instead, he will try to subversively redirect in the service of sovereign power and civil peace.

4

Hobbes "At the Edge of Promises and Prophecies"

Introduction

Recalling the circumstances of his birth, Thomas Hobbes wrote that his mother "gave birth to twins: myself and fear at the same time." His premature birth on April 5, 1588 was caused, Hobbes claimed, by rumors of an approaching Spanish Armada that was bringing England's "last day."[1] These rumors had been circulating for several months and the English awaited the Spanish fleet with a sense of utter dread.

But there were other reasons to expect the last day. The year 1588 had been the focus of apocalyptic expectation and terror for over a century. One prominent fifteenth-century prediction expected that the year would bring "with it woe enough. If this year, total catastrophe does not befall, if land and sea do not collapse in total ruin, yet will the whole world suffer upheavals, empires will dwindle and from everywhere will be great lamentation."[2] During the course of Hobbes's life, there would be an explosion of apocalyptic prophecy that combined fears of the imminent end of the known world with hopes for a radically better future. The chaos and violence of the English Civil War only seemed to

---

[1] Fama ferebat enim diffusa per oppida nostra,
Extremum genti classe venire diem.
Atque metum tantum concepit tunc mea mater,
Ut pararet geminos, meque metumque simul.

See: Thomas Hobbes, "Vita [Verse]," in *Opera Philosophica Quae Latine Scripsit Omnia*, ed. William Molesworth, vol. 1 (London: John Bohn, 1939), lxxxvi.

[2] Garrett Mattingly, *The Armada* (Boston: Mariner Books, 2005), 176. There were numerous similar prophecies circulating at the time of the Armada. See: Mattingly, *Armada*, 172–86. Francis Bacon mentions the quoted prophecy, along with others concerning 1588, in his brief essay "On Prophecies." See: Francis Bacon, "Of Prophecies," in *The Essays of Francis Bacon*, ed. Mary Augusta Scott (New York: Charles Scribner's Sons, 1908), 168–69.

confirm these prophetic revelations. Throughout the kingdom, people waited for God to save the elect and condemn the damned.

I argue here that the English apocalyptic imaginary shaped Hobbes's later work, and *Leviathan* in particular. While some have grappled with his understanding of the political implications of religion, the intentions and beliefs that may be inferred from his scriptural and theological arguments, and his accounts of the origins of the civil war, Hobbes's response to apocalyptic expectations has received little attention.[3] Yet this became one of his central preoccupations. The rich stock of doomsday stories and images proved difficult to contain. Kings and church authorities had initially used apocalypticism as a legitimating tool. By the mid-seventeenth century, a more radical apocalyptic imaginary was abroad in the land.

Hobbes responds to this imaginary not by condemning it, but by redirecting it in the service of sovereign power and civil peace. He fights apocalypse *with apocalypse*. Hobbes pursues two paths in his project – one is overtly scriptural and the other is seemingly secular. His scriptural argument takes aim at both the conveyors and the content of apocalyptic prophecy, ultimately offering a deflationary reinterpretation of Christian eschatology. Hobbes's political argument stages a secular apocalypse, in which the terror and chaos of the state of nature are the narrative prelude to an enduring commonwealth ruled by a mortal God. In pursuing these twin paths, Hobbes does not reject the apocalyptic imaginary. He redirects it and tries to return it safely into sovereign hands.[4]

---

[3] For three notable exceptions that touch on Hobbes's responses to apocalypticism in discussions that are focused on more general questions of eschatology, religion, and prophecy, respectively, see: Pocock, "Time, History and Eschatology"; Aloysius P. Martinich, *The Two Gods of Leviathan: Thomas Hobbes on Religion and Politics* (Cambridge: Cambridge University Press, 1992); Kinch Hoekstra, "Disarming the Prophets: Thomas Hobbes and Predictive Power," *Rivista Di Storia Della Filosofia* 59, no. 1 (2004): 97–153.

[4] As is the case with Machiavelli, much of the scholarly debate about Hobbes's arguments about religion and theology has focused on the sincerity and content of his beliefs. The position shared by several scholars with very different interpretive leanings is that Hobbes was not a sincere (or entirely sincere) Christian and that his apparent professions of Christian faith are either strategic or ironic. Leo Strauss casts Hobbes first as an agnostic (in *Spinoza's Critique of Religion*, first published in German in 1930), then as a sort of deist (in *The Political Philosophy of Thomas Hobbes*, first published in German in 1936), then as a philosopher who sought to create an "a-religious or atheistic society as the solution to the social or political problem" (in *Natural Right and History*, 1950), and finally as an atheist (in "On the Basis of Hobbes's Political Philosophy," first published in French in 1954). According to Strauss, Hobbes's professions of faith and the defenses of episcopacy in his pre-English Civil War work, far from being sincere, were instead meant to conceal his true views from potential persecutors. See: Leo Strauss, *Spinoza's Critique of Religion*, trans. E. M. Sinclair (New York: Schocken Books, 1965), 101; Leo Strauss, *The Political Philosophy of Hobbes: Its Basis and Its Genesis*, trans. E. M. Sinclair (Chicago: University of Chicago Press, 1952), 74–76; Leo Strauss, *Natural Right and History* (Chicago: University of Chicago Press, 1950), 198; Leo Strauss, "On the Basis of Hobbes's Political Philosophy," in *What Is Political Philosophy? And Other Studies* (Chicago: University of Chicago Press, 1988), 171. Edwin Curley, from whose work this account of Strauss's changing interpretations is drawn, argues along similar lines that "Hobbes wanted (a) to undermine the religion

Introduction

This chapter proceeds in three parts. First, I trace the evolution of the apocalyptic imaginary from the late sixteenth century to the English Civil War (1642–1651). We will see that the very apocalyptic ideas that initially supported monarchical power eventually subverted it. Second, I outline Hobbes's scriptural response to the apocalyptic imaginary. Here, I focus on his treatment of the political threat of prophecy, his response to features of apocalyptic prophecy (especially the figure of the Antichrist), and his revisionist accounts of hell and the final judgment. Third, I argue Hobbes's secular political argument relies on some of the narrative structure and imagery of apocalypticism.

of his day, (b) to shelter himself against persecution for disbelief by falsely giving the impression that he was a believer, and (c) to appeal to the religious beliefs of his readers to support his political conclusions." Hobbes's use of irony is the textual "evidence that he would have gone further than he did in the direction of unorthodoxy, if the political situation had permitted him to do so safely." See: Edwin Curley, "'I Durst Not Write So Boldly' Or How to Read Hobbes's Theological-Political Treatise," in *Hobbes E Spinoza: Scienza E Politica*, ed. Daniela Bostrenghi (Naples: Bibliopolis, 1992), 589–90, 512. Quentin Skinner is similarly attuned to Hobbes's use of irony and argues that it is part of a broader set of strategies familiar to humanist rhetoricians. According to Skinner, those interpreters who take Hobbes's own statements as evidence of sincere Christian belief simply fail to recognize that Hobbes "makes systematic use of the various devices recommended by theorists of eloquence for contriving a tone of irony and ridicule." Their interpretations of his beliefs are therefore likely to be "over-simplified." See: Quentin Skinner, *Reason and Rhetoric in the Philosophy of Hobbes* (Cambridge: Cambridge University Press, 1996), 14, 13. David Johnston also directs our attention to Hobbes's use of rhetoric, arguing that Hobbes did not need to challenge the authority of Scripture overtly. Instead, his discussion of Christian doctrine was intended to implant "doubts in the minds of his readers... [and] to subvert many of the central tenets of Christian theology ... and replace them with Hobbes's own rationalized version of Christian doctrine." See: David Johnston, *The Rhetoric of Leviathan: Thomas Hobbes and the Politics of Cultural Transformation* (Princeton: Princeton University Press, 1986), 181. Jeffrey R. Collins largely puts the debate about Hobbes's theism aside and draws together elements of all of the foregoing positions to argue for the essentially esoteric nature of Hobbes's theological project in *Leviathan*. Collins contends that this esoteric strategy was necessary in order to accomplish the two central goals of Leviathan – "to educate rulers in civil science" (which required Hobbes to "undercut Christianity in order to expose the true foundations of politics") and "to serve as a pedagogical tool inculcating obedience among political subjects" (which required Hobbes to preserve Christianity's instrumental value). See: Jeffrey R. Collins, *The Allegiance of Thomas Hobbes* (Oxford: Oxford University Press, 2005), 33. On the other side of this debate about Hobbes's own religious beliefs are those who argue that he was essentially sincere. The most developed argument has been made by Aloysius P. Martinich, who argues that "for the most part Hobbes meant what he said." If the contextually sensitive standard of orthodoxy is "adherence to the propositions expressed by the authoritative Christian creeds of the first four church councils," Martinich seeks to demonstrate that "Hobbes was a sincere, and relatively orthodox, Christian." See: Martinich, *Two Gods of Leviathan*, 16, 2, 1. Sharon A. Lloyd also suggests that Hobbes was a sincere believer, but argues that his aim was to rationalize and redescribe core Christian beliefs in order to make them compatible with the requirements of political obedience and civil peace. It was these attempts at rationalization, rather than Hobbes's own beliefs, that attracted charges of atheism from Hobbes's contemporaries. See: Sharon A. Lloyd, *Ideals as Interests in Hobbes's Leviathan: The Power of Mind over Matter* (Cambridge: Cambridge University Press, 1992), 272–74. I have two suggestions. First, this debate is virtually impossible to resolve based on the evidence we have – Hobbes's writings and those of his

The English Apocalyptic Imaginary

The apocalyptic imaginary that captivated England from the Reformation through the civil war drew on a rich interpretive tradition. Other scholars have captured this richness in fuller detail than I can provide here.[5] I focus on three of the most important and influential theological sources for the apocalyptic imaginary that would come to dominate Hobbes's world: John Bale's *Image of Both Churches* (1547)[6], John Foxe's *Acts and Monuments* (1563)[7], and the

contemporaries. As readers such as Strauss and Curley have argued, the fear of persecution may well have led Hobbes to offer insincere professions of faith. However, this interpretation has difficulty accounting for why, if he so feared persecution, Hobbes *explicitly* made both political and theological arguments that he knew would raise the ire of persecuting authorities. Willis B. Glover, "God and Thomas Hobbes," *Church History* 29, no. 3 (1960): 279–80; Lloyd, *Ideals as Interests in Hobbes's Leviathan*, 17–18; Martinich, *Two Gods of* Leviathan, 30–32; Samuel I. Mintz, *The Hunting of Leviathan: Seventeenth-Century Reactions to the Materialism and Moral Philosophy of Thomas Hobbes* (New York: Cambridge University Press, 1962), 44. The real challenge for those who want to take Hobbes's written professions (or suggestions) of faith at face value is that, according to his own political philosophy, "subjects are obligated publicly to adhere to their sovereign's public theology, and Hobbes's sovereign required his subjects to profess belief in God." See: Arash Abizadeh, "Hobbes's Conventionalist Theology, the Trinity, and God as an Artificial Person by Fiction," *Historical Journal*, published electronically (January 30, 2017), 3, doi: 10.1017/S0018246X16000418. See also: Kinch Hoekstra, "The End of Philosophy (The Case of Hobbes)," *Proceedings of the Aristotelian Society* 106, no. 1 (2006): 54. While Hobbes was certainly accused of atheism by his contemporaries, the label was at that time a general term of abuse and cannot therefore serve as reliable evidence of Hobbes's own sincere beliefs. See: Martinich, *Two Gods of* Leviathan, 19–22. Second, it is not clear that we have to settle the question of the sincerity of Hobbes's beliefs to get an argument about the argumentative and rhetorical strategies of his political-theological argument off the ground. My own argument – that Hobbes reinterprets and redirects the apocalyptic imaginary to make it safe for sovereign power – takes no stand on the question of his religious beliefs. It is an argument that is not logically inconsistent with any of the positions outlined earlier and could reasonably be held by any of their defenders, if they accept that one of Hobbes's primary purposes was to investigate and secure the conditions of political order. As a sincere Christian, a deist, an agnostic, or an atheist, Hobbes would have had good reason to want to undermine the destabilizing potential of the apocalyptic imaginary. The question of his religious beliefs is thus orthogonal to this investigation.

[5] For more detailed accounts, see: Paul K. Christianson, *Reformers and Babylon: English Apocalyptic Visions from the Reformation to the Eve of the Civil War* (Toronto: University of Toronto Press, 1978), 13–92; Katharine R. Firth, *Apocalyptic Tradition in Reformation Britain, 1530–1645* (Oxford: Oxford University Press, 1979); Bernard Capp, "The Political Dimension of Apocalyptic Thought," in *The Apocalypse in English Renaissance Thought and Literature: Patterns, Antecedents and Repercussions*, ed. C. A. Patrides and Joseph Wittreich (Ithaca: Cornell University Press, 1984), 93–124; Crawford Gribben, *The Puritan Millennium: Literature & Theology, 1550–1682* (Dublin: Four Courts Press, 2000), 26–79.

[6] Bale published the work in three parts. The first appeared in 1541, the second in 1545, and the third in 1547.

[7] Foxe published the first edition of *Acts and Monuments*, in Latin, in Basel in 1559. The first English edition, which contained substantial expansions from the Latin version, was published in 1563. Foxe published three subsequent English editions in his lifetime, with varying degrees of revision.

Geneva translation of the Bible (1560, 1599).[8] The choice of these three works is not arbitrary. Historians studying sixteenth- and seventeenth-century English apocalypticism tend to agree that the works of Bale, Foxe, and the translators and annotators of the Geneva Bible are the theological basis for the radical apocalyptic polemics of the seventeenth century.[9] These writers came into frequent contact with one another and with theologians and religious dissidents on the Continent, building upon and integrating one another's ideas into a self-consciously new Protestant apocalyptic tradition.[10] Together, their works voiced a uniquely Protestant reading of the apocalypse that would take on a life of its own in the violence and hopes of the English Civil War.

Like John of Patmos, these apocalyptic writers all wrote in exile. When his powerful protector, Thomas Cromwell, lost King Henry VIII's favor in 1540, John Bale fled to Flanders. He returned briefly after the accession of King Edward VI. But like John Foxe and the translators and annotators of the Geneva Bible, Bale fled to the Continent once again when the violently pro-Catholic Queen Mary inherited the English throne in 1553. Together, these Marian exiles helped forge an English apocalyptic tradition shaped by their persecutions at home and their ties to the Protestant community abroad.[11]

While the works of the Marian exiles would soon inflame radical movements in England, the intentions of their authors were far from revolutionary. Continental Protestants were deeply wary of the destabilizing potential of apocalyptic hopes. Twenty years earlier, the German town of Münster had been rocked by an Anabaptist apocalyptic revolt. Radicals proclaimed the town the New Jerusalem and tried to build a proto-socialist theocracy. Besieged by Catholic forces and cut off from the outside world, the town succumbed to famine and cannibalism. Those who survived eventually surrendered in exchange for the offer of safe conduct, but were instead brutally massacred and their corpses exhibited in cages as a lesson to others attracted to the subversive messages of Revelation.[12] To the Continental Protestants of the 1550s and the Marian

---

[8] There were several versions of the Geneva translation. The first full version appeared in 1560, but was not published in England until 1575/6. In 1599, a new version appeared with Franciscus Junius' newly translated notes on Revelation. In this chapter, I draw on both the 1560 and 1599 editions.

[9] See: Christianson, *Reformers and Babylon*, 13–46; Gribben, *Puritan Millennium*, 26–79; Firth, *Apocalyptic Tradition*, 32–149.

[10] Large parts of Bale's "apocalyptic framework" were absorbed into Foxe's *Acts and Monuments* and the annotations in the Geneva Bible. See: Christianson, *Reformers and Babylon*, 36.

[11] Katharine R. Firth argues: "For the development of the apocalyptic tradition in Britain no six years were more important than those from 1553 to 1559. The period of the Marian exile, during which some eight hundred persons gathered in a few Protestant cities on the continent, was marked by close association and co-operation between the exiles and scholars from all over the Protestant world." See: Firth, *Apocalyptic Tradition*, 69.

[12] Gribben, *Puritan Millennium*, 34–35.

exiles who dwelt among them, Münster was a powerful reminder of the dangers of apocalypticism. Protestant theology would now have to defend with equal vigor against "the twin threats of the totalitarianism of Rome and the danger of sectarian frenzy."[13] The Marian exiles were on the front lines of this effort.

John Bale's *Image of Both Churches* is a sophisticated theological response to these twin threats. Written before the Marian exile, Bale's apocalyptic understanding of history had a profound influence on Foxe's *Acts and Monuments* and the translations and annotations in the Geneva Bible. For Bale, the book of Revelation is a microcosm of scripture: "Not one necessary point of belief is in all the other scriptures, that is not here also in one place or another." It was also essential reading for any faithful Christian, for "he that knoweth not this book, knoweth not what the church is whereof he is a member."[14] Borrowing from Augustine's conception of the two cities, Bale reads Revelation as a prophecy of the unfolding of Christianity. To Bale, the final book of the Bible describes the parallel development and opposition of two churches – the "true Christian church ... the meek spouse of the Lamb without spot ... and the sinful synagogue of Satan."[15] Bale's reading identifies his Protestant contemporaries with the persecuted elect of the "true" church, giving them a past that stretches back to early Christianity. For Bale, the Church establishment in Rome is a false church in the service of Antichrist. As Paul Christianson explains, "By applying the idea of the two churches, Bale stood history on its head. The church establishment of the middle ages, headed by the papacy, became the vassals of antichrist, while many hounded as heretics in the same period became the small, pure, persecuted elect of the true church."[16]

While Bale's historical reading of Revelation gave fodder for the contemporary struggles between Protestants and Rome, he does not offer a call to apocalyptic action. As we shall see, many of his Protestant contemporaries pinned their hopes for apocalyptic transformation on an established political authority – a godly prince who would carry out the events prophesied in Revelation by ending the persecution of the elect and doing battle with the forces of Antichrist. For Bale, however, kings and princes are incapable of such divine tasks. God has not given earthly rulers the power "to subdue these beasts. Only is it reserved to the victory of his living word."[17] The agents of God are not rulers, but rather the persecuted, the oppressed, and those who preach the divine message.

Yet Bale is careful to avoid the kinds of destabilizing doctrines that might fuel radical ambitions. He does not issue a call to arms and, following Augustine, he is cautious when addressing possible futures prophesied in Revelation.[18] His

---

[13] Gribben, *Puritan Millennium*, 35.
[14] John Bale, *Select Works of John Bale*, ed. Henry Christmas (Cambridge: Cambridge University Press, 1849), 252, https://archive.org/details/selectworksofbaloobaleuoft.
[15] Bale, *Select Works*, 251. [16] Christianson, *Reformers and Babylon*, 15.
[17] Bale, *Select Works*, 365.
[18] Gribben, *Puritan Millennium*, 37–38; Firth, *Apocalyptic Tradition*, 56.

The English Apocalyptic Imaginary

commentary on the New Jerusalem simply paraphrases the biblical text and avoids drawing almost any connection to the plight of Protestant reformers.[19] Bale's work gave Protestants an eschatological history, but did not urge them toward a prophetic future.

Like Bale, Foxe focuses his reading of Revelation on the past and present. *Acts and Monuments*, more commonly known as *The Book of Martyrs*, blends an eschatological reading of history with an older genre describing the lives of saints. Using Bale's notion of two churches, Foxe catalogues and details the persecution of the elect in an account that links the Marian exiles back to the apostles in an unbroken trail of blood.[20] The elect are identified by their suffering and the forces of Antichrist are marked by their eagerness to persecute.[21] Yet while their persecution and martyrdom give members of the true church a place in the apocalyptic drama, Foxe does not encourage any direct popular action. Political agitation and subversion are vices practiced by papal supporters: "What kings have been deposed, and emperors stripped from their imperial seat, and all because they would not stoop and bend to the image of the beast, that is, to the majesty and title of Rome."[22]

To the extent that the elect have an active role to play in the apocalypse, it is through their leaders. In the 1563 edition of *Acts and Monuments*, Foxe casts Queen Elizabeth as a new Constantine, a godly ruler who ends the persecution of the elect and "confound[s] the dark and false-valorized kingdom of Antichrist."[23] The work's dedication to Elizabeth makes this connection clear. In the opening lines of the dedication, the capital c in "Constantine" is embellished with a picture of the Queen triumphing over the body of the Pope. Just as Constantine ended the persecution of the early church, Elizabeth will stop the suffering of Protestants. The dedication in the 1570 edition of the book discusses Christ, rather than Constantine. But the capital C in "Christ" bears the same image of Elizabeth.[24] Foxe thus builds on Bale to develop a Protestant identity grounded in history and prophecy, while restricting the active apocalyptic role of the elect to the actions of their godly sovereign.

The Geneva Bible further develops Bale's Protestant apocalyptic theology. This clear and forceful translation was one of the most enduring achievements of the Marian exiles. Rich with detailed annotations, cross-references, indices, woodcut illustrations, and maps of the holy land, it was a mass-produced translation that gave its English readers the world's first study Bible. It gained official

---

[19] Christianson, *Reformers and Babylon*, 18.
[20] Gribben, *Puritan Millennium*, 59; Richard Helgerson, *Forms of Nationhood: The Elizabethan Writing of England* (Chicago: University of Chicago Press, 1992), 256.
[21] Helgerson, *Forms of Nationhood*, 259.
[22] John Foxe, *The Acts and Monuments of John Foxe*, ed. Josiah Pratt, vol. 4 (London: George Seeley, 1870), 106, https://books.google.com/books?id=RDwJAQAAIAAJ&dq.
[23] Foxe, *Acts and Monuments*, vol. 7, 466.
[24] Frances A. Yates, *Astraea: The Imperial Theme in the Sixteenth Century* (Harmondsworth: Penguin, 1977), 42.

status in Scotland, where a 1579 Act of Parliament demanded "every substantial householder [be] required to purchase a copy."[25] While it was never officially recognized in England, it still became hugely influential. The Geneva Bible was Shakespeare's Bible and that of many of other Elizabethan and Jacobean authors.[26] It was one of the Bibles taken to America on the Mayflower and the translation became wildly popular in the colonies.[27] And when Oliver Cromwell's parliamentarian troops went into battle, they carried a *Soldiers Pocket Bible* with verses taken from the Geneva translation.[28]

Influenced by the ideas of Bale and Foxe, the Geneva Bible has an overt anti-Catholic and apocalyptic agenda. While Antichrist plays a small role in the Bible and is mentioned in only three passages[29], the translators of the Geneva version chose to capitalize the name. This decision was not maintained in the later Authorized (King James) Version, a fact that hints at the Geneva translation's "more polemical apocalyptic agenda."[30]

The annotations further support this assessment. "Antichrist" is linked to "the man of sin" and the "son of perdition" of 2 Thessalonians 2:3. This antichristian adversary is then identified with the papacy, and the pope with the second beast in Revelation 13. The second beast inherits the powers of the first, which the notes identify as the Roman Empire. The pope "is the head both of the tyrannical Empire, and also of the false prophets." He "exercises a most wicked and most insolent tyranny over the persons of men...and over their goods and actions."[31] The papacy was part of a chain of antichristian forces, for Antichrist "comprehendeth the whole succession of the persecutors of the church." He "shall not reign without the Church, but in the very bosom of the Church."[32]

The Geneva Bible also seemed to sow the seeds of political radicalism. Several of the rulers of the Old Testament – Pharaoh, Saul, Ahab, and Nahash the Ammonite – are described as "tyrants."[33] Many of the marginal notes sound a similar message. The note on Exodus 1:22, which describes Pharaoh's command to throw newborn males into the Nile, reads: "When tyrants cannot prevail by craft, they burst forth into open rage." When Pharaoh commands the taskmasters to increase the burdens of labor on the Israelites, the relevant note reads: "The more cruelly the tyrants rage, the nearer is God's help."[34] A comment on

---

[25] Maurice S. Betteridge, "The Bitter Notes: The Geneva Bible and Its Annotations," *The Sixteenth Century Journal* 14, no. 1 (1983): 44.
[26] David Daniell, *The Bible in English: Its History and Influence* (New Haven: Yale University Press, 2003), 295.
[27] Betteridge, "The Bitter Notes," 53.   [28] Daniell, *The Bible in English*, 295.
[29] 1 John 2:18, 22; 1 John 4:3; and 2 John 7.   [30] Gribben, *Puritan Millennium*, 28.
[31] 1599 Geneva Bible, note on Rev. 13: 12–16.
[32] 1599 Geneva Bible, note on 2 Thess. 2: 3–4.
[33] Christopher Hill, *The English Bible and the Seventeenth-Century Revolution* (London: Penguin, 1993), 59.
[34] 1599 Geneva Bible, notes on Exod. 1:22 and 5:9.

Daniel sounds an even more radical note: "he did disobey [King Darius'] wicked commandment [in order] to obey God, and so did no injustice to the King who ought to command nothing whereby God should be dishonored."[35] The subversive potential of these notes did not escape James I, who called them "very partial, untrue, seditious and savouring too much of dangerous and traitorous conceits."[36] Looking back from the Restoration, the royalist polemicist Peter Heylyn echoed this view, writing that the notes were "destructive of the persons and powers of kings, and of all civil intercourse and human society."[37]

Despite its religious and political radicalism, the Geneva Bible, like the works of Bale and Foxe, tries to avoid encouraging the kind of Protestant enthusiasm that had been so disastrous at Münster. Indeed, the Bible's annotations were meant to "offer the interpretive guidelines required by those protestants concerned to support the social and religious *status quo*."[38] Sovereigns, not individual Protestants, would destroy Antichrist. The apocalyptic preface to the 1560 Geneva Bible was addressed to Queen Elizabeth. One of the notes on Revelation explains that "Kings and Princes (contrary to that wicked opinion of the Anabaptists) are partakers of the heavenly glory, if they rule in fear of the Lord."[39] While the Geneva Bible claims scriptural authority for the Protestant cause, its challenge to sovereign power is at best uneven.

Bale, Foxe, and the translators and annotators of the Geneva Bible had attempted to avoid encouraging Protestant enthusiasm. But their works became the theological basis for the Puritan apocalypticism of the English Civil War. This fact confronts historians with a puzzle. How did the comparatively moderate Protestant apocalypticism of the sixteenth century become the radical apocalypticism of the seventeenth century?

To understand how this happened, we must trace three important shifts in English apocalypticism that occurred between the reigns of Queen Elizabeth I (1558–1603) and King Charles I (1625–1649). First, England took on a special role in the apocalyptic drama. For Bale and Foxe, the true church was universal and the elect were spread throughout the world.[40] Both writers drew

---

[35] Hill, *English Bible*, 59.
[36] As quoted in Peter Heylyn, *Aerius Redivivus* (1670; Early English Books Online), 247, http://gateway.proquest.com/openurl?ctx_ver=Z39.88-2003&res_id=xri:eebo&rft_id=xri:eebo:citation:12139018.
[37] Heylyn, *Aerius Redivivus*, 247.
[38] Gribben, *Puritan Millennium*, 67. Nevertheless, the Church of England and King James recognized enough anti-monarchical exegesis in the Geneva translation to justify commissioning the Authorized Version to replace it. This move did not decrease the popularity of the Geneva Bible, which was still in widespread use during the English Civil War.
[39] 1560 Geneva Bible, note on Revelation 21:24. As Crawford Gribben explains, "this confirmation of England's establishment would find fewer echoes in succeeding editions of puritan scriptures." This shift is part of a larger transformation in English apocalypticism that I explore in the following pages. See: Crawford Gribben, "Deconstructing the Geneva Bible: The Search for a Puritan Poetics," *Literature and Theology* 14, no. 1 (2000): 5.
[40] Capp, "The Political Dimension," 96.

substantial material from English history, reading the experiences of the country's reformers and Protestants alongside Revelation. However, they did not single England out for a special role in the apocalyptic transformation.[41] This special status developed in the aftermath of England's defeat of the Spanish Armada in 1588, after which the country was increasingly cast as an elect nation with a special role in the end times.[42] The failure of the Gunpowder Plot in 1605 was taken as a further sign that England was under divine protection.[43] This special role for England would be an overtly activist one. As Bernard Capp explains, "English Protestants were no longer merely preachers spreading the Gospel or martyrs suffering patiently" but an army "which would throw down Babylon."[44]

At the same time, there was a second shift in the agent of the apocalyptic transformation. For Bale and Foxe, the principal actors in the apocalyptic drama are martyrs – the persecuted and the oppressed who belong to the true church. But they play a passive role. To the extent that early Protestant apocalypticists envision any active agency, it is in the role of a godly prince who will fight the forces of Antichrist and end the persecution of the true church. This is the role that Foxe and the translators and annotators of the Geneva Bible assign to Queen Elizabeth I.[45] When James I succeeded Elizabeth, he became the focus of similar apocalyptic hopes. This is understandable, given that James had written an extensive commentary on Revelation, which prophesied the imminent overthrow of Catholic nations.[46] James I seemed to have all the right Protestant apocalyptic credentials.

Yet the political decisions he made during his reign did little to satisfy radical apocalyptic hopes. He made peace with Spain, he refused to intervene on the Protestant side in the Thirty Years War, and he proved almost as hostile to Puritans as he was to papists.[47] James' son, Charles I, was even less satisfactory as a candidate for the godly prince. He married a Catholic and supported the Arminian[48] party in the church, which promoted religious ceremonies widely condemned as popish. He was also openly hostile to the identification of the

---

[41] William Haller argues that Foxe did identify England as an elect nation. See: William Haller, *Foxe's Book of Martyrs and the Elect Nation* (London: Jonathan Cape, 1963). Katharine Firth, among others, has convincingly criticized this thesis. See: Firth, *The Apocalyptic Tradition*, 107–08. It is worth noting, however, that Foxe's work was added to substantially over time and later editions did incorporate a stronger role for England. Also, as Bernard Capp has explained, we must remember that the focus on English examples in the works of both Foxe and Bale had the effect of appearing to confirm England's importance in the apocalyptic drama. See: Capp, "The Political Dimension," 96.

[42] Capp, "The Political Dimension," 98.   [43] Christianson, *Reformers and Babylon*, 108.

[44] Capp, "The Political Dimension," 98.

[45] A caveat is in order here. Bernard Capp reminds us that while "most Protestant writers saw Elizabeth as having a major, distinctive or even unique position in the Church's history...they stopped short of ascribing a messianic role to her." See: Capp, "The Political Dimension," 96.

[46] Capp, "The Political Dimension," 102.   [47] Capp, "The Political Dimension," 103.

[48] In the narrowest sense, Arminians were followers of Jacobus Arminius (1560–1609), who proposed a series of revisions to Calvinist theology, most of which were focused on the doctrines of

The English Apocalyptic Imaginary

papacy with Antichrist.[49] With their hopes for a godly prince dashed, radical Protestants in England began to focus on Parliament, or even the community of believers at large, as agents of apocalyptic transformation.[50] The alliance between apocalyptic hope and sovereign power had dissolved.

Finally, and perhaps most importantly, there was a shift in the location of Antichrist. Bale, Foxe, and the translators and annotators of the Geneva Bible had all associated the pope and the institution of the papacy with Antichrist. By Elizabeth's reign, these links had become even more overt. It was entirely respectable to argue that the pope himself was Antichrist. This identification served the interests of sovereign power, unifying England against a common papal enemy – Spain. James I's commentary on Revelation had clearly identified the pope with Antichrist.[51] He viewed papal attempts to meddle in the secular jurisdiction of princes as particularly anti-Christian and as a threat to sovereign power.[52]

During his reign, James seems to have become increasingly aware of the politically destabilizing effects of this identification. It was hard to argue against those who criticized his peace with Spain and his failure to intervene on behalf of Protestants abroad, as these critics were merely seeking action against the Roman Antichrist.[53] Perhaps for this reason, James backed down from his earlier views.[54]

The more radical implications of this identification emerged under Charles I. The Church of England under Archbishop Laud and the Arminians was widely seen by its separatist and radical Puritan opponents as popish and sympathetic to the Catholic Church. Since the pope was Antichrist, argued some Puritans, so too must be his agents in England.[55] The "hatred traditionally directed outwards towards the pope or Hapsburgs was now turned inwards."[56] Realizing that the identification of the pope with Antichrist had become destabilizing,

---

predestination and salvation. In seventeenth-century England, however, Arminianism was associated with a broader set of commitments to uniformity of faith and religious practice, ecclesiastical hierarchy, and liturgical ceremony. Under Charles I, many Arminians rose to prominent positions in the church and the state.

[49] Capp, "The Political Dimension," 104.
[50] Capp, "The Political Dimension," 105; Gribben, *Puritan Millennium*, 45. This shift is on full display in William Prynne's thought. See: Christianson, *Reformers and Babylon*, 192.
[51] James I/VI, *Ane Fruitfull Meditatioun* (1588; Early English Books Online), part 1, http://gateway.proquest.com/openurl?ctx_ver=Z39.88-2003&res_id=xri:eebo&rft_id=xri:eebo:citation:99836897.
[52] Christopher Hill, *Antichrist in Seventeenth Century England* (London: Verso, 1990), 65.
[53] Hoekstra, "Disarming the Prophets," 101. Capp points out that Elizabeth I came to have similar problems. See: Capp, "The Political Dimension," 99.
[54] Hill suggests that James was also "uneasy about the rudeness involved in calling a fellow head of state names." Hill, *Antichrist*, 34.
[55] Christopher Hill quotes an anonymous tract with a note that adds up the values of VVILL LAUD to 666 and adds: "I am the Beast. Count it who can / This is the number. I am the man." As quoted in Hill, *Antichrist*, 68.
[56] Capp, "The Political Dimension," 107.

Laud and the Church of England backed away from this doctrine. The Laudians also censored works that espoused this identification, editing out the relevant passages or refusing to publish them entirely.[57] These efforts proved unsuccessful and the subsequent identification of the bishops of the Church of England with Antichrist soon bled into parliamentary and radical politics. Charles I, as head of the Church of England and a king with a Catholic wife, was increasingly seen as a kind of Antichrist as well. No longer safely abroad, Antichrist was now at home. Sovereign power had been undermined and disobedience had become a religious duty.[58]

While this apocalyptic message circulated among learned students of scripture, the ideas also seeped into the popular political consciousness in Britain. With the breakdown of censorship in 1641, apocalyptic prophecy exploded and was widely available in pamphlets.[59] From late 1640 onwards, apocalyptic preachers also had the ear of Parliament. After a series of successful invited sermons, the House of Commons began an official program of monthly fast sermons in 1642. Most of those who preached before Parliament offered an apocalyptic interpretation of England's recent political and religious unrest.[60]

Stephen Marshall, a Presbyterian churchman who preached to Parliament on several occasions, was particularly forceful in this interpretation. In a sermon commemorating the accession of Queen Elizabeth I, Marshall argued that the Laudians were in league with Satan, who "knowes his time is short" and so "stirres up all his instruments." Dangerous times lay ahead: "Little quiet I feare is to bee expected in *Christendome*, till the Beast his Kingdome be ruined."[61] In a later sermon, Marshall urged God's soldiers to be unflinching in their use of divine violence, not only when they confront "*armed* enemies in the *field*,

---

[57] Hoekstra, "Disarming the Prophets," 102; Hill, *Antichrist*, 37.

[58] William Goffe, a lieutenant-colonel in the New Model Army and a committed Puritan, made just such a case in the 1647 Putney Debates. "It is said," he recounted, "in the Revelation, that the kings of the earth should give up their power unto the Beast, and the kings of the earth have given up their power to the Pope. But some places that have seemed to deny the Pope's supremacy, yet they have taken upon them that which hath been equivalent to that which the Pope himself holds forth." See: Arthur S.P. Woodhouse (ed.), *Puritanism and Liberty: Being the Army Debates (1647–9) from the Clarke Manuscripts with Supplementary Documents* (Chicago: University of Chicago Press, 1951), 39–40.

[59] Hoekstra, "Disarming the Prophets," 99.

[60] Paul Christianson notes: "Of the nineteen sermons preached to the Commons between November 1640 and January 1642, only three failed to present this apocalyptic interpretation of the 1630s." See: Christianson, *Reformers and Babylon*, 184, fn. 16. See also: Hill, *The English Bible*, 90–93. Bernard Capp estimates: "Roughly 70 percent of leading clergy supporting parliament during the revolution, many of whom were moderate Presbyterians, held millenarian ideas." See: Bernard Capp, "The Millennium and Eschatology in England," *Past & Present* 57, no. 1 (1972): 157.

[61] Stephen Marshall, *A Sermon Preached Before the Honourable House of Commons... November 17, 1640* (1641; Early English Books Online), 43–44, http://gateway.proquest.com/openurl?ctx_ver=Z39.88-2003&res_id=xri:eebo&rft_id=xri:eebo:citation:99896500.

but afterward *deliberately* to come into a subdued *City*, and take the *little ones* upon the *speares point*, to take them by the heeles and beat out their *braines against the walles*." Some, Marshall admitted, may think this zealous violence barbarous and inhumane. But they are weak willed. Drawing on the language and images of Psalm 137, he argued: "If this worke be to revenge Gods Church against *Babylon*, he is *a blessed man that takes and dashes the little ones against the stones*."[62] Parliament regularly invited preachers like Marshall, officially thanked them, and often published their sermons.[63]

Marshall's ideas were widely disseminated as fodder for the parliamentarian cause. Edward Symmons, a royalist chaplain, begins his response to Marshall's apocalypticism with a description of an encounter with two Parliamentary prisoners in Shrewsbury in the spring of 1644. The chaplain's account of this exchange is worth quoting at length:

questioning them about their taking up of Armes against their *Soveraigne*, they answered me, that they took up Armes against *Antichrist*, and *Popery*; for (said they) *'tis prophesied in the Revelation, that the Whore of Babylon shall be destroyed with fire and sword, and what doe you know, but this is the time of her ruine, and that we are the men that must help to pull her downe*. I answered that the *Revelation* tells us, that 'tis the *worke of Kings*...to pull downe the whore of Babylon, *to hate her, to make her naked, and to burne her with fire*. But as for them, they (in my apprehension) laboured to keep up the *whore of Babilon*, that shee might not fall, by their endeavouring to *pull downe Kings*, who were appoynted of God *to pull downe her*: they replyed, that *'tis said in the Revelation, that the People, the Multitude and Nations should also pull her downe*: but I reading the verse out of one of their Bibles, shewed them their mistake, *that the People, Multitude and Nations*...were those whom the *Whore* did sit upon, and as it were did *brood* under her, that is, shee did rule over them, had them under their obedience, insomuch that they might rather be said to submit unto her, then to *pull* her downe.[64]

The prisoners then asked whether Symmons believed kings could pull down the Whore of Babylon without the help of their subjects. He answered: "no, nor yet the *People* without their *Kings*, who are appoynted of God; to lead them thereunto, and in whose power alone it is, to *Authorize* people to be active and assistant in such a businesse." The chaplain went on to explain that the prisoners were mistaken in their belief that popery was the Whore of Babylon. For, the Antichrist and the Whore "dwelt at *Rome*, and not here in *England*: and

---

[62] Stephen Marshall, *Meroz Cursed, Or, A Sermon Preached to the Honourable House of Commons...Febr. 23, 1641* (1641[2]; Early English Books Online), 11–12, http://gateway.proquest.com/openurl?ctx_ver=Z39.88-2003&res_id=xri:eebo&rft_id=xri:eebo:citation:12442426.

[63] Christianson, *Reformers and Babylon*, 183; Hoekstra, "Disarming the Prophets," 103; Capp, "The Political Dimension," 109.

[64] Edward Symmons, preface to *Scripture Vindicated from the Mis-Apprehension, Mis-Interpretations, and Mis-Applications of Mr. Stephen Marshall* (1644; Early English Books Online), http://gateway.proquest.com/openurl?ctx_ver=Z39.88-2003&res_id=xri:eebo&rft_id=xri:eebo:citation:99872387. See also: Hoekstra, "Disarming the Prophets," 105–06; Hill, *Antichrist*, 79–80.

it was the very *Roman seat* or City which was to be so abolished." The prisoners replied "that *all the true godly Divines in England* (amongst whom they named in speciall M. Marshall[)] *were of their opinion, that Antichrist was here in* England *as well as at* Rome, *and that the Bishops were Antichrist, and all that did endeavour to support them* ... and therefore they thought, they were bound in Conscience to fight against them."[65] To the horror of royalists such as Symmons, the apocalypticism of parliamentary sermons had penetrated the popular consciousness and was being deployed as a challenge to sovereign power.

The political use of apocalyptic ideas persisted during the English Civil War, as those on both sides justified their actions by citing Revelation. Groups such as the Diggers and the Levellers drew on the apocalyptic tradition to sketch a millennial and egalitarian future. The Fifth Monarchists, who took their name from a prophecy in Daniel, were convinced the end times were at hand and they would rule with Jesus in his millennial kingdom. Several Fifth Monarchists were judges at the trial of King Charles I and ultimately signed his death warrant. It is not clear whether Oliver Cromwell sincerely shared the apocalyptic zeal of such groups as these.[66]

However, Cromwell often surrounded himself with apocalypticists. His 1649 campaign to suppress Irish Royalists was widely interpreted in apocalyptic terms. John Owen, Cromwell's friend and chaplain, saw the Irish as the "sworn vassals of the man of sin" and "followers of the beast."[67] In a speech to the Barebones Parliament, Cromwell himself conveyed a sense of apocalyptic expectation: "Indeed I do think somewhat is at the door: we are at the threshold... You are at the edge of the Promises and Prophecies."[68]

Later, when Cromwell's power was formalized in the Protectorate, he would once again draw on apocalyptic tropes – this time to dash the millennial hopes of groups like the Diggers and the Levellers. At the opening of Parliament under the Protectorate, Cromwell quoted St. Paul's warning to Timothy: "In the latter times some shall depart from the faith, giving heed to seducing spirits, and doctrines of devils; Speaking lies in hypocrisy," and so on.[69] He continued: "And surely it may be feared, these are *our* times. For when men forget all rules of Law and Nature, and break all the bonds that fallen man hath on him... These are sad tokens of the last times!"[70] In the end, however, Cromwell himself would

---

[65] Symmons, "*Scripture Vindicated*," preface.
[66] Christopher Hill, *The Experience of Defeat: Milton and Some Contemporaries* (New York: Viking, 1984), 186.
[67] John Owen, as quoted in Gribben, *Puritan Millennium*, 151.
[68] Oliver Cromwell, "Opening of the Little Parliament (July 4, 1653)," in *Oliver Cromwell's Letters and Speeches with Elucidations*, ed. Thomas Carlyle, vol. 3 (New York: Charles Scribner's Sons, 1903), 65–66.
[69] 1 Timothy 4:2–3.
[70] Oliver Cromwell, "Meeting of the First Protectorate Parliament (September 4, 1654)," in *Oliver Cromwell's Letters and Speeches with Elucidations*, ed. Thomas Carlyle, vol. 3 (New York: Charles Scribner's Sons, 1903), 110.

be the victim of apocalyptic condemnation. The Fifth Monarchists, who had once been Cromwell's allies but were outraged by the creation of the Protectorate, eventually condemned the Lord Protector as the Beast of Revelation and actively sought to undermine his power.[71] Once again, the apocalyptic imaginary refused to remain safely in sovereign hands.

Hobbes's Scriptural Project

As the religious and political conflicts of the English Civil War intensified, Thomas Hobbes's political works became increasingly concerned with the challenge these apocalyptic ideas posed for political order and civil peace. Over time, Hobbes focused more and more on the conflict between secular and religious authority. He circulated *The Elements of Law, Natural and Politic* on May 9, 1640, four days after Charles I dissolved the Short Parliament.[72] Just less than one-fifth of the work deals with scriptural and religious questions.[73] Following some unsuccessful campaigns in Scotland, Charles I was forced to call the Long Parliament in November 1640. Hobbes recounts that "words that tended to aduance the prerogatiue of kings began to be examined in Parliament." He knew that there were some there "that had a good will to haue [him] troubled." Beyond the criticisms to which the circulation of *Elements of Law* had opened him, Hobbes also claims that he saw "a disorder coming" that made it difficult to remain in England.[74] He fled to Paris. Free from the gathering political storm in England, Hobbes busied himself with work on logic, science, geometry, and metaphysics. Some of this work would become the basis for *De Corpore*, which was to have been the first of three sections in his *Elements of Philosophy*. His plan had been to complete the sections in sequence. Once *De Corpore* was finished, he would turn to *De Homine* and then to *De Cive*.

However, soon after his arrival in Paris, he set *De Corpore* aside and hurried the completion of *De Cive*, which was published in 1642. Hobbes turned to *De Cive*, he tells us, because "it happened that my country, some years before the civil war broke out, was already seething with questions of the right of Government and of the due obedience of citizens, forerunners to the approaching war." Among those arguing against monarchical power and absolute sovereignty were preachers, confessors, and casuists who were trying to show that their rebellious doctrines were "consistent with the Word of God." Hobbes wrote *De Cive*, at least in part, to "show that the right of Sovereigns over citizens ... is

---

[71] Capp, "The Political Dimension," 115–16.
[72] This is the date in the dedication for *Elements of Law*. See: Aloysius P. Martinich, *Hobbes: A Biography* (Cambridge: Cambridge University Press, 1999), 122.
[73] I class the following chapters of *Elements of Law* as those dealing with scriptural and religious questions: 11, 18, 25, and 26.
[74] Thomas Hobbes, "Letter from Hobbes to John Scudamore (1641)," in *The Correspondence of Thomas Hobbes*, ed. Noel Malcolm, vol. 1 (Oxford: Clarendon Press, 1994), 15.

not in conflict with the holy Scriptures."[75] Two-fifths of this work deals with scriptural and religious matters, four of which are grouped in their own section at the end.[76] Yet, while Hobbes's attention to these issues was increasing, it is still fair to say "Scriptural and religious questions remained a distinctly subordinate subject" in his early political philosophy.[77]

This would soon change. Hobbes monitored events in England very closely during his exile. He describes a visit in the summer of 1646 from the young Prince Charles and his entourage, who brought fresh news of royalist defeats. The king's enemies, they told Hobbes, were interpreting these defeats as evidence of God's support for the parliamentarian cause. Hobbes tells us that he "could not bear to hear such terrible crimes attributed to the commands of God."[78] A little more than two and a half years after that, he would have received news of the execution of Charles I on January 30, 1649. *Leviathan* was published less than eighteen months later. Hobbes claimed that his primary motivation to write the work was to "absolve the divine laws."[79] *Leviathan* was

---

[75] Hobbes's account of these circumstances occurs in the preface to the revised (1647) edition of *De Cive*. See: Thomas Hobbes, *De Cive*, ed. Richard Tuck, trans. Michael Silverthorne (New York: Cambridge University Press, 1998), 12–14.

[76] I class the following chapters of *De Cive* as those dealing with scriptural and religious questions: 4, 11, 15, 16, 17, and 18.

[77] Johnston, *Rhetoric of Leviathan*, 114.

[78] "pati tot tantaque foeda / Apponi jussis criminal, nolo, Dei." Hobbes, "Vita [Verse]," xcii. I adopt Quentin Skinner's translation here. See: Skinner, *Reason and Rhetoric*, 330–31.

[79] "Divinas statuo quam primum absolvere leges." Hobbes, "Vita [Verse]," xcii. I adopt Quentin Skinner's translation here. See: Skinner, *Reason and Rhetoric*, 330–31. In his verse and prose autobiographies (both composed in the 1670s), Hobbes dates the start of his work on *Leviathan* to the summer of 1646. However, evidence from his own correspondence and that of his close friends and associates suggests that he turned to revisions for the second edition of *De Cive* in 1646 (published in 1647), then subsequently returned to work on *De Corpore*. This work went more slowly than expected, in part because of a serious illness. Hobbes seems to have begun concerted work on *Leviathan* in the latter half of 1649. Hobbes's retrospective dating of the start of his work on *Leviathan* may well have been done with a desire to establish his royalist credentials with the restored Stuarts. However, I do not think we must conclude that his account of his motivations in writing *Leviathan* was similarly clouded. There are two reasons for this. First, the account Hobbes gave in the preface to the revised edition of *De Cive* of the motivations that drove him to write that work (1647), in the thick of immediate circumstances, largely mirrors his later autobiographical account of what turned him to the work of *Leviathan*. Second, the preface to the revised edition of *De Cive*, along with several of the arguments in that work and an even greater number of those in *Leviathan*, shows that Hobbes was deeply concerned with refuting arguments that God's laws justified rebellion against any established sovereign. It also bears noting that one can accept that one of Hobbes's motives in writing Leviathan was to "absolve the divine laws," while still acknowledging that he may have had other motives as well (e.g., justifying submission to the Protectorate). For a review of the evidence regarding the dating of Hobbes's work on *Leviathan*, see: Quentin Skinner, *Visions of Politics*, Vol. 3: Hobbes and Civil Science (Cambridge: Cambridge University Press, 2002), 15–20; Noel Malcolm, introduction to *Leviathan*, vol. 1 by Thomas Hobbes (Oxford: Oxford University Press, 2012), 1–12.

Hobbes's Scriptural Project

published in 1651 and contains Hobbes's most extended treatment of scriptural and religious matters. He includes a completely new chapter on. He positions it at the end of his account of human nature and before his description of the state of nature, which forms the basis for his theory of the basis and rights of sovereign authority.[80] The final two parts of *Leviathan* – "Of a Christian Commonwealth" and "Of the Kingdom of Darkness" – deal, respectively, with scriptural interpretation and scriptural error.[81] These two parts occupy as much space as the first two parts on human nature and the commonwealth. Thus, as Johnston summarizes, "Scriptural and religious questions occupy more space in *Leviathan* than any other topic discussed in the work, including Hobbes's theory of the commonwealth itself."[82] It is reasonable to conclude that the importance that Hobbes places on religious questions in *Leviathan*, and in such later works as *Behemoth* (1668/1681)[83], stemmed from his acknowledgment of the role of scriptural argument in the debates over civil and ecclesiastical authority that animated the English Civil War.[84]

However, *Leviathan* is not only Hobbes's most scriptural work, but also his most eschatological. While *De Cive* has a chapter on Christ's kingdom on earth, *Leviathan* gives a much more detailed and sustained account of Christian eschatology and many of the latter work's scriptural arguments depend on this account. This might seem to pose a problem for Hobbes scholars. As John G. A. Pocock notes: "If we conclude that Hobbes's interest in eschatology increased between 1642 and 1651, this must have occurred during his residence in Paris, in a milieu not usually considered eschatologically-minded."[85]

Why, then, did Hobbes write his most scriptural and eschatological work in Paris, surrounded by intellectuals and early Enlightenment rationalists? There are three related responses to this question. First, Hobbes followed the events of the war closely from Paris, sometimes engaging with them directly.[86] Second, the character of the civil war had changed between 1642 and 1651. The war

---

[80] Johnston, *Rhetoric of Leviathan*, 114.
[81] I class the following chapters of *Leviathan* as those dealing with scriptural and religious questions: 12, 31–47. By word count, these chapters amount to more than half the book.
[82] Johnston, *Rhetoric of Leviathan*, 115.
[83] Hobbes completed *Behemoth, Or the Long Parliament* in 1668, but it was not published until 1681, two years after Hobbes's death.
[84] It is also worth remembering that, as Patricia Springborg notes, "theological argument happened to be the currency in which authority was traded in the seventeenth-century contest between the king and Parliament... Theology belonged within the scope of the problem of authority, and Hobbes's theological arguments are to be judged, therefore, not on the basis of his private religious beliefs but on his public commitment to resolve this problem in the terms in which he understood it." See: Patricia Springborg, "Leviathan and the Problem of Ecclesiastical Authority," *Political Theory* 3, no. 3 (1975): 290.
[85] Pocock, "Time, History and Eschatology," 173, n. 41. I would like to thank Joshua Foa Deinstag for first raising this question.
[86] For instance, Hobbes read and responded to an April 1641 petition to abolish the episcopacy. See: Martinich, *Hobbes*, 171.

did not begin in earnest until 1642. Hobbes may still have hoped the King could survive the challenge. By 1651, the king had been executed, an event that shocked royalists and moderates alike. It was no longer possible to dismiss radical apocalypticism as a fringe phenomenon.[87] The scriptural and apocalyptic arguments that had been made by parliamentarians and political and religious radicals demanded a response. Third, as Pocock himself notes, by the time Hobbes published *Leviathan* in 1651, "the collision between private inspiration and the authority of the civil magistrate had become a staple of political debate. The far greater attention paid to apocalyptic in *Leviathan* than in *De Cive* may perhaps be a consequence of this."[88] Those claiming divine inspiration offered scriptural support for their prophetic claims. Hobbes may well have become convinced that he had to meet these arguments on their own scriptural ground.

His response to the apocalypticism of the English Civil War is idiosyncratic and complex. He combats the politically destabilizing potential of the apocalyptic imaginary not by trying to escape it or condemn it but by attempting to put it back in the service of sovereign power.[89] Hobbes pursues two paths to this end – one is overtly scriptural and the other is seemingly secular and rational.[90] This section of the chapter traces the first path, while the next explores the second.

In examining Hobbes's scriptural response to the apocalyptic imaginary, I argue he condemns the radical Protestant apocalypse as false and reveals a "true" apocalypse that has been safely returned to sovereign hands.[91] This

---

[87] Hoekstra, "Disarming the Prophets," 107.
[88] Pocock, "Time, History and Eschatology," 180.
[89] By his own principles, Hobbes is not able to reject the apocalypse entirely. Those claiming that the end times were imminent during the English Civil War drew support for these prophetic assertions from Revelation. One possible route to deflating these claims might have been to challenge the canonicity of Revelation. Erasmus had done this by denying that John the Evangelist wrote Revelation. However, this route is not available to Hobbes, for whom matters of canonicity are determined by the sovereign. Hobbes's sovereign had pronounced on this matter. Revelation was canonical. This may be one reason why Hobbes is compelled to fight apocalypse with apocalypse. See: Hoekstra, "Disarming the Prophets," 109, n. 60.
[90] Hobbes characterizes the two modes of argument in *Leviathan* by identifying one with reason and the other with scripture. While he is confident in the argument from reason in the first half of Leviathan, he sees the scriptural argument as an alternate route to the same conclusions: "But supposing that these of mine are not such Principles of Reason; yet I am sure they are Principles from Authority of Scripture." I think the characterization of the first two parts of *Leviathan* entirely in terms of rational argument underplays (perhaps deliberately so) their political-theological resonances and appeals to imagination. I will expand on this suggestion in the third part of the chapter. Thomas Hobbes, *Leviathan*, ed. Noel Malcolm (Oxford: Oxford University Press, 2012), chapter 30, 522. Future references will take the following form: 30, 522.
[91] This move of denouncing false apocalypses is, for Jacques Derrida, one of the defining features of the apocalyptic tone. After pointing to the focus in Revelation on identifying and testing false apostles and envoys, he asks: "Shall we thus continue in the best apocalyptic tradition to

Hobbes's Scriptural Project

strategy is best understood as a form of "subversive integration" – Hobbes accepts many of the broad outlines of the radical apocalyptic imaginary while redirecting it toward a different end.[92] He pursues the strategy in his warnings about false prophets, his narrowing of the definition of Antichrist, and his sketch of an alternative Christian eschatology. Together, the three lines of argument cast those who accept the claims of radical apocalypticists as inconsistent and gullible believers and unfit political subjects.

As we have seen, popular apocalypticism flourished in the early 1640s. Parliament had opened its doors to apocalyptic preachers who prophesied and encouraged unrestrained violence. While Hobbes saw these developments as threats to political order, he understood the appeal of prophecy. For him, the roots of religious belief lie in man's Promethean condition, his inescapable tendency to look "too far before him, in the care of future time" and so to have "his heart all the day long, gnawed on by feare of death, poverty, or other calamity."[93] Hobbes will go on to argue that this same anxiety about the future can be harnessed to get men to accept an absolute state.[94]

But it can also subject them to self-proclaimed prophets who play on their anxiety about the future. These prophets offer captivating apocalyptic interpretations of the present and consoling promises about the world to come.[95] In Hobbes's time, they claimed divine inspiration from God or special insight into scripture to authorize their claims. The radical Puritan preachers "vsed the Scripture phrase, whether vnderstood by the people or not, as that no Tragœdian in the world could haue acted the part of a right godly man better than these did."[96] They feigned divine inspiration, giving their sermons the

---

denounce false apocalypses?" See: Jacques Derrida, "Of an Apocalyptic Tone Newly Adopted in Philosophy," in *Derrida and Negative Theology*, ed. Harold Coward and Toby Foshay (Albany: State University of New York Press, 1992), 59.

[92] I am borrowing the term "subversive integration" from Franck Lessay, who uses it regarding Hobbes's covenant theology and contrasts it with a strategy of "criticism and rejection." See: Franck Lessay, "Hobbes's Covenant Theology and Its Political Implications," in *Cambridge Companion to Hobbes's Leviathan*, ed. Patricia Springborg (Cambridge: Cambridge University Press, 2007), 258. We see Hobbes use the same strategy in his idiosyncratic use of the image of *Leviathan*, the biblical symbol of primeval chaos, as a secular symbol of political order.

[93] Hobbes, *Leviathan*, 12, 166.

[94] Stephen Holmes put its well: "If the yet unreal future had no causal power, human beings could never be moved by threats of punishment or fear of violent death." See: Stephen Holmes, introduction to *Behemoth, or the Long Parliament*, by Thomas Hobbes (Chicago: University of Chicago Press, 1990), xiv.

[95] In a remark added to the original manuscript of *Elements of Law*, Hobbes quips: "those that determine of the time of the world's end, and other such points of prophecy" may be numbered "amongst the learned madmen." See: Thomas Hobbes, *The Elements of Law, Natural and Politic*, ed. J. C. A. Gaskin (Oxford: Oxford University Press, 2008), chapter 10, paragraph 9, page 63. Future references will take the following form: 10.9, 63.

[96] Thomas Hobbes, *Behemoth, or The Long Parliament*, ed. Paul Seaward (Oxford: Oxford University Press, 2010), dialogue I, page 138. Future references to *Behemoth* will take the following form: I, 138.

appearance of spontaneity, as if they had in that very moment been "dictated by the Spirit of God within them."[97] These performances were so convincing that their content became less important than their source. Hobbes explains, "I thinke that neither the preaching of Fryers nor Monkes nor of Parochiall Priests tended to teach men *what*, but *whom* to beleeue. For the Power of the mighty has no foundation but in the opinion and beleefe of the people"[98] The basis for authority, then, "is not coercion of the body but captivation of the mind."[99] Apocalyptic prophets succeeded because they captivated the imagination, provoked belief, and secured adherence.

For Hobbes, this creates a problem of divided allegiance. Both the prophet and the sovereign appeal to our anxiety about the future. When what they each ask of us is contradictory, the decision about whom to obey could then rest on whose vision of the future is more compelling. As Stephen Holmes explains, "the struggle for sovereignty is fought on a battlefield of wholly unreal imaginings or rationally unjustifiable assumptions about the future. Whoever controls the future (or the idea people have of the future) has unstoppable power."[100] Because they can give us different and more compelling visions of the future than our sovereign, prophets can undermine civil sovereignty by dividing our allegiances.

---

[97] Hobbes, *Behemoth*, I, 139. For Hobbes, the fault here does not lie entirely with self-proclaimed prophets and their cunning uses of rhetoric, but also with fundamental tendencies of human nature. This marks an important shift for Hobbes. In his earlier work, *The Elements of Law*, he crafted a strong opposition between reason and rhetoric and attributed man's outbursts of irrationality to shrewd rhetoricians. "And such is the power of eloquence," explains Hobbes, "as many times a man is made to believe thereby, that he sensibly feeleth smart and damage, when he feeleth none, and to enter into rage and indignation, without any other cause, than what is in the words and passion of the speaker." Hobbes, *Elements*, 28.14, 171. However, by the time Hobbes comes to consider the problem of prophecy in *Leviathan*, the use of rhetoric is not the only, or even the primary, culprit for man's irrationality. The main source of irrationality is the way in which superstitions and magical beliefs work upon predictable features of human psychology. While they can manipulate such beliefs, rhetoricians do not create them. Rather, these beliefs emerge from a basic human fear of the unknown. "Ignorance of naturall causes disposeth a man to Credulity, so as to believe many times impossibilities." This ignorance of natural causes, along with men's failure to remedy it, instills a fear "of what it is that hath the power to do them much good or harm [and they] are inclined to suppose and feign unto themselves several kinds of Powers Invisible; and to stand in awe of their own imaginations." See: Hobbes, *Leviathan*, 11, 160–62. This analysis draws on Johnston, *Rhetoric of Leviathan*, 60–61, 106–08.

[98] Hobbes, *Behemoth*, I, 128. As Stephen Holmes points out, this statement raises important questions about the centrality of rational self-interest and self-preservation in Hobbes's political theory. What is the true foundation of political authority? Holmes: "Human behavior, no matter how self-interested, remains unpredictable because it is guided partly by assessments of the future, assessments that, in turn, result from irrational traits of the mind (naïve trust in prognostications, a gloomy disposition, etc.), not from the calculations of a rational maximizer." See Holmes, introduction, xv.

[99] Holmes, introduction, xi.   [100] Holmes, introduction, xiv.

Hobbes's Scriptural Project

For Hobbes, "the most frequent praetext of Sedition, and Civill Warre, in Christian Common-wealths hath a long time proceeded from a difficulty, not yet sufficiently resolved, of obeying at once, both God, and Man...when their Commandments are one contrary to the other." The claim of the prophet to speak in God's name allies him with the divine and reduces the sovereign to the status of a mere man. This problem is made worse by our inability or unwillingness to question those who claim to speak in God's name. Dazzled by a prophetic vision of the future, men may fail to identify the "many false Prophets...that seek reputation with the people, by phantasticall and false Doctrines; and by such reputation...govern them for their private benefit."[101] Their anxiety about the future and their reverence toward those who claim to speak in God's name leads men astray, away from the proper obedience owed to their sovereign and toward rebellion and civil war.

Hobbes's solution is to identify those who claim to speak in the name of God against the sovereign as "false prophets." In denouncing them in this way, Hobbes aligns himself with a rich Christian apocalyptic tradition of identifying false prophets announcing the imminent end of the known world.[102] Consistent with this tradition, Hobbes demands that we test those who purport to be prophets. Anyone claiming to speak in the name of God is "worthy to be suspected of Ambition and Imposture; and consequently, ought to be examined, and tryed by every man before, hee yeeld them obedience."[103]

Hobbes first asks men to use their reason to assess what the prophet is telling them and whether this should command belief or adherence. To those prophets who claim that God has spoken to them through scripture, Hobbes responds that this is no different than the way God speaks to "all other Christian men." The prophet claiming inspiration from scripture can therefore have no special status or authority. To the prophet claiming divine inspiration through a dream, Hobbes wryly responds: "to say he hath spoken to him in a Dream, is no more then to say he dreamed that God spake to him; which is not of force to win beleef." A prophet who claims to have had waking visions may do so because he has failed to observe "his own slumbering." Similarly, the prophet's claim of supernatural inspiration may merely amount to "an ardent desire to speak, or some strong opinion of himself, for which hee can alledge no naturall and sufficient reason."[104] These grounds for doubting claims of prophetic inspiration give the individual believer a rational basis to question prophetic authority. But they also seem aimed at revealing the gullibility and eliciting the shame of those who may have accepted such authority in the past.

---

[101] Hobbes, *Leviathan*, 43, 928.
[102] Chapters 2 and 3 of Revelation deal with false prophets and a duty of perseverance. Similarly, the "mini-apocalypse" in the book of Matthew warns that "many shall come in my name, saying, I am Christ; and shall deceive many" and "many false prophets shall rise, and shall deceive many" (24: 5, 11). See also: Mark 13:1–37. Unless otherwise noted, the biblical passages in this chapter are from the King James Version.
[103] Hobbes, *Leviathan*, 36, 674.   [104] Hobbes, *Leviathan*, 32, 580.

Not entirely confident in man's capacity to rationally assess prophetic claims, Hobbes offers a more concrete test for identifying false prophets. He argues that scripture provides "two marks, by which together, not asunder, a true Prophet is to be known. One is the doing of miracles; the other is the not teaching any other Religion than that which is already established."[105] In line with the contemporary doctrine of the Church of England, Hobbes declares that miracles no longer happen. They ceased because belief in them was not necessary for salvation after the work of Jesus and scripture was finished. Scripture replaces miracles and recompenses "the want of all other Prophecy; and from which, by wise and learned interpretation, and carefull ratiocination, all rules and precepts necessary to the knowledge of our duty both to God and man, without Enthusiasme, or supernaturall Inspiration, may easily be deduced."[106] The cessation of miracles alone means that no self-proclaimed prophet can meet Hobbes's test, as the two marks of prophethood must both be present.

Nevertheless, Hobbes also addresses the second mark of a prophet – his consistency with established religious doctrine. The responsibility for establishing and defending doctrine rests entirely with the sovereign. Like Moses, the sovereign of a Christian commonwealth is the sole interpreter of God's commands:

[N]o man ought in the interpretation of the Scripture to proceed further than the bounds which are set by their severall Soveraigns. For the Scriptures since God now speaketh in them, are the Mount Sinai; the bounds whereof are the Laws of them that represent Gods Person on Earth. To look upon them, and therein to behold the wondrous works of God, and learn to fear him is allowed; but to interpret them, that is, to pry into what God saith to him whom he appointeth to govern under him, and make themselves Judges whether he govern as God commandeth him, or not, is to transgresse the bounds God hath set us, and to gaze upon God irreverently.[107]

---

[105] Hobbes, *Leviathan*, 32, 582. Hobbes draws these criteria from Deuteronomy 13:1–5: "If there arise among you a prophet, or a dreamer of dreams, and giveth thee a sign or a wonder, And the sign or the wonder come to pass, whereof he spake unto thee, saying, Let us go after other gods, which thou hast not known, and let us serve them; Thou shalt not hearken unto the words of that prophet, or that dreamer of dreams: for the LORD your God proveth you, to know whether ye love the LORD your God with all your heart and with all your soul. Ye shall walk after the LORD your God, and fear him, and keep his commandments, and obey his voice, and ye shall serve him, and cleave unto him. And that prophet, or that dreamer of dreams, shall be put to death; because he hath spoken to turn you away from the LORD your God, which brought you out of the land of Egypt, and redeemed you out of the house of bondage, to thrust thee out of the way which the LORD thy God commanded thee to walk in. So shalt thou put the evil away from the midst of thee."

[106] Hobbes, *Leviathan*, 32, 584. For a discussion of the cessation of miracles as Church of England doctrine and the debates among Protestants about this doctrine, see: Jane Shaw, *Miracles in Enlightenment England* (New Haven: Yale University Press, 2006), 21–50.

[107] Hobbes, *Leviathan*, 40, 744–46. This marks a change from the positions that Hobbes had adopted in *Elements of Law* and *De Cive*. In *Elements*, the church is the authoritative interpreter of scripture: "our faith, that the Scriptures are the word of God, began from the confidence and trust we repose in the church; there can be no doubt but that their interpretation of

Hobbes's Scriptural Project

Thus, those who claim prophetic status while attempting to subvert the religious interpretation established by the sovereign must necessarily be false prophets.

Beyond challenging claims to prophetic authority, Hobbes also attends to the content of the prophecies that animated the radical hopes of the civil war. In the lead-up to the civil war, the doctrine that the pope was Antichrist had gained wide mainstream acceptance. This became a problem for England when Archbishop Laud and his followers initiated reforms seen by many as undoing the work of the Reformation. If the pope and the papacy were Antichrist and the Church of England had become "popish," then the agents of Antichrist must be in England. With the dissolution of censorship and rising religious tensions, "the explosive accusation of antichristianity could be levelled against anything one disliked, so it was necessary to pin [the accusation] down as something politically harmless."[108] This is precisely what Hobbes attempts to do.

He addresses this question in a lengthy chapter of *Leviathan* that responds to the arguments of Cardinal Bellarmine, a prominent defender of the authority of the pope in secular matters. Most of the chapter deals with Bellarmine's individual claims and reasserts and develops Hobbes's argument that ecclesiastical power does not extend to secular matters. However, when he reaches the point in Bellarmine's argument where the cardinal deals with the question of whether the pope is Antichrist, Hobbes becomes more agreeable.[109] "For my part," he explains, "I see no argument that proves he is so, in that sense the Scripture useth the name; nor will I take any argument from the quality of Antichrist, to contradict the Authority he exerciseth, or hath heretofore exercised in the Dominions of any other Prince or State." While Hobbes aggressively defends the jurisdiction of civil sovereigns against papal interference, he will not do so by identifying the pope with Antichrist.

Hobbes then makes an additional move to render Antichrist politically impotent. Appealing to scripture, he claims Antichrist must possess two characteristics: "One, that he denyeth Jesus to be Christ; and another that he professeth himselfe to bee Christ." From these two attributes of Antichrist, a third follows: "he must also be an *Adversary of Iesus the true Christ*, which is another

---

the same Scriptures, when any doubt or controversy shall arise...is safer for any man to trust than his own, whether reason or spirit; that is to say his own opinion." See: *Elements*, 11.10, 69. In *De Cive*, as in *Leviathan*, Hobbes reasons that civil sovereigns have jurisdiction over spiritual and temporal matters. Nonetheless: "As a Christian, therefore, the holder of sovereign power in the commonwealth is obliged to interpret holy scripture." See: Thomas Hobbes, *On the Citizen (De Cive)*, trans. Michael Silverthorne, ed. Richard Tuck (Cambridge: Cambridge University Press, 1998), chapter 17, paragraph 28, page 233. Future references will be given in the following form: 17.28, 223.

[108] Hoekstra, "Disarming the Prophets," 107.
[109] Bellarmine was among a group of Jesuit controversialists attempting to undermine Protestant apocalypticism. See: Christianson, *Reformers and Babylon*, 93–94.

usuall signification of the word Antichrist."[110] Clearly, then, the pope cannot be Antichrist, as he does not claim to be Christ, nor does he deny that Jesus is the Christ. While the pope is illegitimately usurping the power of Christian kings, "he doth it not as Christ, but as *for Christ*, wherein there is nothing of *The Antichrist*."[111] Hobbes's narrowing of the definition of Antichrist does not only exclude the pope. It also excludes Archbishop Laud, the episcopacy of the Church of England, the royalists, and the parliamentarians, none of whom claimed to be Christ or denied that Jesus is the Christ. The requirement that Antichrist claim to be Christ also excludes the non-Christians historically identified as Antichrist, like Muslims or "Turks." Hobbes thus excludes "almost any conceivable Christian or non-Christian" from the category of Antichrist.[112]

The true Antichrist will come at the end of days, "but that tribulation is not yet come." We will know when it does because we will witness "such tribulation as was not [seen] since the beginning of the world," followed by "a darkening of the Sun and Moon, a falling of the Stars, and a concussion of the Heavens, and the glorious coming again of our Saviour in the cloudes."[113] And if we should be in any doubt about this, we must always remember that our sovereign is the only legitimate interpreter of scripture. Thus, as Kinch Hoekstra puts it, the king himself has the authority "to determine whether or not he [himself] is the Antichrist predicted in the New Testament. And one could expect the stars to fall well before he would give an affirmative answer to this question."[114] Hobbes defines the Antichrist out of political existence.[115]

Hobbes's final scriptural response to apocalypticism is an alternative Christian eschatology divested of subversive potential. Two features of this alternative eschatology are particularly important for our analysis here. First, Hobbes tries to undermine claims that we can know that the apocalypse is imminent. Before and during the English Civil War, many apocalyptic prophets had claimed England was experiencing the end of days foretold in Revelation. They gave England's struggles a divine urgency and lent war a sacred legitimacy. Those who might have been unwilling to challenge sovereign power under presumably normal circumstances were enticed to rebellion by a belief that

---

[110] Hobbes, *Leviathan*, 42, 874–76. Emphasis in original. Hobbes bases the first characteristic on a passage from 1 John: "And every spirit that confesseth not that Jesus Christ is come in the flesh, is not of God: and this is the spirit of antichrist" (4:3). He bases the second characteristic on two passages from Matthew: "For many shall come in my name, saying, I am Christ; and shall deceive many" (24:5) and "Then if any man shall say unto you, Lo, here is Christ, there; believe it not" (24:23).

[111] Hobbes, *Leviathan*, 42, 876. Emphasis in original.

[112] Hoekstra, "Disarming the Prophets," 108.   [113] Hobbes, *Leviathan*, 42, 876.

[114] Hoekstra, "Disarming the Prophets," 109.

[115] Hobbes deploys a similar (and perhaps similarly unpersuasive) definitional strategy in his argument for why sovereign power must be absolute. See: George Kateb, "Hobbes and the Irrationality of Politics," *Political Theory* 17, no. 3 (1989): 361.

Hobbes's Scriptural Project

they were participating in a final battle that would be the prelude to a New Jerusalem.

Hobbes responds to this belief in an imminent apocalypse by condemning it as blatantly false. He explains that the "second coming, not yet being, the Kingdome of God is not yet come, and wee are not now under any other Kings by Pact, but our Civill Soveraigns."[116] We will know when the apocalypse starts because the sun and moon will darken and the stars will fall. We cannot hasten or predict the arrival of the last days. Hobbes summarizes the position of Jesus: "My Kingdome is not yet come, nor shall you foreknow when it shall come; for it shall come as a theefe in the night."[117] In short, Hobbes adopts a conservative eschatology like that of Augustine. In colloquial terms, the argument amounts to this: the apocalypse will come, but we can never understand it to be happening here and now.

Hobbes's second move in offering an alternative eschatology is more original but also distinctly unorthodox. Apocalyptic prophets and godly men had power during Hobbes's time not only because they held out the hope for a millennial future but also because they wielded the threat of eternal damnation. Failure to participate in the battles of the last days would ensure one a place in the fiery depths of hell. A menacing threat indeed. For his part, the only viable threat the sovereign can make is to punish disobedience with mortal death. The clear imbalance in the power of these two threats is politically destabilizing. When the dictates of those threatening eternal damnation conflict with the dictates of the sovereign, who can only threaten death, it is clear whose demands will triumph. "For no one can serve two masters, and the one to whom we believe that obedience is due, under fear of damnation, is no less a Master than the one to whom obedience is due through fear of temporal death, but rather more."[118] Indeed, hardly anything could be more damaging to sovereignty than "for citizens to be turned by the threat of eternal torment from obeying their princes."[119]

It is difficult to overestimate the importance of this problem for Hobbes's political argument. The fear of mortal and violent death is the primary passion inclining men to peace and therefore to the acceptance of and obedience to sovereign authority.[120] For Hobbes, this passion is so fundamentally reasonable it can totally excuse those who violate the laws of the sovereign "by the

---

[116] Hobbes, *Leviathan*, 44, 960.
[117] Hobbes, *Leviathan*, 44, 980. Hobbes echoes Paul (1 Thess. 5:2) here.
[118] Hobbes, *De Cive*, 6.11, 80. See also: Hobbes, *Leviathan*, 29, 510–12; Hobbes, *Behemoth*, I, 125. Here, Hobbes echoes the advice of Matthew 10:28: "And fear not them which kill the body, but are not able to kill the soul: but rather fear him which is able to destroy both soul and body in hell."
[119] Hobbes, *De Cive*, 12.5, 135. See also: Hobbes, *Elements*, 25.5, 144; Hobbes, *Leviathan*, 38, 698.
[120] Hobbes, *Leviathan*, 13, 196. The analysis in this paragraph draws on Johnston, *Rhetoric of Leviathan*, 98–101.

terrour of present death...because no Law can oblige a man to abandon his own preservation."[121] Fear of death is therefore the basis of Hobbes's political argument about the grounds and reach of sovereign power and the rights of subjects.

The problem is that death is not the only object of human fear. We also fear "the Power of Spirits Invisible."[122] These religious fears threaten the stability of the commonwealth. When civil and spiritual powers come into conflict, the former will draw more people because the civil authority is "more visible" and stands "in the cleerer light of naturall reason." Yet the spiritual power may still attract "a party sufficient to Trouble, and sometimes to Destroy a Common-wealth" because "the fear of Darknesse, and Ghosts, is greater than other fears."[123] This is a remarkable admission. It calls into question what is often taken to be the motivational basis of Hobbes's account of the power of sovereigns and the obedience of subjects.

In *Elements of Law* and *De Cive*, Hobbes had dealt with this problem of religious fears by arguing that, properly understood, the dictates of faith coincide with those of reason and the requirements of salvation with those of political order. These arguments persist in *Leviathan*.[124] However, perhaps because he was now convinced there were many religious radicals who were unlikely to

---

[121] Hobbes, *Leviathan*, 27, 468.   [122] Hobbes, *Leviathan*, 14, 216.
[123] Hobbes, *Leviathan*, 29, 510.
[124] Hobbes argues, as he had in his earlier works, that God tells us via scripture that salvation requires obedience to natural laws (which, as Hobbes argues in his secular argument, requires obedience to sovereign power) and faith that Jesus is the Christ. See: Hobbes, *Leviathan*, 43, 928–38. Unfortunately, for many readers, this project seems to exhaust the possibilities of what Hobbes was attempting in his scriptural arguments in *Leviathan*. See, for instance: John Rawls, *Lectures on the History of Political Philosophy* (Cambridge: Belknap Press, 2007), 27–28. There is certainly support for this interpretation. Hobbes praises founders and legislators like Numa and Muhammed for having "had a care to make it believed that the same things were displeasing to the gods which were forbidden by the laws." See: Hobbes, *Leviathan*, 12, 176–78. The advantage, then, of such a reading is that it offers coherent reconstruction of important portions of Hobbes's argument. Its disadvantages are that it assumes too narrow, rational, and homogenous an audience for the work and has difficulty accounting for some of Hobbes's most developed scriptural arguments. The attempt to diminish the threat of hell, for instance, is an argument that would seem to assume that there will still be those for whom duties to God conflict with political obligations. The best argumentative strategy here, Hobbes seems to conclude, is not to convince us that our religious and political obligations align, but rather to make hell less threatening – to tip the balance of obedience in favor of our civil sovereigns. It therefore seems reasonable to assume that Hobbes realized that there were good theological arguments and persuasive religious rhetoric available to support the claim that God demands much more from us than obedience to our secular sovereigns and a minimalist faith that Jesus is the Christ. *Leviathan* might best be seen, then, as an attempt to make several discrete arguments and rhetorical maneuvers aimed to make religious belief safe for sovereign power. See also: Lloyd, *Ideals as Interests*, 18–20; Christopher Scott McClure, "Hell and Anxiety in Hobbes's Leviathan," *Review of Politics* 73 (2011): 22–23; Kateb, "Hobbes and the Irrationality of Politics," 368–69; David Johnston, "Hobbes's Mortalism," *History of Political Thought* 10, no. 4 (1989): 647–63.

Hobbes's Scriptural Project

be persuaded, Hobbes now deploys a new strategy. He offers an unorthodox and mortalist account of the Day of Judgment that denies the possibility of a Christian hell and everlasting torment.[125]

According to Hobbes, we will all die a corporeal death. Upon Christ's return to earth, our bodies will be resurrected and we will be judged. The righteous "shall have their bodies suddenly changed, and made spirituall, and Immortall."[126] However, the sinners will not be subjected to eternal torments. Their punishment is simply that they undergo a second death. Hobbes cites those passages of the Bible that refer to unquenchable fire, weeping, and gnashing of teeth, but concludes this pain is metaphorical. It is a metaphor for "a grief, and discontent of mind, from the sight of that Eternall felicity in others, which they themselves through their own incredulity, and disobedience have lost." Upon witnessing the felicity of the elect, each wicked man will suffer a second death "after which hee shall die no more."[127] It is inconceivable, Hobbes adds later, that a merciful God "should punish men's transgressions without any end of time, and with all the extremity of torture, that men can imagine, and more."[128]

This still leaves Hobbes with the challenge of dealing with those parts of the Bible that suggest the fires and torments are everlasting. These miseries are endless, he responds, because there will be a perpetual supply of the damned. The reprobate, "that are in the estate which Adam left them in, shall marry, and be given in marriage; that is, corrupt, and generate successively; which is an Immortality of the Kind, but not of the Persons of men." The damned and their children "are not worthy to be counted amongst them that shall obtain in the next world, and an absolute Resurrection from the dead; but onely a short time, as inmates of that world; and to the end onely to receive condign punishment for their contumacy."

The punishment and torment of a second death will last, "by the succession of sinners thereunto, as long as the kind of Man by propagation shall endure; which is till the end of the world."[129] In short, biblical references to everlasting torments are not meant to suggest that such punishment is everlasting for any particular person, but rather that the generations of the damned will be perpetually replenished. In promising us merely a second death, Hobbes tries to remove the threat of eternal damnation from the arsenal of those who urge us to act against our sovereign in the name of faith.[130]

---

[125] David Johnston argues that Hobbes's resort to a mortalist eschatology is perhaps best understood as a response to the growing sectarianism and religious enthusiasm of the late 1640s. Christopher McClure makes a similar suggestion. See: Johnston, "Hobbes's Mortalism"; McClure, "Hell and Anxiety."
[126] Hobbes, *Leviathan*, 44, 990.   [127] Hobbes, *Leviathan*, 38, 716–18.
[128] Hobbes, *Leviathan*, 44, 990.   [129] Hobbes, *Leviathan*, 44, 994.
[130] In some of its details, Hobbes's argument anticipates those of later thinkers who would, for various reasons, attempt to interpret away the possibility of eternal torment. See: Daniel P.

If Hobbes's eschatology is indeed an alternative argument aimed at those unlikely to accept his attempted reconciliation of faith and political obedience, we have reason to question whether this new strategy is adequate. Even if we grant that his attempt to eliminate hell from the Christian account of the Last Days has been successful and his arguments scripturally sound, at best he has only leveled the playing field between prophets and preachers, on the one hand, and the civil sovereign, on the other. Both are capable of threatening death in exchange for disobedience. Hobbes is thus back in a position which he has consistently tried to avoid – one in which the godly and the sovereign can make equal claims upon us. And given the choice between an ordinary death at the hands of one's sovereign and a second death in the sight of an enthroned and judging Christ and his elect, the former may still be vastly preferable to the latter. If one adds to this the utter hopelessness of the knowledge that, once damned, one will beget children who will likewise be "doomed to perish utterly without help from the God who visibly and humanly reigns over them,"[131] death at the hands of one's sovereign may be a welcome fate.[132]

Walker, *The Decline of Hell: Seventeenth-Century Discussions of Eternal Torment* (Chicago: University of Chicago Press, 1964).

[131] Pocock, "Time, History and Eschatology," 175.

[132] Hobbes himself seems to have realized that the propagation of the damned undermined his attempt to offer a more humane account of hell. The 1668 Latin *Leviathan* omits reference to the reproduction of the damned. Noel Malcolm summarizes the relevant changes: Hobbes abandons his argument about the reproduction of the damned, "with its scandalous implication that the damned would have the pleasure of sexual intercourse in the afterlife. Instead, he found a new way of reconciling the notion of eternal punishment with his principle that the damned would live finite lives: 'eternal' in this biblical context signified only 'until the end of the world' or 'until the end of the age,' meaning the last age of the world. Despite the awkwardness of this maneuver (which seemed to imply that the 'eternal' life of the elect on earth would also be finite), Hobbes clearly felt that he had made a significant improvement to his theory; the relevant passage in Chapter 44 was amended in the Latin accordingly." See: Malcolm, introduction to *Leviathan*, 180. Aloysius P. Martinich suggests that Hobbes's account of the endless regeneration of the damned "was undoubtedly an unfortunate view. What started off as a humane reinterpretation of hellfire went seriously wrong. There is not enough difference between the eternal suffering of some people and the finite but intense suffering of an infinite number of people. Hobbes eventually came to see that his views about eternal flames were not acceptable." See: Martinich, *Hobbes*, 251. Christopher McClure suggests that Hobbes might never have intended his arguments about hell to be fully persuasive. Rather, his goal was simply to "leave citizens with an indeterminate belief [about whether there is a hell] that they would be averse to examining." This interpretation makes good sense of the strangeness of Hobbes's rhetorical maneuvering on the question of hell, but at the cost of investing him with motivations and endowing him with elaborate rhetorical strategies that I'm not convinced he had. McClure, "Hell and Anxiety," 4. George Kateb suggests that Hobbes "could have found a way of squaring civil peace with the usual Christian beliefs about hell and even found a way of squaring civil peace with the usual Christian beliefs about hell and even found advantage in them. That he does not is part of his emancipatory power. He is repelled by the cruelty of eternal punishment and finds it unbelievable and unworthy of belief." Kateb, "Hobbes and the Irrationality of Politics," 368. This reading provides a potentially plausible explanation for Hobbes's rather tortured scriptural interpretation on the question of hell, but demands that we

Hobbes's Secular Apocalypse

The thrust of Hobbes's scriptural arguments is deflationary. Like Augustine, he tries to interpret away the radical message of apocalypse to ensure political stability. Yet Hobbes's attempt to redirect the apocalyptic imaginary extends beyond his scriptural arguments in the last half of *Leviathan*. The work's first half, whose ostensible purpose is to support an argument for absolute political authority with "Principles of Reason," also plays a part in this strategy of redirection.[133]

As I will argue in this section of the chapter, both the imagery and the narrative features of Hobbes's argument resonate with the seventeenth-century apocalyptic imaginary. Hobbes's innovation was to redeploy this antinomian imaginary in the service of sovereign power and civil peace. He does this by offering a captivating vision of a secular apocalypse in which the terror of the state of nature is the narrative prelude to an enduring commonwealth. Hobbes redirects the stunning visual and rhetorical resources of apocalypticism to secure belief in and obedience to the Leviathan state.

This project begins with his account of the state of nature – the condition in which men find themselves in the absence of political authority. Hobbes's familiar description of this condition merits a close examination:

Whatsoever therefore is consequent to a time of Warre, where every man is Enemy to every man; the same is consequent to the time, wherein men live without other security, than what their own strength, and their own invention shall furnish them withall. In such condition, there is no place for Industry; because the fruit thereof is uncertain: and consequently no Culture of the Earth; no Navigation, nor use of the commodities that may be imported by Sea; no commodious Building; no Instruments of moving, and removing such things as require much force; no Knowledge of the face of the Earth; no account of Time; no Arts; no Letters; no Society; and which is worst of all, continuall feare, and danger of violent death; And the life of man, solitary, poore, nasty, brutish, and short.[134]

Like the threatened apocalypse that haunted his life and work, Hobbes's state of nature is a chaotic moment in which all mankind is driven by a "perpetuall and restlesse desire of Power after power, that ceaseth onely in death."[135] It is a violent rupture in the apparent temporal continuity of history – a war in which there is "no account of time." If the biblical apocalypse is the rupture between this world and the eternity of Christ's kingdom, then Hobbes's state of nature

---

accept that Hobbes had an emancipatory project along the lines of a "liberalism of fear." Given Hobbes's comfort with sovereign cruelty, this strikes me as a difficult suggestion to accept. See: Judith Shklar, "The Liberalism of Fear," in *Political Thought and Political Thinkers*, ed. Stanley Hoffmann (Chicago: University of Chicago Press, 1988), 3–20.

[133] Hobbes, *Leviathan*, 30, 522.   [134] Hobbes, *Leviathan*, 13, 192.
[135] Hobbes, *Leviathan*, 11, 150.

is the rupture between the life of a political order that has dissolved and the creation of the Leviathan state.

When he describes this natural condition, Hobbes performs an apocalyptic "uncreation." He calls to mind all of the markers of life in a stable commonwealth only then to annihilate them – "no place for industry," "no navigation," "no commodious living," "no letters, no society." As Mark Houlahan observes, "the stabbing, anaphoric clauses, all predicated from 'there is no,' mime the uncreation they describe. The effect is paradoxical...that which is described and then negated is powerfully present, only to vanish at the behest of the narrative voice."[136] The focus of Hobbes's frightening account is as much on the annihilation of the commonwealth as on the barbarous condition of natural man. The destruction of man's creations amounts to a devastation far worse than mere barbarism.[137]

Hobbes did not need to confine his apocalypse to the imagination. His account of uncreation describes the effects of civil war. He makes this connection clear. In responding to the potential criticism that his description of the state of nature has no foundation in experience, Hobbes responds: "it may be perceived what manner of life there would be, where there were no common Power to feare; by the manner of life, which men that have formerly lived under a peacefull government, use to degenerate into, in a civill Warre."[138]

Hobbes draws the same connection when he describes the dangers of failing to take one's own "Christian Soveraign, for Gods Prophet." Men who fail to do this are liable to be bewitched into rebellion "and by this means destroying all laws, both divine, and humane, reduce all Order, Government, and Society, to the first Chaos of Violence, and Civill warre."[139] Hobbes's account of the English Civil War in *Behemoth* echoes these claims. However, perhaps the most terrifying description of war as a radical form of uncreation is in his 1629 translation of Thucydides' *History of the Peloponnesian War*:

---

[136] Mark Houlahan, "Leviathan (1651): Thomas Hobbes and Protestant Apocalypse," in *1650–1850: Ideas, Aesthetics, and Inquiries in the Early Modern Era*, ed. Kevin L. Cope, vol. 2 (New York: AMS Press, 1996), 104–05.

[137] There are some parallels between Hobbes's description of the state of nature and Thucydides' description of ancient Hellas in the Archaeology, which likewise calls forth the markers of civilized life (settled populations, agriculture, reliable transportation, etc.) only to then stress their absence. As a translator of Thucydides, Hobbes was deeply familiar with this text. It is not unreasonable to think that Thucydides' description might have influenced Hobbes's own, though the parallels are not overwhelmingly strong. See: Thucydides, *The Peloponnesian War*, ed. David Grene, trans. Thomas Hobbes (Chicago: University of Chicago Press, 1989), I.2, 2. See also: George Klosko and Daryl Rice, "Thucydides and Hobbes's State of Nature," *History of Political Thought* 6, no. 3 (1985): 405–09; Malcolm, *Leviathan: Introduction*, 325; Ioannis D. Evrigenis, *Images of Anarchy: The Rhetoric and Science in Hobbes's State of Nature* (New York: Cambridge University Press, 2014), 199–200.

[138] Hobbes, *Leviathan*, 13, 194.   [139] Hobbes, *Leviathan*, 36, 680.

But as this war, it both lasted long, and the harm it did to Greece was such, as like in the like space had never been seen before. For neither had there been so many cities expunged and made desolate, what by the barbarians and what by the Greeks warring against one another...nor so much banishing and slaughter, some by war, some by sedition, as was in this. And those things which concerning former time there went a fame of, but in fact rarely confirmed, were now made credible: as earthquakes, general to the greatest part of the world, and most violent withal: eclipses of the sun, oftener than is reported of any former time: great droughts in some places, and thereby famine: and that which did none of the least hurt, but destroyed also its past, the plague. All these evils entered together with this war.[140]

Hobbes's translation gives this account of the world-annihilating catastrophe of war a vividness that is rarely matched. His knowledge of Thucydides provided him with a rhetorical and visual vocabulary with which to both imagine and describe an apocalyptic moment of uncreation.

Yet from the ashes of the annihilated commonwealth the people create the Leviathan state, an absolute political authority that promises to prevent a relapse into apocalyptic chaos. There are at least two ways to understand the figure of the Leviathan in light of Hobbes's apocalyptic account of the state of nature. The first is to see this figure as an entity capable of restraining or holding back apocalyptic violence. The second is to see the Leviathan state as the fulfillment of Hobbes's apocalypse, or the secular equivalent of the Kingdom of Christ. I will explore each of these alternatives in turn.

Following insights first made by Carl Schmitt, some scholars have argued that Hobbes's Leviathan is a secularized *katéchon* – a figure that restrains the Antichrist and holds back the apocalypse.[141] As we saw in Chapter 2, the scriptural basis for the *katéchon* is in Paul's second letter to the Thessalonians.[142] In his first letter, Paul had emphasized that Christ's return to the world would be imminent, sudden, and unexpected, "like a thief in the night."[143] Paul's second letter implies that some Thessalonians thought the end had come, leading to disorder in the community. Paul assures them that the final days are not yet at hand. Christ's return will be preceded by events that have not yet happened. Jesus will come only after there has been a "falling away" during which the

---

[140] Thucydides, *Peloponnesian War*, I.23, 14. See also: Houlahan, "Hobbes and the Protestant Apocalypse," 102–03.

[141] Wolfgang Palaver, "Hobbes and the *Katéchon*: The Secularization of Sacrificial Christianity," *Contagion: Journal of Violence, Mimesis, and Culture* 2, no. 1 (1995): 57–74; Jürgen Moltmann, "Covenant or Leviathan? Political Theology for Modern Times," *Scottish Journal of Theology* 47, no. 1 (1994): 30; Tracy B. Strong, "Forward: Carl Schmitt and Thomas Hobbes: Myth and Politics," in Carl Schmitt, *The Leviathan in the State Theory of Thomas Hobbes: Meaning and Failure of a Political Symbol*, trans. George Schwab and Erna Hilfstein (Chicago: University of Chicago Press, 2008), xxiii–xxvi.

[142] Biblical scholars debate whether Paul was the author of 2 Thessalonians. As was the case in our analysis in Chapter 2, the debate over authorship is not particularly important. The letter forms part of a Pauline tradition of political thought/political theology.

[143] 1 Thess. 5:2.

"lawless one" will reveal himself by sitting in the temple of God and "declaring himself to be God."[144] As Paul writes, the "lawless one" is currently restrained: "And you know what is now restraining him, so that he may be revealed when his time comes."[145] Paul continues: "The mystery of lawlessness is already at work, but only until the one who now restrains it is removed. And then the lawless one will be revealed, whom the Lord Jesus will destroy with the breath of his mouth, annihilating him by the manifestation of his coming."[146] The Greek word for the "one who restrains" is *katéchon*, or restrainer. If we take the "man of sin" to be Antichrist, then the *katéchon* is the force restraining Antichrist and, by extension, the arrival of the apocalypse.

Historically, the restrainer was identified with imperial power. For instance, Christian theologians Hippolytus (170–263) and Tertullian (160–220) identified the *katéchon* with the Roman Empire. These identifications appealed to Schmitt, who sympathized with what he took to be Hobbes's attempt to restrain the apocalyptic promise and antinomian danger of Christianity. For Schmitt, the Leviathan state and its sovereign representative perform the same function as Paul's mysterious restrainer.

In an idiosyncratic comparison, Schmitt likens the Leviathan to Dostoevsky's Grand Inquisitor, who arrests the returned Jesus for threatening the stability that has been achieved by offering men happiness in exchange for freedom. Both the Leviathan and the Grand Inquisitor seek to prevent the radical disorder of the Second Coming without doing away with Christianity altogether. Thus, for Schmitt:

Hobbes articulated and provided scientific reason for what the Grand Inquisitor did: to make the effect of Christ harmless in the social and political sphere; to de-anarchize Christianity but to leave it at the same time some kind of legitimating effect in the background and in any case not to do without it. A clever tactician gives up nothing, at least as long as it is not totally useless. Christianity was not yet spent. Therefore, we may ask ourselves: who is closer to Dostoevsky's Grand Inquisitor: the Roman Church or Thomas Hobbes's sovereign?[147]

The Leviathan does not merely restrain the forces of chaos. It also holds back the arrival of Christ on earth.[148] The radical apocalyptic imaginary is a destabilizing force that must be kept in check by sovereign power. If it were loosed, we would revert to primordial chaos.

As we have already seen, Hobbes gives some support for this interpretation, particularly if we accept the connections between anarchy, civil war, and the apocalypse. For Hobbes, the civil war was anarchic in part because of the proliferation of private interpretation and judgment. Private judgments about the

---

[144] 2 Thess. 2:3–8.   [145] 2 Thess. 2:6.
[146] 2 Thess. 2:7–8. I've used the American Standard Version for this passage.
[147] Carl Schmitt, *Glossarium. Aufzeichnungen der Jahre 1947–1951*, as quoted and translated in Palaver, "Hobbes and the *Katéchon*," 67–68.
[148] Palaver, "Hobbes and the *Katéchon*," 68.

Hobbes's Secular Apocalypse

nature of justice and injustice, and good and evil proliferated. In the state of nature, "nothing can be Unjust. The notions of Right and Wrong, Justice and Injustice have there no place. Where there is no common Power, there is no Law: Where no Law, no Injustice. Force, and Fraud, are in warre the two Cardinall vertues."[149] The sovereign puts an end to this moral and semantic anarchy by stabilizing values and language through positive law.[150] Hobbes also locates the roots of England's civil war in a proliferation of private interpretations of scripture. When the Bible was translated into the vernacular, anyone could interpret the potentially radical message of Jesus.[151] This is why Hobbes gives the sovereign the sole authority to interpret scripture.

Finally, Hobbes sees turbulent potential in claims to prophetic inspiration. This problem had become so acute in his own time "that the number of Apostates from natural reason is almost become infinite." The opinion that faith comes from inspiration "began with crazy men, who gote themselves a store of sacred words from reading scripture, and have developed the habit of stringing them together as they preach in such a way that what they say is meaningless, but seems divine to the ignorant; when a man has no rational capacity but his speech appears divine, he will inevitably be thought divinely inspired."[152] To thwart the potentially dangerous effects of this enthusiasm, Hobbes demands that we accept our sovereign as our only prophet.[153] In all of these ways, Hobbes's state and its sovereign representative restrain the anarchic power of apocalyptic Christianity.

However, while I think Schmitt's interpretation is compelling, it misses the way in which the Leviathan *must participate in a secular apocalypse to hold back its Christian counterpart.* Focused so squarely on the anarchic character of the state of nature, the Schmittian reading neglects the ways in which the apocalyptic violence of the state of nature or civil war is the narrative prelude to a secular millennial kingdom. The experience of the horrors of the state of nature (or civil war) drives individuals to subject themselves to an absolute political authority.[154]

---

[149] Hobbes, *Leviathan*, 13, 196.
[150] For a thorough analysis of Hobbes's account of why the state of nature is a state of war and how sovereign authority is supposed to solve this problem, see: Arash Abizadeh, "Hobbes on the Causes of War: A Disagreement Theory," *American Political Science Review* 105, no. 2 (2011): 298–315.
[151] Hobbes, *Behemoth*, I, 135.   [152] Hobbes, *De Cive*, 12.6, 136.
[153] Hobbes, *Leviathan*, 36, 678–80.
[154] There may be grounds for seeing the state of nature not only as a narrative prelude but also as a temporal prerequisite to the Leviathan state. As several interpreters have pointed out, the state of nature seems to perform an educative function, making the fear of violent death especially salient (especially in relation to the fear of "things invisible" or the life-endangering desires for honor and glory). What is worst about the state of nature – "the continuall feare, and danger of violent death" is also what is most productive about it. It's the fear of death that drives us to create and submit to a Leviathan state. Similarly, Hobbes thinks that the English Civil War

As much as Hobbes's political theory aims to offer a stable solution to the problem of anarchy, his political eschatology invests the state of nature with a productive role, though perhaps one that can only be grasped retrospectively when the worst of the violence is behind us. Amidst its profound terrors, the state of nature, like the biblical apocalypse, is an enticing opportunity for an act of political creativity – the construction of an enduring commonwealth from the emptiness of apocalyptic anarchy. Hobbes's secular political argument has an apocalyptic plot.

The state that emerges is a secular mirror image of the Kingdom of Christ. To be sure, there is an important difference between the secular and sacred kingdoms. The secular state must take men as they are, rather than "as they should be."[155] Subjects of the Leviathan state are fearful, vainglorious, and sinful, while those in Christ's millennial kingdom have been saved and secured from sin. While the secular state is governed by enforceable laws, Christ's kingdom has no need for law.[156]

Nevertheless, there are striking similarities between Hobbes's accounts of the secular and sacred kingdoms. Both emerge from a battle with the forces of chaos. The Leviathan state puts an end to the moral and semantic disorder of the state of nature, while Christ/God wins a final victory against primordial anarchy. The resultant kingdoms both have a single locus of political power. In the millennial kingdom, Christ rules both in his spiritual and political capacities. Hobbes is clear that Christ's kingdom, like the Jewish Kingdom of God that existed before it, will be a civil kingdom on earth. The first Kingdom of God, created by a covenant between the people of Israel and God, was "cast off in the election of Saul" and will be restored and ultimately superseded by Christ at the Day of Judgment.[157] Political authority in both the secular and sacred kingdoms is absolute. In the secular kingdom, the sovereign acts as the sole

---

"instructed" Englishmen that the only stable solution to the problem of anarchy requires unified sovereignty. See: Hobbes, *Leviathan*, 13, 192; 18, 278. Leo Strauss describes the educative experience of an unforeseen encounter with violent death as a conversionary experience that wakes man from "the dream of the happiness of triumph, of a glittering, imposing, apparent good." Such a confrontation is, on Strauss' account, "the ideal for self-knowledge." See: Strauss, *Political Philosophy of Hobbes*, 19; Peter J. Ahrensdorf, "The Fear of Death and the Longing for Immortality: Hobbes and Thucydides on Human Nature and the Problem of Anarchy," *The American Political Science Review* 94, no. 3 (2000): 579–93.

[155] Hobbes makes this distinction in his assessment of why the Jewish Kingdom of God was unsuccessful. "For God truly reigns where the laws are obeyed for fear of God, not of men. And if men were as they should be, that would be the best form of commonwealth. But to rule men as they are, there must be power (which comprises both right and strength) to compel." See: Hobbes, *De Cive*, 16.15, 198. The analysis in these two paragraphs draws on Joel Schwartz, "Hobbes and the Two Kingdoms of God," *Polity* 18, no. 1 (1985): 7–24. See also: Nelson, *The Hebrew Republic*, 21–26, 53–56; Meirav Jones, "'My Highest Priority Was to Absolve the Divine Laws': The Theory and Politics of Hobbes's *Leviathan* in a War of Religion," *Political Studies* 65, no. 1 (2016): 248–63.

[156] Hobbes, *De Cive*, 17.8, 212.   [157] Hobbes, *Leviathan*, 35, 644.

Hobbes's Secular Apocalypse

judge.[158] Similarly, Christ acts as the sole judge in his sacred kingdom, passing judgment on all of humanity in a ritual that fuses absolute grace with absolute power. He "shall judge the world, and conquer his Adversaries, and make a Spirituall Common-wealth."[159]

Both the secular and sacred sovereigns bestow salvation. Christ grants immortality to the faithful by transforming their natural and mortal bodies into spiritual and immortal bodies.[160] For Hobbes, this transformation from mortal to immortal bodies is the essence of salvation. He reasons: "because man was created in a condition immortal, not subject to corruption...and fell from that happiness by the sin of Adam, it followeth that to be saved from sin is to be saved from all the evil and calamities that sin hath brought upon us. And therefore, in the Holy Scripture remission of sin, and salvation from death and misery, is the same thing."[161] Through the sin of Adam humanity lost its immortality. The act of salvation is therefore the restoration of immortality to the saved.

While the Leviathan state cannot save men from eventual death or offer redemption from sin, it creates and enforces laws that protect men from the senseless, premature, and violent deaths in the state of nature. Christ, by contrast, cannot offer any kind of redemption or salvation here and now because he will not be an earthly sovereign until the Second Coming. In this world, the Leviathan state is our only savior. The value of this worldly salvation should not be underestimated. As Aloysius P. Martinich explains, "since 'life' and 'death' are meant literally when Hobbes applies them in both his political and religious discussions, salvation here and now is every bit as precious to humans as salvation at the Second Coming will be then."[162]

The analogy between Hobbes's account of Christ's kingdom and that of the secular state goes beyond the text of *Leviathan*. In an admittedly speculative move, I suggest that the Leviathan represented in Hobbes's famous frontispiece (see Figure 4.1) has distinctly Christic features.[163] The upper panel of the

---

[158] Hobbes, *Leviathan*, 18, 270.   [159] Hobbes, *Leviathan*, 42, 918.
[160] Hobbes, *Leviathan*, 42, 918.   [161] Hobbes, *Leviathan*, 38, 720.
[162] Martinich, *Two Gods of* Leviathan, 272.
[163] There are two frontispieces of *Leviathan* – the more familiar engraved image in the 1651 printed edition of the work (the one on which I focus here) and the hand-drawn image in the manuscript copy. Geoffrey Vaughan summarizes the differences between the two as follows: "In the printed version the people making up the body of *Leviathan* are shown almost in full and all have their eyes fixed upon the face of the mortal god. In the penned version the body of *Leviathan* is made of faces looking out in the same direction as the head. There are also some differences in the face of *Leviathan* between the two copies...and a quotation from Job is inserted into the printed version. Some minor discrepancies exist within the landscapes and among the buildings of the city in the foreground. The general impression however, is very much the same." See: Geoffrey Vaughan, "The Audience of *Leviathan* and the Audience of Hobbes's Political Philosophy," *History of Political Thought* 22, no. 3 (2001): 466. Despite the similarity in the "general impression," it is worth emphasizing the importance of the orientations of the people who make up the Leviathan's body. Keith Brown, who has offered one of

FIGURE 4.1. Frontispiece of *Leviathan*, "Head" edition, 1651. Courtesy of the British Museum.

frontispiece depicts a large crowned figure that appears to be emerging from the sea. Bathed in sunlight, the figure holds a sword in his right hand and a crosier in his left. These items are not placed in opposition to one another, "but are pointed in such a way that they would converge above Leviathan's head if they were extended."[164] His body consists of numerous smaller people who are all looking toward the head of this "mortal god." At least a few of these people are kneeling in a gesture of submission. The figure dominates an orderly landscape dotted with fields, churches, and neat rows of houses.

The lower panel of the frontispiece depicts opposed images of secular and ecclesiastical authority. Looking from left to right and top to bottom, these are: a fortification and a cathedral; a coronet and a miter; a cannon (disturbingly pointed at the word "commonwealth" in the work's title) and a thunderbolt (perhaps the thunderbolt of excommunication); the pointed weapons of war and the pointed weapons of scholastic disputation; and a raging battle and a disputation among schoolmen.[165] While scholars disagree about how to interpret the frontispiece, most acknowledge that it conveys the general thrust of Hobbes's political argument, especially those parts that deal with the fusion of secular and religious authority. To the extent that such a fusion is successful, the conflictual opposition of political and religious authority is suppressed, as it is figuratively in the frontispiece.[166]

The most pronounced scholarly disagreements are about the Leviathan's face. Scholars have guessed it is meant to resemble Charles I, Oliver Cromwell, Charles II, or even Hobbes himself.[167] Given that the image represents the fusion of secular and religious authority, is it not also possible that the figure of Leviathan has something of the bearing and manner of Christ?[168] As Martinich suggests, "the size of Leviathan is consonant with a divine figure. His two outstretched arms indicate both divine, or quasi-divine, judicial judgment and

the most detailed analyses of the frontispiece image, suggests that the manuscript version in which the people are looking outwards seems "much better to express the more traditional view...that in his book Hobbes is trying to get as close as possible to asserting that what is done by the sovereign in his official capacity is, quite literally, also done by his subjects." See: Keith Brown, "Thomas Hobbes and the Title-Page of *Leviathan*," *Philosophy* 55, no. 213 (1980): 411. See also: Keith Brown, "The Artist of the *Leviathan* Title Page," *The British Library Journal* 4, no. 1 (1978): 24–36. Given that the manuscript frontispiece predates the 1651 printed frontispiece, Brown and others argue that the earlier version of the image was likely the one over which Hobbes himself had the most input.

[164] Martinich, *Two Gods of* Leviathan, 363.

[165] My description and characterization of this imagery draw most from Skinner, *Hobbes and Republican Liberty*, 190–96. See also: Martinich, *Two Gods of* Leviathan, 364–66; Vaughan, "Audience of *Leviathan*," 466.

[166] Skinner, *Hobbes and Republican Liberty*, 198.

[167] For reviews and evaluations of these possibilities, see: Martinich, *Two Gods of* Leviathan, 362–63; Vaughan, "Audience of *Leviathan*," 467–69; Maurice M. Goldsmith, "Hobbes's Ambiguous Politics," *History of Political Thought* 11, no. 4 (1990): 639–73.

[168] To be sure, the frontispiece image is overdetermined and likely contains a myriad of visual references. My suggestion here is simply that one of those references might be Christic.

universal jurisdiction." The Leviathan assumes an open-armed pose like that of Christ in many Renaissance and Baroque paintings.[169] Like images of Christ at the final judgment, the Leviathan state is a glorious giant figure, backlit, and towering over a scene that is bathed in sunlight.[170] My suggestion is not that the image of Leviathan is meant to be a *representation* of Christ, but rather that the figure partakes of both the secular and the Christic.

Hobbes himself thought that his own sovereign representative, Charles I, was a Christ-like figure:

> For in a Discourse of our present civill warre, what could seem more impertinent, than to ask (as one did) what was the value of a Roman Penny? Yet the Cohaerence to me was manifest enough. For the Thought of the warre, introduced the Thought of the delivering up the King to his Enemies; The Thought of that, brought in the Thought of the delivering up of Christ; and that again the Thought of the 30 pence, which was the price of that treason.[171]

And, as we have seen, there are close connections for Hobbes between the secular kingdom and the kingdom of Christ – both emerge from apocalyptic terror and offer a kind of salvation. The figure that looms over the landscape of the frontispiece will, like Christ, preside over an earthly kingdom of peace. Hobbes holds out the hope that this secular commonwealth, like the millennial Kingdom of Christ, will be "everlasting."[172]

There is another way in which the apocalyptic anarchy of the state of nature is the narrative prelude for the enduring peace of the Leviathan state. Terrifying representations of the state of nature are a way to cultivate a salutary fear of violent death. In order for the Leviathan state to provide a stable solution to the problems of the state of nature and civil war, its sovereign representative must use coercive power and punishment to "bridle mens ambition, avarice, anger, and other Passions."[173] The effectiveness of the Leviathan state in securing peace through obedience depends crucially, then, on the primacy of our fear of violent mortal death.[174] However, by the time he wrote *Leviathan*, Hobbes was not at all confident we could depend on this fear to emerge naturally or to override other fears and desires. As we have seen, while he seems to want to

---

[169] Martinich, *Two Gods of* Leviathan, 363. This pose is comparatively uncommon in representations of sovereign and state authority in images from the same period.

[170] Here I diverge from Skinner's contention about the frontispiece that "there is no suggestion in Hobbes's scheme of things that the power of our rulers may be divine in origin or character." While there is certainly no suggestion in the frontispiece or the pieces of Hobbes's argument that it so powerful renders in visual form that our rulers are of divine origin, it seems premature to rule out the possibility that the image of the state may partake of the divine in other ways – particularly in the kind of spontaneous, submissive awe that it (like Christ) must inspire. See: Skinner, *Hobbes and Republican Liberty*, 191.

[171] Hobbes, *Leviathan*, 3, 40.   [172] Hobbes, *Leviathan*, 30, 522.

[173] Hobbes, *Leviathan*, 14, 210.

[174] Johnston, *Rhetoric of* Leviathan, 120–21; Ahrensdorf, "Fear of Death," 580–87; Collins, *Allegiance of Thomas Hobbes*, 51.

suggest that the fear of death is our most basic and reliable fear, Hobbes worries that "the feare of Darknesse, and Ghosts, is greater than other fears."[175]

If successful, Hobbes's deflationary account of the final judgment and hell would go some way to diminishing our fears of "things invisible." However, our earlier analysis gives some reasons to doubt his success on this score. To make matters worse, not only might the Leviathan state have to contend with subjects whose souls have not been soothed by a comforting revisionist eschatology, it will also have to deal with those willing to risk their lives for the sake of honor or glory. No matter how costly the Leviathan state makes disobedience, there will always be some willing to bear these costs.[176] What is more, the number of such risk-acceptant subjects will tend to increase the longer the peace and security of the Leviathan state endures. For, as Hobbes points out, the subjects most willing to "compete for honours and reputation" are those "who are least distracted by worry about ordinary necessities."[177] Freed from persistent threats of violent mortal death and made comfortable by an effective regime of enforceable law, men's concern with honor and reputation becomes comparatively more powerful. Hobbes gives us little reason to think that the relative salience of transcendent and spiritual interests would not gather similar strength over time.

Several interpreters have emphasized the roles of enlightened education, cultural transformation, and the rationalization and redescription of transcendent interests in Hobbes's strategy for diminishing the political force of these motivational threats.[178] It seems reasonable to conclude that if such strategies are to succeed, they must be complemented by an effort to inflame the fear of violent mortal death that is always at risk of being weakened in a prosperous and secure state.[179] One way in which this might be done is by rhetorically staging the apocalyptic horrors of the state of nature and civil war. If Hobbes intended *Leviathan* to be read and used by sovereigns and taught in universities in order that "Preachers, and the Gentry" might be equipped to "sprinkle" its civil and moral doctrine "upon the People," it seems plausible that he saw the work not only as a source of arguments that might be redeployed but also as a rhetorical example of how to redirect the apocalyptic imaginary.[180] Hobbes's own

---

[175] Hobbes, *Leviathan*, 29, 510.
[176] Hobbes, *Leviathan*, 15, 234; Hobbes, *De Cive*, 3.12, 49; Hobbes, *Elements of Law*, 16.11, 92. See also: Lloyd, *Ideals as Interests*, 36–47 and Ahrensdorf, "Fear of Death," 580–83 for two different versions of this argument, focused on transcendental ideals and passions, respectively.
[177] Hobbes, *De Cive*, 12.10, 138. See also: Hobbes, *Leviathan*, 17, 260; Ahrensdorf, "Fear of Death," 581–82; Julie E. Cooper, *Secular Powers: Humility in Modern Political Thought* (Chicago: University of Chicago Press, 2013), 46–63.
[178] Johnston, *Rhetoric of* Leviathan; Lloyd, *Ideals as Interests*.
[179] For an extended version of this sort of argument, see Ahrensdorf, "Fear of Death," 580–87. See also: Cooper, *Secular Powers*, 63.
[180] Hobbes, *Leviathan*, RC, 1140. For evidence that Hobbes intended the work to be read for current or potential sovereigns, see: Hobbes, *Leviathan*, introduction, 20; 31, 574. For a useful evaluative summary of several of the main positions in the debate about the audience of

terrifying description of the state of nature might serve as a model for harnessing the apocalyptic imaginary to elicit the salutary fear required to secure obedience and maintain the commonwealth.[181] In sum, while Hobbes's state holds back the anarchic possibility of the Christian apocalypse, it does this by emerging from and then imaginatively sustaining a secular apocalypse.

Conclusion

I have argued that Hobbes, like Machiavelli, developed his political thought in an environment marked by widespread fears and hopes about the end of the world. Unlike Machiavelli, Hobbes does not reject the apocalyptic imaginary and embrace a tragic sensibility. Rather, he redirects the imaginary, fighting apocalypse *with apocalypse*. In his scriptural argument, he undermines apocalyptic prophecies and offers a deflationary Christian eschatology aimed at returning the apocalypse safely into sovereign hands.

He complements this scriptural strategy with a secular political argument that uses the temporal, visual, and rhetorical features of apocalypticism. The account I have offered here differs from those that approach Hobbes's political argument as an abstract and rational account of how free and equal individuals might come to be legitimately subject to political authority.[182] Despite their obvious and familiar virtues, such readings fail to account for the ways in which Hobbes's argument relies not only on the persuasive force of deductive and geometric reasoning but also on the power of apocalyptic narratives and imagery.

Leviathan as well as an argument that Hobbes hoped that his *doctrines* (if not the book itself) would reach the widest possible audience, see: Vaughan, "The Audience of *Leviathan*."

[181] I owe the term "salutary fear" to Peter Ahrensdorf who, one presumes, owes it Alexis de Tocqueville. See: Ahrensorf, "Fear of Death," 587. This line of argument is directly at odds with the suggestion made by Richard Tuck that "Hobbes wished to relieve men of their fears ... The basic fear of death cannot be eliminated; but by transferring our judgement to the sovereign, we are relieved of the responsibility of thinking about it." See: Richard Tuck, "The Civil Religion of Thomas Hobbes," in *Political Discourse in Early Modern Britain*, ed. Nicholas Philipson and Quentin Skinner (Cambridge: Cambridge University Press, 1993), 131–32. I find this a rather odd suggestion. To be sure, part of what is so terrible about the state of nature is the persistence not only of the threat of violent death but also the perpetual fear and anxiety about its possibility. However, Hobbes's Leviathan state can only secure obedience and "conforme the wills" of subjects to peace through the "terror" that is inspired by its "Power and Strength." See: Hobbes, *Leviathan*, 17, 260. Even if we grant that Hobbes did want to "relieve men of their fears," his intention (or hope) and what his arguments about the foundations of political order commit him to may well be quite different. I am far more concerned with the latter than with the former.

[182] Rawls, *Lectures on the History of Political Philosophy*, 23–102; Jean Hampton, *Hobbes and the Social Contract Tradition* (Cambridge: Cambridge University Press, 1986); David P. Gauthier, *The Logic of Leviathan: The Moral and Political Theory of Thomas Hobbes* (Oxford: Oxford University Press, 1969).

Conclusion

This reading of Hobbes has several implications for his identification as a political realist. First, as is the case with Machiavelli, Hobbes's realism is deeply contextual. *Leviathan* is often taken to be Hobbes's most politically realist work. Its pessimistic account of human nature, its commitment to a scientific (though certainly not empirical) approach to understanding the political world as it is, its focus on order as "the first political question,"[183] and its attention to the centrality of power all seem to support this reading. It is important, however, that these commitments are inflected and shaped by a civil war rife with apocalypticism. Only by considering these features of Hobbes's context can we understand why half of *Leviathan* is devoted to the assessment of scriptural arguments. This engagement with scripture suggests that Hobbes is a more interesting and complex realist than the familiar caricatures of him suggest. He recognizes that power has both material and imaginative foundations. For the project of a peaceful political order to succeed, the state must monopolize coercive violence and conquer the "invisible" power of religious belief.

Second, the analysis in this chapter suggests there is a formative project at the root of Hobbes's realism. His pessimistic account of man as self-interested, egoistic, and fearful of death is challenged by the hold that the apocalyptic imaginary and other "powers invisible" held over the minds of many of Hobbes's contemporaries. At numerous points in *Leviathan*, Hobbes worries that the influence of prophets and preachers may engender a belief in rewards greater than life and punishments worse than death. He admits that the fear of violent death cannot always be trusted to emerge on its own as our strongest and most dependable source of motivation. The task of *Leviathan*, then, is not to describe men as they are but to offer both a vision of what they should be and a strategy for cultivating politically salutary motivations. Only egoistic, self-interested men who fear violent death will be fit to obey their sovereign. Hobbes does not *assume* the existence of such men. He aims to *create* them.[184]

Finally, Hobbes's engagement with the apocalyptic imaginary suggests that there may be a rhetorically pragmatic character to his realism. He recognizes that the apocalyptic imaginary captivates people, often preventing them from being the kinds of egoistic, self-interested beings that can be reliably subjected to sovereign power. Instead of rejecting the apocalyptic imaginary, as Machiavelli does, Hobbes redirects it. In fighting apocalypse *with apocalypse*, he uses their own tools against religious and political radicals. Both the imagery and the narrative structure of his secular political argument appropriate elements of the seventeenth-century English apocalyptic imaginary. Understood in this way, the philosophical argument of *Leviathan* is not merely an abstract account of the normative basis of political authority meant to persuade through careful

---

[183] Bernard Williams, *In the Beginning Was the Deed: Realism and Moralism in Political Argument*, ed. Geoffrey Hawthorn (Princeton: Princeton University Press, 2005), 1–17.

[184] Michael Williams puts the point similarly (though to somewhat different ends) in Williams, *Realist Tradition*, 14.

deductive and geometric reasoning. It is also an attempt to subvert apocalypticism from within by appropriating its imagery and narrative structure to secure political obedience.

Yet there are important questions about the degree to which such a strategy can be depended upon to combat the antinomian potential of the apocalyptic imaginary. After all, the experience of Hobbes's own time suggests that the apocalyptic imaginary consistently escapes efforts at sovereign control. More importantly for the development of Hobbes's thought, his redirection of the apocalyptic imaginary coincides with his clearest departure from the realist commitment to take man as one finds him. Instead, Hobbes offers the utopian promise that humanity may be transformed and saved through an encounter with a monstrous Leviathan state capable of eliciting the kinds of salutary fears required for an enduring earthly peace.[185] In fighting the apocalypse with apocalypse, then, Hobbes embraces one of its most radical hopes. In the next chapter, I argue that Hans Morgenthau's response to the possibility of nuclear apocalypse presents a similar dilemma in sharper terms.

---

[185] For an argument (though along somewhat different lines) for the utopianism of Leviathan and the formative project demanded by its doctrines, see: Richard Tuck, "The Utopianism of Leviathan," in *Leviathan After 350 Years*, ed. Tom Sorell and Luc Foisneau (Oxford: Clarendon Press, 2004), 125–38.

5

Morgenthau and the Postwar Apocalypse

Introduction

On January 8, 1918, ten months before the end of World War I, President Woodrow Wilson made an eschatological promise to Americans and the world. This war would be the "final and culminating war for human liberty."[1] He had already told Americans that they would be put to the test in a battle to make "the world safe for democracy." A new world would be born not of slow and progressive change, but of "fiery trial and sacrifice" in "the most terrible and disastrous of all wars" – a war for "civilization itself."[2] In imagining World War I in these terms, Wilson cast it as a violent rupture in history, the terrible but necessary prelude to a new world order. Given the staggering number of casualties and the horrors of trench warfare and poison gas, this apocalyptic narrative might have comforted those looking for some purpose and promise in a war that seemed absurd.

But even before the memories of gangrene, gas clouds, and corpses rotting in no-man's-land could fade, the world was witnessing a second war, and one that would fundamentally transform the twentieth-century apocalyptic imaginary. The numbers alone seem to take on apocalyptic proportions: over 60 million total deaths, including 6 million European Jews and millions of others killed in the Nazi genocide, and final death tolls of 135,000 and 50,000 in Hiroshima and Nagasaki, respectively. Yet it is the images, rather than the numbers, that would come to dominate collective visions of the end times –

---

[1] Woodrow Wilson, "Address to a Joint Session of Congress on the Conditions of Peace," The American Presidency Project, January 8, 1918, www.presidency.ucsb.edu/ws/?pid=65405.

[2] Woodrow Wilson, "Woodrow Wilson: Address to a Joint Session of Congress Requesting a Declaration of War Against Germany," The American Presidency Project, April 2, 1917, www.presidency.ucsb.edu/ws/index.php?pid=65366&st=&st1=.

Hitler's rallies, the mass graves at Auschwitz, and the atomic bomb clouds over Japan.

As a German Jew who left his country in 1932 and emigrated to the United States in time to witness the birth of the nuclear age, Hans Morgenthau struggled to envision the prospects for order and survival in a world in which the apocalypse loomed not only as an imminent future but as an experience that had been *lived* in the concentration camps and the burning remains of annihilated cities. His political realism was shaped, then, by a context that initially seems radically different from the Christian apocalyptic movements to which Machiavelli and Hobbes were responding. I will argue, however, that the ways in which the great upheavals of the twentieth century were imagined share some of the narrative features, imagery, and mood of the religious apocalypticism of the Italian Renaissance and the English Civil War. From the Nazi belief in a millennial Reich to the redemptive hopes that nuclear war could usher in a new world of peace and prosperity, the Judeo-Christian apocalypse insinuated itself into the seemingly secular ideas and images of the twentieth century.

Morgenthau's postwar work is centrally concerned with the dangers of this secularized apocalypticism. From the late 1940s to the early 1960s, he takes aim at the eschatological hopes of contemporary political religions. While the memory of Nazism looms large during this period, Morgenthau's primary target is liberal internationalism. In its most aggressive form, this secular religion sees a decisive battle against the forces of tyranny as the prerequisite for a permanent democratic peace. Morgenthau's response to liberal apocalypticism is to reject it. Like Machiavelli, he opposes the apocalyptic longing for the violent birth of a new world with a tragic insistence on the inescapable and undecided struggle of politics.

However, in the early 1960s, in the shadow of the terrifying prospect of thermonuclear war, Morgenthau turns away from tragedy and adopts the Hobbesian strategy of redirection, fighting apocalypse *with apocalypse*. Against dangerously optimistic scenarios of nuclear war, he gives us a terrifying account of an apocalypse without worldly redemption. Faced with the novel threat of global annihilation, he concludes that tragedy is not enough. We must constantly imagine the apocalypse in order to prevent it.

This chapter proceeds in three parts. First, I sketch the contours of the postwar apocalyptic imaginary, with a focus on the ways in which elements of the Judeo-Christian apocalypse were secularized in the narratives and images of Nazism, the Holocaust, and nuclear era. Second, I outline Morgenthau's criticism of the apocalyptic longings of liberal internationalism and the dangers that he diagnoses in a postwar world dominated by crusading political religions with the means to wage total war. I then trace his turn to tragedy as a counter-apocalyptic worldview. Third, I argue that Morgenthau eventually finds this tragic worldview inadequate for confronting the novel dangers of a nuclear world. Instead, he redirects the apocalyptic imaginary to cultivate the existential fear required to prevent nuclear annihilation.

The Postwar Apocalyptic Imaginary

Expectations about the end of the world loomed large over the tumultuous twentieth century. In this section of the chapter, I focus on the apocalyptic dimensions of Nazism, the mass exterminations of the Holocaust, and the development and deployment of the atomic bomb, all of which created a constellation of narratives and images that haunt Morgenthau's work.

At the heart of Nazism lay an apocalyptic myth centered on a millenarian account of time. According to this myth, the present is a moment of both catastrophe and promise.[3] History has reached a turning point that will lead either to salvation for some or the annihilation of all. Hitler's mentor, Dietrich Eckart, announced in 1919:

> Signs and wonder are seen – from the flood a new world will be born. These Pharisees however whine about wretched nest eggs! It's not simply a question of our collapse – it's a question of our Golgotha! Salvation is to befall our Germany, not misery and poverty. No other people on Earth are so thoroughly capable of fulfilling the Third Reich than ours! *Veni Creator spiritus*![4]

This conception of a "Third Reich" as a final and millennial age has its roots in an idiosyncratic appropriation of the writings of Joachim of Fiore.[5] Joachim proposed a tripartite division of history into three ages, or statuses. The third

---

[3] In making the argument that Nazism relied on apocalyptic narratives and images, I am drawing on and echoing the arguments made by: James M. Rhodes, *The Hitler Movement: A Modern Millenarian Revolution* (Stanford: Hoover Institution Press, 1980); Robert Wistrich, *Hitler's Apocalypse: Jews and the Nazi Legacy* (New York: St. Martin's Press, 1986); Thomas Flanagan, "The Third Reich: Origins of a Millenarian Symbol," *History of European Ideas* 8, no. 3 (1987): 283–95; David Redles, *Hitler's Millennial Reich: Apocalyptic Belief and the Search for Salvation* (New York: NYU Press, 2005); David Redles, "'Nazi End Times: The Third Reich as Millennial Reich,'" in *End of Days: Essays on the Apocalypse from Antiquity to Modernity*, ed. Karolyn Kinane and Michael A. Ryan (Jefferson: McFarland and Co., 2009), 173–96. These works elaborate on a set of fragmentary and largely intuitional arguments offered by: Eric Voegelin, *The New Science of Politics: An Introduction* (Chicago: University of Chicago Press, 1952), 110–27; Norman Cohn, *The Pursuit of the Millennium: Revolutionary Messianism in Medieval and Reformation Europe and Its Bearing on Modern Totalitarian Movements*, 2nd ed. (New York: Harper and Row, 1961), 308–14; Michael Barkun, *Disaster and the Millennium* (New Haven: Yale University Press, 1974), 192–94.

[4] Dietrich Eckart, as quoted in Redles, "Nazi End Times," 173. *Veni Creator spiritus* (Come Creator spirit) is a Catholic chant generally reserved for special Church occasions. However, as David Redles explains, "seen from the perspective of Joachite millennialism...the descent of Holy Spirit upon the Earth takes on a more nuanced meaning. 'Golgotha' [is] where the Romans purportedly crucified Jesus. For an anti-Semite like Eckart, however, the linkage of liberation from 'the curse of gold' to the crucifixion is a blaming of Jews for both Germany's economic woes and the death of Jesus." Redles, "Nazi End Times," 189 (n. 1).

[5] It is worth stressing that Nazism is in no way a natural or logical evolution of Joachim's thought. While proto-Nazi and Nazi thinkers drew upon Joachim's notion of a third *status* (i.e., age of the spirit) in their conceptualization of a Third Reich, Joachim never meant "status" to refer to any kind of political entity.

status would begin at the end times, during which a spiritual elect would defeat Antichrist and usher in a final age in which humanity would be transformed. Historians have proposed that the Nazis might have become aware of Joachim's thought through the secular appropriations of it in the work of Gotthold Lessing and in strands of German Idealism,[6] as well as through Henrik Ibsen's *Emperor and Galilean* (1873), which includes a memorable discussion of a coming Third Empire in which emperor and God will be one.[7] These ideas were transformed into a distinctly Nazi understanding of history by Dietrich Eckart and Otto Strasser and through the appropriation of Arthur Moeller van den Bruck's *Das Dritte Reich* (1923), which argued for the replacement of the Weimar Republic with a Third Reich. According to Moeller, humanity must be transformed to "make good again what we have made so bad."[8] The Nazis saw themselves as the harbingers of a new age.

Knowledge of this apocalyptic vision came through experiences of conversion and revelation. Alfred Rosenberg, one of the most powerful authors of Nazi ideology, described this experience: "There comes a moment for anyone who is truly searching when, out of thinking and fighting, suddenly an experience arises. From this moment on, the present, past and the outlook of the future appear to him in an entirely different light than before."[9] For Hitler and Herman Göring, the source of these revelations was a racial identity that called them to an eschatological mission.[10] Nazi organizational reformer Gregor Strasser suggested that this revelation was also a collective experience of giving meaning to inchoate feelings:

More and more the unclear feeling of young Germans in all camps is becoming a clear realization, that the confusion, the decay of the preceding political, economic, and cultural "order" is only the visible expression of one of the most thoroughgoing reformations, of the revolutionary stirrings of a new world view...on August 1, 1914, a revolution broke out which, with the most serious convulsions and struggles – of which the World War was only the necessary beginning – will bring forth a new world.[11]

These "convulsions and struggles" were at once an impetus to revelation and a sign of election. Prior to this, Hitler had claimed in *Mein Kampf* that Germany

---

[6] Flanagan, "The Third Reich," 285.
[7] "JULIAN: Emperor-god; –god-emperor. Emperor in the kingdom of the spirit,–and god in that of the flesh. MAXIMUS: That is the third empire, Julian! JULIAN: Yes, Maximus, that is the third empire. MAXIMUS: In that empire the present watchword of revolt will be realised." Henrik Ibsen, *Emperor and Galilean: A World-Historic Drama*, ed. and trans. William Archer (New York: Scribner and Welford, 1890), act 3; 274, https://books.google.com/books?id=ZYoOAAAAYAAJ. See also: Redles, "Nazi End Times," 174–75; Flanagan, "The Third Reich," 285–86; Steven F. Sage, *Ibsen and Hitler: The Playwright, the Plagiarist, and the Plot for the Third Reich* (New York: Basic Books, 2007).
[8] Dietrich Eckart, *Das Dritte Reich*, as quoted in Redles, "Nazi End Times," 180.
[9] Alfred Rosenberg, *Der völkisch Staatsgedanke* (1924), as quoted in Redles, *Hitler's Millennial Reich*, 77.
[10] Rhodes, *Hitler Movement*, 39.
[11] Gregor Strasser, *Kampf um Deutschland* (1932), as quoted in Rhodes, *Hitler Movement*, 59.

had been singled out as a particular target. The German defeat in 1918, Hitler declared, was "but the deserved chastisement of eternal retribution." If Germans responded to this chastisement with reform and struggle, it could become "the inspiration of a great future resurrection."[12] The German "people," or *Volk*, had been chosen to receive a revelation, undergo a terrible retribution, and usher in a new age.

However, this new age had to be inaugurated by an apocalyptic battle between good and evil. While Nazis agreed that Jews were the cause of this evil, they could not agree why. Hitler argued that Jews could not be considered human "in the sense of being an image of God." They were instead "the image of the devil."[13] He hypothesized that Jews were once "veritable devils" but had taken on human form over time.[14] Other Nazis simply thought Jews behaved in an evil way. Regardless of their disagreements, Nazis agreed that the source of this evil had to be eliminated. If they were successful, this war would give birth to a new world. Yet as Hitler told an audience in 1925, the stakes were high: "As we banded together in this new movement, we made it clear to ourselves that in this contest there are only two possibilities: Either the enemy will walk over our corpses, or we will walk over his."[15]

By 1943, Heinrich Himmler, *Reichsführer* of the *Schutzstaffel* (Reich Leader of the SS), sensed that he had to remind his subordinates of their mission. He argued that while many Germans seemed to support Jewish extermination on principle, "each of them has his 'decent' Jew" whom he thought should be exempt. Himmler continued: "Not one of all those who talk this way has witnessed it...Most of you know what it means when a hundred corpses are lying side by side, or five hundred, or a thousand...We had the moral right, we had the duty to our people, to destroy this people which wanted to destroy us."[16] Upon the success of this extermination effort depended the creation of a new world and the salvation and redemption of the *Volk*.[17] While its aspirations

---

[12] Adolf Hitler, *Mein Kampf* (1925/6), as quoted from the 1943 Ralph Mannheim translation in Rhodes, *Hitler Movement*, 60. Note the absence of agency here. Unlike overtly religious forms of apocalypticism in which God singles out particular people or groups for chastisement, Hitler does not identify a selective agent. The implication is that "fate" or "history" has singled out Germany.

[13] Hitler, *Mein Kampf*, as quoted from the 1943 Mannheim translation in Wistrich, *Hitler's Apocalypse*, 30.

[14] Hitler, *Mein Kampf*, as quoted from the 1943 Mannheim translation in Rhodes, *Hitler Movement*, 45.

[15] As quoted in Rhodes, *Hitler Movement*, 64.

[16] As quoted in Rhodes, *Hitler Movement*, 56. Himmler is making a rhetorical move here that Hannah Arendt diagnoses as an attempt to overcome the animal pity one feels for others in the face of physical suffering. This move consists "in turning these instincts around, as it were, in directing them toward the self. So that instead of saying: What horrible things I did to people!, the murderers would be able to say: What horrible things I had to watch in the pursuance of my duties, how heavily the task weighed upon my shoulders!" See: Hannah Arendt, *Eichmann in Jerusalem: A Report on the Banality of Evil* (New York: Penguin, 1977), 106.

[17] Like other apocalyptic movements, Nazism did not offer a coherent account of the world to come. Some seemed to have thought that Germans would be transformed into divine beings.

for a racially based program of extermination are unique, Nazism shared with the apocalyptic movements of late fifteenth-century Florence and seventeenth-century England a narrative of hope and despair.

The Nazi millennium failed to come. But Hitler's program of extermination did succeed in creating what was for many a *lived* apocalypse. Conventional histories of apocalypticism tell us a lot about the eschatological narratives of Nazism and the development and deployment of the atomic bomb. However, they tell us far less about the ways in which the Holocaust helped shape the twentieth-century apocalyptic imaginary.

There are at least two problems with this neglect. First, it fails to recognize that the apocalypse was the lens through which some survivors and Jewish thinkers came to understand the Holocaust. I take Elie Wiesel's thoughtful and troubling essay, "A Vision of the Apocalypse," as illustrative of such an interpretation.[18] Wiesel explains: "To the extent that my contemporaries believe in the Apocalypse, they refer to the one they lived through. They speak of memory more than vision."[19] For him, the calm slaughter of thousands of Jews in a single day, doctors separating potential experimental subjects from those destined for the gas chambers, and lawyers crafting the Final Solution at the Wannsee Conference mark a fundamental shift in the apocalyptic imaginary. The apocalypse is "no longer great beasts spewing forth flames, or horsemen ushering in destruction, or homes ransacked and collapsing in an earthquake imparting to History a hallucinatory, fiery end." Rather, it is "a spacious and well-lighted office, well-bred technocrats, efficient secretaries. It is government employees working together with or without passion, with or without conviction, first to imagine, then to bring about, Auschwitz."[20] This is an apocalypse devoid of divine or Satanic agency. It is carried out by calm, cultured professionals who "had all read Goethe and admired Schiller."[21]

Yet this account of the experience at Auschwitz shares more with older religious apocalypses than Wiesel admits. Both are ruptures in the temporal

---

Others expected a worldly immortality through the eternal salvation of the *Volk*. For most, the world to come was likely more mundane, though still mythical – a reconstructed Germany that would be protected from future disasters. The common thread in these visions was the transformation of humanity and the founding of a new society, from which, according to Nazi ideology, Jews and German dissenters had been purged. See: Rhodes, *Hitler Movement*, 77–82.

[18] I want to stress two things here. First, Wiesel's essay is illustrative, but by no means representative, of an apocalyptic reading of the Holocaust. In this instance, I do not think any reading could be representative. One could turn to other Jewish émigré scholars for alternative apocalyptic readings of the Holocaust. Second, an apocalyptic reading of the Holocaust is not unproblematic or uncontested. See, for instance: David G. Roskies, *Against the Apocalypse: Responses to Catastrophe in Modern Jewish Culture* (Cambridge: Harvard University Press, 1984); Michael Andre Bernstein, *Foregone Conclusions: Against Apocalyptic History* (Berkeley: University of California Press, 1994).

[19] Elie Wiesel, "A Vision of the Apocalypse," trans. Joan Grimbert, *World Literature Today* 58, no. 2 (1984): 195.

[20] Wiesel, "A Vision of Apocalypse," 196.   [21] Wiesel, "A Vision of Apocalypse," 196.

continuity of history. For Wiesel, even as Auschwitz negates history, it "represents a kind of aberration and culmination of History. Everything brings us back to it. Illuminated by its flames, the present appears more understandable."[22] It is the culmination of a history of anti-Semitism, persecutions, expulsions, and violence. It is a terrifying revelation of truths about European culture that had been hidden or only half visible for centuries. Finally, the Holocaust ushers in a new world – but not one of redemption and salvation. Instead, it is a world that bears symptoms and traces of terrifying and irrevocable events.[23] Wiesel ends his essay by considering whether the apocalypse of Auschwitz could be transposed into the future. He does not warn about a return to ghettos and gas chambers, but rather the possibility that the culture of indifference and apathy that permitted the Holocaust would now fail to prevent a nuclear apocalypse.

The second problem, then, with avoiding the Holocaust in an account of the twentieth-century apocalyptic imaginary is that doing so blinds us to the connections between the Final Solution and the dawn of the nuclear age. For Wiesel, the two constellations of events are clearly linked: "for us, time stopped between Auschwitz and Hiroshima."[24] This connection is by no means particular to Wiesel. For many, the images and direct experiences of Nazi genocide became ways to envision the possibility of nuclear annihilation. A 1952 *New York Times* review of *The Diary of Anne Frank* noted how successful this work is "in bringing us an understanding of life under threat. And this quality brings it home to any family in the world today. Just as the Franks lived in momentary fear of the Gestapo's knock on their hidden door, so every family today lives in fear of the knock of war."[25] In the early 1950s, this knocking hand would certainly have been that of *atomic* war.

Writing in 1962, the German-Jewish philosopher and journalist Günther Anders argued that nuclear war and the concentration camp shared a totalitarian logic. The threat of nuclear war, he suggested, "amounts to blackmail and transforms our globe into one vast concentration camp from which there is no way out."[26] The same year, in a piece in *The Atlantic Monthly*, poet and critic Al Alvarez hypothesized that our fear of nuclear annihilation was one of the reasons the concentration camps had captured the postwar imagination:

There are no limits to the inflationary spiral of destruction. From 1940 to 1945 nearly 4,500,000 people died in Auschwitz. The same number would die in minutes if a hydrogen bomb landed on London. The gap is very small between the comforts of our affluent

---

[22] Wiesel, "A Vision of Apocalypse," 195.
[23] James Berger, *After the End: Representations of Post-Apocalypse* (Minneapolis: University of Minnesota Press, 1999), 61.
[24] Weisel, "A Vision of the Apocalypse," 195.
[25] Meyer Levin, "The Child behind the Secret Door," *New York Times Book Review*, June 15, 1952, 1, https://search.proquest.com/docview/112258545?accountid=14026.
[26] Günther Anders, "Theses for the Atomic Age," *The Massachusetts Review* 3, no. 3 (1962): 495.

society and the bare, animal squalor of Birkenau, or the finality of the Auschwitz crematorium, with its rasping iron trolleys. So, perhaps the concentration camps have kept a tight hold on our imaginations... [because] we see them as a small-scale trial run for nuclear war.[27]

Alvarez's shift from comparative calculations to the *images* of Auschwitz is important here – from the abstract, unthinkable, enormous numbers to the "animal squalor," the crematorium, and the "rasping iron trolleys." The analogy between the concentration camp and the effects of nuclear destruction is not merely or even primarily one based on comparative death tolls, but on a shared visual vocabulary of annihilation.

More than twenty years later, in 1983, nuclear physicist Isidore Isaac Rabi would rely exclusively on imagistic association: "And now we have the nations lined up, like those prisoners at Auschwitz, going into the ovens, and waiting for the ovens to be perfected, made more efficient."[28] It is with these images of extermination, in addition to the haunting reports from Hiroshima and Nagasaki, that postwar Americans imagined nuclear annihilation.

These visual connections emphasize an apocalypse initiated by human and technological agency, after which there is no redemption. This is consistent with the picture of the nuclear age in many scholarly treatments of apocalypticism.[29] The possibility of a nuclear apocalypse seems fundamentally different from past visions of the end of the world. These older apocalyptic visions are part of a religious cosmology in which "human beings are acted upon by a higher power who destroys only for spiritual purposes, such as achieving the 'kingdom of God' – a far cry from our destruction of ourselves with our own tools, and for no discernible purpose."[30] In contrast to the Judeo-Christian apocalypse, there is no system of belief that renders nuclear annihilation meaningful, no theodicy that endows it with ultimate justification, and no promissory narrative that consoles the terrified and trembling. It is instead an apocalypse without redemption – an end that can only be confronted as a naked absurdity.

It is an absurdity wrought by human agency but at the same time unfathomable to the human mind. We are incapable, Anders suggests, of mentally

---

[27] Al Alvarez, "The Concentration Camps," *The Atlantic Monthly*, December 1962, 70. The fact that Alvarez makes this connection in the early 1960s is perhaps not surprising. This was the period in which the Nazi genocide and nuclear annihilation were linked by a shared referent. While the word "holocaust" was only starting in the early 1960s to become the primary referent for the Nazi genocide, it was a common referent for nuclear annihilation. See: Jon Petrie, "The Secular Word HOLOCAUST: Scholarly Myths, History, and 20th Century Meanings," *Journal of Genocide Research* 2, no. 1 (2000): 43–50.

[28] I. I. Rabi, as quoted in Robert Jay Lifton and Eric Markusen, *The Genocidal Mentality: Nazi Holocaust and Nuclear Threat* (New York: Basic Books, 1991), 9.

[29] For a notable exception that deals explicitly with religious and theological visions of nuclear apocalypse, see: Boyer, *When Time Shall Be No More*, 115–51.

[30] Robert Jay Lifton, "Beyond the Nuclear End," in *The Future of Immortality and Other Essays for a Nuclear Age* (New York: Basic Books, 1987), 149.

grasping the realities that our actions have produced. We are "'inverted Utopians': while ordinary Utopians are unable to actually produce what they are able to visualize, we are unable to visualize what we are actually producing."[31]

Perhaps this inability to come to grips with our own apocalyptic agency is what prompted many to invest nuclear technology with an agency of its own – with powers that exceed our capacities for understanding and control. Consider, for example, the popular notion from the 1950s that there were "doomsday buttons" in both the White House and the Kremlin. The world could be ended as easily as turning on a television set or a dishwasher. This notion of a push-button apocalypse "reinforced feelings of helplessness and apocalyptic inevitability. Once the button was pushed, nothing could be done to stop the process because the technology was...overwhelmingly sophisticated and beyond one's understanding and control."[32] It is this sense of helplessness, inevitability, and technological agency that is so effectively satirized in Stanley Kubrick's film, *Dr. Strangelove* (1964), with its sublime portrayal of the absurdity of Mutually Assured Destruction (MAD).

This standard account of nuclear doomsaying captures some important shifts in the imaginary. But it overstates the contrast between nuclear apocalypticism and the more overtly religious movements to which Machiavelli and Hobbes, for instance, were responding. As we have seen in the two previous chapters, apocalyptic agency is rarely left entirely to God. Both Savonarola and the more radical apocalypticists of the English Civil War, for example, saw a substantial role for human agency.

Even more importantly, this standard account of nuclear doomsaying fundamentally ignores the optimistic apocalyptic narratives surrounding the development and deployment of these new weapons. The explicit contrast invoked by the standard account is between a divine apocalypse that promises redemption and a human and technological apocalypse that brings total annihilation. This contrast forces the same false choice that Leonard Cohen presents in his darkly apocalyptic song "The Future": "Give me Christ or give me Hiroshima."[33] As we will see later, the postwar apocalyptic imaginary often blended a hope for worldly renewal with a fear of total annihilation. It gave us both Christ *and* Hiroshima.

For example, it was with profoundly redemptive hopes that J. Robert Oppenheimer, the scientific director of the Manhattan Project, chose the code name for the first full-scale test of the atomic bomb. General Leslie Groves, the director of the Manhattan Project, wrote to Oppenheimer in 1962 to ask why the physicist had coded the test "Trinity." Oppenheimer wrote back: "Why I chose the name is not clear, but I know what thoughts were in my mind. There is

---

[31] Anders, *Theses*, 496.
[32] Daniel Wojcik, *The End of the World as We Know It: Faith, Fatalism, and Apocalypse in America* (New York: NYU Press, 1999), 103.
[33] Leonard Cohen, *The Future* (Columbia, 1992), compact disc.

a poem of John Donne, written just before his death which I know and love. From it a quotation: 'As West and East / In all flatt Maps – and I am one – are one, / So death doth touch the Resurrection.'"[34] These lines are from Donne's "Hymne to God my God, in My Sicknesse" and they establish the theological connection between death and resurrection.[35]

Oppenheimer's letter to Groves continues: "That still doesn't make a Trinity, but in another, better known devotional poem Donne opens, 'Batter my heart, three person'd God'; – Beyond this, I have no clues whatever."[36] Like Donne's "Hymne," this sonnet connects destruction and redemption:

> Batter my heart, three person'd God; for, you
> As yet but knocke, breathe, shine, and seeke to mend;
> That I may rise, and stand, o'erthrow mee,'and bend
> Your force to breake, blowe, burn and make new.[37]

Here, Donne begs God to violently renew and remake him. This connection between destruction and redemption may have been especially meaningful for Oppenheimer, who sustained himself during the Manhattan Project with the hope that nuclear weapons could be used to overpower evil and inaugurate a new world without war.[38]

---

[34] As quoted in Richard Rhodes, *The Making of the Atomic Bomb* (New York: Simon & Schuster, 1986), 571.

[35] John Donne, "Hymne to God my God, in My Sicknesse," *Complete Poetry and Selected Prose*, 271–72. John Donne biographer Robert Stubbs suggests that there may be another possible reading here. Given that Oppenheimer recounted this story to Groves in 1962, "after the McCarthy witch-hunt... he may have been using the reference less to explain the meaning of 'Trinity' than to discredit the bi-polar division of the Cold War world he had helped to create. East and West were illusions of a map; if one put the chart around the globe, those extremities merged together into one." See: John Stubbs, *John Donne: The Reformed Soul* (New York: W. W. Norton & Co., 2007), 477. I find this interpretation difficult to sustain, given that Oppenheimer goes on to cite a second Donne poem that cannot be so easily connected to the Cold War context of the early 1960s.

[36] As quoted in Richard Rhodes, *The Making of the Atomic Bomb*, 572.

[37] The sonnet continues with a combination of military and sexual imagery: "I, like an usurpt towne, to'another due, / Labour to'admit you, but Oh, to no end, / Reason your viceroy in mee, mee should defend, / But is captiv'd, and proves weake or untrue. / Yet dearly'I love you,'and would be loved faine, / But am betroth'd unto your enemie: / Divorce mee,'untie, or breake that knot againe, / Take mee to you, imprison mee, for I / Except you'enthrall mee, never shall be free, / Nor ever chast, except you ravish mee." See: John Donne, "Holy Sonnet XIV," in *Complete Poetry and Selected Prose*, 252.

[38] Richard Rhodes cites Hans A. Bethe, head of the Theoretical Division at the Los Alamos Laboratory, explaining that Oppenheimer developed these ideas about the moral possibilities of nuclear weapons in conversations with Niels Bohr, who put great faith in the potential for international control. See: Rhodes, *The Making of the Atomic Bomb*, 572. In a communication with Robert Lifton, Oppenheimer biographer Nuel Pharr Davis said: "In talking with me about the name trinity Oppenheimer showed himself apologetic about the rather high-flown poetic derivation but not apologetic about the moral assumption." See: Author Robert Jay Lifton, *The Broken Connection: On Death and the Continuity of Life* (New York: Simon and Schuster, 1979), 370.

Upon witnessing the Trinity test on July 16, 1945, he would reach for a much darker and non-Western vision. Oppenheimer recalled the lines from the *Bhagavad Gita*:

> If the radiance of a thousand suns
> Were to burst at once into the sky
> That would be like the splendor of the Mighty One...
> I am become Death,
> The shatterer of worlds."[39]

In contrast to the redemptive hope of Trinity, his remarks here suggest an overwhelming confrontation with death and annihilation.

Brigadier General Thomas Farrell drew on more explicitly Christian imagery in his contribution to General Groves's official report of the Trinity test. This report that was sent to President Truman during the Potsdam Conference with Winston Churchill and Joseph Stalin. Farrell writes:

> The effects could well be called unprecedented, magnificent, beautiful, stupendous, and terrifying... The whole country was lighted by a searing light with the intensity many times that of the midday sun. It was golden, purple, violet, gray and blue. It lighted every peak, crevasse and ridge of the nearby mountain range with a clarity and beauty that cannot be described but must be seen to be imagined. It was that beauty the great poets dream about but describe most poorly and inadequately. Thirty seconds after the explosion came, first, the air blast pressing hard against the people and things, to be followed almost immediately by the strong, sustained, awesome roar which warned of doomsday and made us feel that we puny things were blasphemous to dare tamper with the forces heretofore reserved to The Almighty. Words are inadequate tools for the job of acquainting those not present with the physical, mental and psychological effects. It had to be witnessed to be realized.[40]

Farrell offers an apocalyptic and sublime vision of an event so magnificent that it escapes description. It can only be witnessed. Upon receiving this report, President Truman reached for images of biblical destruction: "We have discovered the most terrible bomb in the history of the world. It may be the fire destruction prophesied in the Euphrates Valley Era, after Noah and his fabulous Ark."[41] Prime Minister Winston Churchill's reaction a few days later was even darker: "This atomic bomb is the Second Coming in Wrath."[42]

---

[39] As quoted in Lifton, *The Broken Connection*, 370.
[40] Thomas F. Farrell, as quoted in Leslie R. Groves, Memorandum for the Secretary of War (July 18, 1945), point 11. This memorandum is reproduced in Appendix P of: Martin J. Sherwin, *A World Destroyed: Hiroshima and the Origins of the Arms Race* (New York: Vintage, 1987), 312.
[41] As quoted in Herbert Mitgang, "Truman's Newly Found Potsdam Notes Show Concerns on A-Bomb," *New York Times*, June 2, 1980, A14, https://search.proquest.com/docview/121109778?accountid=14026.
[42] As quoted in Harvey H. Bundy, "Remembered Words," *The Atlantic Monthly*, March 1957, 57.

If anything, these darkly apocalyptic visions intensified after the United States dropped the atomic bombs on Hiroshima and Nagaski on August 6 and August 9, 1945, respectively.[43] Initially, however, the responses to the news from Japan were triumphant. Upon hearing of the success of the bomb dropped on Hiroshima, President Truman proclaimed: "This is the greatest thing in history!"[44] It was a sign of the unprecedented military and technological power of the United States.

Yet for many, the destruction of Hiroshima and Nagaski did not call forth images of an all-powerful America, but of a vulnerable and exposed country awaiting its own annihilation. In a *New York Times* piece on August 12, Washington correspondent James Reston suggested: "In that terrible flash 10,000 miles away, men here have seen not only the fate of Japan, but have glimpsed the future of America."[45] In a similar vein, broadcast journalist Edward R. Murrow worried: "Seldom, if ever, has a war ended leaving the victors with such a sense of uncertainty and fear, with such a realization that the future is obscure and that survival is not assured."[46] On the brink of Japanese surrender and at the dawn of the nuclear age, many in America stared into the future and saw their own annihilation.[47] These reactions, along with some of the initial

---

[43] In this section of the chapter, I have chosen to focus on those views of nuclear weapons that stress the weapons' radical newness. The fact that the scientists who designed the atomic bomb as well as the president who deployed it stressed its radical newness is significant. However, there were numerous public figures and scholars (including initially Morgenthau) who argued that nuclear weapons did not represent a qualitative shift away from conventional weapons. In the context of the comparative death tolls during World War II, this position was not unreasonable. The firebombing of Tokyo had killed at least 100,000 people, while final death tolls at Hiroshima and Nagasaki were 135,000 and 50,000, respectively. The argument that nuclear weapons did not represent a qualitative shift from conventional weapons became much more difficult to sustain with the advent of the hydrogen bomb.

[44] President Harry S. Truman, as quoted in Sherwin, *A World Destroyed*, 221.

[45] James Reston, "Dawn of the Atom Era Perplexes Washington," *New York Times*, August 12, 1945, E6. https://search.proquest.com/docview/107030672?accountid=14026.

[46] Edward R. Murrow, August 12, 1945 Radio Broadcast, in Edward R. Murrow, *In Search Of Light*, ed. Edward Bliss Jr. (London: Macmillan, 1968), 102.

[47] Paul Boyer suggests that advocates of international control of nuclear weapons deliberately encouraged and exploited this response. "Without international control of the atom, Americans were endlessly warned, the fate of these two cities would be theirs as well. Highly effective as propaganda, this shorthand use of 'Hiroshima' and 'Nagasaki' as abstract cautionary devices further diminished the capacity of Americans to respond directly to the actual fate of two real cities. The emotional thrust of the 1946 fear campaign was directed forward to possible future atomic holocausts, not backward to what had already occurred." See: Paul Boyer, *Fallout: A Historian Reflects on America's Half-Century Encounter with Nuclear Weapons* (Columbus: Ohio State University Press, 1998), 14. Spencer Weart argues that Hiroshima and Nagasaki presented Americans with "dangerously incomplete" images of nuclear annihilation. The United States government released very few photographs of those who were wounded in Japan. Rather, "the commonly seen Hiroshima pictures mostly showed vast landscapes of rubble, empty of victims... The destruction was usually viewed from an Olympian distance, as in the frequently published maps that showed with concentric circles how many square miles of a city would be pulverized." See: Spencer R. Weart, *Nuclear Fear: A History of Images* (Cambridge: Harvard University Press, 1988), 236. To some extent, however, images of nuclear annihilation escaped

The Postwar Apocalyptic Imaginary

responses to the Trinity test, seem to provide support for the standard reading of nuclear apocalypticism. They suggest an apocalypse created by human agents who have let loose a technology that they cannot control and that holds them in awe. There is no suggestion of spiritual or worldly renewal.

Yet for others the dawn of the nuclear age marked the birth of a new world and promised a kind of earthly salvation. William Laurence, the *New York Times* journalist covering the Manhattan Project, had an apocalyptic conversion upon witnessing the Trinity test. He compared it to what the first man might have seen "at the moment of Creation when God said, 'Let there be light.'"[48] Later that day, he found himself saying: "It was like being witness to the Second Coming of Christ!"[49] This narrative of apocalyptic conversion is even stronger in Laurence's description of his reactions to the May 21, 1956 test of an airborne hydrogen bomb in the northern Pacific. He recounts that his first thoughts were of the damage that such a weapon could do to "any of the world's great cities." But reassurance was almost instantaneous: "This great iridescent cloud and its mushroom top, I found myself thinking as I watched, is actually a protective umbrella that will forever shield mankind everywhere against the threat of annihilation in any atomic war." This phenomenal new weapon with over 700 times the power of the bombs dropped on Hiroshima and Nagasaki would "continue shielding us everywhere until the time comes, as come it must, when mankind will be able to beat atomic swords into plowshares, harnessing the vast power of the hydrogen in the world's oceans to bring in an era of prosperity such as the world has never even dared dream about."[50] For Laurence, the devastation wrought by the atomic bombs dropped on Japan and the hydrogen bomb's potential for unimaginable annihilation had already initiated an apocalyptic transformation and the dawning of a new world. The actual deployment of these bombs in populated areas could not even be

---

government control. John Hersey's *Hiroshima*, originally published in a 1946 issue of the *New Yorker*, offered the following narrative of the destruction, re-created with the help of survivor accounts: "He was the only person making his way into the city; he met hundreds and hundreds who were fleeing, and every one of them seemed to be hurt in some way. The eyebrows of some were burned off and skin hung from their faces and hands. Others, because of pain, held their arms up as if carrying something in both hands. Some were vomiting as they walked. Many were naked or in shreds of clothing. On some undressed bodies, the burns had made patterns – of undershirt straps and suspenders and, on the skin of some women (since white repelled the heat from the bomb and dark clothes absorbed it and conducted it to the skin), the shapes of flowers they had had on their kimonos." See: John Hersey, *Hiroshima* (New York: Alfred A. Knopf, 1985), 39–40.

[48] William Leonard Laurence, *Men and Atoms: The Discovery, the Uses, and the Future of Atomic Energy* (New York: Simon and Schuster, 1959), 118. Laurence also wrote the following remarks in his notebook that day: "With the flash came a delayed roll of mighty thunder, heard, just as the flash was seen, for hundreds of miles. The roar echoed and reverberated from the distant hills and the Sierra Oscuro range near by, sounding as though it came from some supramundane source as well as from the bowels of the earth. The hills said yes and the mountains chimed in yes. It was as if the earth had spoken and the sudden iridescent clouds and sky had joined in one affirmative answer. Atomic energy – yes" (120).

[49] Laurence, *Men and Atoms*, 120.   [50] Laurence, *Men and Atoms*, 197.

contemplated. Total war was a thing of the past. We had crossed the threshold into a millennial age.

However, others were willing to contemplate a world that might come into being after thermonuclear war. From the 1950s onward, numerous articles, books, and films considered the possibilities of a postapocalyptic world. These works offered a full range of possibilities – from the dire to the unapologetically optimistic.[51] But the dire scenarios were those that most troubled the U.S. government. Since the end of the Second World War, policymakers had begun to worry that a public captivated by darkly apocalyptic images of nuclear annihilation would be less willing to "support national policies which might involve the risk of nuclear warfare."[52]

As part of a massive public relations campaign aimed at normalizing nuclear weapons, President Eisenhower's National Security Council ordered a classified study of the effects of the threat of nuclear annihilation on American attitudes and behavior. A panel of social scientists completed a report entitled "The Human Effects of Nuclear Weapons Development." The report recommended a widespread program of "town hall meetings," aimed at balancing public awareness of the effects of nuclear weapons with an "increased knowledge and understanding of both the broad aspects of national security... and the specific countermeasures that can reduce the effects of nuclear attack."[53] The report concluded by noting that nuclear war might even provide survivors with an opportunity for heroism and renewal:

The extremity of human disaster might become the opportunity for resolute survivors. It is a brave thing, admittedly, to brace ourselves against the threat of annihilation. It is another, and better, thing to nerve ourselves to make the very best of the very worst. At this historic crossroads we would begin with knowledge and we would end with wisdom. Thus to take counsel with one another, to the very town meeting grass roots, would be to draw inspiration from our forefathers and to point our children to the sources which make all American generations one and which raise hope for a new dynamics for the human race. It is a vision, indeed, but where visions flourish nations endure.[54]

---

[51] For a discussion of some of these books and films, see Kenneth D. Rose, *One Nation Underground: The Fallout Shelter in American Culture* (New York: New York University Press, 2001), 38–77. These works provide a range of attitudes toward the possibilities of survival after a nuclear apocalypse, ranging from the acceptant pessimism of Nevil Shute's novel, *On the Beach* (1957, with a film adaptation in 1959) to an unabashed optimism and faith in the regenerative possibilities of a robust civil defense program in Philip Wylie's *Tomorrow!* (1954).

[52] Memorandum for the president, Val Peterson (Federal Civil Defense Administration) to Dwight D. Eisenhower, as quoted in William F. Vandercook, "Making the Very Best of the Very Worst: The 'Human Effects of Nuclear Weapons' Report of 1956," *International Security* 11, no. 1 (1986): 184.

[53] "The Human Effects of Nuclear Weapons Development" report, as quoted in Vandercook, "Making the Very Best," 193.

[54] "The Human Effects of Nuclear Weapons Development" Report, as quoted in Vandercook, "Making the Very Best," 193.

The Postwar Apocalyptic Imaginary

While "The Human Effects" report was eventually shelved, it suggests a strong concern with tempering fears of nuclear annihilation with a patriotic "apocalyptic mysticism."[55]

Even without the implementation of the report's "town hall" public relations program, some continued to see reasons for optimism in a postapocalyptic future. These optimists turned to the predictions of thinkers like Herman Kahn, a systems theorist at the RAND Corporation, who argued that despite the hostility of a post-nuclear-war environment, survivors might still enjoy "relatively normal and happy lives." He even predicted that within a few years, the standard of living "would be higher than the standards prevalent in the U.S. between 1900 and 1930."[56] These kinds of optimistic predictions, combined with President Kennedy's 1961 civil defense and fallout shelter initiative, helped fuel radical hopes.

In an October 1961 editorial, *Life* magazine argued that a shelter-building campaign "will give all Americans the hope that they, like their forebears, can some day abandon the stockades to cross whatever new mountains of adversity or trial may lie ahead."[57] Later that month, an article in *Time* magazine struck a similar note: "Only two days after the thermonuclear attack, many adults might start emerging from the protection of their shelters for brief periods... With trousers tucked into sock tops and sleeves tied around wrists, with hats, mufflers, gloves and boots, the shelter dweller could venture forth to start ensuring his today and building for his tomorrow."[58] These images of emergence from the cramped "womb" of the fallout shelter suggest a rebirth and an opportunity for a uniquely American exercise of courage – a kind of postapocalyptic pioneer spirit.[59]

What the "Human Effects" report and these more popular images attempt to elicit is not just the hope that Americans could *survive* a nuclear attack. Rather, they go beyond nuclear optimists like Kahn and present an enticing image of a clean slate – an opportunity to create the world anew and engender "a new dynamics of the human race." This is the vision of creative renewal through destruction for which the standard story of nuclear apocalypticism fails to account. But it is a vision that would preoccupy Morgenthau.

---

[55] Robert Jay Lifton, "The New Psychology of Human Survival," in *The Future of Immortality and Other Essays for a Nuclear Age* (New York: Basic Books, 1987), 121. Lifton also notes that the report reveals "the depth of political and social impulse from above (in this case the Eisenhower administration), to impose nuclear normality, even if the whole population must be trained to achieve that normality" (120–21).

[56] Herman Kahn, *Thinking About the Unthinkable* (New York: Horizon Press, 1962), 87.

[57] "Let's Prepare... Shelters," *Life Magazine*, October 13, 1961, 4.

[58] "The Sheltered Life," *Time*, October 20, 1961, www.time.com/time/magazine/article/0,9171, 872787-9,00.html.

[59] The September 15, 1961 issue of *Life* included a picture of a teenaged girl relaxing in a distinctly womb-like fallout shelter, enjoying a bottle of Coca-Cola and chatting on the telephone (107).

In sum, then, the postwar apocalyptic imaginary was comprised of a constellation of images and narratives drawn from the most troubling events of the twentieth century. From the apocalyptic narratives underpinning Nazism, through the *lived* apocalypse of the Holocaust, to the combination of dread and hope of the nuclear age, the postwar imaginary resists easy characterization. What is clear, however, is the hold that both the terrifying violence and the radical hopes of the Judeo-Christian apocalypse had over the modern "secular" imagination.

Apocalypse "Under an Empty Sky"

Morgenthau's postwar work took shape in the context of this apocalyptic imaginary. Having left Germany for Switzerland in 1932, he immigrated to the United States the following year. After teaching briefly at Brooklyn College and the University of Kansas City, he accepted an appointment at the University of Chicago in 1943 and remained there for almost thirty years. His time at Chicago overlapped with that of two other German-Jewish émigré scholars – Leo Strauss and Hannah Arendt. Morgenthau would come to acknowledge both, but especially Arendt, as influences on his own thought.

During his early years at Chicago, Morgenthau completed three of his most influential books – *Scientific Man vs. Power Politics* (1946), *Politics Among Nations* (1948), and *In Defense of the National Interest* (1951). Together, these books helped to secure Morgenthau's status as a founding father of the study of international relations in the United States.[60] His work, particularly the immensely influential *Politics Among Nations*, and the political realist school of which he was a formative member, set the terms of debate in international relations until at least the end of the 1960s.[61]

In what follows, I read Morgenthau's thought in the context of the apocalyptic imaginary of postwar America. I argue that from the late 1940s to the early 1960s, Morgenthau vigorously criticized the apocalyptic tendencies of "political religions." In reading Morgenthau with a political theological eye, my interpretation departs from the dominant portrait of his early postwar work, particularly *Scientific Man vs. Power Politics*, which is often read purely as a critique of rationalism and scientism.[62] To be sure, there is substantial textual

---

[60] Stanley Hoffmann, *Janus and Minerva: Essays in the Theory and Practice of International Politics* (Boulder: Westview Press, 1987), 6.

[61] John Vasquez presents preliminary small-N data (gathered from surveys from the early 1970s) to support these claims. See: Vasquez, *The Power of Power Politics*, 63–69.

[62] See, for instance: Scheuerman, *Hans Morgenthau*, 41–50; Christoph Frei, *Hans J. Morgenthau: An Intellectual Biography* (Baton Rouge: Louisiana State University Press, 2001), 194–201. For a reading of Morgenthau that emphasizes his critique of rationalism, while trying to distance his ideas from those of Schmitt, see: Williams, *The Realist Tradition*, 84–104. I am inclined to agree with Nicolas Guilhot when he argues that Williams overstates the differences between Morgenthau and Schmitt: "Rather than a matter of substantial difference, it is indeed a striking

support for this dominant portrait. Morgenthau's *Scientific Man* reproduces, without ever citing, Carl Schmitt's argument in his 1929 essay "The Age of Neutralizations and Depoliticizations." Echoing Schmitt, Morgenthau argues that liberal rationalism aims at nothing short of the "repudiation of politics." An ideological product of the ambitious hopes of the Enlightenment, liberal rationalism denies that the "lust for power" is both an ineradicable feature of human nature and the root cause of conflict. Liberalism sees the power struggles that define the political condition as the vestiges of the premodern era – embarrassments to be overcome by technical means. Mass education, careful institutional design, free markets, and regimes of international law will form the basis for a new order in which the undesirable aspects of human nature have been overcome and conflict has been replaced with harmony.[63]

My interpretation does not deny that Morgenthau's early postwar work can be read as a critique of liberal rationalism. Instead, I invite the reader to attend with me to the political theological dimensions of Morgenthau's critique.[64] He

example of what Freud called 'the narcissism of small differences': for Morgenthau, cultivating his own distinctiveness was all the more necessary since his position [in this case, on the concept of the political] was largely identical with Schmitt's. In the deteriorating climate of the 1930s, as Schmitt was on his way to becoming the *Kronjurist* of the Reich, minor conceptual differences acquired huge symbolic significance." See: Nicolas Guilhot, "American *Katechon*: When Political Theology Became International Relations Theory," *Constellations* 17, no. 2 (2010): 252, n. 99. This may also offer at least a partial explanation for why Morgenthau fails to cite Schmitt even in those moments at which the former most relies on the arguments of the latter. Another reason might be because Morgenthau thought it prudent to conceal the German sources of his ideas in postwar America. Christoph Frei suggests that this is why Morgenthau fails to citationally signal his debt to Nietzsche. See: Frei, *Hans J. Morgenthau*, 110–11.

[63] This argument is outlined in: Hans J. Morgenthau, *Scientific Man vs. Power Politics* (Chicago: University of Chicago Press, 1946), 41–74. Morgenthau's critique also reflects his rejection of the application of the scientific method to human and social questions. On this point, his intellectual touchstone was Reinhold Niebuhr. On the two thinkers' shared critiques of "scientism," see: Daniel F. Rice, *Reinhold Niebuhr and His Circle of Influence* (Cambridge: Cambridge University Press, 2012), 55–57, 147–49.

[64] I think it is reasonable to assume that Morgenthau's political theological arguments owe a great debt to those of Carl Schmitt, despite the absence of citational evidence for such a connection. On Morgenthau's possible debts to Schmitt and on the relationship between the thinkers more generally, see: William E. Scheuerman, "Carl Schmitt and Hans Morgenthau: Realism and Beyond," in *Realism Reconsidered: The Legacy of Hans Morgenthau in International Relations*, ed. Michael C. Williams (Oxford: Oxford University Press, 2007), 62–92; William E. Scheuerman, *Carl Schmitt: The End of Law* (Lanham: Rowman & Littlefield Publishers, 1999), 225–52. On the Schmitt-Morgenthau connection, see: Guilhot, "American *Katechon*"; Chris Brown, "'The Twilight of International Morality'? Hans J. Morgenthau and Carl Schmitt on the End of the *Jus Publicum Europaeum*," in *Realism Reconsidered: The Legacy of Hans Morgenthau in International Relations*, ed. Michael C. Williams (Oxford: Oxford University Press, 2007), 42–61; Martti Koskenniemi, *The Gentle Civilizer of Nations: The Rise and Fall of International Law 1870–1960* (Cambridge: Cambridge University Press, 2004), 413–509; Frei, *Hans J. Morgenthau*, 118–19, 123–32; Hans-Karl Pichler, "The Godfathers of 'Truth': Max Weber and Carl Schmitt in Morgenthau's Theory of Power Politics," *Review of International Studies* 24, no. 2 (1998): 185–200; Hans J. Morgenthau, "Fragments of an Intellectual Biography," in

argues that the world is mired in explosive conflicts, the likes of which have not been seen since the religious wars of medieval and early modern Europe. The political religions of the postwar period fight to end evil, annihilate their unjust enemies, and remake the world in their own images. While the memory of the secularized apocalypticism of Nazism looms heavily in the background of this diagnosis, Morgenthau focuses his attention on the Cold War confrontation between Soviet Communism and American liberal internationalism.

He devotes his sharpest critical attention to the latter. At its most extreme, liberal internationalism sees a devastating final war for a singular humanity as a prelude to a millennial democratic future. This kind of apocalyptic ideology, combined with a return to total war and the potential for large-scale nuclear annihilation, make the secularized eschatologies of the twentieth century even more dangerous than their religious predecessors. The postwar world, Morgenthau fears, seems headed for another total war, which "may end in world dominion or in world destruction or in both."[65]

This situation is the result of the almost complete dissolution of a Western intellectual and moral consensus that emerged at the end of the Thirty Years' War with the Peace of Westphalia and the beginning of the modern state system. To understand Morgenthau's diagnosis of the twentieth century, one must therefore grasp the general outlines of a much longer historical narrative. Before outlining this narrative, however, it is worth noting that Morgenthau is no historian. He proceeds in broad strokes and presents empirical evidence in a way

---

Truth and Tragedy: A Tribute to Hans J. Morgenthau, ed. Kenneth W. Thompson and Robert John Myers (New Brunswick: Transaction Books, 1977), 15–16. Less attention, however, has been given to Reinhold Niebuhr as an intellectual touchstone in Morgenthau's political theological arguments. As we shall see, Morgenthau argues that Nazism, Marxism, and American liberal internationalism are secular political religions that that reproduce an apocalyptic eschatology. Niebuhr made similar arguments in Reinhold Niebuhr, *Moral Man and Immoral Society: A Study in Ethics and Politics* (New York: Charles Scribner's Sons, 1932), 61–62, 146, 154–56; Reinhold Niebuhr, *The Nature and Destiny of Man: A Christian Interpretation*, vol. 2 (New York: Charles Scribner's Sons, 1943), 18, 240–41; Reinhold Niebuhr, *The Irony of American History* (Chicago: University of Chicago Press, 2008), 65–88. For Christoph Frei, Morgenthau's frequent citation of and praise for Niebuhr is not evidence of the former's profound intellectual debt to the latter, but rather of the former's strategy of making German ideas palatable to an American audience. See: Frei, *Hans J. Morgenthau*, 111. The main challenge for this sort of argument is that it has difficulty accounting for Morgenthau's private acknowledgments of the depth of this intellectual connection. Toward the end of his life, Niebuhr wrote to Morgenthau: "I am forced to ask whether all my insights are not borrowed from Hans Morgenthau." Morgenthau wrote back: "I have asked myself the same question with reference to you, and I am sure I have by far the better of the argument." As quoted in: Rice, *Reinhold Niebuhr*, 147. I have a hard time dismissing Morgenthau's response as merely a kind reassurance to a dying friend.

[65] Hans J. Morgenthau, "World Politics in the Mid-Twentieth Century," *The Review of Politics* 10, no. 2 (1948): 172–73. Parts of this essay are reproduced in chs. 18–20 of Hans J. Morgenthau, *Politics Among Nations: The Struggle for Power and Peace* (New York: Alfred A. Knopf, 1948). When dealing with material that appears in both texts, I will cite only the original article.

Apocalypse "Under an Empty Sky"

that is at best highly selective and at worst willfully blind to established historical facts. His goal, however, is not to offer an accurate account of the history of interstate conflict. Rather, it is to deploy a historical narrative to support a polemical diagnosis of the postwar international order.

Morgenthau argues that in antiquity and the Middle Ages, war was total and "whole populations faced each other as personal enemies."[66] Participants in the religious wars from the Crusades through the early seventeenth century were motivated by an unwavering confidence in the justice of their cause and the imperative of eradicating their evil foes. In such a situation, there can be no meaningful limits on either the tactics or targets of violence. One must either force one's enemies to submit or annihilate them altogether.[67] Morgenthau's argument here is spotty and underdeveloped. Much of it must be inferred from the comparisons he makes between historical religious wars and twentieth-century secular crusades.[68]

However, his point becomes clearer if we supplement it with a strikingly similar historical narrative in Carl Schmitt's work. Schmitt argues that the theological notion of a just war turned the conflicts of the Middle Ages and the creedal wars of the sixteenth and seventeenth centuries into total wars. Instead of limiting the tactics and targets of violence, the doctrine of the just war encouraged each side to see the other as unjust and therefore as the legitimate target of complete annihilation.[69]

Morgenthau appears to be making a similar point when he argues that in the pre-Westphalian era, "belligerents were held to be free, according to ethics as well as law, to kill all enemies regardless of whether or not they were members of the armed forces, or else to treat them in any way they saw fit."[70]

---

[66] Hans J. Morgenthau, "The Twilight of International Morality," *Ethics* 58, no. 2 (1948): 85.

[67] This picture of warfare in Europe during the Middle Ages, along with the more detailed one that Schmitt offers, exemplify the kind of problematic presentation of history that I flagged earlier. To be sure, there were a few examples of the kinds of conflicts Morgenthau describes – the slaughter of Muslims in Palestine by Crusaders (1095–1099, 1147–1149, 1187–1192); attacks on Jews in the Rhineland by the same Crusaders (1096); the Albigensian Crusade against the Cathars in southern France (1209–1229), and some episodes during the religious wars between the mid-sixteenth and mid-seventeenth centuries. While these incidents are significant, they hardly amount to an accurate *general* characterization of the nature of medieval warfare. I am grateful to John Najemy for alerting me to these examples.

[68] See, e.g., Morgenthau, "Twilight," 85–87.

[69] Carl Schmitt, *The Nomos of the Earth in the International Law of Jus Publicum Europaeum*, trans. G. L. Ulmen (New York: Telos Press, 2003), 141–42. *The Nomos of the Earth* was first published in 1950, after Morgenthau had made the historical case outlined here. However, Schmitt was developing these arguments in various works throughout the 1930s and 1940s and it is plausible that Morgenthau would have been familiar with them. For an account of the evolution of the historical narrative and arguments advanced in Nomos, see: G. L. Ulmen, "Translator's Introduction," in Carl Schmitt, Nomos of the Earth, 9–34.

[70] Morgenthau's only evidence on this point is Hugo Grotius's catalog of war atrocities in chapter 4, book 3 of Grotius's *On the Law of War and Peace*. See: Morgenthau, "Twilight," 82, 82–3. However, this passage does help to explain a worry that Morgenthau shares with Schmitt: that

For Morgenthau, as for Schmitt, the 1648 Peace of Westphalia that brought the Thirty Years' War to an end marks a decisive turning point and the beginning of a new era of European international politics. Like Schmitt, he looks back on this period with unapologetic nostalgia.[71] By 1648, "sovereignty as supreme power over a certain territory was a political fact, signifying the victory of the territorial princes over the universal authority of Emperor and Pope, on the one hand, and over the particularistic aspirations of the feudal barons, on the other."[72] At this point, argues Morgenthau, individual citizens found that only their sovereigns could issue and enforce orders. Sovereigns found that they could not exert authority within the territory of other states without first obtaining permission from their sovereign counterpart or by defeating them in war. The doctrine of sovereignty elevated these "facts" into a legal theory.

the twentieth-century revival of the medieval doctrine of just war in secular liberal garb provides the precondition for total wars of annihilation. See: Morgenthau, *Politics Among Nations* (1948), 289; Morgenthau, "Twilight," 87, 97; Schmitt, Nomos *of the Earth*, 259–80.

[71] Morgenthau's and Schmitt's construction of the Peace of Westphalia as an historical turning point that fundamentally reordered both the structural and normative foundations of international politics is now widely recognized as a myth that does not withstand historical scrutiny. On historical grounds, this account makes at least two significant errors. First, it imputes to the two treaties of the Peace of Westphalia doctrines that are to be found nowhere in the documents themselves. The treaties do not confirm the sovereignty or independence of the signatories, nor do they articulate any general principle of sovereignty. See: Andreas Osiander, "Sovereignty, International Relations, and the Westphalian Myth," *International Organization* 55, no. 2 (2001): 260–68. Second, the traditional account of the Peace of Westphalia fails to acknowledge the gradual nature of the development of the modern state system. In fact, modern states of the kind envisioned in the traditional account did not even begin to emerge until the eighteenth century. Before then, the European "state system" was comprised of "dynastic and other pre-modern communities." According to Benno Teschke's detailed historical work, this situation only began to change when the rise of modern capitalism and British power prompted the institutional revolutions that would lead to what we now recognize as modern European statehood. See: Benno Teschke, "Theorizing the Westphalian System of States: International Relations from Absolutism to Capitalism," *European Journal of International Relations* 8, no. 1 (2002): 6, 30–38. In addition, state sovereignty and the associated norm of non-intervention have consistently been violated. As Stephen Krasner summarizes, "Neither Westphalian nor international legal sovereignty has ever been a stable equilibrium from which rulers had no incentives to deviate. Rather, Westphalian and international legal sovereignty are best understood as examples of organized hypocrisy." See: Stephen D. Krasner, *Sovereignty* (Princeton: Princeton University Press, 1999), 24. However, Morgenthau's conventional presentation of the Westphalian story was not unusual for its time. In the same year that he published his own extensive treatment of sovereignty, Leo Gross released his immensely influential article. Leo Gross, "The Peace of Westphalia, 1648–1948," *American Journal of International Law* 42, no. 1 (1948): 20–41. Here, Gross proclaimed that the Peace of Westphalia "represents the majestic portal which leads from the old into the new world" (28). On the influence of Gross' article in international relations, see: Osiander, "Sovereignty, International Relations," 264–66.

[72] Hans J. Morgenthau, "The Problem of Sovereignty Reconsidered," *Columbia Law Review* 48, no. 3 (1948): 341. Parts of this essay are reproduced in ch. 17 of Morgenthau's *Politics Among Nations* (1948). When dealing with material that appears in both texts, I will cite only the original article.

Apocalypse "Under an Empty Sky"

The individual sovereign was the "sole source of man-made law, that is, of all positive law, but was not himself subject to it."[73]

The independence of these sovereign states was maintained by a Western tradition that "imposed moral and legal limitations on the struggle for power on the international scene and...maintained order in the international community."[74] For Morgenthau, this supranational moral consensus was explicitly Eurocentric and aristocratic. It was a consensus among princes, aristocratic rulers, and high-level diplomats, who were connected with their counterparts in other states "through family ties, a common language (which was French), common cultural values, a common style of life, and common moral convictions as to what a gentleman was and was not allowed to do in his relations with another gentleman, whether of his own or of a foreign nation."[75] As sovereigns jostled for power on the international stage, they did so "as competitors in a game whose rules were accepted by all the other competitors."[76] In contrast to the participants in creedal wars, an aristocratic member of the modern state system would not even consider imposing his own particularistic conception of justice on others. In fact, "the very possibility of such an aspiration never occurred to them, since they were aware only of one universal moral code to which they all gave unquestioning allegiance."[77]

For Morgenthau, the most important effect of this supranational moral consensus was that it placed limits on international conflict and humanized warfare. Once enemies were no longer understood as evil foes to be annihilated,

---

[73] Morgenthau, "Problem of Sovereignty," 341. As Nicolas Guilhot notes, Morgenthau's point here is related to Schmitt's proclamation: "Sovereign is he who decides on the exception." See: Carl Schmitt, *Political Theology: Four Chapters on the Concept of Sovereignty*, trans. George Schwab (Chicago: University of Chicago Press, 2006), 5; Guilhot, "American *Katechon*," 240.

[74] Morgenthau, "World Politics," 154. [75] Morgenthau, "Twilight," 88.

[76] Morgenthau, "Twilight," 88. Schmitt makes a similar point when he argues that the rise of the sovereign state made international conflict in Europe analogous to a duel. The justice of a duel is not determined by assessing whether one side or another has a just cause. Rather, a duel is just when "there are certain guarantees in the preservation of the form – the quality of the parties to the conflict as agents, in the adherence to a specific procedure...and, especially, in the inclusion of witnesses on equal footing...A challenge to a duel (*défi*) was neither aggression nor a crime, any more than was a declaration of war." See: Schmitt, *Nomos of the Earth*, 143. As a member of a German dueling fraternity during his early twenties, Morgenthau might have particularly appreciated this analogy.

[77] Morgenthau, "Twilight," 98. For Morgenthau, this moral code is only universal within the European state system. In fact, the expansion of the colonial frontier provided an outlet for state ambitions, thereby helping states to maintain the "universal moral code" among their European partners. In fact, Morgenthau attributes the decline of the nineteenth-century international system, along with the normative consensus that sustained it, in part to the disappearance of the colonial frontier. See: Morgenthau, "World Politics," 164–68. Schmitt makes a similar argument about the European *nomos* (or set of international ordering principles). This Eurocentrism is the condition of possibility for their shared nostalgia. They do not have to seriously consider, for example, the extermination of indigenous peoples and the enslavement of Africans by Europeans and Euro-Americans that occurred during this period.

war began to be seen not as "a contest between whole populations but only between the armies of belligerent states."[78] This shift in the view of war led to the distinction between combatants and noncombatants, prohibited and limited the use of especially destructive and indiscriminate weapons, and restricted the reliance on "war as an instrument of international politics."[79] For Morgenthau, these moral limitations arose gradually and came to full fruition in a series of international treaties and conventions in the nineteenth and early twentieth centuries.[80] The Hague Protocols and the Geneva Convention, for instance, attest to "the existence of a moral conscience which feels ill at ease in the presence of violence or, at least, certain kinds of it on the international scene."[81]

Beyond the legal codification of these moral limits, Morgenthau finds further evidence of a supranational consensus in patterns of state behavior. He considers the hard case of Otto von Bismarck, whose "moves on the chessboard of international politics" in nineteenth-century Europe were "ruthless and immoral." Yet even Bismarck "rarely deviated from the basic rules of the game which had prevailed in the society of Christian princes of the eighteenth century. It was a fraudulent and treacherous game, but there were a few things that no member of that aristocratic society would stoop to do."[82] Bismarck, for instance, could never have contemplated the possibility of eliminating Germany's eastern and western neighbors, even though this might have been desirable from a purely technical perspective. The fact that Hitler could imagine and carry out such a strategy was a symptom of the dissolution of a supranational moral consensus that had previously restrained even the most ambitious states. Morgenthau's point is that the naked and seemingly amoral practice of international politics in the nineteenth century was made possible by an underlying supranational moral consensus. What allowed the "fraudulent and treacherous game" of European politics to operate was the fact that the supranational moral consensus prevented skirmishes and power grabs from erupting into full-scale campaigns of annihilation.

The dissolution of this consensus was, Morgenthau suggests, the unforeseen result of undeniable political progress. As many of Europe's great powers democratized, international politics ceased to be the exclusive purview of princes. It became instead the responsibility of democratically selected officials

---

[78] Morgenthau, "Twilight," 83.   [79] Morgenthau, "Twilight," 84–85.
[80] This is one of the places where Morgenthau's argument differs sharply from Schmitt's. For Schmitt, the Peace of Westphalia marked the rise of the modern territorial state and a secular European *nomos*, which served to "bracket" war between European states. While Schmitt did see cultural homogeneity as an important precondition for this *nomos*, he would have resisted the idea that a universal code (particularly one codified in the international treaties of the nineteenth and early twentieth centuries, which Schmitt sees as a symptom of the dissolution of the European *nomos*) provided the basis for the limited war of Europe's "golden age." See: Brown, "The Twilight," 51.
[81] Morgenthau, "Twilight," 84.   [82] Morgenthau, "Twilight," 81.

Apocalypse "Under an Empty Sky"

who were "legally and morally responsible for their acts, not to a monarch, that is, a specific individual, but to a collectivity, that is, a parliamentary majority, or the people as a whole."[83]

This shift had three consequences. First, officials were no longer recruited exclusively from the ranks of the aristocracy, but from a much broader cross section of the population. These new officials could not be expected to share a supranational moral consensus premised on codes of gentlemanly conduct. Second, regular elections caused frequent turnover of government officials. The lasting personal and cultural ties that held the supranational consensus together evaporated. Finally, and most importantly, the need to appeal to an electorate with diverse moral positions made the possibility of a supranational consensus impossible. Individual voters "may have no moral convictions of a supranational character at all which determine their actions on election day ... or, if they have such convictions, they will be most heterogeneous in content."[84] In this cacophony of diverse moral commitments, "international morality as an effective system of restraints on international policy becomes impossible."[85] The consensus that had held the Westphalian European state system together was crushed under the weight of democracy and pluralism.

The void left in its wake has been filled with the "particularistic and exclusive" convictions of a new nationalism.[86] Morgenthau explains that in the absence of a cohesive and aristocratic international society, the community of Western states fragmented into a plurality of national communities with their own particular moral ideals, each claiming universal validity.[87] Nations became both the supreme form of collective organization and the ultimate repositories of moral allegiances.[88] To be sure, the nineteenth-century golden age for which Morgenthau is so nostalgic had its fair share of nationalism.

---

[83] Morgenthau, "Twilight," 91.   [84] Morgenthau, "Twilight," 92.
[85] Morgenthau, "Twilight," 91.   [86] Morgenthau, "Twilight," 94.
[87] Morgenthau, "Twilight," 95.
[88] Morgenthau, "World Politics," 154. At this point in Morgenthau's argument, a careful reader might well ask: Why would individuals with the diversity and plurality of moral commitments that made a supranational consensus impossible in a democratic age be willing to commit themselves to the moral consensus required by this new form of nationalism? Morgenthau's answer to this question must be reconstructed from several sources. In "Twilight," he offers an explanation that appeals to the moral psychology of the citizen. He argues that the individual recognizes that he lives in an age in which universal moral standards cannot effectively restrain state action. States flout these universal standards and the individual's conscience is "ill at ease." Unable to give up on the idea of a universal ethics, "he pours, as it were, the contents of his national ethics into the now almost empty bottle of universal ethics." While this argument may explain the way in which an individual comes to substitute the moral standards of his own nation for the universal standards of a dying supranational consensus, it does not explain how nationalism can overcome the plurality of moral commitments that had posed such difficulties for the continued viability of an international society. See: Morgenthau, "Twilight," 96. For a more complete answer, we must turn to *Politics Among Nations*, where Morgenthau argues that a shared national identity can unite individuals around common goals, despite the plurality of moral commitments. This happens most effectively where differences and cleavages are

But nineteenth-century nationalism had the more limited goal of national liberation.[89] The nation itself was "the ultimate goal of political action, the end-point of the political development beyond which there are other nationalisms with similar goals and similar justifications."[90]

In contrast, the twentieth-century "nationalistic universalisms" of German Nazism, Soviet Communism, and American liberal internationalism see the nation as "but the starting-point of a universal mission whose ultimate goal reaches to the confines of the political world."[91] Foreign policies become sacred missions. Wars became crusades waged "for the purpose of bringing the true political religion to the rest of the world."[92] Morgenthau's characterization of this new world is striking and worth quoting at length:

> [Nations] oppose each other now as the standard-bearers of ethical systems, each of them of national origin and each of them claiming and aspiring to provide a supranational framework of moral standards which all the other nations ought to accept and within which their international policies ought to operate. The moral code of one nation flings the challenge of its universal claim in the face of another which reciprocates in kind. Compromise, the virtue of the old diplomacy, becomes the treason of the new... Thus, the stage is set for a contest among nations whose stakes are no longer their relative positions within a political and moral world accepted by all but the ability to impose upon the other contestants a new universal political and moral system recreated in the image of the victorious nation's political and moral commitments.[93]

The international system is no longer a chessboard on which monarchs and aristocrats try to improve their relative positions. It is an unlimited war between nationalist political religions with false claims to universality.

But Morgenthau is not simply criticizing the pseudo-religious tendencies of nationalistic universalism, but also the process of secularization that makes them possible.[94] The supranational consensus that had created a genuine "society" of European states was not just moral. It was also religious. The rules that constrained Bismarck in the nineteenth century were the same ones that "had prevailed in the society of *Christian* princes of the eighteenth century."[95] The supranational consensus was composed of "*Christian*, cosmopolitan, and humanitarian elements" and the international society that this moral agreement

---

crosscutting. A might find himself opposed to B on a political issue, yet allied with B on an economic issue. The "plural role of friend and opponent which A plays with regard to a number of his fellows imposes restraints upon him as both a friend and a foe." Morgenthau, *Politics Among Nations* (1954), 471. The implication is that a comparable consensus cannot (yet) exist at the international level. See also: William E. Scheuerman, *The Realist Case for Global Reform* (Cambridge: Polity, 2011), 45–46.

[89] Morgenthau, "World Politics," 155. [90] Morgenthau, "World Politics," 156.
[91] Morgenthau, "World Politics," 156. [92] Morgenthau, *Politics Among Nations* (1948), 77.
[93] Morgenthau, "Twilight," 96–97.
[94] This dimension of Morgenthau's thought has received very little attention in the secondary literature, which tends to ignore the political theological features of his work. Nicolas Guilhot's work is a notable exception and my argument here borrows from the interpretation he offers in "American *Katechon*," 242–43.
[95] Morgenthau, "Twilight," 81. Emphasis mine.

Apocalypse "Under an Empty Sky"

created "had united the monarchs and the nobility of *Christendom*."[96] The instability of the twentieth century became permanent "as a result of the weakening of the ties of the [Western] tradition, *especially in the form of religion*."[97] The nationalist pseudo-religions of the twentieth century are therefore the products not only of the dissolution of supranational ethical standards but also of secularization.[98] Invoking Hobbes, Morgenthau notes: "The state has indeed become a 'mortal God,' and for an age that believes no longer in an immortal God, the state becomes the only God there is."[99]

In the golden era of the European state system, universal religion had been tamed – transformed from the enabling condition of wars of annihilation to part of the background consensus that curbed the worst excesses of power politics. The pseudo-religions of the twentieth century drive the world back to wars of annihilation aimed at the eradication of evil. The nationalistic masses of the twentieth century meet "carrying their idols before them...each group convinced that it executes the mandate of history, that it does for humanity what it seems to do for itself, and that it fulfils a sacred mission ordained by providence, however defined. Little do they know that they meet under an empty sky from which the gods have departed."[100] The destructive nationalism of the twentieth century is a product of secularization.

The three most powerful nationalistic universalisms of Morgenthau's day were German Nazism, Soviet Communism, and American liberal internationalism. Indeed, he dates the ultimate destruction of the supranational moral consensus that had prevailed since 1648 to the rise of the Nazis in 1933.[101] For him,

---

[96] Morgenthau, "Twilight," 95, 93. Emphasis mine.

[97] Morgenthau, *Politics Among Nations* (1948), 77. Emphasis mine.

[98] These are the moments in Morgenthau's argument where he comes closest to overtly endorsing Schmitt's secularization thesis. For Schmitt, the combination of the depoliticizing tendencies of the liberal state and the separation of the political from the religious creates the conditions of possibility for a "mass belief in an antireligious activism...the belief in unlimited power and the domination of man over nature, even over human nature; the belief in the 'receding of natural boundaries,' in the unlimited possibilities for change and prosperity. Such a belief can be called fantastic and satanic, but not simply dead, spiritless, or mechanized soulessness." See: Carl Schmitt, "The Age of Neutralizations and Depoliticizations (1929)," in *The Concept of the Political*, trans. Matthias Konzen and John P. McCormick (Chicago: University of Chicago Press, 2007), 94. However, as Guilhot explains, "Schmitt does not advocate a re-theologization of politics; rather, he defends the autonomy of the political, but also warns that this autonomy is premised on the historical constitution of a territorial order distinct from, but coexisting with, the moral order embodied by the ecclesial institutions of Christianity. Should secularization proceed to the extent that the state no longer understands itself in relation to (and in tension with) this background and conflates its own interests with morality itself – as in the case of liberalism – then it would assume again religious attributes and give rise to dangerous political religions." See: Guilhot, "American *Katechon*," 234.

[99] Hans J. Morgenthau, "The Evil of Politics and the Ethics of Evil," *Ethics* 56, no. 1 (1945): 15.

[100] Morgenthau, "Twilight," 99.

[101] Morgenthau, *Politics Among Nations* (1948), 165. William Scheuerman points to this as another point of divergence between the narratives of decline offered by Morgenthau and Schmitt. For Morgenthau, 1933 marks the complete demolition of the supranational moral consensus that underpinned the Westphalian state system. For Schmitt, the Nazis were "trying

the secularized religious elements of Nazism are quite clear: "It has in Hitler its savior, in S.A., S.S., and party its sacred orders, in *Mein Kampf* its bible, in the immutable twenty-five points of the party program its catechism, in the racial community its mystical body. It has its miracles and rituals, its apostles, martyrs, and saints."[102] At its heart is an apocalyptic dualism in which "the German race is on the side of the angels, and the Jews and other 'racial degenerates' are on the side of the devil; and once the problem is posed in such terms, the solution presents no intellectual or physical difficulties."[103] The solution is the elimination of evil through mass extermination and a worldwide conquest of apocalyptic proportions. It is only through this transformative war that "the hidden will of nature and of racial destiny becomes manifest."[104]

And, like the apocalyptic religions of the creedal wars, Nazism's "claim to acceptance is absolute and not subject to critical doubt."[105] Any form of dissent is "a sacrilegious revolt against the 'voice of the blood,' through which the genius of the race makes itself known."[106] Nazism's promise of worldly salvation was proven false, its prophecies unfulfilled, and its bid for universality lost with Germany's defeat in the Second World War.[107] What is important, however, is that Morgenthau treats Nazism not as an aberrant or unique historical occurrence, but as a case of the broader phenomenon of an apocalyptic political religion whose aim is world transformation and domination.

Nazism lost its bid for universality. The world was left with two remaining political religions whose conflicts would define the postwar world – Soviet Communism and American liberal internationalism. While Morgenthau makes occasional remarks about the pseudo-religious qualities of the former[108], the overwhelming bulk of his critical attention is devoted to the latter. Like religious eschatologies, liberal internationalism has a teleological view of time. History culminates in a final battle, which will purge the forces of evil and inaugurate a world of peace and prosperity.

---

to build on the best elements of the traditional international system while warding off its real foe – the United States." See: Scheuerman, "Carl Schmitt and Hans Morgenthau," 89 (n. 23).

[102] Hans J. Morgenthau, "Nazism," in *The Decline of Democratic Politics* (Chicago: University of Chicago Press, 1962), 228.

[103] Morgenthau, "Nazism," 235.   [104] Morgenthau, "Nazism," 240.

[105] Morgenthau, "Nazism," 228.   [106] Morgenthau, "Nazism," 238.

[107] Morgenthau draws a distinction on this point between genuine religions and political religions. He explains: "All political religions stand and fall with the experimental proof of their truth. In contrast, other worldly religions are based on faith. Nobody has come back from the other world and told us whether the biblical description of heaven corresponds to reality. But a political religion, which pretends to bring salvation to men in this world and which ... pretends that salvation is just around the corner, stands and falls with the experimental proof or the correctness of its prophecies." See: Hans J. Morgenthau, "The Tragedy of German-Jewish Liberalism," in *The Decline of Democratic Politics* (Chicago: University of Chicago Press, 1962), 253.

[108] See, for instance: Morgenthau, *Scientific Man*, 32–33, 52–53; Morgenthau, "Twilight," 97; Hans J. Morgenthau, *In Defense of the National Interest: A Critical Examination of American Foreign Policy* (New York: Albert A. Knopf, 1951), 62–63.

Apocalypse "Under an Empty Sky"

However, liberal internationalism is not apocalyptic from the outset. It begins with a progressive millennial conception of history that anticipates change through gradual and peaceful transformation, rather than through cataclysmic violence. It expects the slow but inevitable spread of democracy to all corners of the world, bringing with it the benefits of education and rationalism. Liberal democracy overcomes the messy antagonisms of politics by replacing them with a rational and efficient plan, effectively reducing the political to the technical.[109] And with democracy, education, and reason comes peace. Violent conflict is "something irrational, unreasonable, an aristocratic pastime or totalitarian atavism which has no place in a rational world. War is essentially a thing of the past."[110]

Once reason becomes the driving force of international affairs, the causes of conflict disappear and any remaining disagreements can be settled peacefully. Because the rationalist philosophy that underpins liberalism identifies the rational with the good, we should also expect to see moral progress. The notion that there is one (more demanding) set of ethical standards for the individual and another (more permissive) set for the state will disappear. As Woodrow Wilson proclaimed in 1917: "We are at the beginning of an age in which it will be insisted that the same standards of conduct and of responsibility for wrong shall be observed among nations...that are observed among the individual citizens of civilized states."[111] In short, without any violent intervention, the world will march toward a more democratic, peaceful, and moral future.

Yet like other frustrated millennialist movements for whom the world fails to transform, liberal internationalists seek explanations for the inability of history to achieve its ends. Faced with uneven evidence of the spread of democracy or the success of international legal reforms, "the internationalists take the appropriateness of the devices for granted and blame the facts for the failure. 'When the facts behave otherwise than we have predicted,' they seem to say, 'too bad for the facts.'"[112] The obstacles are not the schemes themselves or the belief in human perfectibility upon which they are based, but rather "lack of knowledge and understanding, obsolescent social institutions, or the depravity of certain isolated individuals or groups."[113] The failure to overcome the irrationality of war with a democratic peace is blamed on totalitarian and aristocratic states, or on evil and criminal nations which disrupt the normalcy of "peaceful competition and cooperation."[114]

---

[109] Morgenthau, *Scientific Man*, 27–37. Morgenthau's concerns here mirror Schmitt's that liberalism reduces politics to technology. See: Carl Schmitt, "Neutralizations and Depoliticizations," 80–96.
[110] Morgenthau, *Scientific Man*, 47.
[111] As quoted in Morgenthau, *Scientific Man*, 44. This identity of the individual and the state is also central to international law.
[112] Morgenthau, *Scientific Man*, 39.   [113] Morgenthau, *Politics Among Nations*, 1954, 3.
[114] Morgenthau, *National Interest*, 93, 95. See also: Morgenthau, *Scientific Man*, 51.

For Morgenthau, this turns the conflicts of the postwar era into battles of good versus evil. In contrast to the "selfless and moral" foreign policies of the United States, "the foreign policies of other nations are by definition selfish and immoral. Since the United States is the policeman of the world seeking only peace and order and the welfare of all, only evil nations can dare oppose it. They are criminals when they act alone, conspirators when they act in unison."[115] And if criminals cannot be made peaceful through education and reform, "they must be converted with fire and sword."[116]

Liberal idealism thus falls victim to the same dangers as medieval just war thinking. The moral limits on war that were crystallized in the international treaties of the nineteenth and early twentieth centuries become meaningless. When confronting an unjust foe, "the moral duty to spare the wounded, the sick, the surrendering and unarmed enemy, and to respect him as a human being who was an enemy only by virtue of being found on the other side of the fence is superseded by the moral duty to punish and to wipe off the face of the earth the professors and practitioners of evil."[117] Convinced that they have justice on their side, liberal internationalists will fight total wars that can only end in the annihilation or unconditional surrender of the unjust enemy.

Given their abhorrence of war, liberal internationalists justify these battles by investing them with apocalyptic significance. This is what Woodrow Wilson did, for example, when he announced to America and the world in 1918 that World War I would be "the final and culminating war for human liberty." For Morgenthau, such slogans are not propaganda meant to conceal the base power interests of the United States. Rather, "they are the expression of an eschatological hope deeply embedded in the very foundations of liberal foreign policy."[118] That hope is for a world transformation through a final and decisive battle against the irrational forces of evil. The promise of such a battle, as well as the grounds for its moral justification, is that it is the necessary prelude to a permanent peace. The liberal millennium is "a brave new world" in which states do not engage in power politics and where the concept of a national interest becomes meaningless in a "community of interests comprising mankind."[119]

For Morgenthau, who conceptualizes politics as a particularly intense form of antagonism and conflict, the liberal millennium amounts to nothing less than "the repudiation of politics."[120] It is a dangerous apocalyptic fantasy that takes aim at both the individual's desire for power and states' pursuit of their

---

[115] Morgenthau, *National Interest*, 93.   [116] Morgenthau, *National Interest*, 37.
[117] Morgenthau, "Twilight," 87. Morgenthau thought he saw evidence for this shift in World War II, where the violation of these moral limits is "a matter of fact."
[118] Morgenthau, *Scientific Man*, 52.
[119] Morgenthau, *National Interest*, 26. Morgenthau's use of overtly eschatological language is indisputable. He titles a section on utopianism "After the War – The Millennium" in *In Defense of the National Interest*, 92.
[120] Morgenthau, *Scientific Man*, 41. Morgenthau's understanding of the political is strikingly similar to that of Schmitt. However, in this case, the direction of influence is reversed. There is

national interests. Because these desires are unchanging, liberal wars can never be "last wars." Instead, like World War I, they will be merely "the forerunners and pioneers of wars more destructive and extensive than any liberal epoch had witnessed."[121] This possibility loomed large over the postwar world, in which American liberal internationalism had met its crusading foe in Soviet Communism and both had found in nuclear weapons the means to match their totalizing ends.

Like Machiavelli, Morgenthau responds to the apocalyptic political religions of his time by turning to tragedy. While this turn pervades much of his work from the 1940s and 1950s, Morgenthau's clearest articulation of the tragic worldview is in the final chapters of *Scientific Man vs. Power Politics* (1946). Here, he aims to recover a "tragic sense of life" that has been lost in the modern era. At the root of a tragic worldview is "the awareness of unresolvable discord, contradictions, and conflicts which are inherent in the nature of things and which human reason is powerless to solve."[122] Morgenthau's turn to tragedy is often read as a critique of the scientism and rationalism that underpin the liberal tradition.[123] There is certainly ample textual evidence to support this interpretation. However, it does not exhaust the possibilities of Morgenthau's tragic worldview. In the foregoing analysis, I have drawn out the political-theological dimensions of Morgenthau's portrait of crusading liberalism. I suggest here that his tragic turn is a response and an alternative to liberal internationalism's apocalyptic imaginary.

Against the teleology of the liberal millennial and apocalyptic narratives, Morgenthau defends a tragic and cyclical conception of time. The fortunes of states and men rise and decline in an "everlasting and ever undecided struggle" with no hope for a settled end to political conflict.[124] Here, Morgenthau could have looked to classical Greek tragedy or to the rich German revival of the genre in the work of Friedrich Nietzsche and Max Weber, among others.[125] He does

---

good evidence that Schmitt changed his understanding of the political as a result of Morgenthau's criticisms. William Scheuerman summarizes the evidence well. The first edition of Schmitt's *Concept of the Political* had conceptualized "the political as constituting a fundamentally distinct and independent sphere of activity, existing alongside alternative modes of human activity." For Morgenthau, the political denoted a particularly intense form of conflict and antagonism. Thus, any sphere of human activity could become political if it became the site of intense conflict. In response to Morgenthau's criticisms, the second edition of the *Concept of the Political* "dropped the misleading imagery of politics as a distinct or separate sphere, instead following Morgenthau's conceptualization of politics as concerning conflicts characterized by intense enmity." See: Scheuerman, *Hans Morgenthau*, 33.

[121] Morgenthau, *Scientific Man*, 67.   [122] Morgenthau, *Scientific Man*, 206.
[123] Lebow, *The Tragic Vision of Politics*, 48–49, 308; Frei, *Hans J. Morgenthau*, 85–89.
[124] Morgenthau, *Scientific Man*, 206.
[125] We know that Morgenthau was reading Nietzsche as he completed *Scientific Man vs. Power Politics*. He wrote to the head of the University of Chicago library and alerted them to the fact that they had only single volumes of some of Nietzsche's most "indispensable works." See: Frei, *Hans J. Morgenthau*, 188.

not do so overtly.[126] Instead, he draws on the Christian pre-rationalist tradition of Duns Scotus, Augustine, Thomas Aquinas, and Martin Luther, all of whom acknowledge that "the sinfulness of man is...not an accidental disturbance of the order of the world sure to be overcome by a gradual development toward the good but...an inescapable necessity which gives meaning to the existence of man and which only an act of grace and salvation is able to overcome."[127]

Morgenthau's appeal to a language of sin and salvation is taken by some interpreters to be a means of concealing the German origins of his ideas for an American audience only beginning to recover from World War II.[128] However, his use of the Christian pre-rationalist tradition also allows him to make an important anti-apocalyptic move. He asserts: "There is no progress toward the good, noticeable from year to year, but undecided conflict which sees today good, tomorrow evil, prevail; and only at the end of time, *immeasurably removed from the here and now of our earthly life*, the ultimate triumph of the forces of goodness and light will be assured."[129] Morgenthau borrows from the conservative eschatology of Augustine and locates the apocalyptic triumph of good over evil in an unforeseeable future. When and if it ever happens, this triumph will come in the form of a divine act, not as the product of human agency. In the secular world of the here and now, history offers no hope for a final and settled end to conflict. The best one can hope for is to be "passed by for a time by the stream of events" in a tragic drama played out again and again.[130]

Morgenthau argues that any human project that aims at a final and just peace ignores the tragic limits to political action. The effects of our actions always escape our intentions. There are three reasons for this. First, we are caught between our higher moral and spiritual aspirations, on the one hand, and our animal drive to dominate, on the other. As a result, man "is forever condemned to experience the contrast between the longings of his mind and his actual condition as his personal, eminently human tragedy."[131] While

---

[126] The final chapter of *Scientific Man* is rich in unacknowledged Weberian echoes.
[127] Morgenthau, *Scientific Man*, 204.
[128] Frei, *Hans J. Morgenthau*, 189. For a similar argument about other aspects of Morgenthau's thought, see: Guilhot, "American *Katechon*," 240–47.
[129] Morgenthau, *Scientific Man*, 205–06. Emphasis mine.
[130] Morgenthau, *National Interest*, 92.
[131] Morgenthau, *Scientific Man*, 221. Machiavelli makes a seemingly similar point when he argues that "since from nature [men] have the ability and the wish to desire all things and from fortune the ability to achieve few of them, there continually results from this a discontent in human minds." See: Machiavelli, *Discourses on Livy*, preface to book II, 125. However, for Morgenthau the crucial contrast is between the moral or spiritual "longings of the mind" and our capacity to fulfill them, given our animal drive to dominate. For Machiavelli, the crucial contrast is between man's natural insatiable appetites and his capacity to achieve them, given the limits imposed by fortune. Here, then, Morgenthau's tragic vision seems to share more with Paul than with Machiavelli. For Paul, there is a tragic conflict between our intentions and our actions: "For I do not do the good I want, but the evil I do not want is what I do...So then, with my mind I am a slave to the law of God, but with my flesh I am a slave to the law of sin." See: Rom. 7:19, 25.

the age of science promises to engineer "a new man whose powers equal his aspirations and who masters human destiny as he masters a machine," this promise soon reveals itself to be nothing more than "the old *hybris*...in the new vestments of a scientific age."[132] We are condemned to an eternal agonism between our higher aspirations and our lower drives. Thus, we will often be unable to recognize our moral intentions in our political actions.

Second, even if we can temporarily master our urge to dominate, we are unable to control and anticipate the worldly effects of our deeds. Once performed, an action acquires a kind of autonomy, colliding with other actions and provoking responses, leading to consequences that we could never have foreseen and have only a limited capacity to control. These collisions "deflect the action from its intended goal and create evil results of our intentions."[133]

Third, our best intentions may be corrupted even before they are translated into actions. The world confronts us with tragic choices between equally legitimate ends. The necessity of making a choice means that our actions are never wholly good. In pursuing one moral end, we inevitably abandon another. Morgenthau confronts us with the familiar example of the conflict between our religious and secular duties: "While trying to render to Caesar what is Caesar's and to God what is God's, we will at best strike a precarious balance which will ever waver between both, never completely satisfying either."[134] These kinds of conflicts are particularly pronounced in politics, where the connections of the self to others through action multiply.

For Morgenthau, as for Machiavelli, the best statesmen are those who recognize these tragic conflicts and still manage to act:

> To know with despair that the political act is inevitably evil, and to act nevertheless, is moral courage. To choose among several expedient actions the least evil one is moral judgment. In the combination of political wisdom, moral courage, and moral judgment, man reconciles his political nature with his moral destiny. That this conciliation is nothing more than a *modus vivendi*, uneasy, precarious, and even paradoxical, can disappoint only those who prefer to gloss over and to distort the tragic contradictions of human existence with the soothing logic of specious concord.[135]

These precarious and temporary conciliations are the best that we can hope for in a tragic world. The expectation of a final overcoming of this *modus vivendi* is a dangerous illusion. It reflects a desire to escape from the moral conflict and struggle of the political condition.

---

[132] Morgenthau, *Scientific Man*, 221, 222.

[133] Morgenthau, *Scientific Man*, 189. The Weberian echoes are especially pronounced. Weber: "The final result of political action often, no, even regularly stands in completely inadequate and often paradoxical relation to its original meaning. This is fundamental to all history." See: Max Weber, *Politics as a Vocation*, trans. H. H. Gerth and C. Wright Mills (London: Routledge, 2009), 117.

[134] Morgenthau, *Scientific Man*, 190.

[135] Morgenthau, *Scientific Man*, 203. Machiavelli makes a similar point about expediency and moral judgment at least three times. See: Machiavelli, *The Prince*, ch. 21, p. 91; Machiavelli, *Discourses on Livy*, I.6, 22, 1.38, 81–82.

Nuclear Death

Morgenthau would soon come to recognize the limits of this tragic worldview. While tragedy resists apocalyptic thinking, it also struggles to help us confront radically novel threats, like the possibility of total nuclear war. Morgenthau's writings from the 1950s are marked by a struggle to come to terms with this novel threat. In the early 1960s, however, he took a decisive turn away from tragedy and toward a Hobbesian strategy of redirection, or fighting apocalypse with apocalypse. His remarkable 1961 essay "Death in the Nuclear Age" offers a terrifying account of an apocalypse without redemption or renewal. This section of the chapter traces Morgenthau's turn away from a tragic worldview and toward a prophetic attempt to imagine the apocalypse in order to prevent it.

During the late 1940s and 1950s, Morgenthau struggled to grasp the radical novelty of nuclear weapons. His position developed and changed with advances in nuclear capabilities. Initially, he "conventionalized" nuclear weapons, treating them as quantitative "improvements" on the destructive capacities of conventional weapons rather than as part of a qualitative transformation of the nature of war and the prospects for human survival. In the late 1940s, Morgenthau tended to cast nuclear weapons as merely the latest stage in the mechanization of warfare – they represented a development similar in kind to the invention of the machine gun, though far greater in magnitude.[136] However, even in these early writings, he acknowledges that this development, along with the crusading political religions of the twentieth century, makes total war possible.[137]

The obvious solution to this problem is a world state that can extract loyalty from humanity, provide the "citizens" of the world with some measure of justice, and establish a "monopoly of organized violence."[138] The mistake of previous advocates of international government had been to assume that such an institution could be imposed from above. Just as a national state emerges from the bottom-up demands of a society, a world state would first require a world society. Following John Stuart Mill, Morgenthau recognizes that "political machinery does not act of itself. As it is first made, so it has to be worked, by men, and even by ordinary men. It needs, not their simple acquiescence, but their active participation." A viable political order must meet "three conditions. The people for whom the form of government is intended must be willing to accept it; or least not so unwilling as to oppose an insurmountable obstacle to its establishment. They must be willing and able to do what is necessary to keep it standing. And they must be willing and able to do what it requires of them to

---

[136] Morgenthau, *Politics Among Nations* (1948), 296–97.
[137] Morgenthau, "World Politics," 172–73.
[138] Morgenthau, *Politics Among Nations* (1948), 395, 392–400. Interestingly, Morgenthau does not cite Max Weber here. He also replaces "legitimate" with "organized."

enable it to fulfil its purposes."[139] Morgenthau concludes that no such society exists to support a world state.[140]

There is no escaping the fact that most people still invest their highest loyalties in the nation-state. Occasional bursts of international humanitarian assistance aside, there is little evidence of the kind of supranational society required to create a world state. Thus, Morgenthau concludes: "There is no shirking the conclusion that international peace cannot be permanent without a world state, and that a world state cannot be established under the present moral, social, and political conditions of the world." The tragedy, he goes on, is that "in no period of modern history was civilization in more need of permanent peace and, hence, of a world state, and that in no period of modern history were the moral, social, and political conditions of the world less favorable for the establishment of a world state."[141]

Morgenthau's solution is to cast the creation of a world community as a long-term goal, the first step toward which is to minimize the sources of conflict. He therefore concludes *Politics Among Nations* with a nostalgic plea for a return to the tradition of nineteenth-century European diplomacy.[142] This solution rests uneasily with the analysis in the rest of this work. The supranational consensus that made nineteenth-century diplomacy possible has eroded. A return to that past is impossible.[143] In the shadow of the atomic bomb, Morgenthau's prescriptions seemed to assume a world that no longer existed.

During the 1950s, Morgenthau acknowledged the novelty of nuclear weapons, while still clinging to conventional solutions. For him, the successful Soviet test of an atomic bomb in 1949 was "an event of the greatest importance. In comparison with it, all the great issues of the postwar period fade into insignificance."[144] His response to this frightening news was a demand for massive and rapid American rearmament and almost unqualified support for the development of the hydrogen bomb.[145] Morgenthau responded with

---

[139] John Stuart Mill, *Considerations on Representative Government*, in *On Liberty and Other Essays*, ed. John Gray (Oxford: Oxford University Press, 2008), 207.
[140] Morgenthau, *Politics Among Nations* (1954), 478–79. See also: Campbell Craig, *Glimmer of a New Leviathan: Total War in the Realism of Niebuhr, Morgenthau, and Waltz* (New York: Columbia University Press, 2003), 66; Scheuerman, *The Realist Case for Global Reform*, 82–83.
[141] Morgenthau, *Politics Among Nations* (1948), 402.
[142] Morgenthau, *Politics Among Nations* (1948), 419–45. Morgenthau himself seems to recognize that this solution is anachronistic. He writes: "Diplomacy is the best means of preserving peace which a society of sovereign nations has to offer, but, especially under the conditions of modern world politics and of modern war, it is not good enough" (445).
[143] As one of Morgenthau's contemporary critics notes, "such a return to diplomacy is impossible without...the repeal of the nineteenth and twentieth centuries." See: James P. Speer, "Hans Morgenthau and the World State," *World Politics* 20, no. 2 (1968): 222.
[144] Morgenthau, *National Interest*, 174.
[145] Morgenthau, *National Interest*, 178–80; Hans J. Morgenthau, "The H-Bomb and After," in *The Restoration of American Politics* (Chicago: University of Chicago Press, 1962), 119–27.

similar alarm in the aftermath of the 1957 Soviet satellite launches, urging both a conventional weapons build-up and the direction of the "total resources of the nation toward achieving an operational ICBM at the earliest possible moment."[146] In response to the novel threat of nuclear war, Morgenthau still seemed to be reacting with conventional pleas for a balance of power between the United States and the Soviet Union.

Yet lurking behind these prescriptions was a growing suspicion that such responses would be insufficient. For instance, while he acknowledges that nuclear deterrence could be "a force for peace, however precarious,"[147] Morgenthau worries that the psychology of deterrence is dangerously complex and vulnerable to disastrous miscalculations.[148] Similarly, while he urges the United States to prepare for and be willing to fight a limited nuclear war, he worries that the success of such a war rests on leaders with an almost superhuman capacity to determine "just the right atomic dosage" required to avoid defeat without provoking "all-out atomic retaliation."[149]

Only by the end of the decade did these doubts develop into a complete and unwavering conception of the novelty of nuclear era. He concludes:

[The] rational relationship between the means of violence and the ends of foreign policy has been destroyed by the availability of nuclear power as a means to achieve those ends. For the possibility of universal destruction obliterates the means-end relationship itself by threatening the nations and their ends with total destruction. No such radical qualitative transformation of the structure of international relations has ever occurred in history.[150]

Nuclear weapons had not only changed the practice of warfare, but had transformed international politics.[151]

It is hardly surprising that Morgenthau took more than a decade to fully acknowledge the radical novelty of the nuclear era. The tragic worldview that he embraced in the 1940s and 1950s was a powerful counter-apocalyptic vision. But it also resisted any claims of radical novelty. Against an apocalyptic teleology that expects a decisive break with human history, the tragic worldview insists on a cyclical conception of time. The same conflicts repeat themselves again and again. For Morgenthau, the inescapability of our tragic situation is guaranteed by two constants of human nature – the lust for power and the

---

[146] Hans J. Morgenthau, "Russian Technology and American Policy," *Current History* 34, no. 119 (1998): 132.
[147] Hans J. Morgenthau, "Has Atomic War Really Become Impossible?" in *The Restoration of American Politics* (Chicago: University of Chicago Press, 1962), 137.
[148] Hans J. Morgenthau, "Atomic Force and Foreign Policy," in *The Restoration of American Politics* (Chicago: University of Chicago Press, 1962), 160.
[149] Morgenthau, "Atomic War," 140.
[150] Hans J. Morgenthau, "The Intellectual and Moral Dilemma of Politics," in *The Decline of Democratic Politics* (Chicago: University of Chicago Press, 1962), 12.
[151] Scheuerman, *Morgenthau*, 143.

Nuclear Death

will to dominate.[152] These drives condemn us to a world of unresolvable discord whose patterns are so regular that they can be treated as unchanging laws.[153]

The benefit of a tragic worldview is that we can turn to the past for guidance. The conflicts of our age will always have historical analogs. However, the problem with a tragic worldview is not only that it makes us suspicious of claims to radical novelty, but also that it leaves us without any intellectual or normative tools to confront that novelty. Morgenthau's University of Chicago colleague Hannah Arendt had diagnosed a similar problem in the conventional view of twentieth-century totalitarianism.[154] We have a tendency, she explains, to equate "totalitarian government with some well-known evil of the past, such as aggression, tyranny, conspiracy." This is understandable. If the evils of the present were also the evils of the past, we can look to the past for political wisdom.[155] The problem is that "the wisdom of the past ... dies, so to speak, in our hands as soon as we try to apply it honestly to the central political experiences of our own time. Everything we know of totalitarianism demonstrates a horrible originality which no farfetched historical parallels can alleviate."[156] This is the dilemma that Morgenthau confronts when his tragic worldview collides with the radical novelty of nuclear weapons. Tragedy had been a valuable antidote for a "civilization that likes to see novelty in history where there is none." However, it was ill-suited for a world that seemed "to perceive but dimly the genuine novelty with which nuclear power confronts it."[157]

In his remarkable essay, "Death in the Nuclear Age" (1961), Morgenthau adopts a new strategy. He harnesses the darkest fears of annihilation against the radical hope of renewal through nuclear destruction. He calls upon his readers to imagine the apocalypse in order to prevent it. Both the expressive style of the essay and its existential preoccupations mark a definitive break from his

---

[152] Morgenthau, *Scientific Man*, 192.
[153] Morgenthau, *Politics Among Nations* (1954), 4–13.
[154] In "An Introduction *into* Politics," Arendt labels atomic war and totalitarianism as twin threats to politics. See: Hannah Arendt, "An Introduction *into* Politics," in *The Promise of Politics*, ed. Jerome Kohn (New York: Schocken Books, 2005), 109; Jonathan Schell, "In Search of a Miracle: Hannah Arendt and the Atomic Bomb," in *Politics in Dark Times: Encounters with Hannah Arendt*, ed. Seyla Benhabib, Roy T. Tsao, and Peter Verovsek (New York: Cambridge University Press, 2010), 247–58.
[155] Robert Jervis suggests that the tendency to conventionalize nuclear weapons – to deny their radical novelty by treating them as mere quantitative "improvements" on conventional weapons – is intellectually appealing for the same reason. It "allows the analyst to use familiar concepts and apply ideas and arguments which have proven their utility over centuries of experience." See: Robert Jervis, *The Illogic of American Nuclear Strategy* (Ithaca: Cornell University Press, 1985), 57.
[156] Hannah Arendt, "Understanding and Politics (The Difficulties of Understanding)," in *Essays in Understanding, 1930–1954: Formation, Exile, and Totalitarianism*, ed. Jerome Kahn (New York: Schocken Books, 1994), 309.
[157] Morgenthau, "Intellectual and Moral Dilemma," 12.

previous writings.[158] He takes aim at what he sees as a dangerous complacency toward the prospect of a nuclear war.

His most obvious target, and one whom he engages directly in other writings of this period, is RAND strategist Herman Kahn.[159] Throughout the 1950s and 1960s, Kahn argued that a nuclear war would differ only in magnitude, but not in kind, from the wars of the past. The United States could survive a nuclear war and its remaining inhabitants could even resume something like a normal life.[160] As we saw earlier, such predictions formed the basis of even more radical hopes. For some, nuclear destruction would be an opportunity for courage and heroism or, in the words of the 1956 report on "The Human Effects of Nuclear Weapons Development," a chance to "make the very best of the very worst." Popular publications such as *Time* and *Life* magazines offered hopeful images of families emerging from their fallout shelters ready to create the world anew.

For Morgenthau, these are desperate delusions. Implicating both himself and his readers, he warns: "In spite of what some of us know in our reason, we continue to think and act as though the possibility of nuclear death portended only a quantitative extension of the mass destruction of the past and not a qualitative transformation of the meaning of our existence."[161] While he agreed with Kahn that we must be willing to "think about the unthinkable," Morgenthau could accept neither the RAND strategist's economistic optimism nor the redemptive hopes that it fueled. Perversely, the optimistic and redemptive confrontations with the unthinkable seemed to make nuclear annihilation more likely. Hopeful visions convinced some that we could survive and even prosper after a nuclear war and provided others with the moral cover to wage one. Morgenthau needed

---

[158] Part of the explanation for this shift may lie in the fierce public debates about a nuclear test ban treaty in the early 1960s. However, as William Scheuerman has persuasively argued, "it remains difficult to escape the conclusion that Morgenthau's encounter with Karl Jaspers' influential *The Future of Mankind* helped to crystallize as well as funnel longstanding anxieties in a constructive theoretical direction." Hannah Arendt had helped to arrange for the translation of Jaspers's book and appears to have asked Morgenthau to review it. The review was published in *Saturday Review* several months before Morgenthau's essay on nuclear death. Morgenthau praised Jaspers's book as "a work of major importance" and "the only systematic undertaking to integrate the fact of atomic power into a philosophical system." See: Scheuerman, *Morgenthau*, 146; Hans J. Morgenthau, "An Atomic Philosophy," *The Saturday Review*, February 18, 1961, 18.

[159] See, for example: Hans J. Morgenthau, "The Intellectual and Political Functions of a Theory of International Relations," in *The Decline of Democratic Politics* (Chicago: University of Chicago Press, 1962), 70–71; Hans J. Morgenthau, *Science: Servant or Master?* (New York: New American Library, 1972). The relevant portions of the latter work are based on lectures delivered at the University of Chicago in 1962.

[160] Kahn makes these arguments in their strongest form in Herman Kahn, *On Thermonuclear War* (Princeton: Princeton University Press, 1960). He softens them somewhat in *Thinking About the Unthinkable* (1962).

[161] Hans J. Morgenthau, "Death in the Nuclear Age," in *The Restoration of American Politics* (Chicago: University of Chicago Press, 1962), 24.

a strategy to confront the prospect of nuclear annihilation in a way that might render the unthinkable less probable.

By the early 1960s, he had found one. "Death in the Nuclear Age" attempts to wrench readers out of their dangerous complacency by offering a bleak account of a nuclear apocalypse without worldly redemption. Morgenthau claims that the prospect of nuclear annihilation has radically altered man's understanding of himself within time by denying him any hope of immortality. Death, Morgenthau explains, "is the great scandal in the experience of man." It negates everything that "man experiences as specifically human in his existence: the consciousness of himself and of his world, the remembrance of things past and the anticipation of things to come, a creativeness in thought and action which aspires to, and approximates, the eternal."[162]

Man preserves his humanity by transcending death. Historically, he has done this in three ways: he has denied the reality of death through a faith in human immortality, he has sought mastery over death through suicide or heroic sacrifice, and he has conquered death by achieving worldly immortality through his deeds and works. The secular modern age has deprived us of the first strategy, while the looming possibility of nuclear death has made the other two absurd.

Many religious believers transcend death through a belief in the immortality of the person. They may assume "that the finiteness of man's biological existence is but apparent and that his body will live on in another world."[163] Alternatively, they may insist that our specifically human attributes will survive the worldly destruction of our bodies and be preserved in another realm whose shape we can but dimly grasp. Morgenthau argues that religious immortality is no longer available to us in a secular age. And perhaps this is not something that we should lament. If we still had the comfort of religious belief, we could await nuclear death with calm acceptance. Perhaps we could even muster some enthusiasm as we "look forward to the day of the great slaughter as a day on which the preparatory and vain life on this earth would come to an end for most of us and the true, eternal life in another world begin."[164]

Morgenthau's insistence that this strategy is no longer available to modern man seems to ignore the persistence of religious belief in the secular age. One can only guess at the reasons for his insistence. Perhaps it is a rather blunt rhetorical move aimed at quickly dispensing with the possibility of confronting nuclear death with a sense of hopeful anticipation. Or, maybe Morgenthau is convinced that theological beliefs in an afterlife do not have a sufficiently strong hold on us to calm the terror of totalizing annihilation.[165] Perhaps Morgenthau

---

[162] Morgenthau, "Death," 19.   [163] Morgenthau, "Death," 20.
[164] Morgenthau, "Death," 24.
[165] Reflecting on his work with Hiroshima survivors, Robert Jay Lifton suggests that the "theological symbolism of an afterlife may well be insufficiently strong in its hold on the imagination to still inner fears of total severance." He goes on to suggest that religious visions of the afterlife

was simply ignorant of the depth of American religiosity or actively denied it because he considered it foolish.[166] Or, maybe Morgenthau is making a more nuanced point about the effects of secularization. Of course, there remain substantial portions of humanity that do have recourse to beliefs about the immortality of the body or soul. They can still look forward to nuclear destruction as the cataclysmic prerequisite for an eternal life in a new world. However, the doubt and skepticism that define the modern age mean that this strategy is, at best, one that can be privately contemplated by the individual believer. It cannot form the basis of a collective and public attempt to grapple with the meaning of death in a nuclear age.

Without a faith in immortality, modern secular man is left with two alternatives, both of which are rendered absurd in the face of nuclear annihilation. First, he can attempt to master death by choosing to end his life through suicide or sacrifice. The latter choice gives him the best chance of being remembered for posterity. The hero who sacrifices himself for a cause gives his death and his life a larger meaning. However, this meaning depends on the existence of a culture or civilization that will live on to interpret and remember his courageous sacrifice.[167]

Drawing on examples from Greek mythology, Morgenthau reasons: "Patroclus dies to be avenged by Achilles. Hector dies to be mourned by Priam. Yet if Patroclus, Hector, and all those who could remember them were killed simultaneously, what would become of the meaning of Patroclus' and Hector's deaths?"[168] For the heroic individual, the value and meaning of his death may well depend on the assumption that human beings and certain shared understandings will persist when he is gone. Without this expectation, his sacrifice would not be valuable or intelligible to him.[169]

---

may well depend in some way on beliefs about biological persistence. "Whatever the mixed state of religious symbolism in the rest of the world, there is grave doubt as to whether the promise of some form of life after death can maintain symbolic power in an imagined world in which there are none (or virtually none) among the biological living." See: Robert Jay. Lifton, "On Death and Death Symbolism: The Hiroshima Disaster," *Psychiatry* 27, no. 3 (1964): 208.

[166] This was not an uncommon view among European émigré scholars, whose American acquaintances tended to be urban intellectuals. I am grateful to an anonymous reviewer for suggesting this explanation.

[167] Hannah Arendt had made a similar point almost a decade earlier: "Man can be courageous only as long as he knows he is survived by those who are like him, that he fulfills a role in something more permanent than himself." See: Hannah Arendt, "Europe and the Atom Bomb," in *Essays in Understanding, 1930–1954: Formation, Exile and Totalitarianism*, ed. Jerome Kahn (New York: Schocken Books, 1994), 421.

[168] Morgenthau, "Death," 23.

[169] For a philosophical argument for the connection between leading a "value-laden life" and the assumption that one will be survived by a human future, see: Samuel Scheffler, *Death and the Afterlife* (Oxford: Oxford University Press, 2013). For a philosophical argument for the connection between leading a meaningful and intelligible life, on the one hand, and cultural persistence, on the other, see: Jonathan Lear, *Radical Hope: Ethics in the Face of Cultural Devastation* (Cambridge: Harvard University Press, 2006).

Nuclear Death

The mass death that would result from the deployment of a thermonuclear weapon would deprive the individual hero of both the opportunity for a freely willed sacrifice and a surviving culture that could understand and honor this sacrifice. Even if some manage to survive a nuclear war, individual deaths would lose any heroic significance:

> There is meaning in Leonidas falling at Thermopylae, in Socrates drinking the cup of hemlock, in Jesus nailed to the cross. There can be no meaning in the slaughter of the innocent, the murder of six million Jews, the prospective nuclear destruction of, say fifty million Americans and an equal number of Russians. There is, then, a radical difference in meaning between a man risking death by an act of will and fifty million people simultaneously reduced – by somebody switching a key thousands of miles away – to radioactive ashes, indistinguishable from the ashes of their houses, books, and animals.[170]

Like others writing in the postwar era, Morgenthau finds in the Nazi genocide the closest parallel to the prospect of nuclear annihilation. When death tolls are measured in the millions, lives and deaths have no meaning. The specifically human qualities of the dead will be effaced as remnants of persons with minds, experiences, memories, and attachments are irretrievably commingled with the ashes of physical objects and other animals. Human remains will be unsalvageable and therefore unavailable for the individuation of the dead required by almost all practices of mourning and commemoration.[171] The sheer numbers rob the dead of the possibility of worldly immortality through heroic sacrifice. What is remembered, if there is anyone left to remember, is "the quantity of the killed – six million, twenty million, fifty million – not the quality of one man's death as over and against another's."[172] The heroic individual is both physically obliterated by being reduced to radioactive ashes and historically annihilated by being denied the hope of posterity.

So much for heroism and sacrifice. The second way in which, for Morgenthau, modern secular man transcends death is by leaving behind the works of his will and hands as evidence of his existence. He lives on through his children. He creates monuments, leaving behind "an inheritance of visible things not to be consumed but to be preserved as tangible mementos of past generations... 'Roma eterna,' 'the Reich of a thousand years' are but the most ambitious attempts to perpetuate man and his deeds. The tree he has planted, the house that he has built, have been given a life likely to last longer than his own."[173] Perhaps most importantly, man produces works of the imagination – books, poetry, art – that are lasting testaments to a distinctly human capacity for creativity. When he creates, man participates in "an unbroken chain emerging from the past and reaching into the future, which is made of the same stuff

---

[170] Morgenthau, "Death," 23.
[171] To grasp the bleakness of this situation, consider how much scientific knowledge and forensic labor go into identifying human remains in cases of mass death, as well as our horror and sorrow in situations where circumstances render this kind of work impossible.
[172] Morgenthau, "Death," 23.   [173] Morgenthau, "Death," 21.

his mind is made of and, hence, is capable of participating in, and perpetuating, his mind's creation."[174]

These acts of creation are where, as Hannah Arendt suggests, both "the task and potential greatness of mortals lie." Through the production of "works and deeds and words... mortals could find their place in a cosmos where everything is immortal except themselves."[175] Even if it did not lead to human extinction, a nuclear catastrophe would destroy the "common world" that these works, deeds, and words help to build – the artifacts, institutions, and communities that bind us "not only with those who live with us, but also with those who were here before and with those who will come after us."[176]

Without such a common world, the biological immortality of the human species would persist as long as individual members survived. What a nuclear catastrophe would destroy, however, is our knowledge of this immortality. Generations would live and die in ignorance of one another. Even if we were to accept the optimistic assessments that a thermonuclear attack would "only" kill 50 to 100 million Americans, it would nevertheless make it impossible for any individual to envisage a human future that would survive him or her.[177] To the extent that the assumption of such a future is necessary for leading a "value-laden" life, individual survivors would lead lives of depressed motivation and insidious indifference.[178] For Morgenthau, this is the terrifying loss wrought by nuclear catastrophe and the reason all humans have to fear it.

Morgenthau's essay then takes its most decisive turn, as it rhetorically performs the apocalyptic annihilation whose enormity his contemporaries have systematically failed to grasp:

Nuclear destruction is mass destruction, both of persons and of things. It signifies the simultaneous destruction of tens of millions of people, of whole families, generations, and societies, of all things that they have inherited and created. It signifies total destruction of whole societies by killing their members, destroying their visible achievements, and therefore reducing the survivors to barbarism. Thus nuclear destruction destroys the meaning of death by depriving it of its individuality. It destroys the meaning of immortality by making both society and history impossible. It destroys the meaning of life by throwing life back upon itself.[179]

---

[174] Morgenthau, "Death," 22.
[175] Hannah Arendt, *The Human Condition*, 2nd ed. (Chicago: University of Chicago Press, 1998), 19.
[176] Arendt, *Human Condition*, 55.
[177] Jonathan Schell, *The Fate Of The Earth* (London: Jonathan Cape, 1982), 119. I take this to be what is at stake in Morgenthau's insistence that even if there were survivors of a nuclear attack, "civilization" would not be able to withstand the shock. The point is also made in: Hans J. Morgenthau et al., "Western Values and Total War," *Commentary* 32, no. 4 (1961): 281.
[178] Scheffler, *Death and the Afterlife*, 72.
[179] Morgenthau, "Death," 22. There are distinct echoes here of Arendt's arguments about the nature of worldly immortality: "The task and potential greatness of mortals lie in their ability to produce things – works and deeds and words – which would deserve to be and, at least

Nuclear Death

Like Hobbes in his description of the state of nature, Morgenthau calls forth all the markers of civilization and posterity – families, generations, visible achievements – only to annihilate them rhetorically. He offers the reader an apocalypse in which the suffering and deaths of millions are deprived of meaning. Those who survive are not an elect, but a shattered remnant reduced to barbarism. Against the looming prospect of a nuclear apocalypse, Morgenthau stages a rhetorical and imaginative apocalypse to shake his readers from their "thoughtless optimism."[180] He fights apocalypse *with apocalypse*, asking his readers to imagine nuclear annihilation in order to prevent it.

What are we to make of Morgenthau's apocalyptic strategy? One way to see this attempt to redirect the apocalyptic imaginary is as a self-defeating prophecy. The paradigmatic self-defeating prophet, Jonah, reluctantly prophesied the overthrow of Nineveh. Terrified of their fate and at the encouragement of their king, the Ninevites abandoned their evil ways and God decided to spare them, thereby disconfirming Jonah's prophecy. Jonah is angered at an outcome that raises questions about his prophetic credibility. But God insists that the purpose of dark and catastrophic prophecies is repentance and moral reform.[181] These outcomes are ultimately more valuable than prophetic reliability. Morgenthau may well have intended to assume the stance of a self-defeating prophet, foretelling an impending nuclear apocalypse as if it were an inescapable fate, but with the purpose of avoiding this outcome because of his prophecy.[182]

Avoiding such an outcome would, on Morgenthau's view, require more than the right mindset. It would also require an institutional solution. Since the late 1940s, he had been convinced that the only reliable safeguard against total annihilation was a world state with a monopoly on nuclear violence: "It is only when nations have surrendered the means of destruction which

> to a degree, are at home in everlastingness, so that through them mortals could find their place in a cosmos where everything is immortal except themselves." And later: "Without this transcendence into a potentially earthly immortality, no politics, strictly speaking, no common world and no public realm, is possible. For unlike the common good as Christianity understood it – the salvation of one's soul as a concern common to all – the common world is what we enter when we are born and what we leave behind when we die. It transcends our lifespan into past and future alike; it was there before we came and will outlast our brief sojourn in it. It is what we have in common not only with those who live with us, but also with those who were here before and with those who will come after us." See: Arendt, *The Human Condition*, 19, 55. This is precisely the kind of worldly immortality that nuclear destruction makes impossible, according to Morgenthau. While he does not cite Arendt in this passage, we know that Morgenthau held her work, and *The Human Condition* in particular, in high esteem. When asked to name the ten books that had had the greatest intellectual influence on him, Morgenthau included *The Human Condition*, alongside works by Plato, Aristotle, Publius, and Nietzsche. See: Frei, *Hans J. Morgenthau*, 113.

[180] Morgenthau, "Death," 24–25.   [181] Jon. 3–4.
[182] I owe this connection to conversations with Jean-Pierre Dupuy about what it means to be an enlightened "prophet of doom." See: Jean-Pierre Dupuy, *The Mark of the Sacred*, trans. M. DeBevoise (Stanford: Stanford University Press, 2013), 22–33, 191–92.

modern technology has put in their hands to a higher authority – when they have given up their sovereignty – that international peace can be made as secure as domestic peace."[183] Yet such a state was not possible in the absence of a world community. A world community, in turn, requires shared ends and a shared identity. The unity of mankind would have to precede the creation of a world state.

In a world marked by crusading political religions and the absence of any supranational moral consensus, this kind of unity seemed like a dim and futile hope. Morgenthau was skeptical of efforts to achieve unity cultural education and interchange through such international agencies as the United Nations Educational, Scientific, and Cultural Organization (UNESCO). Cultural education and exchange may increase the knowledge and appreciation of other national groups. However, at best this new knowledge and appreciation might create a community of "intellect and sentiments." Such a community would fall well short of the "moral and political transformation of unprecedented dimensions" required for the unity of mankind.[184]

Morgenthau was somewhat more optimistic about a functionalist path to unity. Drawing on David Mitrany's functionalist theory of international integration, Morgenthau argued that states can and do form supranational institutions to solve common problems. To the extent that they perform their tasks effectively, these institutions create "a community of interests, valuations and actions." Over time, effective international institutions begin to extract loyalty from this new community. It is possible that a time may come when this loyalty supersedes "loyalties to ... separate national societies and their institutions."[185] At the moment, however, international institutions simply do not do enough to generate this sort of loyalty.[186]

By the 1960s, however, Morgenthau had begun to see a new route to the unity of mankind. Nuclear annihilation was not just a novel threat; it was also a novel opportunity. It opened the door to the unprecedented "moral and political transformation" required for a world community. An inchoate "awareness of the unity of mankind," long submerged by the political religions of crusading nationalisms, had been sharpened by the common fear of nuclear death.[187] Our longing to give some political and institutional form to this unity had been greatly strengthened in the nuclear age "by the desire, innate in all men, for self-preservation."[188] This desire could now be harnessed, in a way that had

---

[183] Morgenthau, *Politics Among Nations* (1948), 445.
[184] Morgenthau, *Politics Among Nations* (1954), 489.
[185] Morgenthau, *Politics Among Nations* (1954), 493.
[186] William Scheuerman reads Morgenthau as somewhat more enthusiastic about the functionalist route to unity than I do. See: Scheuerman, *Realist Case for Global Reform*, 82–84.
[187] Hans J. Morgenthau, "International Relations," in *The Restoration of American Politics* (Chicago: University of Chicago Press, 1962), 174–75.
[188] This suggestion echoes earlier arguments by Hannah Arendt and Karl Jaspers. See: Arendt, "Europe and the Atom Bomb," 422; Karl Jaspers, *The Future of Mankind*, trans. E. B. Ashton (Chicago: University of Chicago Press, 1961), 4.

Nuclear Death

previously been impossible, to abolish "international relations itself through the merger of all national sovereignties into one world state which would have a monopoly of the most destructive instruments of violence."[189]

However, Morgenthau's essay on nuclear death betrays some doubt about whether we can rely on this innate desire to emerge on its own as a political force. Clinging to the hope of secular immortality, we fail to grasp the enormity of the nuclear threat. Hobbes faced a similar dilemma. While he suggested that the fear of earthly death is our most basic and reliable fear, he worried that it may ultimately be overpowered by the terror of eternal damnation. Our fear of death cannot be relied upon as a natural force. It must be actively cultivated. Hobbes did this, at least in part, by neutralizing the threat of eternal torment and by offering an apocalyptic account of the breakdown of political order.

Morgenthau, I suggest, is attempting a similar rhetorical endeavor as he strips his readers of the comforts of secular immortality and leaves them with a terrifying vision of nuclear annihilation that cultivates a salutary fear. He envisions the radical reform of human nature. No longer would humans be driven by our pursuit of power or our will to dominate. In the shadow of nuclear

[189] Morgenthau, "International Relations," 175. This marks an important departure from Morgenthau's earlier writings on the world state, which tended to acknowledge its necessity as the only reliable safeguard against the prospect of nuclear annihilation, but which questioned not only its feasibility but also its desirability. In the late 1940s, he was willing to accept, with Hobbes, that "society has no substitute for the power of the Leviathan whose very presence, towering above contending groups, keeps their conflicts within peaceful bounds." However, he could not yet bring himself to accept the possibility of a global equivalent to the Hobbesian sovereign, which, without the support of a world community, would have to be a universal tyranny capable of terrorizing an "unwilling humanity" into perpetual peace. He thought that "such a world state would be a totalitarian monster resting on feet of clay, the very thought of which startles the imagination." See: Morgenthau, *Politics Among Nations* (1948), 404. What had changed by the early 1960s was his evaluation of the prospects for the development of a world community willing to support a world state. In his writings from the 1960s, he toys with various alternatives that all fall short of a world state with a monopoly on violence. He considers the possibility of an American-led "free association" of liberal democratic states that would exercise supranational control over nuclear weapons, a concerted effort by the United Nations "to point the world in the direction of replacing national sovereignty with supranational decisions and institutions," and a system of joint Soviet and American sovereignty over the world. See: Hans J. Morgenthau, *The Purpose of American Politics* (New York: Vintage, 1960), 309; Hans J. Morgenthau, "Threat to – and Hope for – the United Nations," in *The Restoration of American Politics* (Chicago: University of Chicago Press, 1962), 284; Hans J. Morgenthau and Reinhold Niebuhr, "The Ethics of War and Peace in the Nuclear Age," *War/Peace Report* 7, no. 2 (1967): 7. All of these solutions fall short of the "New Leviathan" that would be required to guarantee permanent peace and human survival in a nuclear world. Morgenthau's inability to imagine the contours of the world state strikes some of his critics as an intellectual failing – a fundamental theoretical incoherence or an unwillingness fully to abandon a narrow realism that was dangerously unsuited to a nuclear world. I am borrowing the term "New Leviathan" from Campbell Craig's *Glimmer of a New Leviathan*. On Morgenthau's intellectual failings on the question of the world state, see: Speer, "Hans Morgenthau and the World State," 207–27; Scheuerman, *Morgenthau*, 157–58.

apocalypse, self-preservation would become our guiding motivation and the basis for a project of permanent peace. Thus prepared, we may be more willing to accept our common humanity and to contemplate the possibility of a world state, thereby rendering the prophecy of nuclear apocalypse false.

Conclusion

I have argued that Morgenthau's political realism was shaped by the postwar apocalyptic imaginary. In his writings from the late 1940s and 1950s, he was centrally preoccupied with the violent potential of a world divided by crusading political religions that had found in nuclear weapons the means to match their totalizing ends. The bulk of his critical attention is directed at liberal internationalism, at the root of which he sees an apocalyptic hope for a final and decisive war that will usher in an age of permanent peace. Like Machiavelli, Morgenthau rejects the apocalyptic imaginary, turning instead to a tragic worldview that insists on the inescapability of conflict and the limits to transformative political action.

However, this tragic turn left Morgenthau ill-equipped to confront the radical novelty of nuclear weapons. By the early 1960s, he had taken a dramatic turn away from a tragic worldview and toward a Hobbesian strategy of redirection, or fighting apocalypse with apocalypse. Depriving us of any hope for secular redemption in the wake of nuclear annihilation, he asks us to imagine the apocalypse in order to prevent it. In so doing, Morgenthau hopes that we may be able to effect the kind of profound human transformation required to accept a world state.

This argument has several implications for Morgenthau's identification as a political realist. First, as was the case with Machiavelli and Hobbes, this reading suggests that Morgenthau's thought was deeply contextual. Yet his realism does not develop simply from a clear-eyed analysis of material facts on the ground but also from a struggle about how to imagine and interpret the significance of those events. Features of postwar apocalypticism haunt his work. The eschatological underpinnings of Nazism loom in the background of his worries about the apocalyptic basis of liberal internationalism, while the mass exterminations of the Holocaust provide the only possible analog for the unimaginable prospect of nuclear annihilation.

Second, the interpretation I have offered here points to the moral core of Morgenthau's realism. In his tragic phase, he rejects liberal schemes for permanent peace not primarily on the basis of an assessment of their empirical feasibility. Rather, he rejects these schemes because he has principled objections to the conception of politics that underlies them. In his apocalyptic phase, he calls for the reform of human nature. Instead of accepting men as they are, he offers a terrifying vision aimed at transforming them into what they should be – into what they must be, if humanity is to survive.

Finally, this reading asks whether the tragic realism that had defined Morgenthau's early writings may be ill-equipped to confront radically novel threats to human survival. Profoundly troubled by the prospect of nuclear annihilation, Morgenthau abandons a tragic worldview and embraces the rhetorical potential of the apocalyptic imaginary. In so doing, he defended the very kind of aspirational project for perpetual peace that he had once condemned as a "repudiation of politics." Utopia had become a necessity.

6

Conclusion

Over the course of this book, we have seen that Niccolò Machiavelli, Thomas Hobbes, and Hans Morgenthau were deeply engaged with the apocalyptic hopes and fears of their times. We have seen how attending to their responses to apocalypticism gives us a more nuanced understanding of the contexts in which their paradigmatically realist arguments developed and, in some cases, were eventually abandoned.

In their works, Machiavelli, Hobbes, and Morgenthau all recognize the motivating force of the apocalyptic imaginary. All three also struggle to negotiate its dangers. Despite their firm resistance to the possibility of enduring political settlements, all three thinkers succumb at some point to the apocalyptic imaginary's most radical hopes.

In this final chapter, I would like to revisit and assess the three thinkers' responses to apocalypticism. We will see that the strategies of rejection and redirection both carry their own practical and moral costs. Taken together, these encounters with apocalypticism give us an instruction "in the art of living through an age of catastrophe" that is as relevant today as it was in the unique circumstances of their own respective times.[1]

---

[1] When Henri Marrou characterizes the value of Augustine's teaching for modern readers, he writes that the medieval theologian "instructs us by his example in the art of living through an age of catastrophe." See: Henri Marrou, *Saint Augustine and His Influence through the Ages*, trans. Patrick Hepburne-Scott (New York: Harper Torchbooks, 1957), 7. I think that this is also a good characterization of one of the normative projects of political realism. Some might question whether we are indeed living through "an age of catastrophe." They might appeal to an argument along the lines of that of Steven Pinker, that on one important metric (i.e., rates of violent death), we are living in an era of relative peace. See: Steven Pinker, *The Better Angels of Our Nature: Why Violence Has Declined* (New York: Penguin Books, 2011). The two things may be true at once. While we are living in an era of relative peace, it is a peace that is overshadowed by several prospective catastrophes of existential proportions. As I write in late 2017, both U.S.

Political Realism in Apocalyptic Times

Machiavelli, Hobbes, and Morgenthau all came to recognize both the seductions and the dangers of the apocalyptic imaginary. These seductions and dangers are connected. The very features that make apocalypticism politically seductive also render it politically unstable. First, the apocalyptic imaginary is hostile to established political order. In Chapter 2, we considered the ways in which this hostility manifests itself in the books of Daniel and Revelation. Drawing on the symbolic resources of Near Eastern mythology, both books cast sovereign power as a sea beast, a chaos-monster that God must slay to reassert his authority over the world. The appeal of such a message in the face of real or perceived persecution is understandable. For the afflicted, it confirms a suspicion that our world is out of joint. For the comfortable, the message defamiliarizes sovereign power by casting it in a new and terrifying light.

As we saw in Chapter 4, this apocalyptic hostility to established authority was powerfully deployed during the English Civil War. Radical Protestants and parliamentarians identified the Laudian Church and Charles I with Antichrist and the Beast of Revelation, casting established ecclesiastical and royal power as deeply alien and antithetical to God's rule. The danger of seeing things this way is that it legitimizes violent extremism. When one's enemy poses an apocalyptic threat, almost anything goes. As Stephen Marshall advised in a speech before Parliament in 1642: "If this worke be to revenge Gods Church against *Babylon*, he is a *blessed man that takes and dashes the little ones against the stones.*"[2] Those allied with the forces of evil become targets for divinely sanctioned obliteration.

Second, the apocalyptic imaginary makes the crises of the day intelligible. It imposes a narrative coherence on them. The books of Daniel and Revelation made the persecution and trauma of foreign rule meaningful. The suffering of believers was transformed from an experience of inexplicable evil into the birth pangs of a new world. As I discussed in Chapter 3, apocalypticism, especially in its Savonarolan form, imposed a divine plot on the troubles of Florence and Italy. In a matter of days during November 1494, Florence witnessed the crumbling of the Medici regime and invasion by Charles VIII's forces. These were terrifying events whose outcomes seemed radically uncertain. Savonarola promised to give these events both a meaning and an end. He imagined Charles as a divine agent who would purge Florence of its sins and initiate the apocalypse described in Revelation.

President Donald Trump and North Korean leader Kim Jong-un have intensified their saber-rattling nuclear rhetoric. The threat of nuclear terrorism is also quite real. Beyond this, the threat of anthropogenic climate change looms large. The United States, which is well placed to be a leader on climate change, is led by a president who has called the phenomenon a hoax and who has appointed other skeptics to crucial cabinet positions. It seems fair to call this an "age of catastrophe."

[2] Marshall, *Meroz Cursed*, 11–12.

Savonarola's genius lay in his ability to adapt this narrative to suit changing circumstances. When Charles and his forces left Florence intact, the friar claimed that this was proof of the city's elect status. While this narrative appealed to many, its promise of a spontaneous and peaceful transformation masked some important challenges. Building a stable spiritual republic proved to be difficult work that unleashed deep political tensions. Within four years of Charles's invasion, Savonarola had been executed as a heretic and Florence was once again at the mercy of factional conflict. Far from giving the city's political difficulties a meaning and an end, Savaronolan apocalypticism likely made them worse.

Third, the apocalyptic imaginary holds out the seductive promise that difference, disagreement, and conflict can be eliminated. Daniel envisions a new order in which God gathers his people together to be ruled as one. All differences of race, nationality, and language will disappear. Similarly, John of Patmos promises that Jesus' faithful followers will receive new clothes and new names. Markers of individuality will be eliminated as the elect surrender to his transformative omnipotence. With difference and individuality abolished, "death will be no more; mourning and crying and pain will be no more, for the first things have passed away."[3] If politics is defined in part by inescapable conflict and enduring differences, apocalypticism does not just promise an end to crisis and contingency. It promises the end of politics.

As we saw in Chapter 5, Hans Morgenthau diagnoses a secular variant of this hope in American liberal internationalism, which he thinks sees a final war for humanity as the prerequisite to a millennial democratic future. Underlying this seemingly attractive end, writes Morgenthau, is the fantasy of an escape from the political condition. He argues that this apocalyptic vision is at its most dangerous when the expected end fails to materialize. Then, the "final war" becomes the forerunner "of wars more destructive and extensive than any liberal epoch had witnessed."[4] Some might say that Morgenthau's worries were vastly overstated. Others may find them disturbingly prescient. Our own conclusions will depend on an assessment of the wars that the United States has waged in the name of liberty and democracy over the past century.

We might easily conclude that a typically realist suspicion of utopian or idealist schemes insulates these thinkers from the dangers of apocalypticism, at least in its more hopeful expressions. After all, hopes about the end of the world carry utopian or idealist commitments to disturbing extremes. Frustrated with the limited gains of incremental progress toward a utopia or an ideal, apocalyptic enthusiasts anticipate a cataclysmic end to the known world and a violent purging of its attendant evils.

However, there may be less obvious ways in which realists are especially vulnerable to the seductions of apocalypticism. Realists may struggle to remain faithful to a vision of politics as "an infinite process" from which there is no

---

[3] Rev. 21:4. [4] Morgenthau, *Scientific Man*, 67.

final exit. E. H. Carr suggests, not implausibly, that this view of politics "seems in the long run uncongenial or incomprehensible to the human mind. Every political thinker who wishes to make an appeal to his contemporaries is consciously or unconsciously led to posit a finite goal." Carr proposes that the thoroughgoing realist faces both psychological challenges and rhetorical barriers. Citing Machiavelli's *Prince* and the works of Karl Marx and Friedrich Engels as examples, Carr argues that these challenges account for a tendency of "realist" tracts to culminate in an appeal to an ultimate goal that assumes "the character of an apocalyptic vision [which]...acquires an emotional, irrational appeal which realism itself cannot justify or explain."[5] So, we might conclude that while its core commitments make political realism especially attuned to the dangers of apocalyptic thinking, the difficulties of being a thoroughgoing realist lead to unexpected vulnerabilities.

Considered together, Machiavelli, Hobbes, and Morgenthau develop two lines of response to apocalypticism that track this tension. The later Machiavelli and the earlier Morgenthau reject apocalypticism on normative grounds. They each turn toward a tragic worldview that insists on the limits of effective of political action and resists the allure of final solutions. We saw that Machiavelli only comes to this tragic position after having flirted with the apocalyptic imaginary in *The Prince*. His most famous work culminates in an apocalyptic exhortation because he fails to fulfill the opening promise of the book – to make the variability of politics intelligible and subject to mastery.

I find a more developed and tragic realism in the *Discourses*, were Machiavelli subjects apocalyptic hope to serious normative scrutiny. This extended engagement with the apocalyptic imaginary coincides with a maturation of his political realism from an ambitious project of intelligibility and mastery in *The Prince* to the more modest but difficult attempt to cultivate a tragic wisdom in the *Discourses*.

The early Morgenthau responds to the secularized apocalyptic elements of liberal internationalism with a tragic stance that similarly insists on the inescapability of conflict and the limits to transformative politics. For Morgenthau, however, this tragic stance ultimately proves unable to confront the radical novelty of nuclear weapons and the threat they pose to the future of the world.

In the works of Hobbes and the late Morgenthau, we saw a different response to apocalypticism. Rather than turning away from it, Hobbes and the late Morgenthau redirect it. They fight apocalypse *with apocalypse*. That is, they redeploy apocalyptic images and rhetoric to get their audiences to imagine the end of the world in order to prevent it. Hobbes does this in two ways. In his scriptural argument, he offers a deflationary Christian eschatology that affirms important parts of the narratives of Daniel and Revelation while making apocalypticism safe for sovereign power and civil peace.

[5] Carr, *Twenty Years' Crisis*, 90.

Hobbes's secular political argument borrows from the apocalyptic plot, casting the violence and unpredictability of the state of nature as the narrative prelude to an enduring commonwealth ruled by a mortal God. While he might have preferred to persuade the radicals and enthusiasts of his day with rational argument, he was also willing to burrow into the darker corners of the imagination.

Morgenthau adopts a similar strategy in response to the novel threat of nuclear weapons. He offers a terrifying account of an apocalypse without redemption to generate the salutary fear required to avert catastrophe. Both thinkers redirect the apocalyptic imaginary in the pursuit of aspirational projects. For Hobbes, this project is the creation of a stable Leviathan state that he hopes could endure for all time, while for Morgenthau it is the creation of a world state with a monopoly on nuclear violence. The hope that each has for his ambitious project rests uneasily with the core commitments of political realism.

Rejection and the Burdens of Tragedy

So far, I have refrained from any explicit normative evaluation of these two strategies of response. It is now time to turn to this task. The strategy of rejection – the move away from apocalypticism and toward tragedy – is consistent with realist commitments. The tragic worldview recognizes the difficulty of reaching settled solutions to our deepest disagreements. It resists apocalypticism's dangerous moral clarity about the means and ends of politics. It embraces an incrementalist view of politics as "the strong and slow boring through hard boards."[6]

For these reasons, the tragic worldview is equipped to resist the seductions of apocalypticism. An example might help to draw out this point. Looking back on her own reaction to the post-9/11 rhetoric of the Bush administration, feminist theologian Catherine Keller remembers that she was troubled by what she took to be a dangerous apocalyptic certainty at its core. She detected a certainty about the direction of history, about who and what was evil, and about "our" goodness and "our" righteousness.

Like other forms of apocalyptic rhetoric, the discourse of the War on Terror seemed to target the features of the contemporary world that are valued by some and feared by others – its indeterminacy, ambiguity, and pluralism.[7] Bush seemed certain about the direction of history when he proclaimed: "the untamed fire of freedom will reach the darkest corners of our world."[8] He allowed for no moral ambiguity when he declared: "Either you are with

---

[6] Weber, "Politics as a Vocation," 128. [7] Keller, *God and Power*, 12.
[8] Bush, "Inaugural Address" (2005).

us, or you are with the terrorists."[9] And he evinced a faith in America's righteousness when he described the country's mission as the defense of "freedom...civilization...and universal values."[10]

Yet, on Keller's account, Bush and his supporters were not the only ones captured by the apocalyptic imaginary. Those most critical of the president's rhetoric and the policies it was meant to defend were also seduced by the apocalypse. She describes her own reaction:

> Even the progressive U.S. response gets caught in the apocalyptic mirror-game. Chickens come home to roost: the *real* cause is our policy in the Middle East, especially Israel, or the *real* cause is the global economy. While I heard myself in the initial shock laying these propositions on my students, and heard them echoing through my theological community, their indignant certainties rang hollow at ground zero. I needed something more difficult and honest than the monocausal explanations, the warmed-over and misfitting Vietnam-era slogans... Indeed the very model of a monocausal explanation, with its linear predictability and its indignant certainty, echoes with the hoofbeats of secular apocalypse.[11]

The "apocalyptic mirror-game" that Keller describes is a process in which those who most want to resist apocalyptic thinking are nonetheless drawn to it. In this diagnosis, Keller identifies the power of the apocalyptic imaginary – the profound hold it can have even over those who are trying to resist it.

Keller tries to disrupt this mirror-game by adopting what she calls a "counter-apocalyptic" position. This stance resists the linear temporality, righteous certainty, and totalizing violence of the apocalypse while attempting to preserve the radical political traditions of apocalypticism that value "disclosure, rather than final closure."[12]

I think that the tragic sensibility of the late Machiavelli and early Morgenthau can cultivate this counter-apocalyptic stance. Tragedy encourages us to "doubt the providential image of time, reject the compensatory idea that humans can master all the forces that impinge upon life, [and] strive to cultivate wisdom about a world that is neither designed for our benefit nor plastic enough to be putty in our hands."[13] The late Machiavelli and the early Morgenthau further demand that we resist the urge to turn away from our world. They ask us to shore up the resolution needed for political actions whose success is never guaranteed. They counsel us, as Max Weber does, to arm ourselves "with

---

[9] George W. Bush, "Address Before a Joint Session of the Congress on the United States Response to the Terrorist Attacks of September 11," The American Presidency Project, September 20, 2001, www.presidency.ucsb.edu/ws/index.php?pid=64731&st=&st1=#axzz1W1KOUh9B.

[10] George W. Bush, "Remarks on Arrival in Daytona Beach, Florida," The American Presidency Project, January 30, 2002, www.presidency.ucsb.edu/ws/index.php?pid=73243&st=&st1=#axzz1W1KOUh9B.

[11] Keller, *God and Power*, 12–13.   [12] Keller, *God and Power*, 88.

[13] Connolly, *Capitalism and Christianity*, 121.

that steadfastness of heart which can brave even the crumbling of all hopes." Without such resolution, we "will not be able to achieve even that which is possible today."[14]

Nevertheless, the turn to tragedy is not without difficulties and dangers. First, as we saw in chapter 5, Morgenthau's tragic realism seems to leave him ill-equipped to confront the radical novelty of nuclear weapons. The tragic worldview insists on a cyclical conception of political time. Politics is not "one damn thing after another." It is "one damn thing over and over."[15] While this may strike us as bleak, there is optimism here. If we face the same kinds of conflicts and challenges again and again, then the past becomes a source of wisdom. Current challenges will always have historical analogs.

But tragedy's temporal commitments also make it suspicious of claims about radical novelty. The tragic worldview struggles to recognize or guide us through genuinely novel situations. This is one reason why Morgenthau might have turned away from tragedy and toward the apocalyptic imaginary to avert nuclear annihilation. Given its difficulty in coming to grips with novel threats, we might expect the tragic worldview to be similarly unhelpful today in orienting our response to, for example, global climate change. This is, after all, the most complex collective problem that humanity has ever faced.

Second, insofar as it is committed to a severe epistemic and practical humility about politics, the tragic worldview is vulnerable to a familiar charge that it amounts to an apology for the status quo. In the *Discourses on Livy*, Machiavelli offers countless examples of thwarted political intentions and actions whose outcomes could hardly have been predicted. One plausible reading of these examples is that they are aimed at chastening political hubris. Expecting too much of politics is foolish. Promising a collective rebirth through the crucible of violence is potentially catastrophic. Morgenthau makes a similar argument. Let us assume that we can tame our drive to dominate. The complexity of our political world means that we will not be able reliably to control and anticipate the effects of our actions. For both thinkers, epistemic and practical humility about politics is a salutary bulwark against violent utopian and apocalyptic enthusiasm.

However, we can easily imagine how an insistence on the tragic limits of politics might engender a kind of paralysis. Consumed by the worry that our political actions will always escape our intentions, we might fail to act at all. We might leave the status quo – however unjust – in place by default. Machiavelli and Morgenthau each try to resist this paralyzing conclusion. Machiavelli praises those who found and refound states knowing that they will eventually decay. Morgenthau commends statesmen who are able to recognize the tragic

---

[14] Weber, "Politics as a Vocation," 128.
[15] Edna St. Vincent Millay in a letter to Arthur Davison Ficke, as paraphrased by Joan Dash, *A Life of One's Own: Three Gifted Women and the Men They Married* (New York: Harper & Row, 1973), 189.

limits of politics but still manage to act. And yet the combination of epistemic modesty and political decisiveness that both thinkers celebrate seems to be more suited to a world of tragic heroes than one of ordinary humans.

Third, the tragic worldview may well impose deep burdens on those who hold it. Let me approach this point somewhat indirectly. In her attempt to craft "a virtue ethics framework for thinking about oppression," Lisa Tessman argues that the virtues required for liberatory struggle impede the flourishing of those who practice them. Compassion, she suggests, is such a virtue. It requires inviting the pain of others into our own lives, "being pained by their pain." When faced with suffering, "one's felt pain is part of the response to the other that constitutes the morally recommended responsive action."[16] Yet this action may be so painful that it impedes the flourishing of the compassionate agent. For this reason, Tessman calls compassion a *burdened* virtue. If, as Tessman reasons, "the sufferings to which one is attentive were to be experienced firsthand, they would clearly qualify as the sorts of external conditions that could ruin an otherwise potentially flourishing life; the person who takes on these sufferings in a secondary way – and feels pain – becomes burdened too."[17]

In a similar way, the tragic worldview is a *burdened worldview*. While it may, despite its limitations, be a morally appropriate response to the dangers of the apocalyptic imaginary, its insistence on a world so resistant to mastery, so unresponsive to virtuous intentions, so capricious in its rewards for goodness does not offer much consolation. It is a difficult worldview to hold without a painful reckoning and a hardening of the heart.

Redirection and the Politics of Fear

The strategy of redirection – using apocalypticism to fight its own most dangerous enthusiasms – avoids these difficulties, but manages to generate new ones. This strategy is consistent with political realism's sensitivity to context. This sensitivity is grounded in realism's resistance to moralism and utopianism. Instead of formulating and applying abstract normative principles to particular cases, the realist attends to the actual complaints of particular people in specific circumstances.[18]

As a matter of practical political intervention, this means that the realist must be attentive to the ways in which these complaints are understood and expressed. For instance, if they are expressed by appealing to apocalyptic imagery and rhetoric, this is a fact to which the realist should be sensitive. The strategy of redirection, which attends to and incorporates elements

---

[16] Lisa Tessman, *Burdened Virtues: Virtue Ethics for Liberatory Struggles* (New York: Oxford University Press, 2005), 93.
[17] Tessman, *Burdened Virtues*, 96.
[18] I owe this framing of the commitment to conversations with Philip Pettit.

of the apocalyptic imaginary, displays this kind of practical and pragmatic sensitivity.

There may also be cases in which an appeal to apocalyptic imagery and rhetoric is a morally appropriate response. Avoiding nuclear war and averting the worst effects of global climate change may be two such cases. These are particular kinds of catastrophes that pose unique motivational challenges.

Both are *prospective catastrophes*. That is, they are the kind of catastrophes that, given existing patterns of human activity, we have reason to think could or will arise in the future and that pose an existential threat. They are catastrophes with the potential to bring about human extinction or, at the very least, to radically alter the character of human existence in profoundly undesirable ways.

Prospective catastrophes present us with a unique set of challenges. Because the catastrophe is prospective, we can put it out of our minds. In contrast to a contemporary or ongoing catastrophe, "the act of thinking about it is always voluntary, and the choice of not thinking about it is always available."[19] Because the catastrophe is gigantic in its scope, we have difficulty imagining its effects. We are, as Günther Anders notes, "incapable of mentally realizing the realities which we ourselves have produced."[20] Prospective catastrophes are difficult to visualize because they lack imaginative analogs. While some of their likely effects (e.g., widespread radiation sickness, droughts, and floods) have been experienced before, both the vastly increased scale and interaction of these effects mean that imagining prospective catastrophes requires "thinking about the unthinkable."[21]

Yet this thinking is essential if we are to meet the challenges posed by these looming catastrophes. To the extent that we cannot properly conceive of the devastation wrought by nuclear war or global climate change or the part that we might play in bringing either about, avoiding honest confrontations with questions of moral responsibility and guilt becomes much easier. The imaginative challenges of prospective catastrophes enable dangerous forms of denial.

In the nuclear case, this denial took the form of optimism about the capacity to survive and even thrive after a nuclear attack. At its most extreme, nuclear denial held out hope for some kind of redemption through destruction. I have argued that Morgenthau's turn toward a strategy of redirection can be read as a response to these dangerous tendencies.

In the case of global climate change, individual and collective denial have centered on challenging scientific and expert claims about the existence, causes,

---

[19] Schell, *The Fate Of The Earth*, 8.
[20] Anders, "Theses for the Atomic Age," 496. Anders calls this the "Promethean discrepancy" or the "Promethean gap" and associates it with a kind of "inverted utopianism." "While ordinary Utopians are unable to actually produce what they are able to visualize, we are unable to visualize what we are actually producing" (496).
[21] I have borrowed this phrase from Herman Kahn.

and likely effects of the phenomenon. The most powerful instances of global climate change denial have come from organized and well-funded movements whose goal is to generate epistemological and scientific doubt.[22] A different but ultimately complementary strategy has been to accept the scientific findings on climate change but to challenge the seriousness of the problem or the priority of its mitigation relative to other policy goals.[23] These challenges and questions have been amplified by a media environment where the norm of balanced reporting has given members of the denial movement an amount of time and airspace vastly disproportionate to the balance of evidence on the issue.[24]

Given the kinds of difficulties that attend prospective catastrophes, it may be that a strategy of apocalyptic redirection is, all things considered, the most appropriate response. In Chapter 5, we saw that one way to interpret Morgenthau's strategy of redirection is as a self-defeating prophecy – an attempt to cast a nuclear apocalypse as a certain future, but with the hope of escaping this horrifying end. There may well be a good case to be made that such a strategy is also appropriate in other cases of prospective catastrophe as well.

To see how the strategy might be used, let us revisit an example we saw in the introductory chapter. In Davis Guggenheim's *An Inconvenient Truth*, which was marketed as "the most terrifying film you will ever see," Al Gore shows viewers a particularly devastating set of images of communities, neighborhoods,

---

[22] These movements, which bring together fossil fuel industry representatives, politicians, pundits, and think tanks, have used several strategies to achieve this end. For instance, they have attempted to refute and question the scientific evidence of the anthropogenic causes of climate change. This evidence, the suggestion goes, has been manufactured or manipulated for political ends. Using a strategy that had first been perfected by the tobacco industry to discredit scientific findings on the causal link between smoking and cancer, the climate denial movement has effectively deployed scientists (including some who had earlier lent their expertise to the tobacco industry) to raise questions about the finding of the Intergovernmental Panel on Climate Change, and other mainstream climate research. See: Peter J. Jacques, Riley E. Dunlap, and Mark Freeman, "The Organisation of Denial: Conservative Think Tanks and Environmental Scepticism," *Environmental Politics* 17, no. 3 (2008): 349–85; Naomi Oreskes and Erik M. Conway, *Merchants of Doubt: How a Handful of Scientists Obscured the Truth on Issues from Tobacco Smoke to Global Warming* (New York: Bloomsbury Press, 2010).

[23] Bjørn Lomborg, *The Skeptical Environmentalist: Measuring the Real State of the World* (New York: Cambridge University Press, 2001). Whether or not to include positions such as Lomberg's under the heading of climate denial is a matter of understandable debate. Accepting the argument about a strategy of redirection that I make here does not ultimately require taking a stand on the issue.

[24] Maxwell T. Boykoff and Jules M. Boykoff, "Balance as Bias: Global Warming and the US Prestige Press," *Global Environmental Change* 14, no. 2 (2004): 125–36. While it is clear that these denial strategies have helped structure the public debate and actively contributed to political inertia on climate change, their causal effect on patterns of public opinion remains contested. For a quick summary of the evidence on this question, see: Matthew C. Nisbet, "Public Opinion and Participation," in *The Oxford Handbook of Climate Change and Society*, ed. John S. Dryzek, Richard B. Norgaard, and David Schlosberg (Oxford: Oxford University Press, 2011), 358–59.

and landscapes annihilated by "natural" disasters. These images visually perform the task of Hobbes's and Morgenthau's apocalyptic rhetoric. They are metonyms at once of our common worldly life and of its annihilation. Pausing briefly to allow the viewer to take in the force of these images, Gore then notes that they are "like a nature hike through the book of Revelations [sic]."[25]

There is little doubt that, for Gore, the fear elicited by the apocalyptic imaginary is a salutary one. With distinct echoes of Morgenthau, Gore suggests:

> Today, there are dire warnings that the worst catastrophe in the history of human civilization is bearing down on us, gathering strength as it comes... The tragedy of Hurricane Katrina... as horrible as it was, may have been the first sip of a bitter cup which will be proffered to us over and over again until we act on the truth we have wished would go away... This crisis is bringing us an opportunity to experience what few generations in history ever have the privilege of knowing: a generational mission; the exhilaration of a compelling moral purpose; a shared and unifying cause; the thrill of being forced by circumstances to put aside the pettiness and conflict that so often stifle the restless human need for transcendence; the opportunity to *rise*.[26]

We can discern several familiar moves here. First, Gore casts the prospective catastrophe of climate change as both an imminent and a contemporary problem. It is "bearing down on us, gathering strength as it comes." This catastrophe, he notes earlier, "could be set in motion in the lifetime of children already living – unless we act boldly and quickly... We are in grave danger of crossing a point of no return within the next 10 years!"[27]

Second, Gore makes the catastrophic potential of global climate change more vivid by invoking a terrifying contemporary analog – the devastation of Hurricane Katrina, "the first sip of a bitter cup which will be proffered to us over and over again." Beyond echoing Winston Churchill's condemnation of Neville Chamberlain's appeasement policy, the language of "proffered cups" calls to mind the bowls of God's wrath in Revelation. Like Morgenthau, Gore gestures to the totalizing imaginative analog of the Holocaust when he compares the gathering storm of ecological devastation to the "evil threat posed by the Nazis."[28]

Third, also like Morgenthau, Gore discerns in the looming threat of global climate change a transcendent and unifying purpose. It is an opportunity that must compel us to "put aside... the pettiness and conflict" of everyday politics and "to *rise*." For Morgenthau, the looming threat of nuclear annihilation was, if rightly imagined, capable of making individuals conscious of their shared humanity, allowing them to overcome the conflicts, differences, and particularities that normally defined the political condition. Gore's apocalyptic framing

---

[25] Al Gore, *An Inconvenient Truth*, documentary, dir. Davis Guggenheim (Hollywood: Paramount, 2006), DVD.
[26] Al Gore, "The Moment of Truth," *Vanity Fair*, May 2006, www.vanityfair.com/news/2006/05/climate-change-200605. Emphasis in original.
[27] Gore, "Moment of Truth."   [28] Gore, "Moment of Truth."

of climate change seems to rest on a similar set of connections. Rightly imagined, the looming threat of climate change will be an opportunity to put aside the petty conflicts of everyday politics and acknowledge a "compelling moral purpose."[29]

Gore, like Morgenthau, uses apocalyptic images to elicit a salutary fear. Political uses of fear have been criticized as fear mongering. This is not what either Morgenthau or Gore seem to be doing. To see why, consider a clear case of fear mongering – the discourse on crime in the United States during the 1990s. Despite a dramatic drop in violent crime starting at the beginning of the decade, the evening news throughout the 1990s was perpetually punctuated with murders and warnings by pundits about the rise of dangerous young "super-predators." It is estimated that between 1990 and 1998 there was a 600 percent increase in American network news stories on murder.[30] Most Americans are still not aware of the declining trends in violent crime.[31]

This sort of fear mongering relies on predictable patterns of human bias. A recent and easily recalled news story or an emotionally intense invocation of violent crime causes many of us to overestimate the frequency of such events. We will then be more likely to support tougher laws on violent crime. Fear mongering prevents an unbiased evaluation of the risk of crime and encourages support for bad policies.

However, cultivating apocalyptic fears of nuclear war or climate change is not fear mongering in this sense. Morgenthau tried to elicit a salutary fear of nuclear war in order to correct for irrational denial of the threat. In the case of climate change, many are similarly subject to cognitive biases and motivated reasoning that cause them either to ignore or underestimate this global risk.[32] Morgenthau and Gore are not trying to elicit irrational biases; they are trying to cultivate rational fears.

So, evoking apocalyptic fear may be an appropriate response to prospective catastrophes such as nuclear war and global climate change. Yet the strategy

---

[29] Gore, "Moment of Truth."
[30] Barry Glassner, "Narrative Techniques of Fear Mongering," *Social Research* 71, no. 4 (2004): 820.
[31] D'Vera Cohn et al., "Gun Homicide Rate Down 49% Since 1993 Peak; Public Unaware," Pew Research Center, May 7, 2013, www.pewsocialtrends.org/2013/05/07/gun-homicide-rate-down-49-since-1993-peak-public-unaware/.
[32] See, for instance: Max H. Bazerman, "Climate Change as a Predictable Surprise," *Climatic Change* 77, nos. 1–2 (2006): 179–93; David V. Budescu, Stephen Broomell, and Han-Hui Por, "Improving Communication of Uncertainty in the Reports of the Intergovernmental Panel on Climate Change," *Psychological Science* 20, no. 3 (2009): 299–308; Stephen B. Broomell, David V. Budescu, and Han-Hui Por, "Personal Experience with Climate Change Predicts Intentions to Act," *Global Environmental Change* 32 (2015): 67–73; Ezra M. Markowitz and Azim F. Shariff, "Climate Change and Moral Judgement," *Nature Climate Change* 2, no. 4 (2012): 243–47; Per Espen Stoknes, *What We Think About When We Try Not To Think About Global Warming: Toward a New Psychology of Climate Action* (White River Junction, VT: Chelsea Green Publishing, 2015).

is still politically risky. As we have seen throughout this book, apocalypticism resists efforts to contain, tame, and successfully redirect its powerful rhetoric and imagery. Despite the efforts of early Christians such as Paul and church fathers such as Augustine to discipline and redirect the political radicalism of apocalypticism, the imaginary has continued to reemerge as a challenge to sovereign power. While Savonarola tried to deploy apocalypticism in the service of a new republican order in Renaissance Florence, this same imaginary was eventually used to condemn the friar himself as Antichrist.

Similarly, in seventeenth-century England, the apocalypticism that had supported sovereign and ecclesiastical power in the sixteenth century became the basis for a radical challenge, less than a hundred years later. Once loosed upon the world, the rich imaginative and semiotic resources of the apocalypse have consistently proven difficult to control. We have little reason to think that similar dangers would not attend strategic attempts to redeploy the apocalyptic imaginary today.

Beyond acknowledging the difficulty of controlling it, we have good reason to worry that the apocalyptic imaginary leads to three dangerous political postures. The first and most dangerous response is a full-throated embrace of the apocalyptic worldview, one that divides the world into good and evil, vilifies opponents, and pushes the battle for ultimate justice to its violent consummation. This cosmic vision animated the European wars of religion and the English Civil War. Today, its main champion is ISIS.[33]

The remaining postures are less explosive but perhaps more likely. The second response is to withdraw from participation in politics, as John of Patmos encouraged early Christians to do. Those who care about the fate of their souls must not be complicit with evil, he cautions.[34] Christians who accepted this counsel were left with no option but to give up on their political world and await the New Jerusalem. The problem with this focus on the imminent afterlife is that any number of more mundane injustices may go unchecked in the meantime.

The third posture is resignation. The world is going to hell, concludes the apocalyptic believer, but there is nothing to be done. This is a common reaction to apocalyptic images in the climate change debate. While these images make the prospective catastrophe more salient, they tend to decrease people's sense of efficacy. Instead of rousing people to action, these calamitous warnings leave them defeated and disengaged.[35] Faced with terrifying and often overtly apocalyptic representations of the effects of climate change, many are inclined

---

[33] McCants, *The ISIS Apocalypse*. [34] Revelation 18.
[35] Julia Metag et al., "Perceptions of Climate Change Imagery Evoked Salience and Self-Efficacy in Germany, Switzerland, and Austria," *Science Communication* 38, no. 2 (2016): 197–227; Saffron J. O'Neill et al., "On the Use of Imagery for Climate Change Engagement," *Global Environmental Change* 23, no. 2 (2013): 413–21; Saffron J. O'Neill and Sophie Nicholson-Cole, "'Fear Won't Do It' Promoting Positive Engagement With Climate Change Through Visual and Iconic Representations," *Science Communication* 30, no. 3 (2009): 355–79.

to conclude – not entirely without good reason – that any actions they can take will be futile.

Do these risks mean that the strategy of apocalyptic redirection should be abandoned entirely? We need not be so hasty. In cases of prospective catastrophe, our judgment about the strategy of redirection must hinge on how effectively it helps us avert the unwanted end while guarding against the risk of perverse apocalyptic politics.

In the end, much of the normative work of political realism is about cultivating the art of living through catastrophe without apocalyptically surrendering to it. The experiences of the thinkers in this book suggest that, regardless of the strategy one ultimately adopts, this is a practice to which one must repeatedly recommit without any reliable hope of success.

References

Abizadeh, Arash. "Hobbes on the Causes of War: A Disagreement Theory." *American Political Science Review* 105, no. 2 (2011): 298–315.
"Hobbes's Conventionalist Theology, the Trinity, and God as an Artificial Person by Fiction." *Historical Journal*. Published electronically January 30, 2017. doi: 10.1017/S0018246X16000418.
Ahrensdorf, Peter J. "The Fear of Death and the Longing for Immortality: Hobbes and Thucydides on Human Nature and the Problem of Anarchy." *The American Political Science Review* 94, no. 3 (2000): 579–93.
Alvarez, Al. "The Concentration Camps." *The Atlantic Monthly*, December 1962.
Amira, Dan. "A Conversation With Harold Camping, Prophesier of Judgment Day." *New York Magazine: Daily Intelligencer*, May 11, 2011. http://nymag.com/daily/intelligencer/2011/05/a_conversation_with_harold_cam.html.
Anders, Günther. "Theses for the Atomic Age." *The Massachusetts Review* 3, no. 3 (1962): 493–505.
Arendt, Hannah. "An Introduction *into* Politics." In *The Promise of Politics*, edited by Jerome Kohn, 93–200. New York: Schocken Books, 2005.
Eichmann in Jerusalem: A Report on the Banality of Evil. New York: Penguin, 1977.
"Europe and the Atom Bomb." In *Essays in Understanding, 1930–1954: Formation, Exile and Totalitarianism*, edited by Jerome Kohn, 418–422. New York: Schocken Books, 1994.
The Human Condition. 2nd ed. Chicago: University of Chicago Press, 1998.
"Understanding and Politics (The Difficulties of Understanding)." In *Essays in Understanding, 1930–1954: Formation, Exile, and Totalitarianism*, edited by Jerome Kohn, 307–27. New York: Schocken Books, 1994.
Arnold, Isaac Newton. *The History of Abraham Lincoln, and the Overthrow of Slavery*. Chicago: Clarke & Co., 1866.
Ascoli, Albert Russell. "Machiavelli's Gift of Counsel." In *Machiavelli and the Discourse of Literature*, edited by Albert Russell Ascoli and Victoria Kahn, 219–57. Ithaca: Cornell University Press, 1993.

References

Augustine of Hippo. *Concerning the City of God against the Pagans*. Translated by Henry Bettenson. Harmondsworth: Penguin, 1972.

Augustine. *The Works of Saint Augustine* [Electronic Edition], vol. 2, no. 3. Translated by Roland Teske. Charlottesville: InteLex, 2001. http://pm.nlx.com/xtf/view?docId=augustine_iii/augustine_iii.00.xml;chunk.id=div.aug.pmpreface.1;toc.depth=2;toc.id=div.aug.pmpreface.1;hit.rank=0;brand=default.

Aune, David E. "The Apocalypse of John and the Problem of Genre." *Semeia* 36 (1986): 65–96.

Bacon, Francis. "Of Prophecies." In *The Essays of Francis Bacon*, edited by Mary Augusta Scott, 165–70. New York: Charles Scribner's Sons, 1908.

Bale, John. *Select Works of John Bale*. Edited by Henry Christmas. Cambridge: Cambridge University Press, 1849. https://archive.org/details/selectworksofbaloobaleuoft.

Barkun, Michael. *Disaster and the Millennium*. New Haven: Yale University Press, 1974.

Baron, Hans. "The Principe and the Puzzle of the Date of Chapter 26." *Journal of Medieval and Renaissance Studies* 21, no. 1 (1991): 83–102.

Bazerman, Max H. "Climate Change as a Predictable Surprise." *Climatic Change* 77, nos. 1–2 (2006): 179–93.

Bell, Duncan, ed. *Political Thought and International Relations: Variations on a Realist Theme*. Oxford: Oxford University Press, 2009.

——— "What Is Liberalism?" *Political Theory* 42, no. 6 (December 1, 2014): 682–715.

Benner, Erica. *Machiavelli's Prince: A New Reading*. Oxford: Oxford University Press, 2013.

Berger, James. *After the End: Representations of Post-Apocalypse*. Minneapolis: University of Minnesota Press, 1999.

Berlin, Isaiah. "The Originality of Machiavelli." In *Against the Current: Essays in the History of Ideas*, edited by Henry Hardy, 25–79. London: Hogarth Press, 1980.

Bernstein, Michael Andre. *Foregone Conclusions: Against Apocalyptic History*. Berkeley: University of California Press, 1994.

Betteridge, Maurice S. "The Bitter Notes: The Geneva Bible and Its Annotations." *The Sixteenth Century Journal* 14, no. 1 (1983): 41–62.

Bisaha, Nancy. *Creating East and West: Renaissance Humanists and the Ottoman Turks*. Philadelphia: University of Pennsylvania Press, 2006.

Bottici, Chiara. "Imaginary, The." In *Encyclopedia of Political Theory*, edited by Mark Bevir, vol. 1. Thousand Oaks: SAGE, 2010.

Boucher, David. *Political Theories of International Relations: From Thucydides to the Present*. Oxford: Oxford University Press, 1998.

Bousquet, Antoine. "Time Zero: Hiroshima, September 11 and Apocalyptic Revelations in Historical Consciousness." *Millennium* 34, no. 3 (2006): 739–64.

Boyer, Paul. *Fallout: A Historian Reflects on America's Half-Century Encounter with Nuclear Weapons*. Columbus: Ohio State University Press, 1998.

——— *When Time Shall Be No More: Prophecy Belief in Modern American Culture*. Cambridge: Harvard University Press, 1992.

Boykoff, Maxwell T., and Jules M. Boykoff. "Balance as Bias: Global Warming and the US Prestige Press." *Global Environmental Change* 14, no. 2 (2004): 125–36.

Broomell, Stephen B., David V. Budescu, and Han-Hui Por. "Personal Experience with Climate Change Predicts Intentions to Act." *Global Environmental Change* 32 (2015): 67–73.

Brown, Alison. "Introduction." In *Selected Writings of Girolamo Savonarola: Religion and Politics, 1490–1498*. Translated by Anne Borelli and Maria Pastore Passaro, xv–xxxv. New Haven: Yale University Press, 2006.

——— "Savonarola, Machiavelli and Moses: A Changing Model." In *Florence and Italy: Renaissance Studies in Honour of Nicolai Rubinstein*, edited by Peter Denley and Caroline Elam, 1–71. London: Committee for Medieval Studies, Westfield College, University of London, 1988.

——— *The Return of Lucretius to Renaissance Florence*. Cambridge: Harvard University Press, 2010.

Brown, Chris. "'The Twilight of International Morality'? Hans J. Morgenthau and Carl Schmitt on the End of the *Jus Publicum Europaeum*." In *Realism Reconsidered: The Legacy of Hans Morgenthau in International Relations*, edited by Michael C. Williams, 42–61. Oxford: Oxford University Press, 2007.

Brown, Keith. "The Artist of the *Leviathan* Title Page." *The British Library Journal* 4, no. 1 (1978): 24–36.

——— "Thomas Hobbes and the Title-Page of *Leviathan*." *Philosophy* 55, no. 213 (1980): 410–11.

Buck-Morss, Susan. *Dreamworld and Catastrophe: The Passing of Mass Utopia in East and West*. Cambridge: MIT Press, 2000.

Budescu, David V., Stephen Broomell, and Han-Hui Por. "Improving Communication of Uncertainty in the Reports of the Intergovernmental Panel on Climate Change." *Psychological Science* 20, no. 3 (2009): 299–308.

Bundy, Harvey H. "Remembered Words." *The Atlantic Monthly*, March 1957.

Burd, Arthur L. Introduction to *The Prince*, by Niccolò Machiavelli, 1–71. Edited by Arthur L. Burd. Oxford: Clarendon Press, 1891.

Burke, Edmund. "A Philosophical Inquiry into the Origin of Our Ideas of the Sublime and Beautiful with Several Other Additions." In *On Taste, On the Sublime and Beautiful, Reflections on the French Revolution, Letter to a Noble Lord*, 27–148. New York: P. F. Collier and Son, 1909.

Bush, George W. "Address Before a Joint Session of the Congress on the State of the Union." The American Presidency Project. January 29, 2002. www.presidency.ucsb.edu/ws/?pid=29644.

——— "Address Before a Joint Session of the Congress on the State of the Union." The American Presidency Project. January 28, 2003. www.presidency.ucsb.edu/ws/index.php?pid=29645#axzz1UZTKZP00.

——— "Address Before a Joint Session of the Congress on the United States Response to the Terrorist Attacks of September 11." The American Presidency Project. September 20, 2001. www.presidency.ucsb.edu/ws/index.php?pid=64731&st=&st1=#axzz1W1KOUh9B.

——— "Address to the Nation Announcing Strikes Against Al Qaida Training Camps and Taliban Military Installations in Afghanistan." The American Presidency Project. October 7, 2001. www.presidency.ucsb.edu/mediaplay.php?id=65088&admin=43.

"Inaugural Address." The American Presidency Project. January 20, 2005. www.presidency.ucsb.edu/ws/index.php?pid=58745.

"Remarks on Arrival in Daytona Beach, Florida." The American Presidency Project. January 30, 2002. http://www.presidency.ucsb.edu/ws/index.php?pid=73243&st=&st1=#axzz1W1KOUh9B.

Capp, Bernard. "The Millennium and Eschatology in England." *Past & Present* 57, no. 1 (1972): 156–62.

——— "The Political Dimension of Apocalyptic Thought." In *The Apocalypse in English Renaissance Thought and Literature: Patterns, Antecedents and Repercussions*, edited by C. A. Patrides and Joseph Wittreich, 93–124. Ithaca: Cornell University Press, 1984.

Carey, Frances, ed. *The Apocalypse and The Shape of Things to Come*. Toronto: University of Toronto Press, 1999.

Carr, Edward Hallett. *The Twenty Years' Crisis, 1919–1939*. New York: Harper and Row, 1964.

Carruthers, Mary. *The Craft of Thought: Meditation, Rhetoric, and the Making of Images, 400–1200*. New York: Cambridge University Press, 1998.

Cassirer, Ernst. *The Myth of the State*. New Haven: Yale University Press, 1946.

Chabod, Frederico. *Machiavelli and the Renaissance*. Cambridge: Harvard University Press, 1960.

Christianson, Paul K. *Reformers and Babylon: English Apocalyptic Visions from the Reformation to the Eve of the Civil War*. Toronto: University of Toronto Press, 1978.

Clifford, Richard J. "The Roots of Apocalypticism in Near Eastern Myth." In *The Continuum History of Apocalypticism*, edited by Bernard J. McGinn, John J. Collins, and Stephen J. Stein, 3–29. New York: Continuum, 2003.

Cohen, Leonard. *The Future*. Columbia, 1992. Compact Disc.

Cohn, D'Vera, Paul Taylor, Mark Hugo Lopez, Catherine A. Gallagher, Kim Parker, and Kevin T. Maass. "Gun Homicide Rate Down 49% Since 1993 Peak; Public Unaware." Pew Research Center. May 7, 2013. www.pewsocialtrends.org/2013/05/07/gun-homicide-rate-down-49-since-1993-peak-public-unaware.

Cohn, Norman. *The Pursuit of the Millennium: Revolutionary Messianism in Medieval and Reformation Europe and Its Bearing on Modern Totalitarian Movements*. 2nd ed. New York: Harper and Row, 1961.

Colish, Marcia L. "Republicanism, Religion, and Machiavelli's Savonarolan Moment." *Journal of the History of Ideas* 60, no. 4 (1999): 597–616.

Collingwood, Robin G. *An Autobiography*. Oxford: Oxford University Press, 1939.

Collins, Adela Yarbro. *Cosmology and Eschatology in Jewish and Christian Apocalypticism*. Leiden: Brill, 1996.

——— *Crisis and Catharsis: The Power of the Apocalypse*. Philadelphia: Westminster Press, 1984.

——— "The Book of Revelation." In *The Continuum History of Apocalypticism*, edited by Bernard J. McGinn, John J. Collins, and Stephen J. Stein, 195–217. New York: Continuum, 2003.

Collins, Jeffrey R. *The Allegiance of Thomas Hobbes*. Oxford: Oxford University Press, 2005.

Collins, John J. "Apocalypses and Apocalypticism: Early Jewish Apocalypticism." In *The Anchor Bible Dictionary*, edited by David Noel Freedman, vol. 1, 282–88. New York: Doubleday, 1992.
— "Daniel, Book of." In *The Anchor Bible Dictionary*, edited by David Noel Freedman, vol. 2, 29–37. New York: Doubleday, 1992.
— "From Prophecy to Apocalypticism: The Expectation of the End." In *The Continuum History of Apocalypticism*, edited by Bernard J. McGinn, John J. Collins, and Stephen J. Stein, 64–88. New York: Continuum, 2003.
— *The Apocalyptic Imagination: An Introduction to Jewish Apocalyptic Literature*. 2nd ed. Grand Rapids, MI: William B. Eerdmans, 1998.
— "The Zeal of Phinehas: The Bible and the Legitimation of Violence." *Journal of Biblical Literature* 122, no. 1 (2003): 3–21.
— "Towards the Morphology of a Genre: Introduction." *Semeia* 14 (1979): 1–20.
Connolly, William E. *Capitalism and Christianity, American Style*. Durham: Duke University Press Books, 2008.
Cooper, Julie E. *Secular Powers: Humility in Modern Political Thought*. Chicago: University of Chicago Press, 2013.
Coyle, Kevin J. "Augustine and Apocalyptic: Thoughts on the Fall of Rome, the Book of Revelation, and the End of the World." *Florilegium* 9 (1987): 1–34.
Craig, Campbell. *Glimmer of a New Leviathan: Total War in the Realism of Niebuhr, Morgenthau, and Waltz*. New York: Columbia University Press, 2003.
Cranston, Maurice. *Political Dialogues*. London: British Broadcasting Corporation, 1968.
Cromwell, Oliver. "Meeting of the First Protectorate Parliament (September 4, 1654)." In *Oliver Cromwell's Letters and Speeches with Elucidations*, edited by Thomas Carlyle, vol. 3, 103–26. New York: Charles Scribner's Sons, 1903.
— "Opening of the Little Parliament (July 4, 1653)." In *Oliver Cromwell's Letters and Speeches with Elucidations*, edited by Thomas Carlyle, vol. 3, 40–73. New York: Charles Scribner's Sons, 1903.
Crossan, John Dominic. *Jesus: A Revolutionary Biography*. San Francisco: Harper, 1994.
Crouter, Richard. *Reinhold Niebuhr: On Politics, Religion, and Christian Faith*. New York: Oxford University Press, 2010.
Curley, Edwin. "'I Durst Not Write So Boldly' Or How to Read Hobbes's Theological-Political Treatise." In *Hobbes E Spinoza: Scienza E Politica*, edited by Daniela Bostrenghi, 497–593. Naples: Bibliopolis, 1992.
Daniell, David. *The Bible in English: Its History and Influence*. New Haven: Yale University Press, 2003.
Dash, Joan. *A Life of One's Own: Three Gifted Women and the Men They Married*. New York: Harper & Row, 1973.
de Grazia, Sebastian. *Machiavelli in Hell*. Princeton: Princeton University Press, 1989.
Derrida, Jacques. "Of an Apocalyptic Tone Newly Adopted in Philosophy." In *Derrida and Negative Theology*, edited by Harold Coward and Toby Foshay, 25–72. Albany: State University of New York Press, 1992.
Di Maria, Salvatore. "Machiavelli's Ironic View of History: The *Istorie Fiorentine*." *Renaissance Quarterly* 45, no. 2 (1992): 248–70.

References

Dietz, Mary G. "Trapping the Prince: Machiavelli and the Politics of Deception." *The American Political Science Review* 80, no. 3 (1986): 777–99.

Donne, John. "Holy Sonnet XIII." In *The Complete Poetry and Selected Prose of John Donne*, edited by Charles M. Coffin, 252. New York: Modern Library, 1952.

"Holy Sonnet XIV." In *The Complete Poetry and Selected Prose of John Donne*, edited by Charles M. Coffin, 252. New York: Modern Library, 1952.

"Hymne to God my God, in My Sicknesse." In *The Complete Poetry and Selected Prose of John Donne*, edited by Charles M. Coffin, 271–72. New York: Modern Library, 1952.

Donnelly, Jack. *Realism and International Relations*. Cambridge: Cambridge University Press, 2000.

Dunne, Tim. "Theories as Weapons: E. H. Carr and International Relations." In *E. H. Carr*, edited by Michael Cox, 217–33. Basingstoke: Palgrave Macmillan, 2000.

Dupuy, Jean-Pierre. *The Mark of the Sacred*. Translated by M. DeBevoise. Stanford: Stanford University Press, 2013.

Ehrman, Bart D. *Jesus: Apocalyptic Prophet of the New Millennium*. Oxford: Oxford University Press, 1999.

The New Testament: A Historical Introduction to the Early Christian Writings. New York: Oxford University Press, 2008.

Emmerson, Richard K., and Ronald B. Herzman. *The Apocalyptic Imagination in Medieval Literature*. Philadelphia: University of Pennsylvania Press, 1992.

Euben, J. Peter. "The Politics of Nostalgia and Theories of Loss." In *Vocations of Political Theory*, edited by Jason A. Frank and John Tambornino, 73–83. Minneapolis: University of Minnesota Press, 2000.

The Tragedy of Political Theory: The Road Not Taken. Princeton: Princeton University Press, 1990.

Evrigenis, Ioannis D. *Images of Anarchy: The Rhetoric and Science in Hobbes's State of Nature*. New York: Cambridge University Press, 2014.

Fiorenza, Elisabeth Schüssler. *The Book of Revelation: Justice and Judgment*. Minneapolis: Fortress Press, 1985.

Firth, Katharine R. *Apocalyptic Tradition in Reformation Britain: 1530–1645*. Oxford: Oxford University Press, 1979.

Flanagan, Thomas. "The Third Reich: Origins of a Millenarian Symbol." *History of European Ideas* 8, no. 3 (1987): 283–95.

Forde, Steven. "Varieties of Realism: Thucydides and Machiavelli." *Journal of Politics* 54, no. 2 (1992): 372–93.

Foxe, John. *The Acts and Monuments of John Foxe*. Edited by Josiah Pratt. Vol. 4. London: George Seeley, 1870. https://books.google.com/books?id=RDwJAQAAIAAJ&dq.

Fredriksen, Paula. "Apocalypse and Redemption in Early Christianity: From John of Patmos to Augustine of Hippo." *Vigilae Christianae* 45, no. 2 (1992): 151–83.

From Jesus to Christ: The Origins of the New Testament Image of Christ. New Haven: Yale University Press, 2000.

Freeman, Samuel. Foreword to *John Rawls, Lectures on the History of Political Philosophy*. Edited by Samuel Freeman, ix–xvi. Cambridge: Belknap/Harvard University Press, 2007.

Frei, Christoph. *Hans J. Morgenthau: An Intellectual Biography.* Baton Rouge: Louisiana State University Press, 2001.
Friesen, Steven J. *Imperial Cults and the Apocalypse of John: Reading Revelation in the Ruins.* Oxford: Oxford University Press, 2001.
Frye, Northrop. *Anatomy of Criticism.* Princeton: Princeton University Press, 2000.
Fukuyama, Francis. *The End of History and the Last Man.* New York: Free Press, 1992.
"Full Transcript: Donald Trump NYC Speech on Stakes of the Election." *POLITICO.* June 22, 2016. www.politico.com/story/2016/06/transcript-trump-speech-on-the-stakes-of-the-election-224654.
Galston, William A. "Realism in Political Theory." *European Journal of Political Theory* 9, no. 4 (October 1, 2010): 385–411.
Gauthier, David P. *The Logic of Leviathan: The Moral and Political Theory of Thomas Hobbes.* Oxford: Oxford University Press, 1969.
Geuss, Raymond. *Philosophy and Real Politics.* Princeton: Princeton University Press, 2008.
Gilbert, Felix. "The Humanist Concept of the Prince and *The Prince* of Machiavelli." *The Journal of Modern History* 11, no. 4 (1939): 449–83.
Gilpin, Robert. "The Richness of the Tradition of Political Realism." In *Neorealism and Its Critics*, edited by Robert O. Keohane, 301–21. New York: Columbia University Press, 1986.
Glassner, Barry. "Narrative Techniques of Fear Mongering." *Social Research* 71, no. 4 (2004): 819–26.
Glover, Willis B. "God and Thomas Hobbes." *Church History* 29, no. 3 (1960): 275–97.
Godman, Peter. *From Poliziano to Machiavelli: Florentine Humanism in the High Renaissance.* Princeton: Princeton University Press, 1998.
Goldsmith, Maurice M. "Hobbes's Ambiguous Politics." *History of Political Thought* 11, no. 4 (1990): 639–73.
Gore, Al. *An Inconvenient Truth.* Documentary. Directed by Davis Guggenheim. Hollywood: Paramount, 2006. DVD.
   Our Choice: A Plan to Solve the Climate Crisis. Emmaus, PA: Rodale Books, 2009.
   "The Moment of Truth." *Vanity Fair*, May 2006. www.vanityfair.com/news/2006/05/climate-change-200605.
Gray, John. *Two Faces of Liberalism.* New York: New Press, 2000.
Greene, Thomas M. "The End of Discourse in Machiavelli's 'Prince.'" *Yale French Studies*, no. 67 (1984): 57–71.
Gribben, Crawford. "Deconstructing the Geneva Bible: The Search for a Puritan Poetics." *Literature and Theology* 14, no. 1 (2000): 1–16.
   The Puritan Millennium: Literature & Theology, 1550–1682. Dublin: Four Courts Press, 2000.
Gross, Leo. "The Peace of Westphalia, 1648–1948." *American Journal of International Law* 42, no. 1 (1948): 20–41.
Gruen, Erich S. "Hellenism and Persecution: Antiochus IV and the Jews." In *Hellenistic History and Culture*, edited by Peter Green, 238–64. Berkeley: University of California Press, 1993.
Guilhot, Nicolas. "American *Katechon*: When Political Theology Became International Relations Theory." *Constellations* 17, no. 2 (2010): 224–53.

References

Gutierrez, Cathy. "The Millennium and Narrative Closure." In *War in Heaven/Heaven on Earth: Theories of the Apocalyptic*, edited by Stephen D. O'Leary and Glen S. McGhee, 46–58. London: Equinox, 2005.

Guzzini, Stefano. *Realism in International Relations and International Political Economy: The Continuing Story of a Death Foretold.* London: Routledge, 1998.

Habermas, Jurgen. *Between Facts and Norms: Contributions to a Discourse Theory of Law and Democracy.* Translated by William Rehg. Cambridge: MIT Press, 1998.

Hall, John R., Philip D. Schuyler, and Sylvaine Trinh. *Apocalypse Observed: Religious Movements and Violence in North America, Europe and Japan.* New York: Routledge, 2000.

Haller, William. *Foxe's Book of Martyrs and the Elect Nation.* London: Jonathan Cape, 1963.

Hammill, Graham. *The Mosaic Constitution: Political Theology and Imagination from Machiavelli to Milton.* Chicago: University of Chicago Press, 2012.

Hampton, Jean. *Hobbes and the Social Contract Tradition.* Cambridge: Cambridge University Press, 1986.

Hanson, Paul D. "Apocalypses and Apocalypticism: The Genre." In *The Anchor Bible Dictionary*, edited by David Noel Freedman, vol. 1, 279–88. New York: Doubleday, 1992.

——— "Apocalypticism." In *Interpreter's Dictionary of the Bible, Supplementary Volume*, edited by Keith Crim, et al. Nashville: Abingdon Press, 1976.

——— *The Dawn of Apocalyptic: The Historical and Sociological Roots of Jewish Apocalyptic Eschatology.* Philadelphia: Fortress Press, 1975.

Hatfield, Rab. "Botticelli's Mystic Nativity, Savonarola and the Millennium." *Journal of the Warburg and Courtauld Institutes* 58 (1995): 89–114.

Hayes, Christine. *Introduction to the Bible.* New Haven: Yale University Press, 2012.

Helgerson, Richard. *Forms of Nationhood: The Elizabethan Writing of England.* Chicago: University of Chicago Press, 1992.

Hersey, John. *Hiroshima.* New York: Alfred A. Knopf, 1985.

Heylyn, Peter. *Aerius Redivivus: Or, the History of the Presbyterians.* Reprint of the 1670 edition, Early English Books Online. http://gateway.proquest.com/openurl?ctx_ver=Z39.88-2003&res_id=xri:eebo&rft_id=xri:eebo:citation:12139018.

Hill, Christopher. *Antichrist in Seventeenth-Century England.* London: Verso, 1990.

——— *The English Bible and the Seventeenth-Century Revolution.* London: Penguin, 1993.

——— *The Experience of Defeat: Milton and Some Contemporaries.* New York: Viking, 1984.

Hobbes, Thomas. *Behemoth, or the Long Parliament.* Edited by Paul Seaward. Oxford: Oxford University Press, 2010.

——— *De Cive.* Edited by Richard Tuck. Translated by Michael Silverthorne. New York: Cambridge University Press, 1998.

——— "Letter from Hobbes to John Scudamore (1641)." In *The Correspondence of Thomas Hobbes*, edited by Noel Malcolm, vol. 1, 114–15. Oxford: Clarendon Press, 1994.

——— *Leviathan.* Edited by Noel Malcolm. Oxford: Oxford University Press, 2012.

——— *The Elements of Law, Natural and Politic.* Edited by J. C. A. Gaskin. Oxford: Oxford University Press, 2008.

"Vita [Verse]." In *Opera Philosophica Quae Latine Scripsit Omnia*, edited by William Molesworth, vol. 1, lxxxv–xcix. London: John Bohn, 1939.

Hoekstra, Kinch. "Disarming the Prophets: Thomas Hobbes and Predictive Power." *Rivista Di Storia Della Filosofia* 59, no. 1 (2004): 97–153.

———. "The End of Philosophy (The Case of Hobbes)." *Proceedings of the Aristotelian Society* 106, no. 1 (2006): 25–62.

Hoffmann, Stanley. *Janus and Minerva: Essays in the Theory and Practice of International Politics*. Boulder: Westview Press, 1987.

Hollerich, Michael. "Carl Schmitt." In *The Blackwell Companion to Political Theology*, edited by Peter Scott and William T. Cavanaugh, 107–22. Malden: Blackwell, 2004.

Holmes, Stephen. Introduction to *Behemoth, or the Long Parliament*, by Thomas Hobbes, vii–l. Chicago: University of Chicago Press, 1990.

———. *Passions and Constraint: On the Theory of Liberal Democracy*. Chicago: University of Chicago Press, 1995.

Honig, Bonnie. *Political Theory and the Displacement of Politics*. Ithaca: Cornell University Press, 1993.

Houlahan, Mark. "Leviathan (1651): Thomas Hobbes and Protestant Apocalypse." In *1650–1850: Ideas, Aesthetics, and Inquiries in the Early Modern Era*, edited by Kevin L. Cope, vol. 2, 95–109. New York: AMS Press, 1996.

Hultgård, Anders. "Persian Apocalypticism." In *Continuum History of Apocalypticism*, edited by Bernard J. McGinn, John J. Collins, and Stephen J. Stein, 30–63. New York: Continuum, 2003.

Ibsen, Henrik. *Emperor and Galilean: A World-Historic Drama*. Edited and translated by William Archer. New York: Scribner and Welford, 1890. https://books.google.com/books?id=ZYoOAAAAYAAJ.

Intergovernmental Panel on Climate Change (IPCC). *Climate Change 2014: Impacts, Adaptation, Vulnerability*. Cambridge: Cambridge University Press, 2014.

Jacobitti, Edmund E. "The Classical Heritage in Machiavelli's Histories: Symbol and Poetry as Historical Literature." In *The Comedy and Tragedy of Machiavelli*, edited by Vickie B. Sullivan, 176–92. New Haven: Yale University Press, 2000.

Jacques, Peter J., Riley E. Dunlap, and Mark Freeman. "The Organisation of Denial: Conservative Think Tanks and Environmental Scepticism." *Environmental Politics* 17, no. 3 (2008): 349–85.

James I/VI. *Ane Fruitfull Meditatioun Contening Ane Plane and Facill Expositioun of Ye 7.8.9 and 10 Versis of the 20 Chap. of the Reuelatioun in Forme of Ane Sermone*. Reprint of the 1588 edition, Early English Books Online. http://gateway.proquest.com/openurl?ctx_ver=Z39.88-2003&res_id=xri:eebo&rft_id=xri:eebo:citation:99836897.

James, Scott. "From Oakland to the World, Words of Warning: Time's Up." *The New York Times*, May 19, 2011. www.nytimes.com/2011/05/20/us/20bcjames.html.

Jaspers, Karl. *The Future of Mankind*. Translated by E. B. Ashton. Chicago: University of Chicago Press, 1961.

Jervis, Robert. *The Illogic of American Nuclear Strategy*. Ithaca: Cornell University Press, 1985.

Johnston, David. "Hobbes's Mortalism." *History of Political Thought* 10, no. 4 (1989): 647–63.

The Rhetoric of Leviathan: *Thomas Hobbes and the Politics of Cultural Transformation.* Princeton: Princeton University Press, 1986.

Jones, Meirav. "'My Highest Priority Was to Absolve the Divine Laws': The Theory and Politics of Hobbes's Leviathan in a War of Religion." *Political Studies* 65, no. 1 (2016): 248–63.

Jordheim, Helge. "Conceptual History Between *Chronos* and *Kairos* – The Case of 'Empire.'" In *Redescriptions: Yearbook of Political Thought and Conceptual History*, Vol. 11, edited by K. Lindroos and Kari Palonen, 115–45, 2007.

Jurdjevic, Mark. *A Great and Wretched City: Promise and Failure in Machiavelli's Florentine Political Thought.* Cambridge: Harvard University Press, 2014.

Kahn, Herman. *On Thermonuclear War.* Princeton: Princeton University Press, 1960.

Thinking About the Unthinkable. New York: Horizon Press, 1962.

Kahn, Paul W. *Political Theology: Four New Chapters on the Concept of Sovereignty.* New York: Columbia University Press, 2011.

Kateb, George. "Hobbes and the Irrationality of Politics." *Political Theory* 17, no. 3 (1989): 355–91.

Keller, Catherine. *Apocalypse Now and Then: A Feminist Guide to the End of the World.* Boston: Beacon Press, 1996.

God and Power: Counter-Apocalyptic Journeys. Minneapolis: Fortress Press, 2005.

Kermode, Frank. *The Sense of an Ending: Studies in the Theory of Fiction (with a New Epilogue).* New York: Oxford University Press, 2000.

Klein, Naomi. *The Shock Doctrine: The Rise of Disaster Capitalism.* New York: Picador, 2008.

Klosko, George, and Daryl Rice. "Thucydides and Hobbes's State of Nature." *History of Political Thought* 6, no. 3 (1985): 405–09.

Koskenniemi, Martti. *The Gentle Civilizer of Nations: The Rise and Fall of International Law 1870–1960.* Cambridge: Cambridge University Press, 2004.

Krasner, Stephen D. *Sovereignty.* Princeton: Princeton University Press, 1999.

Landes, Richard. *Heaven on Earth: The Varieties of the Millennial Experience.* New York: Oxford University Press, 2011.

"Lest the Millennium Be Fulfilled: Apocalyptic Expectations and the Pattern of Western Chronography 100–800 CE." In *The Use and Abuse of Eschatology in the Middle Ages*, edited by Werner Verbeke, Daniel Verhelst, and Andries Welkenhuysen, 137–211. Leuven: Leuven University Press, 1988.

"Roosters Crow, Owls Hoot: On the Dynamics of Apocalyptic Millennialism." In *War in Heaven/Heaven on Earth: Theories of the Apocalyptic*, edited by Stephen D. O'Leary and Glen S. McGhee, 19–46. London: Equinox, 2005.

"The Fear of an Apocalyptic Year 1000: Augustinian Historiography, Medieval and Modern." *Speculum* 75, no. 1 (2000): 97–145.

"What Happens When Jesus Doesn't Come: Jewish and Christian Relations in Apocalyptic Time." In *Millennial Violence: Past, Present and Future*, edited by Jeffrey Kaplan, 243–74. London: Frank Cass, 2002.

Lane, Melissa. "Doing Our Own Thinking for Ourselves: On Quentin Skinner's Genealogical Turn." *Journal of the History of Ideas* 73, no. 1 (2012): 71–82.

Langton, John, and Mary G. Deitz. "Machiavelli's Paradox: Trapping or Teaching the Prince." *The American Political Science Review* 81, no. 4 (1987): 1277–88.

Laurence, William Leonard. *Men and Atoms: The Discovery, the Uses, and the Future of Atomic Energy.* New York: Simon and Schuster, 1959.

Lear, Jonathan. *Radical Hope: Ethics in the Face of Cultural Devastation.* Cambridge: Harvard University Press, 2006.

Lebow, Richard Ned. *The Tragic Vision of Politics: Ethics, Interests and Orders.* Cambridge: Cambridge University Press, 2003.

Lefort, Claude. *Machiavelli in the Making.* Translated by Michael B. Smith. Evanston: Northwestern University Press, 2012.

Lessay, Franck. "Hobbes's Covenant Theology and Its Political Implications." In *The Cambridge Companion to Hobbes's* Leviathan, edited by Patricia Springborg, 243–70. Cambridge: Cambridge University Press, 2007.

"Let's Prepare...Shelters." *Life Magazine*, October 13, 1961.

Levin, Meyer. "The Child behind the Secret Door." *New York Times Book Review*, June 15, 1952, https://search.proquest.com/docview/112258545?accountid=14026.

Levine, Amy-Jill. "Daniel: Introduction and Notes." In *The New Oxford Annotated Bible, New Revised Standard Version with Apocrypha*, edited by Michael D. Coogan, 4th ed., 1233–57. Oxford: Oxford University Press, 2010.

Lifton, Robert Jay. "Beyond the Nuclear End." In *The Future of Immortality and Other Essays for a Nuclear Age*, 10–27. New York: Basic Books, 1987.

———. "On Death and Death Symbolism: The Hiroshima Disaster." *Psychiatry* 27, no. 3 (1964): 191–210.

———. *The Broken Connection: On Death and the Continuity of Life.* New York: Simon and Schuster, 1979.

———. "The New Psychology of Human Survival." In *The Future of Immortality and Other Essays for a Nuclear Age*, 111–35. New York: Basic Books, 1987.

Lifton, Robert Jay, and Eric Markusen. *The Genocidal Mentality: Nazi Holocaust and Nuclear Threat.* New York: Basic Books, 1991.

Lloyd, Sharon A. *Ideals as Interests in Hobbes's* Leviathan: *The Power of Mind over Matter.* Cambridge: Cambridge University Press, 1992.

Lomborg, Bjørn. *The Skeptical Environmentalist: Measuring the Real State of the World.* New York: Cambridge University Press, 2001.

Lovelock, James. *The Revenge of Gaia: Earth's Climate Crisis and the Fate of Humanity.* New York: Basic Books, 2006.

Lovin, Robin W. *Reinhold Niebuhr and Christian Realism.* Cambridge: Cambridge University Press, 1995.

Machiavelli, Niccolò. *Discourses on Livy.* Translated by Harvey C. Mansfield and Nathan Tarcov. Chicago: University of Chicago Press, 1996.

———. "First Decennale." In *The Chief Works and Others*, translated by Allan Gilbert, vol. 3, 1444–57. Durham: Duke University Press, 1989.

———. "History of Florence." In *The Chief Works and Others*, translated by Allan Gilbert, vol. 3, 1025–1435. Durham: Duke University Press, 1989.

———. *The Prince.* Translated by Harvey C. Mansfield. Chicago: University of Chicago Press, 1998.

Machiavelli, Niccolò et al. *Machiavelli and His Friends: Their Personal Correspondence.* Dekalb: Northern Illinois University Press, 2004.

Macpherson, Crawford B. "The History of Political Ideas." *Canadian Journal of Economics and Political Science* 7, no. 4 (1941): 564–77.
Malcolm, Noel. Introduction to *Leviathan*, vol. 1, by Thomas Hobbes, 1-325. Oxford: Oxford University Press, 2012.
Mansfield, Harvey C. *Machiavelli's Virtue*. Chicago: University of Chicago Press, 1996.
Mantena, Karuna. "Another Realism: The Politics of Gandhian Nonviolence." *American Political Science Review* 106, no. 2 (May 2012): 455–70.
Markowitz, Ezra M., and Azim F. Shariff. "Climate Change and Moral Judgement." *Nature Climate Change* 2, no. 4 (2012): 243–47.
Markus, Robert A. *Saeculum: History and Society in the Theology of St Augustine*. Cambridge: Cambridge University Press, 1970.
Marrou, Henri. *Saint Augustine and His Influence through the Ages*. Translated by Patrick Hepburne-Scott. New York: Harper Torchbooks, 1957.
Marshall, Stephen. *A Sermon Preached Before the Honourable House of Commons...November 17, 1640*. Reprtint of the 1641 edition, Early English Books Online. http://gateway.proquest.com/openurl?ctx_ver=Z39.88-2003&res_id=xri: eebo&rft_id=xri:eebo:citation:99896500.
Meroz Cursed, Or, A Sermon Preached to the Honourable House of Commons...Febr. 23, 1641. Reprint of the 1641[2] edition, Early English Books Online. http://gateway.proquest.com/openurl?ctx_ver=Z39.88-2003&res_id=xri: eebo&rft_id=xri:eebo:citation:12442426.
Martelli, Mario. "Da Poliziano a Machiavelli: Sull'epigramma dell'Occasione E Sull'occasione." *Interpres* 2 (1979): 230–54.
"La Logica Provvidenzialistica E Il Capitolo XXVI Del Principe." *Interpres* 4 (1982): 262–384.
"Machiavelli E Savonarola: Valutazione Politica E Valutazione Religiosa." In *Girolamo Savonarola: L'uomo E Il Frate*, 121–59. Spoleto: Centro Italiano di studi sull'alto medioevo, 1999.
Martinez, Ronald L. "Tragic Machiavelli." In *Comedy and Tragedy of Machiavelli*, edited by Vickie B. Sullivan, 102–19. New Haven: Yale University Press, 2000.
Martinich, Aloysius P. *Hobbes: A Biography*. Cambridge: Cambridge University Press, 1999.
The Two Gods of Leviathan: Thomas Hobbes on Religion and Politics. Cambridge: Cambridge University Press, 1992.
Mason, Steve. "Jews, Judaeans, Judaizing, Judaism: Problems of Categorization in Ancient History." *Journal for the Study of Judaism* 38, no. 4 (2007): 457–512.
Mattingly, Garrett. "Machiavelli's *Prince*: Political Science or Political Satire?" *The American Scholar* 27, no. 4 (1958): 482–91.
The Armada. Boston: Mariner Books, 2005.
McCabe, David. *Modus Vivendi Liberalism: Theory and Practice*. Cambridge: Cambridge University Press, 2010.
McCanles, Michael. *The Discourse of Il Principe*. Malibu: Undena, 1983.
McCants, William. *The ISIS Apocalypse: The History, Strategy, and Doomsday Vision of the Islamic State*. New York: St. Martin's Press, 2015.
McClure, Christopher Scott. "Hell and Anxiety in Hobbes's *Leviathan*." *Review of Politics* 73, no. 1 (2011): 1–27.

McCormick, John P. "Addressing the Political Exception: Machiavelli's 'Accidents' and the Mixed Regime." *American Political Science Review* 87, no. 4 (1993): 888–900.

Machiavellian Democracy. Cambridge: Cambridge University Press, 2011.

McGinn, Bernard. *Anti-Christ: Two Thousand Years of the Human Fascination With Evil.* New York: Columbia University Press, 1999.

"Revelation." In *The Literary Guide to the Bible*, edited by Robert Alter and Frank Kermode, 523–41. Cambridge: Harvard University Press, 1990.

Visions of the End: Apocalyptic Traditions in the Middle Ages. New York: Columbia University Press, 1998.

McIntosh, Donald. "The Modernity of Machiavelli." *Political Theory* 12, no. 2 (1984): 184–203.

McKinley, Jesse. "Despite Careful Calculations, The World Does Not End." *The New York Times*, May 21, 2011. www.nytimes.com/2011/05/22/us/22doomsday.html.

"An Autumn Date for the Apocalypse." *The New York Times*, May 23, 2011. www.nytimes.com/2011/05/24/us/24rapture.html.

McQueen, Alison. "Political Realism and Moral Corruption." *European Journal of Political Theory*. Published electronically August 30, 2016. doi: 10.1177/1474885116664825.

"Political Realism and the Realist Tradition." *Critical Review of International Social and Political Philosophy* 20, no. 3 (2017): 296–313.

"The Case for Kinship: Political Realism and Classical Realism." In *Politics Recovered: Essays on Realist Political Thought*, edited by Matt Sleat, chapter 10. New York: Columbia University Press, 2018.

Mearsheimer, John J. "Hans Morgenthau and the Iraq War: Realism versus Neo-Conservatism." *openDemocracy*, May 19, 2005. www.opendemocracy.net/democracy-americanpower/morgenthau_2522.jsp.

Mearsheimer, John J., and Stephen M. Walt. "An Unnecessary War." *Foreign Policy*, no. 134 (2003): 50–59.

Meinecke, Friedrich. *Machiavellism: The Doctrine of Raison d'Etat and Its Place in Modern History.* Translated by Scott Douglas. New Haven: Yale University Press, 1962.

Ménissier, Thierry. "Prophétie, Politique et Action Selon Machiavel." *Les Études Philosophiques* 3, no. 66 (2003): 289–313.

Metag, Julia, Mike S. Schäfer, Tobias Füchslin, Tjado Barsuhn, and Katharina Kleinen-von Königslöw. "Perceptions of Climate Change Imagery Evoked Salience and Self-Efficacy in Germany, Switzerland, and Austria." *Science Communication* 38, no. 2 (2016): 197–227.

Mill, John Stuart. "Considerations on Representative Government." In *On Liberty and Other Essays*, edited by John Gray, 203–468. Oxford: Oxford University Press, 2008.

Mintz, Samuel I. *The Hunting of Leviathan: Seventeenth-Century Reactions to the Materialism and Moral Philosophy of Thomas Hobbes.* New York: Cambridge University Press, 1962.

Mitgang, Herbert. "Truman's Newly Found Potsdam Notes Show Concerns on A-Bomb." *New York Times*, June 2, 1980, https://search.proquest.com/docview/121109778?accountid=14026.

Moltmann, Jürgen. "Covenant or Leviathan? Political Theology for Modern Times." *Scottish Journal of Theology* 47, no. 1 (1994): 19–42.
Morgenthau, Hans J. "An Atomic Philosophy." *The Saturday Review*, February 18, 1961.
——. "Atomic Force and Foreign Policy." In *The Restoration of American Politics*, 155–61. Chicago: University of Chicago Press, 1962.
——. "Death in the Nuclear Age." In *The Restoration of American Politics*, 19–28. Chicago: University of Chicago Press, 1962.
——. "Fragments of an Intellectual Biography." In *Truth and Tragedy: A Tribute to Hans J. Morgenthau*, edited by Kenneth W. Thompson and Robert John Myers, 1–17. New Brunswick: Transaction Books, 1977.
——. "Has Atomic War Really Become Impossible?" In *The Restoration of American Politics*, 134–41. Chicago: University of Chicago Press, 1962.
——. *In Defense of the National Interest: A Critical Examination of American Foreign Policy*. New York: Albert A. Knopf, 1951.
——. "International Relations." In *The Restoration of American Politics*, 167–75. Chicago: University of Chicago Press, 1962.
——. "Nazism." In *The Decline of Democratic Politics*, 227–40. Chicago: University of Chicago Press, 1962.
——. *Politics Among Nations: The Struggle for Power and Peace*. New York: Alfred A. Knopf, 1948.
——. *Politics Among Nations: The Struggle for Power and Peace*. 2nd ed. New York: Alfred A. Knopf, 1954.
——. "Russian Technology and American Policy." *Current History* 34, no. 119 (1998): 129–35.
——. *Science: Servant or Master?* New York: New American Library, 1972.
——. *Scientific Man vs. Power Politics*. Chicago: University of Chicago Press, 1946.
——. "The Evil of Politics and the Ethics of Evil." *Ethics* 56, no. 1 (1945): 1–18.
——. "The H-Bomb and After." In *The Restoration of American Politics*, 119–27. Chicago: University of Chicago Press, 1962.
——. "The Intellectual and Moral Dilemma of Politics." In *The Decline of Democratic Politics*, 7–15. Chicago: University of Chicago Press, 1962.
——. "The Intellectual and Political Functions of a Theory of International Relations." In *The Decline of Democratic Politics*, 62–78. Chicago: University of Chicago Press, 1962.
——. "The Problem of Sovereignty Reconsidered." *Columbia Law Review* 48, no. 3 (1948): 341–65.
——. *The Purpose of American Politics*. New York: Vintage, 1960.
——. "The Tragedy of German-Jewish Liberalism." In *The Decline of Democratic Politics*, 247–56. Chicago: University of Chicago Press, 1962.
——. "The Twilight of International Morality." *Ethics* 58, no. 2 (1948): 79–99.
——. "Threat to – and Hope for – the United Nations." In *The Restoration of American Politics*, 279–85. Chicago: University of Chicago Press, 1962.
——. "World Politics in the Mid-Twentieth Century." *The Review of Politics* 10, no. 2 (1948): 154–73.
Morgenthau, Hans J., and Reinhold Niebuhr. "The Ethics of War and Peace in the Nuclear Age." *War/Peace Report* 7, no. 2 (1967): 3–8.

Morgenthau, Hans J., Sidney Hook, H. Stuart Hughes, and Charles P. Snow. "Western Values and Total War." *Commentary* 32, no. 4 (1961): 277–304.

Mouffe, Chantal. *On the Political*. London: Routledge, 2005.

Murrow, Edward R. *In Search Of Light*. Edited by Edward Bliss Jr. London: Macmillan, 1968.

Najemy, John M. *A History of Florence 1200–1575*. Malden: Wiley, 2006.

—— *Between Friends: Discourses of Power and Desire in the Machiavelli-Vettori Letters of 1513–1515*. Princeton: Princeton University Press, 1993.

—— "Papirius and the Chickens, or Machiavelli on the Necessity of Interpreting Religion." *Journal of the History of Ideas* 60, no. 4 (1999): 659–81.

Nederman, Cary J. "Amazing Grace: Fortune, God, and Free Will in Machiavelli's Thought." *Journal of the History of Ideas* 60, no. 4 (1999): 617–38.

Nelson, Eric. *The Hebrew Republic: Jewish Sources and the Transformation of European Political Thought*. Cambridge: Harvard University Press, 2010.

Newell, Waller R. "How Original Is Machiavelli?: A Consideration of Skinner's Interpretation of Virtue and Fortune." *Political Theory* 15, no. 4 (1987): 612–34.

Newey, Glen. *After Politics: The Rejection of Politics in Contemporary Liberal Philosophy*. Houndmills: Palgrave Macmillan, 2001.

Niccoli, Ottavia. *Prophecy and People in Renaissance Italy*. Edited by Lydia G. Cochrane. Princeton: Princeton University Press, 1990.

Niebuhr, Reinhold. "Augustine's Political Realism." In *The Essential Reinhold Niebuhr: Selected Essays and Addresses*, edited by Robert McAfee Brown, 123–41. New Haven: Yale University Press, 1986.

—— *Moral Man and Immoral Society: A Study in Ethics and Politics*. New York: Charles Scribner's Sons, 1932.

—— *The Irony of American History*. Chicago: University of Chicago Press, 2008.

—— *The Nature and Destiny of Man: A Christian Interpretation*. 2 vols. New York: Charles Scribner's Sons, 1943.

Nisbet, Matthew C. "Public Opinion and Participation." In *The Oxford Handbook of Climate Change and Society*, edited by John S. Dryzek, Richard B. Norgaard, and David Schlosberg, 355–68. Oxford: Oxford University Press, 2011.

Nordhaus, Ted, and Michael Shellenberger. "Apocalypse Fatigue: Losing the Public on Climate Change by Ted Nordhaus and Michael Shellenberger: Yale Environment 360." *Yale Environment 360*, November 16, 2009. http://e360.yale.edu/feature/apocalypse_fatigue_losing_the_public_on_climate_change/2210/.

—— "Global Warming Scare Tactics." *The New York Times*, April 8, 2014. www.nytimes.com/2014/04/09/opinion/global-warming-scare-tactics.html.

O'Leary, Stephen D. *Arguing the Apocalypse: A Theory of Millennial Rhetoric*. New York: Oxford University Press, 1994.

O'Neill, Saffron J., Maxwell Boykoff, Simon Niemeyer, and Sophie A. Day. "On the Use of Imagery for Climate Change Engagement." *Global Environmental Change* 23, no. 2 (2013): 413–21.

O'Neill, Saffron J., and Sophie Nicholson-Cole. "'Fear Won't Do It': Promoting Positive Engagement With Climate Change Through Visual and Iconic Representations." *Science Communication* 30, no. 3 (2009): 355–79.

Oreskes, Naomi, and Erik M. Conway. *Merchants of Doubt: How a Handful of Scientists Obscured the Truth on Issues from Tobacco Smoke to Global Warming*. New York: Bloomsbury Press, 2010.

Orr, Robert. "The Time Motif in Machiavelli." In *Machiavelli and the Nature of Political Thought*, edited by Martin Fleisher, 185–208. New York: Atheneum, 1972.
Orwin, Clifford. "Machiavelli's Unchristian Charity." *The American Political Science Review* 72, no. 4 (1978): 1217–28.
Osiander, Andreas. "Sovereignty, International Relations, and the Westphalian Myth." *International Organization* 55, no. 2 (2001): 251–87.
Pagels, Elaine. *Revelations: Visions, Prophecy, and Politics in the Book of Revelation.* New York: Viking, 2012.
Palaver, Wolfgang. "Hobbes and the *Katéchon*: The Secularization of Sacrificial Christianity." *Contagion: Journal of Violence, Mimesis, and Culture* 2, no. 1 (1995): 57–74.
Palmer, Ada. "Reading Lucretius in the Renaissance." *Journal of the History of Ideas* 73, no. 3 (2012): 395–416.
Pangle, Thomas L., and Peter J. Ahrensdorf. *Justice Among Nations: On the Moral Basis of Power and Peace*. Lawrence: University Press of Kansas, 1999.
Petersen, David L. "Eschatology." In *The Anchor Bible Dictionary*, edited by David Noel Freedman, vol. 2, 575–79. New York: Doubleday, 1992.
Petrie, Jon. "The Secular Word HOLOCAUST: Scholarly Myths, History, and 20th Century Meanings." *Journal of Genocide Research* 2, no. 1 (2000): 31–63.
Philp, Mark. *Political Conduct*. Cambridge: Harvard University Press, 2007.
Pichler, Hans-Karl. "The Godfathers of 'Truth': Max Weber and Carl Schmitt in Morgenthau's Theory of Power Politics." *Review of International Studies* 24, no. 2 (1998): 185–200.
Pinker, Steven. *The Better Angels of Our Nature: Why Violence Has Declined*. New York: Penguin Books, 2011.
Pitkin, Hanna Fenichel. *Fortune Is a Woman: Gender and Politics in the Thought of Niccolò Machiavelli*. Chicago: University of Chicago Press, 1984.
Pocock, John G. A. *The Machiavellian Moment: Florentine Political Thought and the Atlantic Republican Tradition*. Princeton: Princeton University Press, 2003.
——— "'The Onely Politician': Machiavelli, Harrington and Felix Raab." *Historical Studies: Australia and New Zealand* 12, no. 4 (1966): 265–96.
——— "Time, History and Eschatology in the Thought of Thomas Hobbes." In *The Diversity of History: Essays in Honour of Sir Herbert Butterfield*, edited by J. H. Elliott and H. G. Koenigsberger, 149–98. Ithaca: Cornell University Press, 1970.
Polizzotto, Lorenzo. *The Elect Nation: The Savonarolan Movement in Florence, 1494–1545*. Oxford: Clarendon Press, 1994.
Popkin, Richard H. "Savonarola and Cardinal Ximines: Millenarian Thinkers and Actors at the Eve of the Reformation." In *Millenarianism and Messianism in Early Modern European Culture*, edited by Karl A. Kottman, vol. 2, 15–26. Boston: Kluwer, 2001.
Preus, J. Samuel. "Machiavelli's Functional Analysis of Religion: Context and Object." *Journal of the History of Ideas* 40, no. 2 (1979): 171–90.
Prezzolini, Guiseppe. *Machiavelli*. Translated by Gioconda Savini. New York: Noonday Press, 1967.
——— "The Christian Roots of Machiavelli's Moral Pessimism." *Review of National Literatures* 1, no. 1 (1970): 26–37.
Rahe, Paul. "In the Shadow of Lucretius: The Epicurean Foundations of Machiavelli's Political Thought." *History of Political Thought* 28, no. 1 (2007): 30–55.

Ranke, Leopold von. *Sämtliche Werke, Vol. 34: Zur Kritik Neuerer Geschichtschreiber.* Leipzig: Duncker und Humblot, 1874.
Rawls, John. *Lectures on the History of Political Philosophy.* Cambridge: Belknap Press, 2007.
"Read Trump's Speech on the Orlando Shooting." *Time.* June 13, 2016. http://time.com/4367120/orlando-shooting-donald-trump-transcript/.
Redles, David. *Hitler's Millennial Reich: Apocalyptic Belief and the Search for Salvation.* New York: NYU Press, 2005.
———. "'Nazi End Times: The Third Reich as Millennial Reich.'" In *End of Days: Essays on the Apocalypse from Antiquity to Modernity*, edited by Karolyn Kinane and Michael A. Ryan, 173–96. Jefferson: McFarland and Company, 2009.
Reeves, Marjorie. *Joachim of Fiore and the Prophetic Future.* New York: Harper & Row, 1977.
———. *The Influence of Prophecy in the Later Middle Ages: A Study in Joachimism.* Oxford: Oxford University Press, 1969.
Reston, James. "Dawn of the Atom Era Perplexes Washington." *New York Times*, August 12, 1945. https://search.proquest.com/docview/107030672?accountid=14026.
Rhodes, James M. *The Hitler Movement: A Modern Millenarian Revolution.* Stanford: Hoover Institution Press, 1980.
Rhodes, Richard. *The Making of the Atomic Bomb.* New York: Simon & Schuster, 1986.
Rice, Daniel F. *Reinhold Niebuhr and His Circle of Influence.* Cambridge: Cambridge University Press, 2012.
Ridolfi, Roberto. *The Life of Girolamo Savonarola.* Translated by Cecil Grayson. New York: Knopf, 1959.
———. *The Life of Niccolò Machiavelli.* Translated by Cecil Grayson. Chicago: University of Chicago Press, 1963.
Roosevelt, Theodore. "The Case Against the Reactionaries (June 17, 1912)." In *Selected Speeches and Writings of Theodore Roosevelt*, edited by Gordon Hunter, 159–72. New York: Vintage, 2014.
Rose, Kenneth D. *One Nation Underground: The Fallout Shelter in American Culture.* New York: New York University Press, 2001.
Roskies, David G. *Against the Apocalypse: Responses to Catastrophe in Modern Jewish Culture.* Cambridge: Harvard University Press, 1984.
Rossi, Enzo, and Matt Sleat. "Realism in Normative Political Theory." *Philosophy Compass* 9, no. 10 (October 1, 2014): 689–701.
Ruffo-Fiore, Silvia. *Niccolò Machiavelli.* Boston: Twayne, 1982.
Sage, Steven F. *Ibsen and Hitler: The Playwright, the Plagiarist, and the Plot for the Third Reich.* New York: Basic Books, 2007.
Sasso, Gennaro. "Il 'Principe' Ebbe Due Redazioni?" In *Machiavelli E Gli Antichi: E Altri Saggi*, vol. 2, 197–276. Milan and Naples: R. Ricciardi, 1988.
———. "Machiavelli E La Teroria Dell'anacylosis." *Rivista Storica Italiana* 70, no. 3 (1958): 333–75.
———. *Niccolò Machiavelli: Storia Del Suo Pensiero Politico.* Bologna: Società Editrice Il Mulino, 1980.
———. *Niccolò Machiavelli, Volume 1: Il Pensiero Politico.* Bologna: Società Editrice Il Mulino, 1993.

Savonarola, Girolamo. *A Guide to Righteous Living and Other Works*. Translated by Konrad Eisenbichler. Toronto: Centre for Reformation and Renaissance Studies, 2003.
   Prediche Sopra L'Esodo. Edited by Pier Giorgio Ricci. Rome: Belardetti, 1955.
   Selected Writings of Girolamo Savonarola: Religion and Politics, 1490–1498. Translated by Anne Borelli and Maria Pastore Passaro. New Haven: Yale University Press, 2006.
Schedler, Andreas. "Mapping Contingency." In *Political Contingency: Studying the Unexpected, the Accidental, and the Unforeseen*, edited by Ian Shapiro and Sonu Bedi, 54–78. New York: New York University Press, 2007.
Scheffler, Samuel. *Death and the Afterlife*. Oxford: Oxford University Press, 2013.
Schell, Jonathan. "In Search of a Miracle: Hannah Arendt and the Atomic Bomb." In *Politics in Dark Times: Encounters with Hannah Arendt*, edited by Seyla Benhabib, Roy T. Tsao, and Peter Verovsek, 247–58. New York: Cambridge University Press, 2010.
   The Fate Of The Earth. London: Jonathan Cape, 1982.
Scheuerman, William E. "Carl Schmitt and Hans Morgenthau: Realism and beyond." In *Realism Reconsidered: The Legacy of Hans Morgenthau in International Relations*, edited by Michael C. Williams, 62–92. Oxford: Oxford University Press, 2007.
   Carl Schmitt: The End of Law. Lanham: Rowman & Littlefield Publishers, 1999.
   Hans Morgenthau: Realism and beyond. Cambridge: Polity Press, 2009.
   The Realist Case for Global Reform. Cambridge: Polity, 2011.
   "The Realist Revival in Political Philosophy, or: Why New Is Not Always Improved." *International Politics* 50, no. 6 (November 2013): 798–814.
   "Was Morgenthau a Realist? Revisiting *Scientific Man Vs. Power Politics*." *Constellations* 14, no. 4 (2007): 506–30.
Schlosser, Joel Alden. "Herodotean Realism." *Political Theory* 42, no. 3 (June 1, 2014): 239–61.
Schmidt, Brian C., and Michael C. Williams. "The Bush Doctrine and the Iraq War: Neoconservatives Versus Realists." *Security Studies* 17, no. 2 (2008): 191–220.
Schmitt, Carl. *Crisis of Parliamentary Democracy*. Translated by Ellen Kennedy. Cambridge: MIT Press, 1988.
   Political Theology: Four Chapters on the Concept of Sovereignty. Translated by George Schwab. Chicago: University of Chicago Press, 2006.
   "The Age of Neutralizations and Depoliticizations (1929)." In *The Concept of the Political*, translated by Matthias Konzen and John P. McCormick, 80–96. Chicago: University of Chicago Press, 2007.
   The Concept of the Political: Expanded Edition. Translated by George Schwab. Chicago: University of Chicago Press, 2007.
   The Nomos of the Earth in the International Law of the Jus Publicum Europaeum. Translated by G. L. Ulmen. New York: Telos Press, 2003.
Schwartz, Joel. "Hobbes and the Two Kingdoms of God." *Polity* 18, no. 1 (1985): 7–24.
Schweitzer, Albert. *The Quest of the Historical Jesus*. Translated by W. Montgomery. London: Adam and Charles Black, 1910.
Shakespeare, William. *Romeo and Juliet*. Edited by Jill L. Levenson. Oxford: Oxford University Press, 2000.

Shaw, Jane. *Miracles in Enlightenment England*. New Haven: Yale University Press, 2006.
Sherwin, Martin J. *A World Destroyed: Hiroshima and the Origins of the Arms Race*. New York: Vintage, 1987.
Shklar, Judith. "The Liberalism of Fear." In *Political Thought and Political Thinkers*, edited by Stanley Hoffmann, 3–20. Chicago: University of Chicago Press, 1988.
Skinner, Quentin. "A Genealogy of the Modern State." *Proceedings of the British Academy* 162 (2009): 325–70.
Hobbes and Republican Liberty. Cambridge: Cambridge University Press, 2008.
Introduction to *The Prince*, by Niccolò Machiavelli, ix–xxiv. Edited by Quentin Skinner. Translated by Russell Price. Cambridge: Cambridge University Press, 1988.
Liberty before Liberalism. Cambridge: Cambridge University Press, 1998.
Machiavelli. New York: Hill and Wang, 1981.
"Meaning and Understanding in the History of Ideas." *History and Theory* 8, no. 1 (1969): 3–53.
Reason and Rhetoric in the Philosophy of Hobbes. Cambridge: Cambridge University Press, 1996.
The Foundations of Modern Political Thought, Vol. 1: The Renaissance. Cambridge: Cambridge University Press, 1978.
"The Limits of Historical Explanations." *Philosophy* 41, no. 157 (1966): 199–215.
"The Rise of, Challenge to and Prospects for a Collingwoodian Approach to the History of Political Thought." In *The History of Political Thought in National Context*, edited by Dario Castiglione and Iain Hampsher-Monk, 175–88. Cambridge: Cambridge University Press, 2001.
Visions of Politics, Vol. 3: Hobbes and Civil Science. Cambridge: Cambridge University Press, 2002.
Sleat, Matt. *Liberal Realism: A Realist Theory of Liberal Politics*. Manchester: Manchester University Press, 2013.
"Realism, Liberalism and Non-Ideal Theory or, Are There Two Ways to Do Realistic Political Theory?" *Political Studies* 64, no. 1 (2016): 27–41.
Speer, James P. "Hans Morgenthau and the World State." *World Politics* 20, no. 2 (1968): 207–27.
Springborg, Patricia. "Leviathan and the Problem of Ecclesiastical Authority." *Political Theory* 3, no. 3 (1975): 289–303.
Squarotti, Giorgio Bàrberi. *La Forma Tragica del "Principe" e Altri Saggi Sul Machiavelli*. Florence: L. S. Olschki, 1966.
Stoknes, Per Espen. *What We Think About When We Try Not to Think About Global Warming: Toward a New Psychology of Climate Action*. White River Junction: Chelsea Green Publishing, 2015.
Strauss, Leo. *Natural Right and History*. Chicago: University of Chicago Press, 1950.
"On the Basis of Hobbes's Political Philosophy." In *What Is Political Philosophy? And Other Studies*, 170–96. Chicago: University of Chicago Press, 1988.
Spinoza's Critique of Religion. Translated by E. M. Sinclair. New York: Schocken Books, 1965.
The Political Philosophy of Hobbes: Its Basis and Its Genesis. Translated by E. M. Sinclair. Chicago: University of Chicago Press, 1952.

"The Three Waves of Modernity." In *An Introduction to Political Philosophy: Ten Essays by Leo Strauss*, edited by Hilail Gildin, 81-98. Detroit: Wayne State University Press, 1989.

Thoughts on Machiavelli. Chicago: University of Chicago Press, 1958.

Strong, Tracy B. "Forward: Carl Schmitt and Thomas Hobbes: Myth and Politics." In *Carl Schmitt, The Leviathan in the State Theory of Thomas Hobbes: Meaning and Failure of a Political Symbol*, translated by George Schwab and Erna Hilfstein, vii–xxviii. Chicago: University of Chicago Press, 2008.

Stubbs, John. *John Donne: The Reformed Soul*. New York: W. W. Norton, 2007.

Sullivan, Vickie B. Introduction to *The Comedy and Tragedy of Machiavelli: Essays on the Literary Works*, edited by Vickie B. Sullivan, ix–xxi. New Haven: Yale University Press, 2000.

"Neither Christian nor Pagan: Machiavelli's Treatment of Religion in the 'Discourses.'" *Polity* 26, no. 2 (1993): 259–80.

Symmons, Edward. *Scripture Vindicated from the Mis-Apprehension, Mis-Interpretations, and Mis-Applications of Mr. Stephen Marshall*. Reprint of the 1645 edition, Early English Books Online. http://gateway.proquest.com/openurl?ctx_ver=Z39.88-2003&res_id=xri:eebo&rft_id=xri:eebo:citation:99872387.

Tarcov, Nathan. "Quentin Skinner's Method and Machiavelli's *Prince*." *Ethics* 92, no. 4 (1982): 692–709.

Tarlton, Charles D. "The Symbolism of Redemption and the Exorcism of Fortune in Machiavelli's *Prince*." *The Review of Politics* 30, no. 3 (1968): 332–48.

Taylor, Charles. *Modern Social Imaginaries*. Durham: Duke University Press, 2004.

Teschke, Benno. "Theorizing the Westphalian System of States: International Relations from Absolutism to Capitalism." *European Journal of International Relations* 8, no. 1 (2002): 5–48.

Tessman, Lisa. *Burdened Virtues: Virtue Ethics for Liberatory Struggles*. New York: Oxford University Press, 2005.

"The Sheltered Life." *Time*, October 20, 1961. www.time.com/time/magazine/article/0, 9171,872787-9,00.html.

Thompson, Leonard L. *The Book of Revelation: Apocalypse and Empire*. New York: Oxford University Press, 1990.

Thucydides. *The Peloponnesian War*. Edited by David Grene. Translated by Thomas Hobbes. Chicago: University of Chicago Press, 1989.

"TRANSCRIPT: Donald Trump's Speech Responding To Assault Accusations." *NPR.org*. October 13, 2016. www.npr.org/2016/10/13/497857068/transcript-donald-trumps-speech-responding-to-assault-accusations.

"Transcript of the New Hampshire GOP Debate, Annotated." *Washington Post*. February 6, 2016. www.washingtonpost.com/news/the-fix/wp/2016/02/06/transcript-of-the-feb-6-gop-debate-annotated/.

Trexler, Richard C. *Public Life in Renaissance Florence*. New York: Academic Press, 1980.

Tuck, Richard. "The Civil Religion of Thomas Hobbes." In *Political Discourse in Early Modern Britain*, edited by Nicholas Philipson and Quentin Skinner, 120–38. Cambridge: Cambridge University Press, 1993.

"The Utopianism of Leviathan." In *Leviathan After 350 Years*, edited by Tom Sorell and Luc Foisneau, 125–38. Oxford: Clarendon Press, 2004.

Vacano, Diego A. von. *The Art of Power: Machiavelli, Nietzsche, and the Making of Aesthetic Political Theory.* Lanham: Lexington Books, 2007.
Valentini, Laura. "Ideal vs. Non-Ideal Theory: A Conceptual Map." *Philosophy Compass* 7, no. 9 (September 1, 2012): 654–64.
Vandercook, William F. "Making the Very Best of the Very Worst: The 'Human Effects of Nuclear Weapons' Report of 1956." *International Security* 11, no. 1 (1986): 184–95.
Vasquez, John A. *The Power of Power Politics: From Classical Realism to Neotraditionalism.* Cambridge: Cambridge University Press, 1998.
Vatter, Miguel. "Machiavelli and the Republican Conception of Providence." *Review of Politics* 75, no. 4 (2013): 605–23.
Vaughan, Geoffrey. "The Audience of Leviathan and the Audience of Hobbes's Political Philosophy." *History of Political Thought* 22, no. 3 (2001): 448–71.
Viroli, Maurizio. "Machiavelli and the Republican Idea of Politics." In *Machiavelli and Republicanism*, edited by Gisela Bock, Quentin Skinner, and Maurizio Viroli, 143–72. Cambridge: Cambridge University Press, 1990.
——— *Machiavelli's God.* Translated by Antony Shugaar. Princeton: Princeton University Press, 2010.
——— *Redeeming* The Prince: *The Meaning of Machiavelli's Masterpiece.* Princeton: Princeton University Press, 2013.
Voegelin, Eric. *The New Science of Politics: An Introduction.* Chicago: University of Chicago Press, 1952.
Walker, Daniel P. *The Decline of Hell: Seventeenth-Century Discussions of Eternal Torment.* Chicago: University of Chicago Press, 1964.
Walzer, Michael. *Exodus And Revolution.* New York: Basic Books, 1985.
——— "On the Role of Symbolism in Political Thought." *Political Science Quarterly* 82, no. 2 (1967): 191–204.
"War with Iraq Is Not in America's National Interest." Ad published in *The New York Times*, September 26, 2002. www.bear-left.com/archive/2002/0926oped.html.
Weart, Spencer R. *Nuclear Fear: A History of Images.* Cambridge: Harvard University Press, 1988.
Weber, Max. "Politics as a Vocation." Translated by H. H. Gerth and C. Wright Mills, 77–128. London: Routledge, 2009.
Weinstein, Donald. "Machiavelli and Savonarola." In *Studies on Machiavelli*, edited by Myron P. Gilmore, 253–64. Florence: G. C. Sansoni Editore, 1972.
——— "Millenarianism in a Civic Setting: The Savonarola Movement in Florence." In *Millennial Dreams in Action: Essays in Comparative Study*, edited by Silvia L. Thrupp, 187–203. The Hague: Mouton, 1962.
——— *Savonarola and Florence: Prophecy and Patriotism in the Renaissance.* Princeton: Princeton University Press, 1970.
——— *Savonarola: The Rise and Fall of a Renaissance Prophet.* New Haven: Yale University Press, 2011.
——— "The Myth of Florence." In *Florentine Studies: Politics and Society in Renaissance Florence*, edited by Nicolai Rubinstein, 15–44. Evanston: Northwestern University Press, 1968.
White, Hayden. *Metahistory: The Historical Imagination in Nineteenth-Century Europe.* Baltimore: Johns Hopkins University Press, 1973.

Wiesel, Elie. "A Vision of the Apocalypse." Translated by Joan Grimbert. *World Literature Today* 58, no. 2 (1984): 194–97.
Williams, Bernard. *In the Beginning Was the Deed: Realism and Moralism in Political Argument*. Edited by Geoffrey Hawthorn. Princeton: Princeton University Press, 2005.
———. "Realism and Moralism in Political Theory." In *In the Beginning Was the Deed: Realism and Moralism in Political Argument*, edited by Geoffrey Hawthorn, 1–17. Princeton: Princeton University Press, 2005.
Williams, Michael. *The Realist Tradition and the Limits of International Relations*. Cambridge: Cambridge University Press, 2005.
Wills, Lawrence M. "Daniel: Introduction and Annotations." In *The Jewish Study Bible, Tanakh Translation*, edited by Adele Berlin and Mark Zvi Brettler, 1640–42. New York: Oxford University Press, 2004.
Wilson, Woodrow. "Address to a Joint Session of Congress on the Conditions of Peace." The American Presidency Project. January 8, 1918. www.presidency.ucsb.edu/ws/?pid=65405.
———. "Woodrow Wilson: Address to a Joint Session of Congress Requesting a Declaration of War Against Germany." The American Presidency Project. April 2, 1917. www.presidency.ucsb.edu/ws/index.php?pid=65366&st=&st1=.
Wistrich, Robert. *Hitler's Apocalypse: Jews and the Nazi Legacy*. New York: St. Martin's Press, 1986.
Wojcik, Daniel. *The End of the World as We Know It: Faith, Fatalism, and Apocalypse in America*. New York: NYU Press, 1999.
Wolin, Sheldon S. *Politics and Vision: Continuity and Innovation in Western Political Thought*. Expanded ed. Princeton: Princeton University Press, 2006.
Woodhouse, Arthur S.P., ed. *Puritanism and Liberty: Being the Army Debates (1647–9) from the Clarke Manuscripts with Supplementary Documents*. Chicago: University of Chicago Press, 1951.
Wright, Paul. "Machiavelli's City of God: Civic Humanism and Augustinian Terror." In *Augustine and Politics*, edited by Kevin L. Hughes and Kim Paffendorf, 297–336. Lanham: Lexington Books, 2005.
Yates, Frances A. *Astraea: The Imperial Theme in the Sixteenth Century*. Harmondsworth: Penguin, 1977.

Index

1 Thessalonians, 45–6
2 Thessalonians, 46, 52, 112, 135–6
9/11. *See* September 11, 2001 terrorist attacks

Acts and Monuments (Foxe), 108, 110, 111
Adam, 139
Afghanistan, war in, 3–4
Ahab (king), 112
Al Qaeda, 7
Alexander the Great, 32
Alexander VI (pope), 72
Alvarez, Alfred, 153–4
Amos, 25
Anabaptist rebellion (Münster), 60
Anders, Günther, 153, 154, 200
anti-apocalypticism, 12–13
Antichrist
  Bale on, 110
  Catholic Church as, 110
  destruction of, 113
  Foxe on, 111
  Hobbes on, 127–8
  in 2 Thessalonians, 46, 135–6
  in Geneva Bible, 112
  in seventeenth-century England, 115–16, 117–18, 193
  Joachim of Fiore on, 150
  pope as, 112, 114–16
  Savonarola denounced as, 76, 204
Antiochus IV Epiphanes, 25, 29–33, 34, 41, 57
Aphrodisias, 34, 35f, 36f
apocalypse
  as literary genre, 27–8

Augustine (St.) on, 13, 20, 47–51, 110, 129, 133, 176, 204
belief. *See* apocalypticism
biblical. *See* apocalypse, Judeo-Christian
cataclysm, 2, 57–8
concept, 18, 23–4, 56–9
description, 1–2
evil, 42, 58
historical, 28
Hobbes on, 119–44
imagery, 55–6
imminence, 2, 24, 27, 37, 45–6, 49–50, 57
in political discourse, 3–6
Judeo-Christian, 20, 23–42, 154
Machiavelli on, 84–91
Morgenthau on, 162–75
Paul (St.) on, 20
revelation, 59
rupture, 2, 58–9
symbolism, 55–6, 61–2
apocalypticism, 2–6, 24–7
  and fall of Rome, 47
  and the Holocaust, 152
  as imaginary. *See* imaginary; apocalyptic
  as political theodicy, 26
  as utopianism, 12, 194
  early Christian, 45
  features, 26–7
  in Nazism, 149–52
  in Renaissance Florence, 8–9, 20, 74–9, 193, 194
  in seventeenth-century England, 9, 113–19, 204

Index

nuclear, 153–62
political effects of, 193–4
Protestant, 108–13
psychological effects of, 14, 61–2
secular, 19–20, 21, 56, 84–7, 133–44, 149–62
semiotic arousal, 61
study of, 12–13
vs. anti-apocalypticism, 12–13
Aquinas, Thomas (St.), 176
Arduini, Oliviero, 76
Arendt, Hannah, 181
 influence on Morgenthau, 162, 186
Aristotle
 regime theory, 98
Arminians, 114, 115
Asia Minor, 33, 36, 37, 38
Assyrians, 24
Athenians, 85
Augustine (St.)
 apocalyptic context, 47–8
 as political realist, 7, 42, 44–5
 City of God, 49
 Morgenthau on, 176
 on apocalypse, 13, 20, 47–51, 110, 129, 133, 176, 204
 on the city of God, 103
 use of tragedy, 48–9
Aum Shinrikyo, 2
Auschwitz, 152–4

Babylon, 30, 33
 in book of Revelation, 39, 43, 48, 114, 117–18
Babylonian captivity. *See* Babylonian exile
Babylonian exile, 24–5, 29
Babylonians, 24
Bale, John, 109, 113–14, 115
 Image of Both Churches, 108, 110–11
 on Antichrist, 110
Barebones Parliament, 118
Battle of Ravenna, 84
beasts of Revelation. *See* Revelation, book of; beasts
Becchi, Ricciardo, 81, 82
Behemoth (Hobbes), 121, 134
Bellarmine, Robert, 127
Bhagavad Gita, 157
Bible
 Geneva translation, 109–10, 111–13, 114, 115
  Antichrist, 112

Hebrew, 28–9, 112
 King James Version, 112
Bismarck, Otto von, 168, 170
Book of Martyrs. *See* Acts and Monuments (Foxe)
Borgia, Cesare, 92
Botticelli, Sandro, 76
Branch Davidians, 2
Buck-Morss, Susan, 54
Burke, Edmund, 55
Bush, George W., 3–4, 196, 197
 administration, 6, 7, 196

Camping, Harold, 1–4
Capp, Bernard, 114
Carr, Edward H.
 as political realist, 7
 on apocalypticism, 195
 on realism, 195
 on Woodrow Wilson, 7–8
catastrophe, prospective, 200, 202, 204
Chamberlain, Neville, 202
Charlemagne
 prophecy, 68, 74
Charles I (king), 113, 114–16, 119, 141, 142, 193
 execution of, 120
 trial of, 118
Charles II (king), 120, 141
Charles VIII (king), 66, 67–8, 73, 74, 76, 193–4
Chronica de origine civitatis, 75
Church of England, 115–16, 126, 128
City of God (Augustine), 49
civil defense, 161
Claudius, 34, 36f
climate change, 2, 5, 22, 56, 200–3
 denial, 200–1
Clizia (Machiavelli), 98
Cohen, Leonard
 Future, The, 155
Cold War, 164
Collingwood, Robin G., 16
Collins, Adela Yarbro, 41
Collins, John, 28
Communism, Soviet, 164, 172, 175
Constantine I (emperor), 47, 111
contextualism, 15–17
 on doctrines, 16–18
 on traditions, 16–17
contingency, 61, 73–4, 86, 87–8, 93, 95, 103

Coyle, J. Kevin, 48
Cromwell, Oliver, 9, 112, 118–19, 141
Cromwell, Thomas, 109
Crucixion (Botticelli), 76
Crusades, 165
Cyrus, 83, 85

Daniel, book of, 26, 28–33, 37, 118, 195
  beasts, 31, 40–1
  Christian view, 29
  criticism of imperial power, 40–1
  criticism of sovereign power, 40–1
  dating, 29
  end of politics, 42, 194
  evil, 42, 58
  historical context, 29–30
  imminence, 31, 54, 57
  narrative coherence, 193
  political quietism, 42–3
  political radicalism, 43–4, 193
  revelation, 59
  rupture, 58
  sovereignty of God, 41–2, 193
  symbolism, 43–4, 58, 61–2
  violence, 44
Dante, 28
Darius I (king), 113
Das Dritte Reich (Moeller), 150
Day of Judgment, 29, 32, 40, 50, 67, 131
De Cive (Hobbes), 119, 122, 130
  religion, 119–20
  scriptural arguments, 119–20
De Corpore (Hobbes), 119
De Homine (Hobbes), 119
Dead Sea Scrolls, 26
death
  Morgenthau on, 183–4
Death in the Nuclear Age (Morgenthau), 178, 181–7
Diary of Anne Frank, The, 153
Diggers, 118
Discourses on Livy (Machiavelli)
  conception of time, 99–100
  corruption, 101–2
  everlasting republic, 103
  redemptive prince, 101–2
  Rome, 102–3
  Savonarola, 83
  tragic sensibility, 97–103, 195, 198
Divine Comedy (Dante), 28
Domenica da Ponzo, 75
Domitian (emperor), 34

Donne, John, 46, 155–6
  Hymne to God my God in my sicknesse, 156
Dostoevsky, Fyodor M., 136
Dr. Strangelove (Kubrick), 155
Duns Scotus, John, 176

Eckart, Dietrich, 149, 150
Edward VI (king), 109
Egypt, 30, 33, 38, 56
Ehrman, Bart, 25
Eisenhower, Dwight D., 160
Elements of Law, The (Hobbes), 119, 130
Elements of Philosophy (Hobbes), 119
Elizabeth I (queen), 113, 115, 116
  as godly prince, 111, 114
Emperor and Galilean (Ibsen), 150
emplotment, 54, 80, 84, 85, 86
Engels, Friedrich, 195
English Civil War, 9, 204
  apocalypticism in, 9, 20–1, 115–19, 193
  debates over ecclesisatical authority, 121
Enlightenment, the, 163
eschatology, 23–4
evil, 44, 45
  in apocalypse. *See* apocalypse, evil
  rhetoric of, 3
Exodus, book of, 38, 56, 72, 82, 85, 112
Ezekiel, 25

fallout shelter, 161, 182
Farrell, Thomas, 157
fast sermons, 116
fear, 203
  Hobbes on, 130–1, 142–4, 189
  Morgenthau on, 189–90, 203
  of violent death, 43
Ficino, Marsilio, 76
Fifth Monarchists, 118, 119
Final Solution, 152, 153
First Decennale (Machiavelli), 82
Florence
  apocalypticism. *See* apocalypticism, in Renaissance Florence
  French invasion (1494), 66, 67, 194
  identity, 75
  politics, 66, 69–71, 194
  role in apocalyptic prophecy, 9, 69, 194
Florentine Histories, The (Machiavelli), 98, 99
fortune. *See Prince, The* (Machiavelli), fortune
Foxe, John, 108, 109–10, 111, 113–14, 115
  on Antichrist, 111
Future, The (Cohen), 155

Index

Geneva Bible. *See* Bible, Geneva translation
Geneva Convention, 168
Goethe, Johann Wolfgang von, 152
Gore, Al, 5–6, 201–3
Göring, Herman, 150
Grand Inquisitor, 136
Greece, 32, 33
Groves, Leslie, 155, 156, 157
Guicciardini, Francesco, 97
Gunpowder Plot, 114

Hague Protocols, 168
Hannibal, 92
Heaven's Gate, 2
hell, 39, 40, 129–32, 143
Hellenistic wars, 32, 33
Henry VIII (king), 109
Heylyn, Peter, 113
Himmler, Heinrich, 151
Hippolytus of Rome, 136
Hiroshima
  atomic bombing of, 153, 154, 155, 158–60
History of the Peloponnesian War (Thucydides), 134–5
Hitler, Adolf, 150, 151, 152, 168, 172
Hobbes, Thomas
  apocalyptic context, 9–10, 20–1, 105–6, 108–19
  as political realist, 7, 8, 15, 18
  Behemoth, 121, 134
  De Cive, 119, 122, 130
  De Corpore, 119
  De Homine, 119
  Elements of Law, The, 119, 130
  Elements of Philosophy, 119
  Leviathan, 9, 120–44
  Morgenthau's use of, 171
  on Antichrist, 127–8
  on apocalypse, 10, 12, 13–14, 20–1, 119–44, 155, 192–3, 196, 202
  on civil war, 134–5
  on divided allegiance, 124–5
  on fear, 130–1
  on fear of death, 130–1, 142–4, 189
  on hell, 129–32, 143
  on kingdom of God, 138–9
  on Leviathan state, 135–44
  on miracles, 126
  on priority of order, 11
  on prophecy, 123–7, 137
  on religion, 119–32

  on state of nature, 133–4, 138, 142–3
  scriptural arguments, 9, 20–1, 119–32
Hoekstra, Kinch, 128
Holmes, Stephen, 13, 124
Holocaust, 9, 185, 202
  and nuclear war, 153–4
  as apocalypse, 152–3
Hosea, 25
Houlahan, Mark, 134
Human Effects of Nuclear Weapons Development, The (report), 160–1, 182
Hume, David, 7
Hurricane Katrina, 202
Hussein, Saddam, 7
hydrogen bomb, 159
Hymne to God my God in my sicknesse (Donne), 156

Ibsen, Henrik
  Emperor and Galilean, 150
Image of Both Churches (Bale), 108, 110–11
imaginary
  apocalyptic, 20, 51–62, 133, 136, 193–4
  concept, 52–6
  social, 53–4
In Defense of the National Interest (Morgenthau), 162
Inconvenient Truth, An (Guggenheim), 6, 201–2
Iraq, war in, 6
Isaiah, 25
Islamic State (ISIS), 2, 204
Israel, 25
Israel, kingdom of, 24
Israelites, 24, 25, 26, 85, 88, 112
Italian Wars, 64, 84
Italy
  French invasion (1494), 66, 67–8
  in *The Prince* (Machiavelli), 84–91, 96
  prevalence of prophecy, 64, 74–5

J.G.A. Pocock, 121
James I (king), 113
  commentary on book of Revelation, 114–15
  on apocalypse, 114–15
Jeremiah, 25, 32
Jerusalem, 32, 37
  New Jerusalem, 40, 42, 69, 71, 86, 103, 111, 204
  temple, 30, 32, 33, 34, 37

Jesus, 46, 126
  as apocalyptic prophet, 27, 45, 50
  as judge, 29, 40, 132, 139, 142
  in book of Revelation, 37, 38, 39, 40, 42
Jewish-Roman wars, 34
Joachim of Fiore, 74
  Nazi uses of, 149, 150
John of Patmos, 33–4, 37, 59, 109, 194, 204
Johnston, David, 121
Jonah, book of, 187
Jonestown, Guyana, 2
Judah, kingdom of, 24
Judea, 30, 33
Julius II (pope), 95
Jurdjevic, Mark, 82

Kahn, Herman, 161, 182
katechon, 46, 135–6
Keller, Catherine, 196–7
Kennan, George, 7
Kennedy, John F., 161
kingdom of God, 32, 38, 41, 129, 138–41
Kubrick, Stanley
  Dr. Strangelove, 155

Landes, Richard, 12, 61
Laud, William (Archbishop of Canterbury), 115–16, 127, 128, 193
Laudians, 116
Laurence, William, 159–60
Lefort, Claude, 90
Lessing, Gotthold, 150
Levellers, 118
Leviathan (Hobbes)
  Antichrist, 127–8
  apocalypse, 121–44
  civil war, 134–5
  divided allegiance, 124–5
  fear, 130
  fear of death, 130–1, 142–4
  frontispiece, 139–42
  hell, 129–32, 143
  kingdom of God, 138–9
  Leviathan state, 135–44
  miracles, 126
  prophecy, 123–7, 137
  religion, 120–32
  scriptural arguments, 9, 120–32
  state of nature, 133–4, 138, 142
Leviathan (sea beast), 40–1
liberalism
  Morgenthau's critique of, 163, 164, 172–5

Lincoln, Abraham, 4
Livy, 85
Long Parliament, 119
Lorenzo de' Medici (Lorenzo the Magnificent), 65, 66, 75
Lovelock, James, 5
Luther, Martin, 176

Maccabean Revolt, 30, 42
Machiavelli, Niccolò
  apocalyptic context, 8–10, 20, 64–79
  as political realist, 7, 8, 15, 18, 104, 195
  as tragic thinker, 97–103, 195, 197, 198
  Clizia, 98
  conception of time, 99–100
  Discourses on Livy, 83, 97–100, 101–3, 195, 198
  epistemological ambitions, 18
  First Decennale, 82
  Florentine Histories, The, 98, 99
  Mandragola, 98
  on apocalypse, 10, 12, 13, 14, 20, 72, 75, 84–91, 96, 155, 192–3, 195
  on corruption, 101–2
  on death of Lorenzo de' Medici (Lorenzo the Magnificent), 75
  on distinctiveness of politics, 10
  on fortune, 86, 91, 93–6
  on Moses, 83
  on Rome, 102–3
  on Savonarola, 83
  on the redemptive prince, 85, 86–7, 101–2
  on utopianism, 11–12
  Prince, The, 9–10, 20, 83–96, 101–2, 195
  Savonarolan influence on, 84–90
  strategy of rejection, 195
  view of Savonarola, 79–84
Machiavellian moment, 72–3
Mandragola (Machiavelli), 98
Manhattan Project, 155–7, 159
Marian exiles. *See* Mary I (queen), Marian exiles
Marshall, Stephen, 116–18, 193
Martinich, Aloysius P., 139, 141
Marx, Karl, 195
Marxism
  apocalyptic features, 58
Mary I (queen), 109
  Marian exiles, 109–10, 111
McCormick, John, 102
Mearsheimer, John, 7
Media, 32

Index

Medici
  Lorenzo de' Medici (Lorenzo the
    Magnificent), 65, 66, 75
  Machiavelli's advice to, 90
  Piero de' Medici, 66, 68
  regime in Florence, 66, 68, 84, 90, 193
Mein Kampf (Hitler), 150, 172
Mill, John Stuart, 178
millennialism
  progressive, 60–1
millennium, 39, 49, 50, 59, 138
Mitrany, David, 188
Moeller van den Bruck, Arthur, 150
  Das Dritte Reich, 150
moral consensus, supranational
  Morgenthau on, 167
Morgenthau, Hans J.
  apocalyptic context of, 9–10, 21
  as political realist, 7, 8, 15, 18, 162
  critique of liberalism, 163, 164, 172–5, 194, 195
  Death in the Nuclear Age, 178, 181–7
  In Defense of the National Interest, 162
  influence of Schmitt, 163, 165–7
  nuclear war, 195
  on apocalypse, 10, 12, 13–14, 21, 61, 162–75, 192–3, 194, 195, 196, 200, 201, 202
  on conflictual nature of politics, 11
  on death, 183–4
  on fear, 189–90, 203
  on Hobbes, 171
  on immortality, 182
  on nationalism, 169–72
  on nationalistic universalism, 169–72
  on Nazism, 171–2, 202
  on nuclear death, 181–7
  on nuclear war, 164, 178–90, 196
  on political religion, 170–1
  on secularization, 170–1
  on sovereignty, 166–7
  on supranational moral consensus, 167
  on total war, 164, 178
  on unity, 187–9, 202
  on utopianism, 12
  on Woodrow Wilson, 8, 173, 174–5
  on world government, 178–9, 187–8
  on world state, 178–9, 187–8
  Politics Among Nations, 162, 179
  redirection, 181–7
  Scientific Man vs. Power Politics, 162, 163
  tragic worldview, 14, 175–7, 180–1, 195, 197, 198
  use of self-defeating prophecy, 187, 201
Moses, 72, 83, 85, 126
Münster. *See* Anabaptist rebellion
  Anabaptist rebellion, 109–10, 113
Murrow, Edward R., 158
Mutually Assured Destruction, 155
Mystic Nativity (Botticelli), 76

Nagasaki
  atomic bombing of, 154, 158–60
Nahash of Ammon (king), 112
nationalism
  Morgenthau on, 169–72
nationalistic universalism
  Morgenthau on, 169–72
Nazism, 164
  apocalyptic elements, 149–52, 171–2
Nebuchadnezzar, 30, 31
Nero, 34, 35f
Nietzsche, Friedrich, 7, 175
Nineveh, 187
nuclear deterrence
  Morgenthau on, 180
nuclear war, 2, 9, 14, 21, 200, 203
  and Holocaust, 153–4
  apocalyptic imaginary, 154–62
  Morgenthau on, 164
Numa, 82

Old Testament. *See* Bible, Hebrew
Oppenheimer, J. Robert, 155–7
Owen, John, 118

Parenti, Piero, 74
parousia. *See* Second Coming
Paul (St.), 44–6, 118, 204
  as political realist, 42, 44–5
  letters to Thessalonians, 45–6, 51, 52, 135–6
  on apocalypse, 20, 45–6, 51–2, 135–6
Peace of Westphalia, 164, 166
Peoples Temple, 2
Persia, 32
Persians, 85
Pharaoh, 112
Pico della Mirandola, 65, 76
Piero de' Medici, 66, 68
Pocock, John G.A., 72–3, 102, 121, 122
political theology, 18
Politics Among Nations (Morgenthau), 162, 179

Polybius, 99
Pope
  as Antichrist, 112, 115–16, 127, 128
Pope Alexander VI, 81
Potsdam Conference, 157
Prayer for the Church (Savonarola), 65
Prince, The (Machiavelli), 195
  epistemological ambitions, 90–3, 195
  final chapter, 9–10, 20, 84–91, 96, 97, 195
  fortune, 86, 91, 93–6
  Moses, 83
  redemptive prince, 85, 86–7, 101–2
  Savonarola, 83
  Savonarolan influence, 84–90
prophecy
  in Renaissance Italy, 64, 74–5
  Jeremiah's, 32
  self-defeating, 187, 201
Protectorate, 118–19
Psalm 16–18, 117

Rabi, Isidore I., 154
rapture, 1
Reagan, Ronald, 4–5
realism, political
  as doctrine, 16–18
  as tradition, 16–18
  criticism of war in Iraq, 7
  definition, 6–7, 10–12
  on conflictual nature of politics, 10–11
  on distinctiveness of politics, 10
  on priority of order, 11
  on utopianism, 11–12, 194, 199
  response to apocalypticism, 8–14, 194–5
redirection
  as response to apocalypticism, 14, 199–205
  Hobbes's use of, 14, 20–1, 122–44, 195, 196
  Morgenthau's use of, 14, 21, 181–7, 195, 196, 201
Reeves, Marjorie, 74
rejection
  as response to apocalypticism, 13–14, 196–9
  Machiavelli's use of, 14, 20, 97–103, 195
  Morgenthau's use of, 14, 21, 175–7, 195
religion, political
  Morgenthau on, 170–1
Renaissance, the, 75, 78
Reston, James, 158
resurrection, 29, 33, 39, 40, 43, 49, 59, 131, 139
Revelation, book of
  Augustine (St.) on, 49–51
  Bale's interpretation of, 110–11
  beasts, 38–9, 40–1, 49, 116, 119, 193
  Camping's use of, 1–2
  cataclysm, 57
  criticism of imperial power, 40–1
  criticism of sovereign power, 40–1
  dating, 34
  end of politics, 42, 194
  evil, 42, 58
  four horsemen, 38
  Gore's reference to, 202
  historical context, 34–7
  imagery, 55–6
  imminence, 37, 54, 57
  James I's commentary on, 114–15
  Lincoln's use of, 4
  literary structure, 37
  millennium, 39
  narrative, 33–42, 195
  narrative coherence, 193
  political quietism, 42–3
  political radicalism, 43, 193
  Protestant interpretations of, 114
  revelation, 59
  rupture, 58
  seven bowls, 37, 39, 202
  seven seals, 37, 38
  seven trumpets, 37, 38
  seven vials. *See* Revelation, book of; seven bowls
  sovereignty of God, 41–2, 50, 193
  symbolism, 43–4, 55–6, 58, 61–2
  Symmons' interpretation of, 117–18
  violence, 44
  Winberger's reference to, 5
Ridolfi, Roberto, 98
Rome, 30, 34, 35, 46, 102
  apocalyptic significance, 39, 47–8
  as Babylon. *See* Babylon, in book of Revelation
  imperial cult, 35–7
  in *Discourses on Livy* (Machiavelli). *See Discourses on Livy* (Machiavelli), Rome
  sack of, 47
Romulus, 83, 102
Roosevelt, Theodore, 4
Rosenberg, Alfred, 150

Satan, 38, 39, 40, 41, 49, 116
Saul (king), 112
Savonarola, Girolamo
  apocalyptic agency, 71, 86
  denounced as Antichrist, 76

early life, 64–5
execution, 71–2
Florence as holy republic, 69–71, 194
influence on Machiavelli, 84–8
Machiavelli's view of, 79–84
moral reform, 70–1
on apocalypse, 9, 20, 63, 65–72, 155, 193, 194, 204
political role, 69–71
political theory, 69–71
Prayer for the Church, 65
sermons, 63, 66–8
Savonarolan moment, 63, 72–4, 83, 96, 103
Schiller, Friedrich, 152
Schmitt, Carl, 135
  as political realist, 7
  influence on Morgenthau, 163, 165–7
  on political theology, 18–19
Scientific Man vs. Power Politics (Morgenthau), 162, 163, 175–7
Scipio, 92
Second Coming, 45–6, 131, 136, 139, 159
secularization
  Morgenthau on, 170–1
Seleucid Empire, 30
semiotic arousal. *See* apocalypticism, semiotic arousal
September 11, 2001 terrorist attacks, 3–4, 6
Shakespeare, William, 112
Short Parliament, 119
Signorelli, Lucca, 76–8
Skinner, Quentin, 15–17, 90
sovereignty
  Morgenthau on, 166–7
Spanish Armada, 105, 114
Sparta, 102
Stalin, Joseph, 157
state of nature
  Hobbes on, 133–4, 138
Strasser, Gregor, 150
Strasser, Otto, 150
Strauss, Leo, 162
sublime, 55
Symmons, Edward, 117–18

Taylor, Charles, 53–5
Tertullian, 136
Tessman, Lisa, 199
Theseus, 83, 85
Third Reich, 149
Thirty Years' War, 114, 164, 166
Thucydides, 7, 16, 17, 134

History of the Peloponnesian War, 134–5
Titus (emperor), 37
total war
  Morgenthau on, 164
tragedy
  as response to apocalypticism, 13–14, 196–9
  Augustine's (St.) use of, 48–9
  Machiavelli's use of, 20, 97–103
  Morgenthau's use of, 14, 21, 175–7
Trinity test, 155–7, 159
Truman, Harry S., 157, 158
Trump, Donald, 5
Turks
  apocalyptic significance, 67

UNESCO, 188
unity
  Morgenthau on, 187–9

Venice, 102
Vettori, Francesco, 72, 91
virtù, 93, 101
  in *Prince, The* (Machiavelli), 82, 84, 85

Waltz, Kenneth, 7
Walzer, Michael, 54
Wannsee Conference, 152
War on Terror, 196
Weber, Max
  as political realist, 7
  as tragic thinker, 197
  influence on Morgenthau, 175
Weinberger, Caspar, 5
Weinstein, Donald, 75
whore of Babylon. *See* Babylon, in book of Revelation
Wiesel, Elie, 152
Williams, Michael, 17
Wilson, Woodrow
  idealism of, 7–8, 61
  Morgenthau's critique of, 173, 174
  progressive millennialism, 61, 147, 174–5
world government
  Morgenthau on, 178–9, 187–8
world state
  Morgenthau on, 178–9, 187–8
World War I, 174, 175
World War II, 172, 176
worldview, apocalyptic. *See* apocalypticism

Zion, 41